THE
ALPINE JOURNAL
2003

Frontispiece: Paul Ramsden on the seventh pitch of the first day of the first ascent of the N Face of Siguniang. (*Mick Fowler*) (p28)

THE
ALPINE JOURNAL
2003

The Journal of the Alpine Club

A record of mountain adventure
and scientific observation

Edited by Ed Douglas

Assistant Editors:
José Luis Bermúdez and Geoffrey Templeman

Production Editor: Johanna Merz

Volume 108

No 352

Supported by the
MOUNT EVEREST FOUNDATION

Published jointly by
THE ALPINE CLUB & THE ERNEST PRESS

THE ALPINE JOURNAL 2003
Volume 108 No 352

Address all editorial communications to the Hon Editor :
Steve Goodwin, 1 Ivy Cottages, Edenhall, Penrith, CA11 8SN
e-mail : sg@stephengoodwin.demon.co.uk

Address all sales and distribution communications to:
Cordée, 3a De Montfort Street, Leicester, LE1 7HD

Back numbers:
Apply to the Alpine Club, 55 Charlotte Road, London, EC2A 3QF
or, for 1969 to date, apply to Cordée, as above.

© 2003 by the Alpine Club

First published in 2003 jointly by the Alpine Club and the Ernest Press
Typesetting by Johanna Merz
Illustration reproduction by Digital Imaging, Glasgow
Printed and bound in Great Britain by St Edmundsbury Press Ltd,
Bury St Edmunds, Suffolk

A CIP catalogue record for this book is
available from the British Library

ISBN 0 948153 72 5

Foreword

It has been an exceptional summer in the Alps, and for all the wrong reasons. Weeks of sweltering heat have had an unprecedented impact on the mountains and mountaineering, making both more dangerous. First the Matterhorn was closed following massive rockfalls, next Mont Blanc was deemed too dangerous by any of its more commonly used routes because of rockfall and unstable glaciers. The story has been the same the length of the Alps, with huge rockfalls on the Dru and glaciers apparently sprinting back up the slopes they had covered for aeons.

It would be interesting to hear the opinion of one of the Club's former Presidents on these momentous events. Thomas Bonney was born in 1833, educated at Uppingham and St John's College, and became an influential professor of geology at University College, London after starting life as a mathematics master at Westminster. He was a pioneer in his chosen field and a pioneer climber in the Alps, and so we can assume not overwrought by the shock of the new. Someone who can sit down and write with confidence a book entitled *The Story of our Planet* isn't going to be wildly surprised by the kind of upheavals witnessed in 2003, 180 years on from his birth, and just 90 since his death.

The science of the melting of the Alps, however, would fascinate him and he would grasp the importance and urgency of it being fully understood. Days after the dramatic events that saw around 70 climbers airlifted from the Matterhorn to escape the mountain's perilous state, the International Permafrost Association met in Zurich to discuss the implications of the rapid warming of the Alps.

Given the colossal scale of Alpine tourism, those implications are sobering. In Bonney's day, the infrastructure that has bored, tunnelled and draped itself through and over the Alps was in its infancy. Another famous Club member with an interest in geology, John Ruskin, warned against what he saw as the desecration of mountain areas by engineers and sportsmen treating the mountains as an arena rather than an environment. His warnings now seem grimly prophetic as the overbearing confidence shown by the engineers who built that infrastructure becomes, quite literally, unstuck. The general principle of treading softly on the Earth's high places is not just attractive to mountaineers wishing to preserve climbing challenges for future generations. It makes good environmental sense too.

For me, the appeal of Victorian mountaineers like Thomas Bonney was the depth and range of their interest in the mountains. They made valuable contributions on how mountains were understood in our popular culture. If, in the modern era, we treat mountains as merely the backdrop for sporting endeavour, then climbing will become marginalised still further and our influence will shrivel.

Mountaineering was the focus of a great deal of public attention last year, largely because of the 50th anniversary of the first ascent of Everest. Given the scale of coverage already afforded this subject and the plethora of new books written to coincide with the celebrations, the Alpine Journal has restricted its interest in this subject compared to the volume published for the 40th anniversary. It is worth stressing, however, that the events of 1953 still capture the public's imagination in a positive way, which in a cynical age is testament to the teamwork and integrity shown by the climbers involved.

Yet it would be wrong if the public assumed that the courage and exploratory drive that characterised that era is missing from the present one. This year's Journal is full of accounts of hard new climbs done in good style in remote corners of the world by today's young adventurers. Public funding in Britain for mountaineering has looked shaky in recent months, partly because there are simply no more Everests to climb in the public imagination. But the future of mountaineering is full of opportunities for those enterprising enough to look for them.

After five years as Honorary Editor, I shall be handing over to Stephen Goodwin for the 2004 edition. It has been a privilege to oversee the Journal, and one that I could not possibly have managed without the unfailing support of Johanna Merz in her role as Production Editor. Nor could I have coped without the Journal's excellent Assistant Editors Geoff Templeman and José Luis Bermúdez, who is this year stepping down after seven years editing the Area Notes. To all of them, I am very grateful.

Ed Douglas

Contents

SKETCH MAPS AND DIAGRAMS

Illustrations

46. Johnnie Lees with Vic Bray during a reunion at RAF Valley in 1993. (*Derek Walker*)
47. Johnnie Lees on Kaisergebirge Wall in the early 1950s. (*Ray Tanter*)
48. The most likely birthplace for Tenzing Norgay, the holy lake of Tshechu overlooking the Kama valley and opposite Makalu on the eastern side of Everest. (*Ed Douglas*)
49. Elijah Walton's 'Bedouin Encampment in the Desert with the artist sitting in his tent looking at a sketch' dated 28 February, 1864. (*Courtesy of the Victoria and Albert Museum*)
50. Gabriel Loppé's 'Sunrise on the Grandes Jorasses seen from Mont Blanc', 1869.
51. Lower Kumdan Glacier – Shyok. (T E Gordon, *The Roof of the World*, 1876)
52. Kila Panja on the Oxus – looking east. (T E Gordon, *The Roof of the World*, 1876)
53. The Karakoram Peak – from the southern side of the pass – looking NW. (T E Gordon, *The Roof of the World*, 1876)
54. Aktash Valley – looking NW. (T E Gordon, *The Roof of the World*, 1876)
55. Andrew Dalgleish and his Yarkand household including Abyssinian servant and Yarkandi wife. (John Keay, *When Men and Mountains Meet*, 1977)

Appearing between pages 308 and 309
56. Tschingelhorn (centre) from the Gamchilücke. (*C M Sleeman*) (*Alpine Club Photo Library*)
57. Rulten, Austvågøy, Lofoten Islands. (*J N Collie*) (*Alpine Club Photo Library*)
58. S (left) and N peaks of Ushba from the south-east. (*W Weckert*) (*Alpine Club Photo Library*)
59. Members of Dr and Mrs Workman's party leaving Srinagar, 26 May 1903. (*Reproduced from Ice-Bound Heights of the Mustagh, 1908*)
60. View from Mount Huber, Canadian Rockies. (*Reproduced from AJ25, 1910-11*)
61. André Roch, 1906-2002, with Peter Lloyd. (*F B Goodfellow*) (*Alpine Club Photo Library*)
62. Chris Brasher, 1928-2003. (*John Cleare*)
64. Gisèle Pighetti de Rivasso, 1905-2002. (*Marcel Bozon*)
65. Jean François Saltet, 1920-2003, on the West Face of the Aiguille de la Tsa, 1957. (*Robbert Leopold*)
66. Gino Buscaini, 1931-2002. (*foto Altamura*)
67. Oliver Turnbull, 1933-2002.
68. John 'Andy' Anderson, 1944-2002. (*Henry Day*)
69. Peter Lloyd CBE, 1907-2003. (*John Cleare*) (*Alpine Club Photo Library*)

Everest

GEORGE BAND

Everest Golden Jubilee 1953-2003

(*Plates* 14–23)

The Alpine Journal of 1993 was very much a 40th Anniversary volume, including contributions from all the surviving members of the 1953 Everest team. As so many more Everest books were published in conjunction with the 50th Anniversary in comparison to the 40th, the Editor decided that a brief round-up of the celebratory events to mark the Golden Jubilee (May 2003) was more appropriate for this Journal, and asked me to do it.

As with the 40th, the Mount Everest Foundation (MEF) was the natural body to take the lead in this, representing the Alpine Club (AC) and the Royal Geographical Society with the Institute of British Geographers (RGS). The MEF set up a small ad hoc committee and brought in Dr Charles Clarke to chair it, as he had previously been involved with the 40th Anniversary events and would himself become Chairman of the MEF during 2003. This was a considerable commitment on his part on top of his professional duties, but he took it on willingly and cheerfully and it was a pleasure for all of us to work with him.

The other members of this group initially were Richard Morgan, the MEF Hon Treasurer; Bill Ruthven, MEF Hon Secretary; Nigel Winser, Deputy Director RGS, and his assistant Rebecca Trumble to take the minutes; Glyn Hughes, AC Hon Secretary later succeeded by Martin Scott and Toto Gronlund; Andy McNae from the British Mountaineering Council; and myself as a member of the original 1953 team, particularly to provide the link with the surviving team members.

The 1953 Team

Sadly, our leader, John Hunt, died in November 1998 so we lacked his guiding inspiration. Tom Bourdillon, Wilfrid Noyce, Charles Evans, Griffith Pugh, Tom Stobart and Tenzing Norgay had also passed away. But half the original team of fourteen still survive: Ed Hillary, Charles Wylie, George Lowe, Alf Gregory, Mike Ward, Mike Westmacott and myself, not forgetting our redoubtable non-climbing correspondent from *The Times*, James, now Jan Morris.

Most people's memories do not stretch back fifty years. Such was the continuing publicity given to Hillary and Tenzing that many folk now call us the 'Hillary Expedition' thinking he was the leader. Although Everest certainly changed his life his greatest satisfaction over the last forty years has probably come from the creation and running of his Himalayan Trust which has helped to improve the lives of the Sherpas in North-east Nepal. So he understandably felt his first priority should be to celebrate the Jubilee with his many Sherpa friends and their community in Kathmandu before coming to join us in London. Alfred Gregory, now in his 90th year, living in the Dandenong hills near Melbourne, felt the journey to be too long and expensive to justify. Sadly, Michael Ward also had to miss most of the celebrations as he was recovering from injuries following a serious car accident (for which he was blameless) followed by heart surgery.

We were very keen to have some of our Sherpa friends join us in London to mark the essential role they played on numerous Himalayan expeditions. Fortunately Tenzing's nephew Nawang Gombu was able to do so. He had been one of the youngest High Altitude Sherpas in 1953, just 17 at the time, and was the first person to climb Everest twice, with the Americans in 1963 and the Indians in 1965, and is an Honorary Member of the AC. Tenzing's eldest daughter Pem Pem also graced the occasion, as did his son Dhamey (by his third wife, Daku) who now lives in Switzerland.

Purpose

Our MEF sub-committee first met on 19 April 2000 and agreed that the purpose should be 'To celebrate the 50th Anniversary of the first ascent of Everest in 1953, a British Commonwealth, mountaineering achievement in the Coronation year, and to raise substantial funds for the MEF.' We started with a clean slate and all ideas were welcome; many of these did not come to fruition and others evolved gradually into their final form. It would be tedious to give too much detail so I will concentrate mostly on the final outcome.

'Endeavour on Everest'

It was decided to hold the main fundraising event, a Royal Gala Celebration entitled 'Endeavour on Everest', on the anniversary day itself, Thursday 29 May 2003, to be followed by a Reception. After considering venues such as the RGS and the Royal Albert Hall, we settled on the Odeon, Leicester Square where the BAFTA Awards are held. It was close to the Warner Theatre where Tom Stobart's Everest film had been given its Royal Premiere on 21 October 1953. The graceful ambience of Spencer House in St. James's Place was made available for the Reception. Through the Queen's Private Secretary, Sir Robin Janvrin, we learnt that our invitation to Her Majesty and Prince Philip, Patron of the MEF, was likely to receive favourable consideration. As the organisational workload increased, we realised that professional help was required so we engaged an experienced public relations consultant, Sarah Turner, who later brought in Annie Taylor to assist and Mandy Duncan-Smith of Media Natura to orchestrate the Performance itself and discipline us participants to conform to a tight schedule. We cannot thank these three ladies enough for their vital contribution to the success and undoubted enjoyment of this magnificent occasion. Jamie Buchanan Dunlop handled all the complex ticketing without losing his cool.

As to the programme itself, there were two showings, a matinée and a full 1800 capacity, for the evening performance. Sir David Attenborough kindly compered a galaxy of speakers, using a mix of film-clips and slides: Charles Clarke, Chris Bonington, Stephen Venables, Doug Scott, four of the 1953 team: Band, Westmacott, Wylie and Lowe, with a video message from Hillary, and an eloquent coda by Jan Morris. Seven members of the Royal Family agreed to attend. It was an evening of drama, nostalgia, pride and joy which many people found very moving. They will not easily forget Charles Wylie's emotional description of the Great Carry by his team of Sherpas to the South Col, or the allegorical part played in the adventure by Jan, then James Morris, the confirmed Welsh republican, in dashing back down the Icefall with Mike Westmacott, to get the news back in time for the Queen's Coronation: 'The message went on to ring the world and 50 years on is still giving innocent pleasure, is it not – to the Queen and her husband I hope, and to all the rest of us this very day here in the heart of London.'

The Media – Films, Exhibitions and Books

The original team members were astonished by the great interest shown by the media, almost as much as in 1953. Every newspaper and magazine seemed to carry feature articles or special supplements, notably *The Times*, *Geographical*, and the *National Geographic Magazine*. Even *Hello!* had a picture of the 'Everest adventurers' meeting the Queen, beside another of Hillary being honoured by King Gyanendra in Nepal where, under the auspices of the Nepal Mountaineering Association, there was a great gathering of 'Everest summitters' in conjunction with numerous other sporting events.

Most UK TV channels ran special programmes, notably the BBC's *Race for Everest* produced by Mick Conefry, in which 80 hours of filming were condensed to an authoritative and balanced one-hour programme. Other countries – Germany and Brazil – made special programmes and, in particular, New Zealand produced *On Top of the World* and *Hillary on Everest* highlighting Sir Edmund's early years and his extraordinarily varied and crowded later life. Similarly the Auckland Museum mounted a major Exhibition *Sir Edmund Hillary: Everest and Beyond* opened by the New Zealand Prime Minister on 25 October 2002.

One TV production company, Mentorn Barraclough Carey, was very keen to replicate an Everest Expedition 'in the style of 1953', where a young team of top British tigers unfamiliar with Everest would attempt the climb using old-fashioned crampons and long ice-axes, but equipped with the latest mini-cameras to beam live images to viewers back home. A potential leader, Iain Peter from Plas y Brenin, was appointed and at least six months spent on developing the concept and seeking sponsorship, but in the aftermath of the September 11 catastrophe insufficient sponsorship was available and the project was aborted. Happily, one of the short-listed leaders, Lt. Colonel Nick Arding of the Royal Marines, refused to admit defeat and instead persuaded the Royal Navy to mount its first expedition to Everest, the Army having climbed it in 1976 and the Royal Air Force in 2000. Under his leadership, they succeeded by the north ridge on 22 May 2003. Their innovative oxygen equipment, pressured to 300 bar, weighed only half that of ours in 1953 and was shown on *Blue Peter* and *'Tomorrow's World' Road Show*.

There was always the intention to mount a major Everest Exhibition to mark the anniversary in the UK; various venues in the South-east were discussed at different times: the RGS, Somerset House, the Science Museum, but all of these collapsed for one reason or another, despite a lot of effort expended, particularly by Julie Summers of the Ashmolean, a great-niece of Sandy Irvine. Only the Gurkha Museum in Winchester contrived a display highlighting the role of Gurkha officers and men on successive Everest expeditions. In the end it was the 'National Mountaineering Exhibition' at Rheged, Penrith, which secured the vital financial support of the NW Development Fund to remodel its current exhibition in record time with a full Everest theme from May 2003 to April 2004, as well as showing the Everest IMAX film. Rheged included a special series of Everest lectures in May and June culminating in one on 14 June, repeated on 8 August, by Lowe, Westmacott and Band in a joint presentation reminiscent of the 1953 performances at the Festival Hall and other major locations.

There was no shortage of books published to mark the occasion, but many of these were reprints of early classics, jumping on the Anniversary bandwagon: Hillary's *High Adventure*, Morris's *Coronation Everest*, Bonington's *Everest*, Krakauer's *Into Thin Air* and others less memorable. An exception, conceived by our sub-committee, was a limited edition facsimile of John Hunt's *The Ascent of Everest* with Heaton Cooper's original dust jacket and the signatures of the complete team.

Regarding new books, I was invited by HarperCollins to write yet another on Everest and this was accepted by the MEF as its Official History, and formally supported by both the AC (who had to invent a new logo for it!) and the RGS, who provided most of the 300 illustrations. *Everest: 50 years on Top of the World* was duly published on 6 May 2003 and for two weeks even hit the hardback best-seller lists! I rashly included a section on some of the more remarkable record ascents, hardly expecting several of them to be broken in the very month of publication when over 200 more climbers reached the summit: the fastest was 36-year-old Sherpa Lhakpa Gelu in a crazy 10hrs 56mins; the youngest, a girl of 15, Mingkipa Sherpa, together with her brother and sister; and the oldest, a sprightly 70-year-old Japanese, Yiuchiro Miura, who in 1970 failed to reach the summit but gained instant fame as 'the man who skied down Everest', being filmed in a spectacular parachute-assisted ski descent from the South Col and subsequent fall down the Lhotse Face. They may all have contributed to the festive spirit but

Everest is turning into a circus. 'This is not mountaineering,' commented Reinhold Messner. 'It has been prepared like a piste. The Nepalese government has a choice: it can leave it as it was, or sell it to Disneyland!'

The RGS provided its own super coffee-table book: *Everest – Summit of Achievement* to publicise and profit from its magnificent archive of some 20,000 Everest images donated to it with all rights in 1974 by the MEF. Various writers contributed essays, with Stephen Venables being the Senior Consulting Editor. Stephen also wrote a delightful new book for children *To The Top – The Story of Everest*.

Two other new books were Michael Ward's wide-ranging monograph *Everest, A Thousand Years of Exploration,* covering mountaineering, geographical exploration, medical research and mapping, and our own Alpine Journal Editor's most revealing and readable biography *Tenzing. Hero of Everest*. In the 1950s we had thought Tenzing had been born in Thame, in North-east Nepal, but Ed Douglas's diligent research revealed the full extent of Tenzing's long and astonishing climb to fame from the obscurity of an illiterate yak herder born in a sacred Tibetan valley in the shadow of Everest. Standing together on the summit, it was Hillary who gazed at the surrounding virgin peaks waiting to be climbed, whereas Tenzing saw the valleys and the past beneath his feet: 'the monasteries and the farms, the rivers and forests of his youth. No wonder a mere handshake with Hillary was not enough!'

Other Initiatives

On the agenda of our first sub-committee meeting was a proposal to the Royal Mail for a set of commemorative postage stamps. To our delight this was accepted but extended to a series of six, issued on 29 April 2003, entitled 'Extreme Endeavours' depicting British explorers and adventurers. Although only one represented the Everest team it was the most widely used first class stamp, showing Hillary and Tenzing high on the South-east ridge. Traditionally, the sovereign is the only living person to appear on UK stamps, but again Hillary had broken the mould!

During his short stay in the UK in early June, Sir Edmund, together with Lady Hillary and the rest of the team, were privileged guests at the service in Westminster Abbey on 2 June to mark the 50th Anniversary of the Queen's Coronation. The following evening the MEF hosted a charity dinner at the RGS to honour Sir Edmund and to generate funds for his Himalayan Trust. Since its inception, George Lowe has served as Chairman of the UK Branch of the Trust, with his wife Mary as Secretary. Thanks to some spirited auctioneering by Rebecca Stephens, over £8,000 was raised. Further celebrations with the American Himalayan Foundation in California prevented Ed from joining us at the traditional private party at Pen-y-Gwryd on 7 June, generously given by Jane Pullee, where 42 members of the extended 'Everest Family' sat down for dinner after a full day on Snowdon.

Since the establishment of the MEF, in 48 years nearly 1400 expeditions have been helped. One of the most successful of this year's initiatives has been the 'Leaders Appeal', Charles Clarke writing to invite donations from all those leaders who have benefited from grants in years gone by, using Bill Ruthven's comprehensive database of MEF expeditions. So far, with only half the letters sent out, over £20,000 has been raised.

We had several meetings at the RGS in conjunction with *The Times* (the major sponsor in 1953) and *Geographical*, inviting firms to sponsor packages for the various events. We would like to thank all those who responded generously and who were mentioned in the souvenir programme, notably 20th Century Fox, Odeon Leicester Square, JP Morgan, Dixon Wilson, American Express, Glenmorangie, Shaeffer UK, Stanfords Books, Champagne Taittinger and Hatch Mansfield Agencies, Audi Cars, Go Outdoors, Simpkins of Sheffield, Jagged Globe, Lyon Equipment, Berghaus, Canal + (for use of 'The Conquest of Everest'), British Pathé, Far Frontiers, Think Publishing, M &A Security, Westminster City Council, The Travellers Club, The High Commissioner for New Zealand and numerous individuals.

Of all the Anniversary events, the Alpine Club's own party on 28 May was one of the friendliest and most informal, held in our own premises at Charlotte Road and surrounded by our collection of Howard Somervell's watercolours, augmented for the occasion by an exhibition of newly-processed Everest photographs.

At this stage one would like to give a succinct summary of the total funds raised for the MEF by all these initiatives, but our Hon. Treasurer is on a well deserved holiday in the Alps and the final figure must await his return. Let us say that we anticipate at least £50,000 has been raised.

One of the great pleasures of the Anniversary has been the renewal of contacts with friends old and new. For instance, meeting J J Asper of the Swiss 1952 expedition, the first person to cross the great crevasse at the head of the Khumbu Icefall to enter the Western Cwm, and my seeing for the first time the film clip of him doing so.

Finally, only as I began to write this narrative did I receive a friendly letter from our member Sir Edward Peck in Tomintoul. 'You may be interested to know that in August 1924, as a young boy of 9, I climbed the Haute Cime of the Dents du Midi to be greeted on the top by General Charles Bruce who had come up the North face with his Champery friend Montaignier. This made a great impression on me as a small boy and inspired my enthusiasm for the mountains which has never left me, even though at nearly 88 I can no more than just about totter up a small hill here in the Cairngorms. Though it may mark me down as one of the oldest members of the AC, I treasure this direct link with Charlie Bruce – perhaps the only living one.'

O longum memoranda dies! – Oh day, long to be remembered!

JOHN B WEST

The G I Finch Controversy of 1921-1924

New physiological and medical insights

The 50th anniversary of the first ascent of Everest in 1953 has prompted a renewal of interest in the early expeditions to Everest. One of the strangest stories of the first three expeditions, in 1921, 1922 and 1924, was the controversy surrounding George Ingle Finch (1888-1970).

In 1919, shortly before permission was given by the Tibetan authorities for the first British Everest expedition, J P Farrar, President of the Club, consulted many mountaineers and concluded that George Finch and his brother Maxwell were the strongest climbers for the summit party. Then, early in 1921, the design of oxygen equipment for climbing at extreme altitudes was discussed at length and Finch took a leading role. This was natural because he was a well-trained physical chemist with a special interest in gases and none of the other climbers had these skills. But most remarkable of all, when Finch was studied in a high-altitude chamber in March 1921, he exhibited an extraordinary degree of fitness and tolerance to low oxygen. In fact a survey of the physiological literature to the present day shows that Finch's performance when acutely exposed to extreme simulated high altitude was almost unique, being equalled by only one other person, the Italian physiologist Margaria.

It would be natural to assume from all this that Finch would play a pivotal role in the first three Everest expeditions. However, this was not to be, in spite of the fact that during the 1922 expedition he and his companion Geoffrey Bruce attained the altitude record of 8320m, and in the process clearly demonstrated the enormous value of climbing oxygen. As expected, Finch was invited to join the 1921 expedition, but then amazingly the invitation was withdrawn because he was declared unfit only one week before his extraordinary demonstration of fitness in the low-pressure chamber. Even stranger was that after his record ascent during the 1922 expedition and his subsequently being asked to modify the oxygen sets for 1924, he was not invited to be a member of that expedition. The story is a fascinating one of personality conflicts with an outcome that was to the great disadvantage of everybody concerned.

Background of George Finch

Much has been written about Finch and we are particularly fortunate that his son-in-law, Scott Russell, prepared a detailed memoir which was included in the 1988 reprint of Finch's fine book *The Making of a Mountaineer*.

Briefly, George Finch was born in 1888 in Orange, New South Wales, then a small country town west of Sydney. He first became interested in climbing at the age of thirteen when he was entranced by the view of Orange from a nearby hill. The family moved to Europe when George was only fourteen and his mother, Laura, fell in love with Paris and decided to stay there while her husband Charles returned to Australia. It is said that he never saw his wife again. George's schooling presented something of a crisis. While it would have been natural for him to go to an English public school because the Finch family had strong links with Britain, Laura felt that the restrictions were too repressive and she arranged for George and his younger brother Maxwell to be privately tutored in Paris. Around this time George and his brother demonstrated their climbing initiative by scaling Beachy Head by a particularly dangerous route, and ascending the cathedral of Notre Dame in Paris.

George enrolled briefly at the École de Médecine in Paris but soon felt that he would be more comfortable in one of the physical sciences. At the suggestion of Laura's friend, Sir Oliver Lodge, George moved to the Eidgenossische Technische Hochschule (ETH) in Zurich where he studied from 1906 to 1911 with great academic success. He and his brother spent the weekends and vacations climbing in the Alps, and George became an outstanding mountaineer and president of the prestigious Zurich Academischer Alpen Club.

George returned to England in 1912 and soon became associated with the Imperial College of Science and Technology in London, which was to become his scientific base for the next forty years. During the Great War he served with the Royal Field Artillery in France, and also the Ordnance Corps. working on explosives in Salonica. He was awarded the military MBE, was mentioned in dispatches, and demobilised with the rank of captain. He married briefly in 1916 and there was a son, Peter Finch, who became the famous actor. After a divorce, a second marriage in 1921 was very happy and there were three daughters, one of whom, Anne, married Scott Russell.

Physiological studies
Early in the preparations for the 1921 expedition Finch became involved in improving the operation of Primus stoves at extreme altitude. In 1920, Kellas and Moreshead on Kamet had found that their Primus stove would not work above about 6100m. Finch and P J H Unna, a member of the Oxygen Subcommittee of the 1921 expedition, went to Oxford in March 1921 to see tests of the Primus stove in the low-pressure chamber in the laboratory of Georges Dreyer, the Professor of Pathology. Dreyer was originally from Copenhagen and his primary interest was in bacteriology. However, during the First World War he was a consultant to the Royal Flying Corps and became very knowledgeable about the effects of oxygen deprivation on

flying personnel. His design of oxygen equipment for aviators was a major advance and was widely used including in the USA.

The stoves were modified for high-altitude use and then Dreyer raised the issue of supplementary oxygen for climbers. He stated: 'I do not think you will get up [Everest] without it, but if you do succeed you may not get down again.' Finch visited Oxford again on 25 March together with Unna and Farrar, and Finch stayed in Oxford overnight so that Dreyer could carry out experiments on him in the high-altitude chamber the following day.

The results of these experiments clearly showed that Finch was outstandingly fit and furthermore that he had an extraordinary ability to exercise while acutely exposed to the severe oxygen deprivation of high altitude. Specifically, the altitude of the chamber was set at 6400m and Finch stepped up on a chair, first with one foot and then with the other, twenty times in succession while carrying a load of 16kg slung over his shoulder. The stepping rate was chosen to correspond to a fairly rapid climbing pace and he exercised in this way for two and a half minutes. Finch first carried out this task while breathing air, and then again while breathing oxygen. As expected, he tolerated the severe exercise much better with the oxygen, as evidenced by his better colour, ease of movement, lower pulse rate and slightly shorter time for the task.

The exceptional performance of Finch while breathing air is highlighted by the fact that there are almost no comparable experiments in the whole of the physiological literature to this day. The only similar study which has been reported is that of the Italian physiologist, Rodolfo Margaria in 1929 who studied three students aged 22 and himself aged 27 years in a low-pressure chamber at an altitude of 6500m while they exercised on a bicycle ergometer. However two of the students were unable to sit on the bicycle and ended up lying on the floor of the chamber, where their skin became pale, their lips were blue, and they lost consciousness. The third student was not studied at this altitude, and only Margaria was able to exercise under these conditions. In fact Margaria was able to work up to an altitude of 7000m, a feat that Finch equalled in another set of experiments in 1922. Incidentally, it is extremely unlikely that these experiments performed on Finch would be allowed under present guidelines for human investigations because of the dangers of the extremely severe oxygen deprivation.

Dreyer had carried out a substantial number of tests on the effects of oxygen lack on young men and it was quite clear to him that Finch's performance was outstanding. In a four-page letter to Farrar dated 28 March 1921 describing the experiments he stated: 'The tests in the low-pressure chamber proved that Captain Finch possesses quite unusual powers of resistance to the effects of high altitudes. Among the large number of picked, healthy, athletic young men we have examined, more than 1,000 in all, we have not come across a single case where the subject possessed the resistance power to the same degree.' The inescapable conclusion from all this is that in March 1921 Finch was phenomenally fit and that his exercise ability at simulated extreme altitude was second to none in the published physiological literature to the present day.

Medical reports

We now come to the strangest chapter of the Finch story. The members of the 1921 expedition were required to have a routine medical examination and on 17 and 18 March, just one week before the low-pressure chamber experiments described above, Finch was examined by two Harley Street doctors. Amazingly they concluded that Finch was unfit and soon after this his invitation to join the expedition was withdrawn. The two medical reports still exist and make astonishing reading for someone with a medical training. The first by Dr H Graeme Anderson, a surgeon, is absurdly brief with vague statements such as 'Nutrition poor. Spare. Flabby.' and concludes: 'His physical condition at present is poor.' The second report by Dr F E Larkins, a physician (internist), is longer but includes no objective data on which to base his conclusion that 'This man is not at the moment fit.' There was a mild degree of anemia, often seen in athletes, and a single test suggesting that the urine contained sugar, a finding in diabetes. This test should have been repeated. Dreyer performed the same test a week later when the result was normal and when the test was repeated eight months later it was normal again.

An obvious omission from these two medical reports was any test of Finch's exercise ability. Fitness in the context of the 1921 expedition implies an ability to withstand the rigours of climbing, ideally under conditions of oxygen deprivation as is seen at high altitude. The two medical reports are essentially irrelevant in this context. By contrast, the outstanding performance of Finch in the low-pressure chamber just one week later is enormously convincing. There is a dramatic disparity between the medical reports and the physical performance of Finch, which raises the question of whether the reports were biased.

The decision to rescind Finch's invitation

The implication that the two medical reports were biased, and that Dreyer's report was intentionally suppressed, is a serious one and necessitates a closer look at how the decision to rescind Finch's invitation was reached. The make-up of the expedition was the responsibility of the Everest Committee which was formed by four members of the Royal Geographical Society (RGS) and four from the Alpine Club (AC). A R Hinks was the Secretary of the RGS and became the Secretary of the Everest Committee. The other three members from the RGS were Sir Francis Younghusband, Col E M Jack and Edward Somers-Cocks. From the AC there were J E C Eaton, Norman Collie, Capt J P Farrar and C F Meade.

It was quite reasonable for the Everest Committee to require that the members of the expedition should undergo a medical examination.

Presumably, the two doctors who examined Finch were selected by the official expedition doctor, A F R Wollaston. The choice of Wollaston as expedition doctor might be queried because his decision to study medicine was taken reluctantly and only so that he could take part in expeditions, as he stated himself. He once wrote to his father, 'medical practice as a means of a livelihood does not attract me – in fact I dislike it extremely'. On the other hand, it is true that Wollaston distinguished himself as a surgeon in the Royal Navy during the First World War when he was awarded a DSC.

Wollaston's choice of Graeme Anderson was reasonable because the latter had written the first book on the medical and surgical aspects of aviation and was knowledgeable about oxygen deprivation and the selection of aviators. Of course there is an obvious difference between a seated aviator and someone climbing at high altitude but very little was known about the medical selection of mountaineers at the time.

The choice of F E Larkins is curious because he was a paediatrician chiefly interested in the health of school children. It is possible that Wollaston asked Anderson to suggest a second doctor and he recommended Larkins. Both Anderson and Larkins had the same address and telephone number in Harley Street and presumably were partners in a practice. This raises the question of whether the two reports were really as independent as they should have been.

The reports themselves are clearly inadequate because their conclusions do not fit with the findings of the examinations. The only abnormal test was that for sugar in urine and, as indicated above, this was probably an error and should have been repeated. However, the most glaring inconsistency in the treatment of Finch is the enormous discrepancy between the results of the medical tests and Finch's extraordinary demonstration of fitness one week later in the low-pressure chamber. The results of these tests were sent by Dreyer to Farrar who was a member of the Everest Committee on 28 March only five days after the medical reports were sent to Hinks. It seems inconceivable that Farrar who was a strong supporter of Finch did not communicate this information to the other members of the Everest Committee as soon as possible. Yet Mallory stated in a letter to Winthrop Young that 'Wollaston told me that there could be no question of taking Finch after the doctor's report.' This statement by Wollaston suggests that he was biased against Finch. He was apparently willing to ignore Dreyer's report.

How is it possible then to explain Finch's rejection? As has been discussed extensively elsewhere, Finch had strong supporters like Farrar, but powerful enemies including Hinks, Secretary of the Everest Committee. There had been several instances in the past where Hinks's animosity towards Finch had been clearly demonstrated and it may be that he and perhaps others were looking for an excuse to reject Finch. The most likely scenario, unpleasant as it is, is that the wishes of the Everest Committee to rescind Finch's invitation were made known to the two examining physicians, and further that the evidence from Dreyer's low-pressure chamber experiments was deliberately suppressed.

There is another possible sequence of events that might be considered. Suppose that Farrar had learned from meetings of the Everest Committee, or private conversations with some of the members, that Hinks and perhaps others were determined to reject Finch, and planned to use the medical reports as the excuse. Farrar then tells Dreyer who carries out the high-altitude test a week after the medical tests. Dreyer then writes his letter specifically to counter Hinks's plans. However, the Everest Committee recognizes that this is why Dreyer did the test, and Dreyer's letter is therefore suppressed. According to Scott Russell it did not surface until 1986 when Mrs Christine Kelly, the RGS Archivist, unearthed it for Scott Russell in a file connected with Primus stoves. Perhaps this explanation is a little gothic but it is interesting.

1922 Expedition

Eight months later, in November 1921, Finch was re-examined by Dr Larkins and declared fit. He reported 'I have also re-examined G I Finch today. He is now absolutely fit and has lost his glucosuria [sugar in the urine]. In my first report on him I stated that I thought all he needed was to get into training.' Finch was accordingly selected for the 1922 expedition and in January 1922 was tested again by Dreyer in the low-pressure chamber. This time the chamber altitude was set at 7010m and Finch performed the stepping test with a 14kg load. We have to marvel first at Finch's outstanding performance, and secondly at Dreyer's bravado in carrying out such a dangerous test. Incidentally, T H Somervell was also tested using the same protocol but was stopped after the fifth step and oxygen was forcibly administered to prevent him from fainting.

Because of the obvious value of oxygen as shown in the low-pressure chamber studies, the Everest Committee agreed that equipment should be prepared for the 1922 expedition and Finch took a leading role in developing this. Dreyer contributed much expertise because he had very successfully designed oxygen for use at high altitude by aviators during and after the First World War. It is interesting that the equipment that was developed had many similarities with that used to such great effect in 1953.

The story of the 1922 expedition is well known and will not be repeated here. The use of oxygen was controversial and some of the climbers tended to ridicule the equipment. Mallory went so far as to refer to its use as a 'damnable heresy' which mystified Finch who pointed out that mountaineers used many other technical advances to improve their performance at high altitude. Finch had a rigorous professional attitude derived from his scientific training and this was evident in other logistical aspects of the expedition as well.

Finch and Geoffrey Bruce carried out the first trials of the oxygen equipment at high altitude towards the end of May 1922 and immediately

FINCH WEARING HIS OXYGEN EQUIPMENT ON THE 1922 EXPEDITION

obtained convincing results. It was clear that climbers who used oxygen could outpace those who were breathing air. Estimates of the extent to which oxygen increased the climbing rate varied from 50 per cent to 300 per cent. Eventually Finch and Bruce reached an altitude of 8320m using oxygen, higher than any human had been before. However they had been considerably weakened by a fierce storm that kept them tent-bound for two nights and a day, and they had to retreat although they were only a little over 500m from the summit.

1924 and after
The final chapter in the Finch controversy was in many ways as mysterious as the first. In 1922 Finch had clearly demonstrated the value of oxygen for climbing at extreme altitude and indeed had, with Bruce, attained the altitude record. Furthermore, Finch was a professional scientist with strong engineering skills, and he had been intimately involved with the design of the equipment for the 1922 expedition. There is no doubt that Finch knew more about the technical aspects of high-altitude oxygen than any other mountaineer of his day. It was not surprising therefore that when the plans for the 1924 expedition were discussed in June 1923, Finch was invited to advise the Everest Committee on the use of oxygen. It would be natural to conclude that in the light of all these qualifications, Finch would be an obvious choice for the 1924 expedition. However he was not selected by the Everest Committee and indeed never again had an opportunity to test the value of oxygen at extreme altitude.

The reasons why Finch was not invited to join the 1924 expedition have been discussed in detail by Scott Russell and others and will only be briefly referred to here. First there was a bitter dispute with Hinks about lectures that Finch was invited to give in Switzerland about the 1922 expedition. Stringent limitations were laid down and Finch argued that they were unreasonable. But there were other tensions as well which have been described elsewhere. Finch had a reputation for being an outspoken, unconventional Australian in a setting where these characteristics created controversy. His schooling and university training on the Continent contrasted with the public school and Oxbridge or military background of most members of the first three Everest expeditions. He was very much a square peg in a round hole in the setting of the Alpine Club in the early 1920s.

Finch went on to become an eminent physical chemist at Imperial College and was elected a Fellow of the Royal Society in 1938. His research was particularly directed to the surface chemistry of metals but included the properties of lubricants and electron diffraction in small crystals. Happily, in spite of his early differences with the Alpine Club, he was eventually elected as its President and served in that position from 1959 to 1961 immediately following the term of John Hunt.

Finally it could be argued that the pioneering work which Finch carried out on high-altitude oxygen equipment in 1922 played a role in the first ascent of Everest in 1953. Several features of the 1924 equipment, such as the economiser to reduce wastage of oxygen, were used in the 1953 sets. John Hunt was under no illusions about the value of oxygen in the first ascent. He wrote after the expedition: 'Among the numerous items in our inventory, I would single out oxygen for special mention. Many of our material aids were of great importance; only this, in my opinion, was vital to success. But for oxygen, without the much-improved equipment which we were given, we should certainly not have got to the top.'

Hunt also alluded tangentially – and in the nicest possible way – to the Finch controversy when he wrote a foreword to the 1988 reprint of *The Making of a Mountaineer*, which was edited by Scott Russell. He referred to Finch's exclusion from the 1921 expedition on 'dubious medical grounds' and added: 'The chapter on the Everest expedition in 1922 added a dimension of realism to the heroic and romantic character of the attempt on the summit which followed two years later. I felt that George Finch, who had done so much to show how the physiological problems might be solved, might well have played an important – perhaps a decisive – part in the ill-fated 1924 expedition.'

History is replete with 'what ifs.' But the temptation to ask the question here is overwhelming. What if Finch had been allowed to take part in the 1921 expedition and had worked on the development of climbing oxygen? Would this have improved the equipment that was used in 1922, allowed him to reach an even higher altitude, and defused some of the antagonism towards oxygen? Finally, with Finch's input in 1924, would oxygen finally have come into its own enabling Finch to go much higher, perhaps to the summit, and Mallory and Irvine to do the same?

This article is based on a more technical and extensive analysis of the physiological and medical aspects of the Finch controversy which was published in the Journal of Applied Physiology 94, 1710-1713, 2003. That article also includes detailed references to the sources of the information.

MICHAEL WARD

A New Map of the Everest Area

Scale 1:5,000 with 5-metre contours

Everest (Chomolungma) has been known to the inhabitants of South Tibet and the Rongbuk Valley since AD 800. The name first appeared, as 'Tchoumour Lancma', on a European map in 1733 on d'Anville's 'Nouveau Atlas de Chine'. Although Everest lies on the Nepal-Tibet border, the Nepalese name 'Sagarmatha' was not given to it until the 1960s. The height and position of Everest were identified in the middle of the 19th century by the Survey of India from the plains of India over a hundred miles away; for political reasons, closer access was not possible at that time. The first on-the-ground identification was made by Henry Wood, an officer of the Survey, from Nepal in 1903 and from Tibet in 1904.

The first detailed survey and mapping was carried out during the first Everest expedition, a reconnaissance from the north, Tibetan side, in 1921. This was completed by E O Wheeler, who later became Surveyor-General, and H T Morshead, together with three Indian surveyors. They were so efficient that they had produced a map before the main party left India.

A further photogrammetric survey, of the north side only, was done by Michael Spender in 1935. The first photographs of the unknown southern, Nepalese side were taken during an aerial survey in 1933. From these a map was drawn by A R Hinks and M D Milne of the Royal Geographical Society. This map lay forgotten in the archives of the Society until, with the help of Ian Mumford, a geography student doing a holiday locum, I disinterred it in early 1951. It was vital to the discovery of the route by which Everest was first climbed, which was confirmed on the ground during the autumn reconnaissance of that year. During this expedition I made a 'Pundit style' compass traverse to the west of Everest and in the Gaurisankar-Menlungste range.

Further exploration and mapping south of Everest were made by R C Evans and J O M Roberts in the autumn of 1953, and in 1955 Dennis Davis completed a plane table survey west of Namche Bazar and north of the Tesi Lapcha pass. In 1954 and 1955 Norman Hardie mapped the south and east quadrant of the Everest region, south and east of Makalu, thus filling in the last big blank on the map of the Everest region.

Between 1954 and 1957 French and Austrian cartographers produced maps of the south side of the Everest region only. But the first comprehensive map of the region, including both the Tibetan and Nepalese sides, was drawn by G S Holland of the RGS in 1961 and updated in 1975.

Since then many maps have been produced by cartographers for different countries, including Nepal and China.

In 1980 Bradford Washburn, founding Director of the Museum of Science, Boston, wished to increase the accuracy of Everest maps to help geographers and glaciologists. Following flights over Everest, a 1:50,000 map was published in conjunction with the National Geographic Society and the Swiss Federal Office in Berne. A second edition in 1991 showed different routes up Everest.

The present map, published in 2003, is at a scale of 1:5,000 with 5-metre contours, and extends from the South Col and Geneva Spur to the North Col (Chang La). Various points, such as the Hillary Step, the First and Second Steps, and the site of Mallory's body, are marked. Without doubt, this is the most detailed map of all and was made by Swissphoto of Zurich (Erich Keller) and edited by Bradford Washburn.

This is a welcome and important addition to the cartographic canon of Everest.

BRADFORD WASHBURN

The Location of Camp IX

(Plate 1)

Over quite a number of years, there was a friendly disagreement between John Hunt and Ed Hillary about the exact line and altitudes of their route from the South Col to where Ed and Tenzing had their final camp, on the night before their famous ascent.

In May 1993, at the time of the 40th Anniversary of their climb, I was in London and managed to get Hunt and Hillary together to settle this little matter, once and for all. The accompanying photograph by Dolf Reist of Switzerland is the basis on which the two of them agreed on exactly where they went.

These altitudes are all based on the new GPS height of the South Col and the contours are those on my new map of the upper part of Everest on the very large scale of 1:2,000.

- South Col GPS Station: 25,890ft
- Remains of the Swiss 1952 tent: 27,265ft
- Where Hunt and Sherpa Da Namgyal left their loads: 27,395ft
- Site of Hillary and Tenzing's final camp: 27,640ft
- The Balcony: 27,690ft
- The Altitude of Everest's South Summit: 28,710ft
- The Altitude of Everest's Summit: 29,035ft

It is interesting to note that the height of the final campsite of Hillary and Tenzing on the night before their first ascent of Everest on May 29, 1953 was 1750 feet higher than today's regular South Col camp, involving a summit climb of 1395 vertical feet against today's final climb of 3145 feet, significantly more than twice the Hillary-Tenzing summit climb.

Everest above its South Col (25,890ft/7890m). (*Dolf Reist*) (p20)

Significant points on the summit pyramid from the 1950s are detailed, following research by Brad Washburn and interviews with the principals in 1993. The points marked on the photograph are listed below:

1. Remains of Lambert and Tenzing's tent from the Swiss 1952 expedition (27,265ft/8310m)

2. Point at which John Hunt and Da Namgyal left food and other equipment for Ed Hillary and Tenzing (27,395ft/8350m)

3. Hillary and Tenzing's final campsite, 28 May 1953 (27,640ft/8424m)

4. The Balcony (27,690ft/8440m)

5. The South Summit (28,710ft/8751m)

The altitude of Everest's summit is 29,035ft/8850m.

2. Do not adjust your set. Kenton Cool peers out of a vertically pitched tent at the end of day two during the five-day second ascent of the Denali Diamond. (*Ian Parnell*) (p23)

Expeditions

IAN PARNELL

Hell to Pay: On Denali's Diamond

(Front cover and Plate 2)

This is my third year in the Central Alaskan Range. I come not just for the mountains, but also for the sense of hope, shared desire and belief that exudes from the climbers here. The mountains, with their 8,000 to 10,000ft faces, offer some of the world's best alpine challenges but it is the people here that are really special. Most climbers gather at the same base camp. A bit like Yosemite's Camp 4 on ice, with your neighbours ranging from wannabe Messners to some of America's leading alpinists, from *voie normale* weekend warriors through to single-push fanatics. For most of us, this is the promised land. We've worked hard to earn the pennies to get here amongst our long-dreamt-of summits. With so many fought-for ambitions it would be easy for brutal competition to breed. Instead there is a real sense of community. Every success seems shared, raising the collective experience, bolstering a belief in what might be possible. Each year I make lifelong friends, meet great people, who share that innocent joy of pure climbing.

2001 was an exceptional season in the Central Alaskan Range, with perfect weather and conditions. Party after party nipped up world-class test-pieces in the lightest of alpine style. It seemed anything was possible and as the mental barriers tumbled and myths evaporated you could sense the collective growth in confidence. May and June 2002 again saw the gathering of the top US alpinists, with a handful of crack Euros thrown in. Buoyant from last year's successes, most had their sights set high, hard and very, very fast. But things had changed; nothing is for certain in the mountains. Amongst the flux, this year's most popular target, the *Moonflower Buttress* on Mount Hunter, lay untouched as a huge rockfall guarded its base. The nearby *Deprivation*, another coveted line, led suitors on with a flirtation of ice that on closer acquaintance revealed vertical ribbons of slush. Everywhere, climbers' attentions were being spurned and despite some bold efforts even Hunter held out, unclimbed so far this year.

Some climbers feel a mystical contact with the hills. Top Slovenian mountaineer Tomaz Humar has even developed his own religion around them saying: 'Every rock face breathes life with its lungs and emanates an energy that is proper only to itself.'

The mountains are a place I love, where I feel most at home, but to me they are still piles of snow and stones. But as I broke through the sun-crust, up to my chest in ball-bearing snow, I couldn't help thinking they weren't on my side. Kenton Cool and I were nearing the end of our second day on the 'six-hour' approach to Mount Foraker's *Infinite Spur* whose glistening back, bare of the usual soft coat of snow, loomed mockingly above us. Perhaps Humar was right and we had used up our alpine karma last year, managing two first ascents and one near-first free ascent. This season it was the mountain's turn for revenge; somewhere someone was laughing. It was an evil humour.

If I'm honest I'd have to admit it wasn't only the mountains with revenge in mind. I'd left the UK with stinging criticism from one particular climbing magazine's comments ringing in my ears. I knew it had little to do with my actual climbing and more to do with selling reputations and magazines, but their accusations still hurt. In the climbing world talk is cheap, meaningless without action, so my determination grew to expose their posturing with an ascent that they couldn't ignore.

Things weren't quite going to plan though. Kenton and I hoped to pioneer a 9000ft new route on Mount Foraker before nipping over to Denali for the coveted second ascent of the *Denali Diamond*. It didn't take us too long to realise that the new route wasn't going to happen this year, or any year, riddled as it was with tottering séracs. The attempt on the *Infinite Spur* was supposed to be our consolation but that wasn't going too well either.

'I hate this place. I want the first flight out of here!' screamed Kenton as he fell through the snow for a final time. Kenton wears his emotions on his sleeve. It's one of the reasons I climb with him. I'm fed up with macho bullshit in the mountaineering world, the inability to be honest about fear and risk. It's carefully calculated reticence, followed closely by jealousy of those who share their stories, and the attitude that promotes someone who travels around the world festival circuit but slags off those who get out into the mountains and try.

I shared Kenton's feelings. We were boiling in frustration and needed some vertical action soon. I put it bluntly: 'Kenny you've got until the end of today to get your whinging out of your system and then let's quit messing about down here and head up onto the Diamond.'

Within 24 hours we were refuelled and leaving base camp with a perfect, stable forecast. Our friends Jimmy and Russ, Kelly and Scott were poised for their prospective return matches with Hunter. That sense of collective energy was growing again. I even began to feel nostalgia for our initial single-push plans. Instead we had opted to go traditional alpine style although in a rather lightweight manner with only one-season sleeping bags plus the novel 'Babu' tent.

Designed for the Sherpa Babu Chhiri during his record camp on the summit of Everest, the tent was certainly strong but not very long – Babu was five-foot-two. With two six-footers lying on top of each other, our shelter took on all the comforts of a primary school play tent but at least it was light. The theory was to climb during the night and slumber in the warmth of the afternoon sun. And after making the approach during the cold of early morning, we spent the day sunbathing at the base of the SW Face, congratulating ourselves on our cunning plan.

Twenty-four hours later and we had begun to test the hypothesis. Of course the mountains are no respecters of mere theories. As the snow began on the first night, it soon became obvious that our forecast was a hollow tease. The test was changing and we'd have to adapt quickly to survive this one.

The tales from the first ascent of the *Denali Diamond* are legendary. Having forgotten half their gear, Brian Becker and Rolf Graage took their single 9mm rope and two ice screws to the 8000ft SW Face of Denali anyway. Seventeen days later they emerged frostbitten and hungry with their Diamond and the first Alaskan grade 6+. I relived their epic story again and again but the line that I couldn't get from my mind was what they'd found on the penultimate technical pitch, 3500 feet up – a great A3 roof, 25 feet wide. My mind leapt at the challenge, could it go free? In the months prior to landing on the glacier here I'd found myself startled awake, head full of images of me struggling across the overhang before the aching void caught my fall. Each time I dreamt I got further toward that virtual lip, gradually convincing myself it might be possible. Last season our friends, Slovenian Marko Prezelj and American Stephen Koch, had pioneered a new line close to the *Denali Diamond* in an astonishing 48-hour push. As striking as their speed was the difficulty. While Marko declined to offer a grade, Stephen, who followed the crux, reckoned it might be M8, as hard as anything yet freed in the mountains. I wanted such a challenge.

The climbing was fantastic, a natural line weaving up ribbons of beautiful ice between towering granite. Gradually the gully narrowed and the walls steepened. An alpine Petra, the Diamond eased its way into ever more improbable terrain until a sudden opening revealed the test. Above us, out of the snow-flurries, loomed a series of huge roofs dripping with spindrift avalanches. There were only three vague weaknesses from the overhung bay – the least likely a hideous flared chimney, blocked by a huge chockstone that implausibly had hoared up to create a 20-foot horizontal ice roof. To our right lay the infamous '25-foot roof crack', in reality a steeply-leaning wall rather than a roof. In places, however, the fissure widened to off-width and as our biggest gear was a Friend 3, that left only one real option. The cracked wall seemed to offer plenty of protection and the possibility of hooks for my ice axes but in places it bulged alarmingly. It would be the steepest mixed climbing I had ever tried.

Again things started badly. An initial attempt, late in the day, ground to a halt in continuous spindrift avalanches. Kenton, lashed to the belay and unable to move, fared the worst, shivering and drowning in the icy torrents. Calling a premature halt to proceedings, we vainly searched for a campsite but had to make do with Kenton's original belay. A couple of hours spent chopping blunted our picks and yielded just two shallow bum-scoops. Eventually we 'pitched' the tent vertically, hanging it from the belay anchors over us as we slumped into the bite of our harnesses. Not only did it look like we might have to climb Scottish 8 to get up this thing but we would have to do it without sleep and without the use of our blood-starved legs. Finally, as if the challenge hadn't been racked up enough notches, I chose this moment to drop my axe.

Strangely, the following morning, despite a little grogginess, I feel ready for whatever this climb might throw at me. I have Kenton's axes, leaving him a puzzle of improvisation to follow. Unlike the imagined screaming struggle a calmness comes over me as I pull the torqued axes home and my picks find improbable hooks at full stretch. After a heroic struggle to follow the pitch with only one axe, an exhausted Kenton declines the next lead, so on the rush of momentum I jump at the challenge. Strength and confidence seem to flood through my veins. Caught within feet of the top of the final steep wall by a freight train of avalanching spindrift, I relax and intuitively release the axe in the centre of its tracks. The snow thunders past, knocking me aside to swing on my remaining axe. Just for these moments I feel like I could climb anything. This was my day and I was relishing every minute. I had passed my test.

Twelve hours later and I feel I can't get any lower. Now I'm having my worst day in the mountains. Perhaps I'm exhausted from the previous day's efforts or perhaps it's due to our third sleepless night. Whatever, I'm really paying for it now. The irony is that after a day spent climbing technically harder ground than I've ever done before, I'm about to fail on 45-degree snow. Twice I've come close to blacking out, fighting nausea as I drop to my knees every other step. The snow has continued to fall, blanketing the black ice beneath, offering a promise of progress as I step up, then letting me down several steps as I break through the crust to skitter on the ice.

Kenton waits patiently for the umpteenth time today. As I reach him I lose it completely, openly sobbing, collapsed in the snow. 'I'm sorry, I'm sorry, I've let you down,' I babble. Kenton's been breaking trail all day. He's not enjoying this much either but he has no doubt about summiting. 'Don't worry mate, it's only a climb,' he reassures me. I feel that I'm losing not only my dreams but breaking Kenton's too. But his calm words break through my despondency. His strength feels like it could pull us both through. If only I can keep moving, no matter how slow or how much snow, we will make it. I remember Kenton last year trying to explain to a non-climber the unique bond of two people climbing. Once again I feel the power of our partnership. As long as one of us keeps working we'll be okay.

This should be our last day on the climb. Last night we had a pleasant surprise as Americans Hank and Jeff emerged out of the swirling snow after climbing the lower two-thirds of the *Cassin*. We made an agreement to wake early and share trail-breaking. Throughout this climb, however, great ideas had been exposed, in the light of the real world, for what they really were. When Hank managed less than a hundred yards on the first stint, I thought he might just need a little warming up and took over. But when the Americans stopped for lunch at 9.30am it became clear we would be doing all the snow-ploughing today. Luckily the exhaustion I felt earlier had lifted somewhat and Kenton was on form yet again. Working together, we waded through knee-deep crust, squinting through the whiteout until suddenly the angle eased. Euphoria and sheer relief welled up and we hugged each other at the top of the *Cassin Ridge*.

We took the hour-long horizontal plod to the summit, the top ticked for the critics, but with no view the highest point seemed superfluous to our climb. Back atop the *Cassin* we joined up once again with Hank and Jeff, combining for the descent across the featureless football field. Zero visibility and a few sloughs of windslab had the Americans nervously enquiring if we knew where we were. We could only answer 'not exactly' but that we were on a bearing and would deal with whatever came in our way. This did little for Hank and Jeff's confidence and so they opted to put up camp and await better weather. With the tent poles broken after our vertical bivvy and our one-season bags useless clumps of mushy down, we had little option. We began to rehearse our lines to the Rangers at the high camp. Would they mind being woken up? Would they have any shelter for us?

Emerging through the cloud at midnight, 5000ft below the summit, we were surprised to see a crowd of climbers ringing the edge of camp. Perhaps 50 climbers and Rangers watched our chaotic descent. We hurriedly stumbled downwards in case they disappeared to bed.

Little did we know but the alert was out. With the poor weather most climbers had been tent-bound, with time to worry about the epic-prone 'bad-ass Brits'. With rescue services poised, friends at base camp had even delayed their flights out in case their help was needed. As we staggered the last few steps to camp the crowd was still there waiting for us. A stranger walked out and shook my hand. Another pressed a mug of steaming tea towards me. I recognised a face. One of the rangers, John Evans, smiled: 'Welcome home boys, we've got a tent ready.' It was all I could do to keep the tears back.

As we were pampered by the Rangers, with a tent that actually worked, huge five-season down bags and a cooked breakfast, I realised I hadn't thought of revenge or reputations once over the last five days. The purity of action had cut away the crap and shown what really mattered. Belief, partnership and the support of our friends on the hill had pulled us through. We'd paid our dues to the real boss.

Summary: A personal account of the second ascent of the *Denali Diamond* (8,000ft , VIII, 8, A3) on the SW Face of Denali (Mt McKinley, 6194m), Alaska, by Kenton Cool and Ian Parnell over 5 days in late May 2002.

Acknowledgements: The Expedition would like to thank the BMC, the Mount Everest Foundation and UK Sport for their financial support and The North Face UK, Mountain Hardwear, Blizzard, Big Stone, Snow and Rock and Urban Rock for their valuable equipment support.

PAUL RAMSDEN
The North Face of Siguniang

(Frontispiece and Plate 5)

The Peak District, along with the rest of the country, had been closed to climbers for six months thanks to foot and mouth. But today, midsummer, Stanage had reopened. You'd expect the place to have been heaving, but things were fairly quiet. Maybe the word hadn't got out yet.

Mick Fowler was easy to spot from a long way off. He had come straight from the tax office and forgotten his climbing clothes. He was, inevitably, the only person on the crag wearing suit trousers and a white collared shirt

'Mick! Careful you don't spoil those nice pants!' I shouted.

'Ah, Mr Ramsden! It's good to be out on the grit again.'

A pleasant evening was interrupted by encroaching darkness and a plague of midges. At the Little John in Hathersage we settled in with a few beers, before descending into the usual round of climbing bullshit and tall stories.

'So, Mr Fowler, have you got any plans for a big trip next year?'

'Well actually I noticed some rather disturbing pictures in the new AAJ. They have definitely given me the urge.'

'You mean the ones of China?' I came back perhaps a bit too quickly. Looking surprised and a bit concerned Mick responded that perhaps we should get together and come up with a plan before someone else did.

A few e-mails later and we were sorted. Some mountain called Siguniang had an unclimbed north face. We weren't sure how high the mountain was, how high the face was or quite how to get to it but we were going next April. Later in the year Mick phoned up to mention that he couldn't really manage much more than three and a half weeks. Doing a bit of quick arithmetic I figured that would give us about two weeks above base camp after travel and bureaucracy. And only if nothing went wrong. It wasn't really long enough for text-book acclimatisation.

'Ah, an added challenge for the Ramsden body!' he replied. What can you say to that kind of irrepressible optimism?

A week to departure. Pre-trip training had gone badly. Which is to say there wasn't any. I went through my cupboards patching holes in gloves, duct-taping up the weak spots in the bivi tent. I hate packing. On the morning we departed, I got out of the shower and stepped onto the scales. Thirteen stones. Plenty of bivi fat, then.

The team met for the first time at the airport. Mick and I were going to attempt Siguniang. Accompanying us to base camp were Mike Morrison and Roger Gibbs who were planning to try some of the other unclimbed peaks in the area. At check-in the minor problem of an excess luggage bill of £1,200 was soon smoothed over by Mick with all the efficiency of a senior civil servant.

'Do you realise we are an official British mountaineering expedition? Sponsored by the government?' The rest of us just stood back to watch some masterful bullshitting. Half an hour later we had an apology and an unlimited baggage allowance.

In China we had employed – over the internet – a local 'fixer' who called himself 'Lion'. He was a young lad but efficient and soon had us on the bus out of Chengdu and onto the road-head at Rilong in the Qionglai Mountains of Sichuan Province. Once in Rilong we stayed with Mr Marr, a friend of Lion's. Mr Marr is the local mountain guide and pony transportation sorter. His English is pretty basic but he is a good bloke with a strange propensity to strip naked on the summit of mountains, as his scrap book showed. Ponies were arranged and then loaded. At dawn we were following the relatively popular trail into the mountains. Base camp was established two days later, in a hanging alp below Siguniang's north face. Home sweet home.

A quick look at the diary and we realised how short of time we really were. It was tempting to go straight on to the route but we agreed that some form of acclimatisation, however brief, was essential. Now the acclimatisation outing on any trip is a strange thing. Basically you set off with a sackful of kit up some obscure and not too technical hillside until you collapse with exhaustion, the obligatory throbbing head and nausea. At the place you collapse you pitch the tent, cook dinner, throw up and try to sleep. On each subsequent day you repeat day one. It's such a laugh. After three days of this we had reached an unimpressive 5200 metres, had finished our books and were desperate to get onto something a bit more interesting. A retreat to base camp seemed in order and, disturbingly, we only took three hours to get down.

We spent a day binge eating, rucksack packing, rucksack unpacking and rucksack repacking. I admit to being totally obsessed with the weight of my gear. The scissors were in action cutting off extraneous features, labels and so on. Mick on the other hand just threw everything in his huge pack and topped it off with the latest Harry Potter.

We set off early next morning, intending to establish our first camp on the flat glacier shelf below the face. Occasionally I would gaze up at the route and watch the constant spindrift avalanches fall in parallel lines down the lower half of the face. Our first camp was idyllic, flat and sunny. Once inside the tent you could forget where you were, almost.

The initial section of the route took the form of a huge open couloir consisting of partially iced slabs threatened by séracs on the left-hand side. Mick set off up the first pitch, which soon developed into an insecure, snowed-up steep slab. Following, I found it hard and disturbing. And it got much steeper above. Mick hung at the stance with a big cheesy grin on his face, obviously glad to be back on technical ground.

Similar pitches led to an ice field one pitch short of the start of a central gully line. It was obvious we would be a long way up this before we found a decent bivi spot, so here would have to do. After a few hours hacking away beneath a small roof we had a ledge 12 feet by 12 inches. Mick hung in the Gemini tent at the far end while I made do with my bivi bag. We ate dinner watching the sun set and I was actually enjoying myself. Things soon changed the following morning.

Mick managed about 30 feet of the gully before shouting down: 'It's steeper than it looks. I'm going to have to leave my sack here and haul it later. And the ice is a bit thin here. The screws won't go in fully but there is some nice shale basalt beneath!'

My heart sank. This was going to be another typical Fowler outing.

'Added challenge!' I shouted back positively, without feeling it. Two steep mixed pitches were followed by a vertical icefall 150 feet high. The problem was that we only had five ice screws. Two in the belay left two for the next belay and only one for protection in the pitch. The only option was to occasionally clip into our tools and rig Abalakov threads as runners.

All too soon it became obvious we would have to find somewhere to bivi. I was perched on a steep smear of ice below a protective roof but the belay was poor. I brought Mick up and we started to excavate the slope by our feet, only to find the ice inches deep.

Mick thought he saw a ledge off to the side. I was not convinced but the desire to find somewhere to at least sit down was too much. Mick headed off and immediately got involved in some difficult snowed-up rock. It started to get dark. No ledge was forthcoming but there was a bomber single nut belay. It would have to do.

The spindrift increased in intensity. Getting into our pits without soaking them was out of the question, as was cooking. In the end we spent the night standing with the tent draped over our heads. I don't remember much of that night; it seemed better to forget it.

The following day saw us back on steep ice. This time it got fat for several pitches but with a corresponding increase in angle being around vertical for much of the day. We settled into a routine of climbing in spurts until lack of oxygen and cramping forearms brought us to a panting halt. The exposure became truly head-spinning.

The third bivi was on an ice smear a pitch out to the left of the gully line. There was no chance of pitching the tent but we did find ice thick enough to hack out a bum ledge. Again we used the tent as a double bivi bag with the stove hanging on a screw to one side. After the first brew however the spindrift started up again giving us little choice but to retreat into the tent without dinner yet again.

Every time we leaned forward, spindrift went down the gap between our backs and the recess chipped in the ice. Over time this wedge built up until after a few hours we were prised off and left hanging from our harnesess. As Mick slid off his ledge, slack in his belay system meant that he ended up stood in the bottom of the tent. His weight was thus neatly transferred to the top of the tent that was braced against my head. Hours passed slowly as I drifted into a state of semi-consciousness, my legs numbed, my neck straining against Mick's weight and the cold damp tent fabric pressed against my face. I hate bivvies.

Next day Mick pulled off a very fine lead up an overhanging groove where the gully had been bisected by a horizontal band or sill that created an overhang. I seconded the line of loose basalt flakes and thin rotten ice with my sack on. Halfway up the pitch I became concerned that my lungs might burst from my desperate effort to suck in more oxygen. Steep climbing at altitude really hurts.

A few more pitches and I managed to climb out onto the rib that bound our gully on the right-hand side. It looked like we were only a few pitches from the point where the gully eased back and onto the slopes below the summit sérac band. However, the next section looked steep so we opted to bivi where we were. Mick scouted around and found a ledge big enough to sit on comfortably behind a small flake. But that wasn't enough. Mick was determined to pitch the tent. It took some creative thinking and advanced dry-stone walling skills.

My side of the ledge was the most undercut, but by piling up some loose blocks I managed to balance the cantilevered stone that was to be my bed. Once inside, however, it was soon clear that the mere fact of pitching the tent would not make us comfortable. At least we were able to cook in relative comfort for the first time in three days. But the night was one of the grimmest with my head below my feet, a rock spike in the small of my back and Mick's feet on my head.

'I slept quite well,' Mick chirped in the morning. I bit my tongue. Smug bastard.

As we packed up, a sense of urgency developed. We were keen to get out of this vertical world onto some easier slopes. I led off, onto what for me would be the crux pitch of the route. Good ice led up to a band of roofs. To the left was a very steep pillar of ice separated from the rock behind. Now the wind got up and spindrift engulfed the ice at regular intervals. Leaving a good screw, I swung onto the front of the pillar, which unfortunately proved to consist of soft, rotten ice with a fragile crust on top of it. Ice screws could be pulled straight out by hand.

I pushed on and it got steeper. I was repeatedly engulfed in spindrift. My lungs pumped like bellows and my forearms burned with real pain. Then, in a white blur, it was over. Above, the angle eased back into classic fifty-degree alpine ice slopes towards the sérac barrier up and out to the right.

The initial plan had been to sneak through the séracs on the left-hand side along a ramp line we had supposedly spotted from below. Intimate contact with the séracs and their fearsome angle soon changed our minds. The only feasible option was a long traverse rightwards beneath the séracs, looking for a weakness in the barrier above. Several calf-pumping pitches later we arrived beneath a gully that led directly up to the summit. By now it was almost dark so we carried on traversing right onto a short rib that looked sheltered from the avalanche slopes above. A small rock flake provided a reasonable half-sit-down ledge and a decent belay so we settled down for a long night.

Dawn was beautiful. A cloud inversion filled the valley and the surrounding peaks glistened under the heavy mantle of snow that had fallen during the night. It had snowed right down to the valley yet again. Today was summit day. One more pitch of steep ice and we were onto the final slopes. Deep snow slowed progress, as did the lack of oxygen on top of our already low energy levels. A fairly steep step and we were onto the summit cornice and there was nowhere else to go. Feeling no real desire to edge out onto the final thin bit we sat down on flat ground for the first time in a week. On every side we could see nothing but endless unclimbed peaks.

Mick grinned. 'The potential is most disturbing.'

It was still morning, but we dropped down a short way and stamped out a flat ledge. We needed a rest and a good feed. The simple pleasure of getting out of a properly pitched tent and urinating without a harness on is very rewarding. Over dinner the subject of descent came up in conversation. Mick with his insatiable appetite for exploration convinced me it would be more rewarding as well as more aesthetic to descend the as yet unclimbed north ridge that bound our face on the left.

The north ridge took two days to descend and its razor sharp but not quite vertical angle made abseiling difficult. Added to that were problems of giant unconsolidated snow mushrooms and a bit of loose rock thrown in for good measure. At least the halfway bivi was good, even palatial. The tent *almost* fitted on to the ledge.

The 5000 feet of descent swallowed up much of the rack and the endless Abalakov anchors required us to shorten one of the ropes considerably. A last flounder down the glacier and we collapsed onto the boulder field in the sun. Handshakes, congratulation, cheesy grins then silence. After days and days of heightened awareness to all the dangers around, safety almost leaves you deflated.

The return to civilization was simple and rapid. Loads carried down to the valley to meet the ponies, a stroll down to Rilong, then the bus to Chengdu for our flight home. Once at home, I stepped onto the bathroom scales. Eleven stone three pounds. I'd lost almost two stone in three weeks. That's some diet.

MARTIN MORAN

The Seven Pillars of Satling

(Back cover and Plates 3 and 4)

Sometimes it is hard to find logic in the footsteps of mountaineers. The Khatling Glacier and Bhilangna River drain one of the largest valley systems of the Garhwal Himalaya. At their head is the magnificent south wall of Thalay Sagar (6904m), ringed by peaks between 5500m and 6500m in altitude and just a few miles from the honeypots of Shivling and the Gangotri Glacier, visited by thousands of trekkers, pilgrims and climbers each year. Yet nobody seems bothered to climb up in the Khatling and only a few trekking parties visit en route to the Shastra Tal or the Maiali Pass and Kedarnath. What the masses miss is a valley of exquisite sylvan beauty and mountaineering potential that has barely been tapped.

The last official climbing party to visit the valley was the British Thalay Sagar expedition of 1992. All of this is bad news for the local people who have missed out on the trekking and climbing boom. It is small wonder then that we were fêted as special visitors when our team of seven climbers arrived at Ghuttu, the Bhilangna roadhead, in late April 2002.

We were enticed by photographs, taken by the 1992 team, showing a range of striking granite spires and towers ringing a side glacier on the eastern rim of the basin. Their local name is 'Sat-ling', which means seven phalluses or pillars. The 1992 team gave some of them individual names appropriate to their shape and features, for example The Cathedral and Rabbit's Ears. To our knowledge the peaks were entirely untouched. The pictures showed the highest of the summits to be capped by two hammer-heads of granite, around 5850m in altitude and defended by steep walls and ridges. This was provisionally named 'Double-Headed Peak'.

The range promised a feast of technical rock and ice climbing at modest altitude. How could such gems have been untouched when Ghuttu is only 12 hours' driving from Delhi?

We left Delhi at 1.30am on 27 April. The night ride to Rishikesh was swift and peaceful, the silent plains of Uttar Pradesh acquiring a ghostly beauty under a waning moon. The springtime heat became intense as our bus wound its way over the foothills through Chamba and then down to Tehri, where the largest dam project in the subcontinent is in an advanced state of construction. The massive dam plugs a narrowing in the Bhagirathi valley, just downstream from old Tehri town, already partially submerged. New settlements have been built on the west side of the valley. The scale of the earthworks, concrete spillway, overflow tunnels and labour camps was awesome, almost threatening. Yet 20km beyond, in the lower Bhilangna

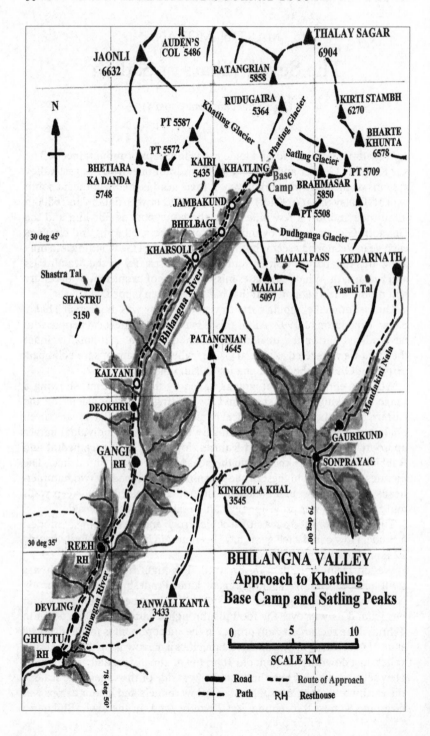

BHILANGNA VALLEY
Approach to Khatling
Base Camp and Satling Peaks

SCALE KM

— Road   - - - Route of Approach
-- Path   RH   Resthouse

valley, the timeless tranquillity of rural life was regained. We reached the roadhead at Ghuttu (1524m) at 6.15pm and took quarters in a large but otherwise empty resthouse.

Our 35 porters were recruited from Ghuttu and surrounding villages. In two days of 10km each we walked to Reeh (2132m) and Gangi (2650m). At both villages large resthouses provided accommodation, their comforts depreciated by collapsing floorboards and colonies of rats. The valley scenery was of a high order, the villages attractively sited on terraces and surrounded by freshly tilled fields of potato mounds and wheat. The local women wore nose jewellery, usually a disc pendant, and they were shy and resentful of any photographic intrusion. The kids were more forthcoming, yelling a chorus of 'Mithai, Mithai' – sweeties – as we passed.

The 18km trek to Kharsoli (2950m) was favoured by wonderfully clear weather. The valley makes a V-shaped trench, thickly clad in olive-needled pines interspersed with the spring-green foliage of chestnuts. Rhododendron was profuse, although its flowers were past their most vivid display. The track linked several forest clearings where goats are grazed in summer. The final eight kilometres followed the riverbank. Save for the obstacles of fallen tree trunks, the trail was distinct and the going good, but the undulations of the route made for a fatiguing day. Kharsoli is a large grazing area at the confluence of the Kairi Gad with the main Bhilangna valley. The porters were lodged variously in caves and tents. The remnants of winter were now visible in the form of a 60-metre icefall high in a gorge and wide fans of avalanche debris in all the side nalas.

The final march to base camp was made stressful by a steady gain in altitude, the sighting of a bear at Bhelbagi alp, a widening cover of snow and a temporary porter strike. At its end we were safely installed at 3720m, in line with our most optimistic schedule. A heavy snowfall commenced just after the porters were embarked on their return trek. Base camp was located by a large boulder in a wide ablation valley under the Phating Glacier lateral moraine. A metre of snow covered the alluvial flats but a healthy stream was flowing under the pack. We spent two hours digging out an area of ground for the mess tent, but pitched personal tents on the snow, which melted rapidly over the next two weeks. A sizeable lake appeared 100 metres away and our tents were left perched on ice platforms.

Entry to the Satling Glacier

All members took an exploratory walk up towards the Satling Glacier, climbing to the moraine crest overlooking the Phating Glacier. From here the brown rock wall of Thalay Sagar's South Face was impressively displayed, but our eyes were more immediately drawn to the array of granite pinnacles up to the right where the side glacier of the Satling tumbled down to meet the main glacier. A short excursion out on to the Phating Glacier brought into view the citadel of Pt. 5541, christened The Fortress. On its left the Satling icefall bridged the valley, but a weakness on its left-hand

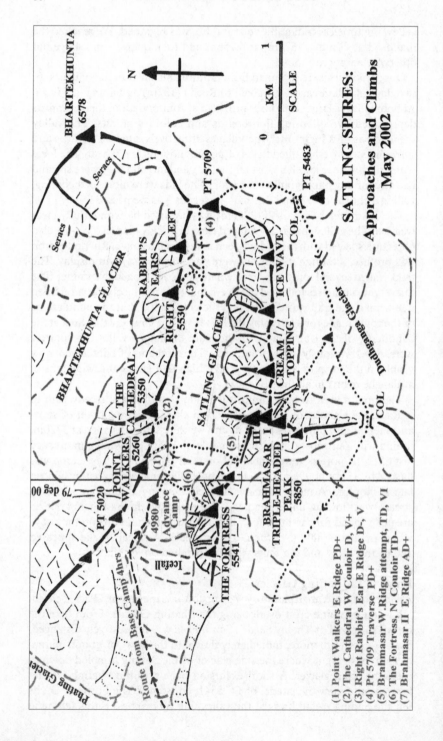

SATLING SPIRES:
Approaches and Climbs
May 2002

SCALE

N

BHARTEKHUNTA
6578

BHARTEKHUNTA GLACIER

Seracs

PT 5709

RABBIT'S EARS

LEFT

RIGHT 5530

THE CATHEDRAL 5350

5260

POINT WALKERS

PT 5020

79 deg 00

Route from Base Camp 4hrs

Phating Glacier

Icefall

4980 Advance Camp

THE FORTRESS 5541

SATLING GLACIER

CREAM TOPPING

ICE WAVE

COL

PT 5483

BRAHMASAR I
TRIPLE-HEADED II
PEAK III
5850

Dudhganga Glacier

COL

0   KM   1

(1) Point Walkers E Ridge PD+
(2) The Cathedral W Couloir D, V+
(3) Right Rabbit's Ear E Ridge D-, v
(4) Pt 5709 Traverse PD+
(5) Brahmasar W Ridge attempt, TD, VI
(6) The Fortress, N. Couloir TD-
(7) Brahmasar II E Ridge AD+

side offered a route to the upper glacier where we hoped to place an advance camp.

Our team now split. Rupert and Sally Bennett planned an exploratory trip up the Phating Glacier towards Rudugaira (5364m) and Ratangrian (5858m). The Satling candidates formed two teams, the first comprising Mark Davidson, John Venier and myself, and the second Keith Milne and Gordon Scott, who had been on the 1992 trip and had now come back to claim some prizes. On 3 May five of us plus high altitude porter Mangal took substantial loads up the Satling valley to a height of 4500m. The intense midday heat persuaded us to make a temporary dump. The distance to the gentle snowfields of the upper glacier was further than we had at first imagined. Early next morning we left for the decisive push to establish our advance base with help from both porters, Mangal and Hari. Above 4500m, with loads well over 20kg each, our pace slowed to an agonised plod.

For 200 metres the route traversed sloppy snow above a considerable drop into the jaws of the icefall, then climbed diagonally up to the lip of the upper plateau. After a seemingly endless trudge the glacier folded into a flat-bottomed hollow ideal for a camp site. The altitude was around 4950m and the time 12.30pm but what a site! Exhaustion turned to elation as we viewed the scything ridges of 'Double-Headed Peak' across the glacier. We were sited close under 200m walls of pristine granite and had a 180-degree outward panorama ranging from Thalay Sagar round to Jaonli and Bhetiara-ka-Danda. In its foreground rose an 80 metre fang of rock, which beckoned to be photographed with a climber perched on its summit in the dramatic fashion of Pierre Tiarraz's pictures of the Chamonix aiguilles. While Mangal and Hari ploughed down the snows back to base camp we lay outside all afternoon enjoying the peerless weather.

On 5 May after retrieving all remaining kit from our dump, we walked up the glacier to view potential objectives. Though not in the top league in terms of scale, in all other respects this is a cirque of superlatives. Every gradation of rock geometry from brown and sunny aiguilles to blank and bulging walls of unweathered granite was displayed. Caps of blue ice and a topping of white spring snow completed the spectacle. At the left end of the glacier twin domes of granite, named 'The Rabbit's Ears' by the 1992 team, looked particularly appealing. Our threesome decided to attempt the nearer of these next day.

The Rabbit's Ear and The Cathedral

At dawn on 6 May we tramped up the glacier until below the east col of the nearer tower. The views en-route demanded a prolonged stop for photo-graphy and for examination of possible objectives. Our route itself proved a little more serious than expected. After two long pitches on 50° snow and grade II mixed ground we gained the East Ridge of the tower, which was poised above an impressive drop down to the shaded Bhartekhunta Glacier. The other Rabbit's Ear sported a sheer granite face of some 400m or 500m vertical height on its north-west side. The hanging séracs of Bhartekhunta's South Face formed an appropriately savage back-cloth. After a varied pitch of III+ up the arête, our way was barred by the bulging summit block. But there was a neat solution in the form of a strenuous grade V hand traverse round its left side, which led to easier shelves and the snow-capped summit. We were on top at 12.30pm, guessing our altitude at c.5530m, and regained the glacier at 2.15pm after three 60-metre abseils. Rumbles of thunder heralded our return and the start of a two-hour snowstorm.

Rising 800m from the upper Phating Glacier is a slender rock steeple, which had been named The Cathedral. From the Satling side this was an accessible objective with its summit just 400 metres above our camp. Here the peak presented us with a pair of fierce rock pillars split by a steep central chimney. We left at 8.30am and soloed a grade I couloir to the col beneath the central gully where we changed into rock shoes and left our plastic boots. Carefully avoiding snow and ice patches, we climbed four varied pitches to the brèche between the two aiguilles, the hardest a strenuous crack of V+ standard. The south top was patently inaccessible in rock shoes and we pinned our hopes on being able to surmount the north top. However, it was impossible to tell whether it was the higher of the two. After some delicate moves up the arête we faced a smooth final five-metre tower. To our joy an exposed but easy traverse went round its right side where a short slab gained the pinpoint summit. Better still, we considered ourselves a metre or so higher than the south top so could make unequivocal claim to the first ascent. Two full 60-metre abseils straight off the summit ridge regained our sacks and we scurried back to our tent as storm-clouds threatened.

A lovely mellow evening allowed us to cook outside. Here was Himalayan living at its most enjoyable. Despite glorious weather we now needed a short rest at base camp.

The Fortress North Couloir

While we engaged the Rabbit's Ear Keith and Gordon made an abortive attempt to climb the attractive West Ridge of Pt. 5260m immediately behind our camp. Foiled by the snowstorm, they planned instead to attempt the first ascent of The Fortress (5541m), which sported an attractive north couloir, gleaming with ice in its lower part, then zigzagging to the summit.

Leaving at 6am Gordon and Keith completed the climb in 10 hours, enjoying two pitches of Scottish grade IV and V in standard, several of III/IV and long sections of steep snow. They were shielded from sight of storm-clouds gathering from the south, and continued to the summit notch in ignorance of the threat. Luckily, the promised thunderstorm did not materialise and they reached the top at 4pm. The descent was made part by abseil and part by down-climbing. They regained camp at around 10pm after an excellent climb.

Discussion during our rest day at base camp centred on the topography of our main objective. A third hammer-headed summit had been spotted on our Double-Headed Peak rendering its name obsolete. Triple-Headed Peak seemed dull and prosaic so with respect for our Hindu hosts we settled on Brahmasar or Brahma's Head, the God Brahma being depicted with three heads. Climbing the thing would be rather more difficult. We guessed that the south side of the peak might be rather shorter of approach and easier in angle, but with our camp and all kit on the Satling Glacier to its north, we were bound to go back that way. Mark, John and I decided to try the West Ridge. Meanwhile Keith and Gordon would go over a col at the head of the Satling and try to access the south face for a lightweight attempt. Early on 10 May we climbed back to our Satling camp.

Brahmasar West Ridge
At the ungodly hour of 2.10am we set out into a perfect clear night, progressing in relaxed fashion to the bergschrund, then plugging steadily up compact dry snow at 55°. When the snow petered out we had to traverse right into a runnel of glassy ice which led direct to the west col in three pitches of Scottish grade III. A short grade IV rock chimney brought us to the ridge crest and a welcome burst of sunshine at 8.30am. We changed into rock shoes, and packed boots, axes and crampons in the sacks. Our fatigue was eased by the delightful climbing that followed. A fierce gendarme could be by-passed with ease on its right-hand side. We ambled along a veritable *vire aux bicyclettes* with a beautiful backdrop of snow peaks and glaciers to the south. The triple heads of Brahmasar soared above us. From the next notch the rock progressively steepened. An excellent 50-metre pitch of IV+/V led up the crest to a sizeable terrace.

Confidence was rising and our altimeter showed us only 150 metres from the top. It was still only 11am so we decided to dump all bivouac kit here in expectation of completing the climb and returning by abseil that evening.

Almost immediately we made the first big route-finding mistake. I climbed a delicate unprotected arête to find myself on top of a pinnacle with no onward connection. Luckily, I could fix a five-metre sling round the top and lowered off. The episode wasted 30 minutes and significant energy. Awkward grade IV and V climbing on the left flank of the crest brought us to a levelling in the ridge before it swept up to an obvious crux section of smooth vertical rock. Two grade IV pitches brought us to its base.

At a six-metre bulge I left my sack to be hauled. Happily a good jam crack cut diagonally left through this, giving a few strenuous moves. Two delicate sections of similar standard gained easier ground. Clever manœuvres were needed to haul my sack up the arête and this grade VI pitch consumed much energy. Already the time was 4.30pm.

There was no sign of the easy ground we anticipated beneath the first summit. A frustrating diagonal pitch of mixed snow and rock produced dilemmas of route choice. We now reached a level shoulder just 15 metres below the first summit. We had to traverse leftwards under this but the terrain remained stubborn, in the grade IV/V range, with much loose rock. After 15 metres of this traverse the alarm bells sounded. Retreat, especially at night, was looking increasingly problematic. The traverses would be especially difficult to reverse and, had we continued, two hours of daylight looked insufficient to tackle the smooth summit tower. You accept a disappointment and frustration that will last for months to come when turning back so close. After 15 pitches of TD climbing we were less than 60 metres below the top.

The difficulty of retreat down the arête soon confirmed the wisdom of our decision. To keep the ropes centred on the ridge I had to clip the ropes into intermediate runners on my way down. A rope jam would have been disastrous especially on the grade VI pitch. Horizontal sections of ridge had to be down-climbed to find new abseil points. Evening cloud licked our ridge and the rock glowed orange in the lowering light. When darkness came, John discovered his torch wasn't working and Mark and I had to guide him down with our torch beams.

We regained the ledge at 9.15pm. Luckily all breezes had subsided and a clear moonless night was established. After prolonged operations to arrange belays and get into extra clothing we crawled into bivouac bags at 11pm. There was just enough ice on the terrace to make a couple of brews. We had no sleeping bags but survived well enough. I awoke shivering several times but quickly dropped back to a deep sleep. Only when the dawn sun touched Jaonli's summit at 6am did we fully rouse ourselves.

We made two abseils down to the notch before the gendarme, and rappelled four more rope lengths directly down austere chimneys towards the snowfield of our approach. We down-climbed the final 200 metres to meet the sunshine just as we crossed the bergschrund. In baking heat we dragged our bodies over the glacier and crashed out at camp at 11am. Despite ultimate failure we had enjoyed a magnificent climb.

We quit the Satling Glacier at 8.15am on 13 May, somehow strapping all remaining kit into loads of 30kg with which we staggered down to a safe dumping spot at 4700m. Leaving some 20kg to be collected the next day by Mangal, we continued down to reach base camp at 10.30am.

The Satling Circuit and Brahmasar II

On their return to the Satling camp Gordon and Keith planned a busy three-day schedule with the aim of getting round to the south-east side of Brahmasar, from where the summit might be more easily tackled. First they made the first ascent of Pt.5260m – named Point Walkers in respect to our biscuit sponsors! – by its snowy east ridge, a short and pleasant climb of PD+ standard. Then came the hard work of moving camp and 20kg loads to the head of the Satling Glacier.

The watershed was crossed to the Dudhganga basin via a snow arête and summit close to Pt 5709m. After a delicate descent of the east side they crossed a subsidiary col to make camp in the basin under Brahmasar's South-east Face. A steep narrow couloir led up to a col between the central and highest top, Brahmasar I, and the southern summit, Brahmasar II. A shorter grade I couloir led up to the col between Brahmasar I and Cream Topping at the foot of B I's East Ridge. However, this East Ridge looked hard. The intense daytime sun could create conditions ripe for rockfall or avalanche in either gully by mid-morning. Gordon and Keith chose the longer left-hand couloir, on the logic that it would allow them access to either B I or B II.

With a night start the left couloir was climbed quickly to the notch, giving one pitch of grade IV standard. On viewing the 60-metre summit block of BI from the notch, they could see no direct way up without hard aid climbing or even drilling. Gordon and Keith decided instead to bag B II, which was both accessible and technically feasible. A grade IV chimney-crack led to the summit, from which B I looked between 10 and 20 metres higher, a worthy 'inaccessible pinnacle'. The descent was made in three hours.

In the afternoon they packed and crossed another col south of Brahmasar to gain the névé leading under the east side of the Fortress and back to the Phating Glacier. They reached base camp just in time for dinner at 6.30pm.

Conclusions and Recommendations

Weather
The weather was impeccable throughout the trip. Late April and early May seem an ideal time to climb on peaks in the 5000m to 6000m range. By mid-May unstable rising air from the hot plains makes inroads to the Himalayan chain.

Snow Conditions
Given good weather the snow was stable and well-packed giving ideal climbing conditions. Approach gullies were largely filled with snow yet the ridges were sufficiently clear that rock shoes could be worn on more technical routes. At the end of April the snow cover was continuous down to 3700m; there is potential for ski-touring at this time of year and ski-ascents of many peaks around 5500m could be attempted.

Trekking Route and Porters
The Bhilangna valley is not often visited but local porters were well organised and easily available despite competing demands of ploughing and sowing in the village fields at this time of year. Beyond Ghuttu it is difficult or impossible to purchase basic foodstuffs, so the party and porters must be self-sufficient. The high-level trekking routes are not clear of snow until mid-May.

Other Climbing Objectives
Our team only scratched the surface of the potential of the Satling range. Future objectives include the first ascents of the remaining pinnacles and the first ascent of the crowning peak of Brahmasar. The North Ridge and North-West Buttress of Brahmasar would give hard challenges. There are also ice goulottes some 500m in length between Brahmasar and its neighbouring tops. The West Face of The Fortress offers several mixed rock and ice lines. Finally, there are some compact big walls of 500m height on The Rabbit's Ears and the buttresses east of Brahmasar.
Any teams wishing to climb on the Satling should book the peak Brahmasar with the Indian Mountaineering Foundation. Brahmasar is now an officially recognised peak. Whatever your objectives some delectable climbing awaits.

GUY ROBERTSON

Kyzyl Asker

(Plate 26)

Dreams are a bit like sugar. They're a great source of energy. They're an integral part of what makes us 'alive'. They give us endless inspiration and motivation. They say a man without dreams is as well to be dead. From that perspective, failure's easier to swallow, as it helps to keep our dreams alive. This is why climbers have it so easy. Irrespective of where, how hard or with whom we climb, our lifeblood flows readily and our dreams come on tap. And the moment a dream is born can be as exciting and rewarding as living the dream itself.

This summer, on a small expedition to a remote part of the Tien Shan mountains, we unearthed a dream. Hidden amongst the rich climbing treasures of the western Kokshal Too, with an unspoilt view over the vast wilderness that forms the western fringes of China, lies the awesome South-east Face of Kyzyl Asker. I desperately want to climb that face, and so does my friend Es Tressider. It's become our dream.

The 2002 Scottish Kyzyl Asker Expedition was originally put together to attempt the impressive 1300m North-west Face, alpine style. Climbed once previously, on the only recorded ascent of the mountain to date, by a stubborn Russian competition outfit, it used much aid and was rated highly – a worthy objective for our small, free-climbing team. However, heavy rain during the early part of the year put paid to those plans as our truck driver steadfastly refused to attempt the last few miles off road, pointing at large puddles and gesticulating in a decidedly unenthusiastic manner. His wisdom ultimately proved correct, as two neighbouring expeditions lost their trucks to the terrible swamp monster during the following weeks.

There were four of us, myself, Es Tressider, Neal Crampton and Blair Fyffe. I was the 'granddaddy' of the expedition, being the only thirty-something in a team of otherwise young tigers. As well as youth there was talent amongst us, with past exploits on E6 rock, A4 aid and Scottish winter VIII to our credit. The only thing we lacked was high-altitude experience. But that was why we were there.

Base Camp was soon established at the snout of the Komorova Glacier amid a myriad of world-class bouldering. To our immediate south, three huge glaciers sprawled leisurely down from an impressive array of dazzling peaks, most of which sat between the 5000m-5500m level. At over 5800m, Kyzyl Asker dominated the vista, looking huge, the North Face itself a huge glacial spill falling over 2000m directly from the summit. Left of this, each glacier – east, central and west in turn – presented impressive retaining walls and peaks, all of which we knew sported just a handful of routes.

The impression was one of big sky and much space, a bit like an outsized version of the northern Cairngorms. This feeling was exaggerated by a huge open 'delta' that rolled off northwards from the snout of the glaciers next to camp. Our approaches were going to be lengthy affairs, a day at least it seemed, unless we confined ourselves to the smaller routes on the glacier walls. But why doodle in the margins when a vast blank canvas awaits?

We decided to divide into pairs as it was soon apparent we had very different ambitions. Es and I were into something long, hard and free in alpine style – with the emphasis on the hard. Blair and Neal were more relaxed, simply looking to bag some peaks, gain high-altitude experience, and hopefully get some decent climbing into the bargain. (They succeeded, but that's another story). Having seen a quite literally eye-popping photo in the *American Alpine Journal*, Es and I were intent on having a crack at Kyzyl's South-east Face.

After two weeks of acclimatisation, including successful forays up to peaks of 4500m-5000m, we went our separate ways. Es and I decided that with only a fortnight and no knowledge of our route, we would have to move an Advanced Base to the foot of the face. This wasn't easy, necessitating a 15km hike over a 4700m col with more or less every bit of food and gear we possessed. It was three days before we were fully ensconced at the desired location but it was worth the effort.

On first acquaintance the South-east Face of Kyzyl resembles something from a Tolkein fable, a mile-high Gothic cathedral laced with glittering streams of diamonds and pearls. Viewed head-on from the glacier it forms an almost symmetrical triangle of vertical rock, composed on either side of monolithic towers rising up towards the apex at the mountain's summit. From the summit to the glacier falls a giant arête, one and a half times the size of El Cap, a worthy challenge for those pushing envelopes in the field of aid and suffering. Immediately left of this was our own intended route, an icy gully-cum-groove that also ran the entire height of the face.

Neither of us had ever entertained anything quite like this. It resembled something akin to a giant version of the hardest of Scottish gullies except without a definite crux. It was simply vertical, overhanging or extremely thin and tenuous all the way to the top. It seemed clear that the lower half would be ascended on pure steep ice, whereas the upper section would require the mixed skills of a Jedi. Route-finding high up wasn't obvious either.

Shortly after relocating Base Camp another storm came in. The air temperature rocketed and plummeted with beguiling speed and frequency, engendering a sense of objective uncertainty that we could have done without. But we had gradually learned to ignore the weather throughout the first part of the trip. Our barometer hadn't budged despite countless severe weather changes, from baking heat through to electric snowstorms, and we had long since abandoned any hope of accurate prediction. The only certainty was that the weather wouldn't stay fair, which in reality meant we were likely to be under pressure high up. We had agreed that starting out in a storm wasn't rational behaviour, though in retrospect it may have been, and that as soon as it cleared we'd make our first move. After two days the snow stopped.

We left camp at around three in the afternoon, hoping to rattle up the introductory pitches and find a bivouac before dark while the sun was off the route. This would leave us well placed for an early attack at first light, before the sun had risen on the far side of the glacier and started to wreak havoc on the thin ice above us. On such an inescapable fall line, this was a major concern that proved ultimately to be our nemesis. We took synthetic sleeping-bags, a small home-made bivvy shelter, a stove and enough food for five days. Our estimate was for a maximum of four up and one down. Our rack was minimal, mainly ice screws and pegs, and roughly equating to that suitable for an icy Scottish winter route but with a small sprinkling of aid gear lest an emergency arose. The weather could only be described at best as 'showery'.

After about 300m of straightforward 60° ice and a fruitless pitch searching for a bivouac site out of the firing line, we eventually gave up and simply made one from the ice. It was never going to be comfy but at least in this instance it seemed safe, despite Es very nearly demonstrating the speed of his sleeping-bag on an unplanned descent. Fortunately he had the presence of mind to attach himself first.

The next morning wasn't promising. Around 2.00am, after a few hours of rest but little sleep, we made a brew and talked tactics. Despite the sky clearing to a myriad of stars, the temperature still only hovered around zero, far from ideal with a million tonne guillotine of ice hanging over our heads. But it seemed to be getting colder and much quieter, so we decided to give it a go.

Starting out in the dark and making reasonable progress over Scottish V ground, we soon reached the base of the route's most prominent singular feature, a giant cul-de-sac sporting a 250m ice smear, and crowned by a threatening ring of Damoclesian icicles. At this point the sun slowly started to make its presence felt, the heart-lurching 'whrrrrrrr' of falling ice steadily becoming more continuous and rapidly heightening our awareness. I led a particularly nasty and crumbly icy mixed pitch to the right of the gully bed before Es set off very gingerly back onto the main fall. He was hardly three placements from the belay when I suggested we might want to take refuge before our options ran out. He agreed. We cowered uncomfortably under an overhang. And sure enough the deluge began.

We knew that during the night it hadn't been particularly cold, but this was getting genuinely hot, very hot, and it soon became ridiculous. Within two hours of the sun's rays reaching the line of the route the water was flowing. By lunchtime what had been a continuous plume of the most impeccable, creamy water ice had a veritable river running straight down the middle of it, so that all we could do was sit and wait – and hope. Even if it became colder out of the sun in the afternoon, it was going to take a day at least to refreeze, and that meant another wet, uncomfortable bivvy. There was no choice but to retreat.

Back at camp we assessed the situation. The weather would undoubtedly soon turn and we'd need a day at least to recover, mentally as well as physically. Moreover, by a serious oversight on the planning front, we hadn't bargained on making multiple attempts so our available food supplies were running low. Perhaps most worrying of all was our new-found uncertainty about the route – did that kind of thaw take place every day? If not, what was the extent of a more 'normal' thaw, and could we climb through it, especially higher up?

On the positive side, despite the torrent of water and falling ice we had witnessed, stonefall had been infrequent, which suggested the thaw didn't usually run quite as deep. We rationalised that with a much earlier start, a more typically hard overnight frost and colder air during the day, we were in with a chance of success. With sufficient food, we could also take a more relaxed approach and simply bivouac and wait when the sun came onto the line. If we were really lucky, we reasoned, we'd get cloudy cold weather.

Our food situation required a return journey to Base Camp, 15km back up over the col, which gobbled up more precious time. We were getting fitter though, and had returned in three days. That left nine days until our driver would return to pick us up. Five days at most on the route, a day of rest, a day to walk out, and then a day to pack up – perfect! Of course things didn't work out like that. On such a long, difficult and tactically complex route, we were naïve to think that such a hostile world would simply revolve around us.

Up until this point in the trip the weather had been reasonable. While the changes in temperature had ensured that climbing conditions had changed almost daily on the higher peaks, there had been few storms and not much in the way of snow. But on our return trip to Advanced Base the snow began to fall. It was heavy at first, whiteout conditions, necessitating careful navigation over the col and down through the crevasses on its southern aspect. We pressed on under the assumption that the weather would clear up by the time we had rested.

At Advanced Base the snow continued and continued – and continued. On the morning after it had started I awoke to complete silence. 'At last!', I thought, quickly doing the necessary arithmetic in my head to work out if we had sufficient time left for an attempt. But alas, the tent door was opened to reveal a solid wall of wind-packed snow blocking out all noise and light. We had quite literally been buried. I slumped back into the tent and resigned myself to yet another day of chapati-making fun, with some digging to relieve the boredom.

On the evening of 15 August the snow stopped. We had exactly five full days left. It would take at least a full day to dig the tent out, return to Base, and pack everything up in time to leave, and there was no chance of setting foot on a route until two metres of fresh snow had been given the chance to settle down.

Next morning we sat outside the tent and watched gargantuan avalanches pouring down in all shapes and sizes and on all aspects around us. It certainly knows how to snow in the Kokshal Too. One particular slide, draining the gully immediately to the left of our own intended route, created a snow cloud fully a quarter the height of the face itself, prompting Es to quiver. 'Er – you don't think that's big enough to come over here do you?' Fortunately it wasn't, but we subsequently found the col over which we had approached obliterated by blocks the size of caravans.

If the weather held out, we'd have one last chance. We knew three days wasn't likely to be enough but we had become obsessed. Seeing a photograph of this line is one thing but it's another entirely to live and breathe in its shadow for a week or more. Our tactics had changed slightly, we would now leave camp late evening and climb as far as possible in the dark, aiming at the very least to gain the start of the ice smear in the back of the cul-de-sac. We hoped to clear this just as the sun appeared, leaving what looked like a couple of easier rope lengths to a large snow ledge on the left. From there, we could either fuel up and keep going or, if the sun was again causing problems, take a bivouac and then continue very early the following day.

It went extremely well at first, with conditions near perfect. We literally raced to our previous high point in a mere four hours, being fitter and able to climb directly this time up ice in the gully bed. After a heady cocktail of baby food, Blueberry Soup and Powerbars we launched onto the smear. We were stunned. It was quite unlike anything either of us had experienced, sustained for fully four 60m rope lengths at 80° to 95°. And this was just one feature on a 1400m route. The ice was indescribably user-friendly right up until the point where Es pulled through the icicles adorning the rim of the cul-de-sac. At this point things once again took a turn for the worse. For a long and worrying time he tried desperately to find an anchor on which to bring me up, while I hung below on a brace of screws watching the dreaded sun making its presence felt. I felt strangely helpless and vulnerable as the first tinkles of ice rolled by and Es cursed increasingly loudly from his precarious position in the groove above.

Eventually the usual calls indicated Es was safe and it seemed that all was well. However, as I cranked desperately through the steepest section at the icicles, my head popping up over the lip, I was greeted by a disturbing sight. Es was quite obviously extremely uncomfortable and, judging by the look on his face, most probably unsafe. I couldn't see what he was belayed to but I thought it best not to ask. More worrying still was the heat of the sun. The thaw wasn't as bad as it had been previously but it was sufficient to thaw the ice here, which was now only a few heart-stopping inches thick.

After we had exchanged unpleasantries I traversed out onto a very thinly-iced wall on the right, accepting without choice what was inevitably going to be a soul-searching lead. The next half-an-hour is etched indelibly onto my climbing memory. The wall steepened gradually from 80° through to 90°, the ice itself becoming thinner and progressively more detached from the rock underneath. With no protection whatsoever, 25 metres from a non-existent belay, the final ten feet on detached, inch-thick vertical ice were undoubtedly among the most frightening I have ever climbed. Slumped onto the edge of a little hanging ice slope above the wall, I struggled to cope with a combined wave of nausea, euphoria and overwhelming relief.

The only feeling missing was hope. The sun had struck again. With the ice on this section of the route much thinner than expected, our progress was halted. After another brew and some food we inspected the options but nothing would yield. We climbed up and down and across, this way and that, but everywhere the ice was thin and melting and simply couldn't justify an attempt. We thought of using aid but this wasn't appropriate on a route that will undoubtedly go free with the right approach.

And so it was, after a long wait for the temperature to fall, we retreated once more, with no time to hang around, limited by the heat of the sun. We were unlucky, perhaps, to be stalled by so much snow, but then it's easy to make excuses. It's more likely that this is simply a route that needs a bit of perseverance, understanding and a lot of climbing hard at night, all of which can be programmed into memory banks for next time round. And there will be a next time.

As we trudged snail-like back over the col at the start of the long haul back to Base Camp, the sun belting down, our gigantic rucksacks cutting grooves in our shoulders, I felt no disappointment. I had enjoyed some of the most challenging and spectacular ice climbing of my life, I was fit and well and I was sharing a laugh with new-found friends. But most important of all I was inspired and motivated. A new dream had been born and I'd never felt more alive.

ACKNOWLEDGEMENTS

The Scottish Kyzyl Asker Expedition 2002 would like to thank the following organisations for their generous support: Mount Everest Foundation, British Mountaineering Council, Mountaineering Council of Scotland, Nick Estcourt Award, Liam Elliot Award, Shipton-Tilman Award from WL Gore, Lyon Equipment Award, Mountain Equipment and Scarpa. This article appears courtesy of www.scottishoutdoors.com.

PAT LITTLEJOHN

Misión Improbable: Climbing in Tenerife

(Plate 29)

It was just like the picture in the travel book. A little boat moored beneath gigantic ochre-coloured cliffs, which seemed to smoulder in the evening sun. Knowing nothing about the rock, we sat on the harbour wall at Los Gigantes and sketched an imaginary line up the steepest and cleanest part of the cliff. We would only do one climb, so it must take the best line, forging directly up the open faces, grooves and cracks. In our dreams! The cliff would quickly cut us down to size.

Rising to 600m and extending for 10km along the south-west coast of Tenerife, El Risco de Los Gigantes is the biggest vertical sea cliff in southern Europe and North Africa. According to the tourist guidebooks there are even bigger 'sea cliffs' in the Canaries but to the climber the others aren't true cliffs, more like the steep vegetated slopes of Slieve League in Ireland.

On the first day we planned to make a reconnaissance by traversing along the base of the cliff from the port of Los Gigantes. Before long we discovered that there was an aqueduct running exactly where we wanted to go, about 50ft up, and we made rapid progress following this for about a mile. It ended at a streambed, which emerged from a hanging valley. We tried to traverse beyond it but were but were stopped by the sea, so we followed the stream way and found that the aqueduct continued across the cliff at a higher level, about 200m up. Here it took the form of an old steel pipe fractured in places and no longer carried water. Going along it was akin to a very scary *via ferrata* with no protection, with just the pipe to grab if you slipped or the ledge you were on crumbled, which it often did. There was a section of climbing around a gated section, and then the pipe swung round to the main bit of the cliff, a huge amphitheatre with a couloir at the back. We looked at several lines and decided that the couloir was the only feasible route as far as the pipeline, above which there looked to be more options. It was too late to begin climbing so we decided to carry on along the pipe. This ended in a 300m crawl through a tunnel in pitch darkness, arms and shoulders aching with the weight of rucksacks full of ropes and climbing gear, till we finally we emerged in a hanging valley *behind* the main cliff and climbed up to the jagged ridge forming the clifftop. The way off from here involved hours of ridge climbing – 'half the bloody Cuillin Ridge' – to a point over 1000m above the sea before we could head back towards the port of Los Gigantes. A knackering day but we had at least grasped the scale of the place.

Next day we hitched a ride with a diving team in a big inflatable, straight to the base of the line. The couloir led to the pipe in five pitches, two of which were 'XS'. So far the XS grade seems to be a peculiarly British phenomenon. Normal traditional climbing grades apply to rock that most people would consider to be okay for climbing. You can get anomalies like routes graded E3 5b, like Wendigo on Gogarth, where the rock might be a little worrying. But the standard system caters for this. In some parts of the country however, most notably the coasts of North Cornwall and the Lleyn Peninsula in North Wales, there is another category of climb on rocks which have always been considered unsuitable for climbing, that are too loose, too soft, too brittle. This is the home of the 'XS'. These climbs may not be that hard technically but they are demanding in every other way – strenuous, serious, committing, hard to protect, needing good judgement and experience. For their size they usually represent a 'big adventure' and this is their attraction. Los Gigantes is 'XS' territory on a grand scale.

Back on the climb, above the pipeline the rock improved and a pleasant rib followed by an exciting E4 pitch led to the base of a deep recess. That was it for the day so we abbed back to the pipeline and followed it down to the port.

We made a pre-dawn start next day as we thought we might make the top. Having regained our highpoint by 10am, an easy pitch to the back of the recess took us to the start of the massively overhanging chimney which led to its lip, some 100ft away and about 60ft out in space. The rock was the worst yet, everything you touched or stood on broke away, and the only protection was a couple of slings draped around loose material precariously wedged. After 10m I decided it was madness, the chimney from hell, and reversed amid a shower of debris. We abbed back to the pipeline. Some 100m to the right was another possible line. I led a deceptively steep pitch up to a cave with a poor belay. Steve led through but was stopped by a crumbling overhang.

'What do you make of the rock Steve?'

'On a scale of one to ten I'd give it one'.

I gave the pitch a try but bad gear and the rotten belay forced me back. We abbed carefully from all our belay points, packed up the kit and left. We'd failed but were happy to have survived some very serious climbing.

We clipped bolts for a couple of days like normal people and explored the north coast, but Los Gigantes was still nagging. I couldn't help thinking of some shallow grooves I'd spotted on the buttress right of the hellish chimney. There was a slim chance they might lead somewhere. After all our struggles I was almost embarrassed to ask Steve if he'd make another attempt, but he was up for it since the prospect of sport-climbing away the rest of the trip was none too riveting. So next morning we made our fourth journey along the pipe.

After two pitches on familiar ground we headed off into the first of the grooves. The rock was flaky but at least it was culm. It was like on-sight pioneering at Blackchurch, in North Devon. There was the odd bit of gear which inspired confidence. Hundreds of feet below us pleasure boats laden with tourists cruised beneath the cliff, playing classical music appropriate to the majesty of the surroundings and hooting when they spotted us. By now we felt like a fixture on this part of the cliff, having spent two days trying to get up the same section. On the next pitch the rock became more and more compact till I came to a dead halt at a blind corner. A small wire went halfway in but the game was up. This line wasn't going to go and it was the last option. It was early afternoon. We had two choices: forget the whole thing or return to the chimney of horror.

So, inevitably, I'm back at my highpoint in the chimney, in the half-light deep inside the huge recess, everything as horrible as I remember it. Anything like a positive hold just breaks, the only way to make progress is to use opposing pressure holds to force a way upwards. It is closer to extreme caving than it is to the sunny sport climbing on the rest of Tenerife. An hour later my T-shirt is in shreds, I'm filthy, bleeding, and every muscle aches, but at least I'm at the top of the chimney. I fix one of my ropes so I'll never have to do it again as long as I live, and knock off for the day. By dark we're back in the port of Los Gigantes sinking the beers, more confident now but aware that we're still only halfway up the cliff.

Back again. Steve got a fun pitch on near-perfect rock above the chimney and we cruised onwards but were heading for another massive recess. As we got closer we could see it was capped by a roof at least 30m across so we broke right and tried a steep wall, which should lead to the continuation of the couloir line. Like everything else it was four grades harder than it looked and started to gobble up time. Our priority was to get up the cliff rather than climb the most direct route, so we retreated again and traversed 80m right on a ledge system to a rib of granite-like rock. Steve led it, a nice 'normal' 5c pitch, which inspired false optimism that the rock might be improving. It led to a complex but lower-angled area of cliff. This must surely go somewhere but we were out of time so again it was lots of abseils back to the pipe and eventually the bar. Purists would have bivouacked, I know.

Summit day and our sixth spent on Los Gigantes. We made another pre-dawn start and toiled back to our highpoint. Now the climbing was serious rather than hard with infrequent anchors, various rock types but always weak and brittle. Get there slow and careful or not at all. We half expected a nasty sting in the tail as anything could happen on Los Gigantes, but the ground became more and more amenable and we topped out at 1pm. We still had to get down of course, but for a happy half-hour we drank all our water, ate fig rolls and basked in the Spanish sun. Misión accomplished.

Summary: *Misión Improbable*, 18/19 pitches, XS, 5c/6a. FA: Pat Littlejohn and Steve Sustad (varied leads) over five climbing days + one reconnaissance day, 14 to 22 Jan, 2003. Gear taken: set of nuts to Rock 10 + spares, cams to Camalot 3. Long slings.

DUNCAN WILSON
Kyajo Ri, Khumbu

(Plates 6–9)

The alarm went off at midnight. We had hardly even dozed, too tired or excited by the prospect of finally reaching the summit of this beautiful unclimbed mountain that had eluded us at the first attempt and was beginning to wear us down. A quick look at our remaining provisions as I prepared our morning tea confirmed that this would be the last day of food. Dinner would be waiting for us at base camp in the evening, or else we would spend a hungry night in Camp 2 at 5500m before heading down tomorrow morning.

At 1am the weather was perfect. A full moon lit up brilliantly the icy peaks, which soared above us on three sides, and in the monochromatic light the Kyajo glacier extended majestically to the south like a huge frozen lake. A delicate route across a steep loose boulder field led us to a glacier we planned to traverse in order to gain access to the mixed South-west Ridge. From there the summit looked accessible. At the far side of the glacier we were turned back by a compact, overhanging, 40-metre rock wall. With no other feasible routes from here, we turned back and returned to Camp 2 at 5am. Day was breaking and the pressure was now on.

Sure, we had left it late and not sufficiently reconnoitred the previous day but if we wanted to try for the summit, it was now or never. Exhausted and demoralized by the night's efforts, my wife Véronique, along with our friends Julien and Laurent, pulled out. A bitter blow for the team, harder still for the individuals concerned, knowing they had sacrificed their last chance. As Véronique's brother Vincent and I headed off, they offered us their last chocolate bars, as if handing us their remaining resolve and courage.

No time to lose. Vincent raced off and I hoped he would have something left for later when the going gets tougher. The sun was already licking the summits around us, and by the time we had to negotiate the first delicate passage, beneath an unstable sérac, the ice was glistening with the sun's heat. The biting –15°C cold of the night had gone and the climbing was pleasant in the warm sunshine. By 8am we were established on the south-west col, and roping up we got our first proper view of the difficulties ahead. The ridge was fairly uniform in slope, steepening here and there between rock outcrops, threatened by a few small séracs higher up, but apparently leading all the way to the summit. Old avalanche debris at the col reminded us chillingly of the advancing hour, and we were soon moving together up the ridge.

The 700m North Ridge of Brahmasar (5850m) above the Satling Glacier.
The West Ridge is on the right-hand skyline in shadow. (*Martin Moran*) (p33)

4. The difficult pitch of VI on the North Ridge of Brahmasar. (*Martin Moran*) (p33)

5. The North Face of Siguniang. Fowler and Ramsden's route took a prominent ice goulotte hidden from view. (*Mick Fowler*) (p28)

6. The E face of Kyajo Ri (6158m) seen from the village of Machherma in Khumbu. Base camp was established on the valley floor, Camp 1 on snowfields at the foot of the face, below the hanging glacier. (*Duncan Wilson*) (p52)

7. Looking East towards Camp 2, nestled below the SE Col of Kyajo Ri, with Everest and the Nuptse-Lhotse wall appearing beyond. (*Duncan Wilson*) (p52)

Vincent Marché climbing the rock outcrop 100m below the summit, on the SW Ridge, the SW Col below. (*Duncan Wilson*) (p52)

Also on 20 October, Vincent Marché sits astride the summit of Kyajo Ri with Everest, Nuptse and Lhotse beyond to the North-east and Ama Dablam to the East. (*Duncan Wilson*) (p52)

10. The Central Buttress on the South Face of Quitaraju (6040m). Powell and Bullock's route began at the black buttresses at the bottom of the face and followed the line up and slightly right to the summit. (*Nick Bullock*) (p73)

1. Al Powell following the crux pitch on the Central Buttress of Quitaraju. (*Nick Bullock*) (p73)

12. From Centennial Hut. (*Paul Knott*) (p116)

13. Looking across Graham Saddle to the NW. (*Paul Knott*) (p116)

We swapped leads as the terrain varied between 55° and 60° snow and ice to a compact rock outcrop, sharing the difficulties according to our respective strengths. The 6000m threshold was now below us, but the excitement of reaching this altitude for the first time brought little relief to our breathless fatigue. Our hope of reaching the summit by 11am had receded, and each rope length seemed to take an age. Only one more chocolate bar each, and the water bottles were almost empty. But the promise of my altimeter reading kept us focused on our goal. As Vincent joined me on what we expected to be the last belay before the summit, he looked tired and dizzy.

'Are you OK?'

'Yeah, I think so, just feel like I'm hearing things through a fog, a bit like what the high-altitude boys describe in those books we've been reading.'

At once my mind flooded with unpleasant recollections of *Into Thin Air* and *Touching the Void* that have been circulating at Base Camp. 'If you're in a bad way we'd better head down right now,' I offered, not really believing my own words.

'No, let's do one more length and see how things are then, hey?'

I certainly wasn't going to argue with that, confident that we were so close to our goal, and I set off immediately up the final snow slope, steep at first, the climbing delicate on a soft and sugary layer of ice, barely covering the rocks. Each step took ten breaths to recover, and I soon found myself setting goals. That block of ice in ten minutes, I would promise, only to discover to my tremendous delight that in just three minutes I'm there. I buried the deadman, knowing what little resistance it would provide against my weight in the event of a fall.

'End of rope!' Vincent yells up from below. So this is the summit fever we've read about. Just above me the slope is flattening off as we approach the summit ridge, and I know nothing can stop us now. We'll just have to top out moving together, and now neither of us is allowed to slip. Suddenly I'm there, perched precariously on the highest point of the mountain, a 40cm-wide ridge of snow, separating the steep South and North-east Faces. Vincent joins me, after what seems like an age, in the pit I've dug on our little roof of the world, exhausted and a little hazy from the altitude.

'Well, that's our first time above 6000m, our first new route, and our first unclimbed summit, all in one!' I gushed, the emotion overwhelming me.

'I hadn't noticed on the map but Kyajo Ri is the highest peak in its massif. These views are fantastic!' replied Vincent. 'I feel I could just reach out and touch Everest – Ama Dablam seems small from here!"

The summit offered fine unrestricted views across the Khumbu, a few clouds lapping harmlessly around the valleys. And yet we felt vulnerable up there, so far from our friends at Camp 2, a world away from the small Base Camp visible deep down in the shadows of the Machherma valley, almost 2000m below. We shared memories of the weeks leading to this point, of the yaks deserting us one night during the walk-in. I thought of

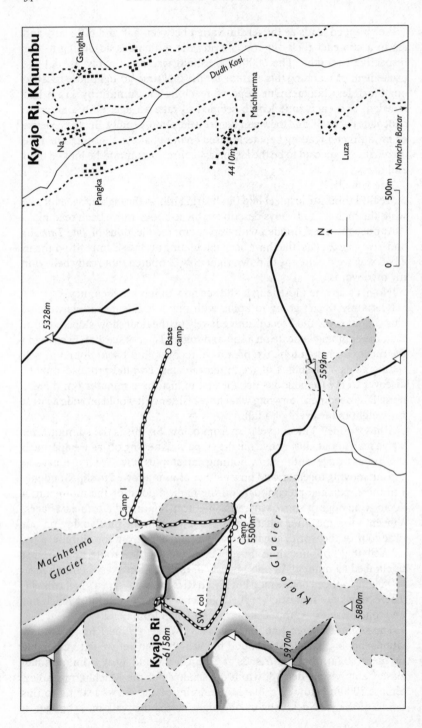

Kyajo Ri, Khumbu

the beautiful puja ceremony at Base Camp when Dawa our sirdar had presided over the blessing of our expedition, throwing rice to the gods through the thick smoke of burning juniper. Then we had set to work, forging a technical route from Camp 1 to Camp 2 with the rest of the team, all three of them now in the safety of Camp 2 anxiously awaiting our return from the summit.

We stayed on the summit for an hour celebrating. We ate and drank our remaining provisions, took no end of photos, unrolled and partially buried a string of prayer flags and then sat back and took in the fantastic landscape. Impossibly steep ice faces extended in all directions: Everest, Cho Oyu, Makalu, Shishapangma, even the Annapurnas and Manaslu visible in the distance. The wind blew lightly, although never enough to cool the sun's heat, lifting the prayer flags in short breaths, carrying those Buddhist chants to the far corners of the world. For a while a thin misty veil covered the summit but five minutes later it had evaporated. By 3pm we were off, down-climbing in 100m lengths between precarious belays on the few rocky outcrops, wary of making errors after 14 hours of climbing and three days above 5500m. Each pitch seemed to last forever as the sun raced towards the western horizon. With the coming night the temperatures plummeted to below –20°C, and my toes lost some feeling that they failed to recover even after painful rewarming. That worried me. Fatigue and lack of sleep, nutrition or water were taking their toll.

'Vincent,' I forced myself to say, as we headed to the top of the steep rock wall that had barred our way during the previous night, 'be careful – I'm very tired – you're going to have to make decisions for both of us from now on.' Fortunately Vincent had recovered from his difficulties near the summit, and we abseiled safely down the overhanging rock face that had rebuffed us 15 hours earlier on the way up.

The final hour's walk back to Camp 2 was made more comfortable by the sight of three bobbing headlamps coming to meet us. What a welcome sight! The reunion with the others was tearful, joyful, hot and cold all in one. It was now past 9pm and we shared rapidly our impressions and experiences of the long day while swallowing whole pieces of *comté* cheese and dried sausage, secretly brought all this way by Laurent, before heading for the warmth of our sleeping bags. We still had over 1100m of descent tomorrow, some of it over technical ground, before reaching Base Camp and rest. Falling into a fitful sleep, buffeted by a violent snowstorm, my mind wandered over our achievement, mixed with the regret of not getting everyone to the summit. At least tomorrow we would all enjoy a good *dahl bhat*, and be awoken the following morning with a piping hot mug of sweet tea, served in the warmth of our sleeping bags! There was just time to think of a name for the route. A Franco-British team, lying now in harmony in our little tents, after a historic – for us at least – first ascent. '*En Tente Cordiale!*'

Summary: The first ascent of Kyajo Ri (6186m) in the Khumbu, Nepal by Duncan Wilson (UK) and Vincent Marché on 20 October, 2002 in lightweight style with no Sherpa support, with climbing up to Difficile/60°. Other team members were Laurent Beurel, Julien Ferrera and Véronique Marché-Wilson.

ACKNOWLEDGEMENTS

We would like to thank our friends and family for their moral support, apologise to those who suffered in the absence of news, and express our gratitude to those who helped us financially, namely www.Expé.fr, Au Vieux Campeur and Murmur.

DEREK BUCKLE, ROBERT DURRAN,
ROY RUDDLE AND DAVE WILKINSON

Citrus Delights

Greenland's North and South Lemon Mountains

(*Plates 44, 45*)

Roy Ruddle writes: 'I had wanted to visit Greenland for almost 25 years.
When I was still in my mid-teens an adult friend had shown me some
pictures of an impressive mountain they had attempted that summer
somewhere in the east of the country. Even though I had yet to take
up climbing, I knew for sure that this was a place I desperately wanted
to go to. I nearly went to Greenland in 1985 for my first major
expedition, but instead I visited Peru's Cordillera Huayhuash, inspired
by Al Rouse's article in *Mountain*. Time passed and opportunity
remained elusive. Then in the summer of 2001, with personal
circumstances changing, urgent action had to be taken. I recruited a
climbing partner and set out to organise a suitable team to help me
achieve a long-held dream.'

The 2002 Alpine Climbing Group/Alpine Club Greater Ranges Meet
was organised, on an ad-hoc basis like its predecessors, to places such
as the Caucasus, the Karakoram, and the Cordillera Blanca. Roy Ruddle
put forward the idea and, if there were sufficient takers, offered to organise
it. The trip started with an e-mail circular and entry in the Club's Newsletter,
inviting anyone interested to contact Roy and, if possible, meet at his house.
The agenda was to find an area, alpine in nature, which allowed exploratory
ski touring and had easy unclimbed peaks, with potential for more technical
new routes up to TD+. Oh, and preferably had an unclimbed Walker Spur.

Eight people turned up, including Paul Walker of Tangent Expeditions
International, who had been asked to provide the logistics. Aided by curry
and copious bottles of wine, we gradually narrowed down the possibilities,
helped enormously by Paul's unparalleled knowledge of Greenland's various
mountain ranges, a carousel of his slides, some aerial photos, and various
back issues of the *Alpine Journal*. By midnight the Lemon Mountains had
been chosen and the core of a team had formed.

The Lemon Mountains can be divided into two roughly equal areas. The
South Lemons had been visited by nine previous expeditions that picked
plums from the various side glaciers of the Frederiksborg. However, it was

a picture of one of the routes that they left untouched which gave us our 'Walker Spur', the North Spur of Mitivagkat East (*AJ* 1993, plate 44).

The North Lemons cover some 300km² and were completely unexplored. Phil Bartlett reinforced this, stating that they were 'unvisited and contained some fine objectives' (*AJ* 1999). By landing in a ski plane near the famous Cathedral (2600m), first ascended by Bartlett and Luke Hughes, we could focus our collective attention on both Mitivagkat and the vast potential that lay further north. This included peaks as high as, but of much larger scale than, anything in the South Lemons and access via any one of four glaciers.

Four pairs of climbers signed up for the trip: Roy Ruddle and Robert Durran, Dave Wilkinson and Geoff Cohen, Andy and Rachel Gallagher, and Derek Buckle and Martin Scott. For official purposes, we were known as the *British Lemon Mountains Expedition 2002*, but in practice we operated as four independent pairs. Our objectives were: the first ascent of the 800m North Spur of Mitivagkat East in the South Lemons; exploration and first ascents in the unexplored Courtauld glacier region of the North Lemons; and major unclimbed lines on the north and west side of Cathedral and Minster in the South Lemons.

We flew to Iceland on 13 July, and on to Greenland in a Twin Otter ski plane two days later to join our equipment that had already been deposited on the edge of the ice cap. We knew that our landing site was two days' ski from where we had intended, the change forced by the accelerated glacial melt of an unusually warm summer. That meant Roy and Robert had to spend a frantic Sunday trying to locate additional pulks to allow us to transport all of our gear in one go.

To get to Greenland we first took a scheduled flight to Isfajordur in North-west Iceland, where we were due to meet a chartered Twin Otter that would take us into the mountains to land on skis. However, after landing in rain and low cloud, we were met by a phone message. It transpired that the weather over the Lemon Mountains was marginal and forecast to get worse. As we were liable for any extra flying time, and an aborted trip to the ice cap would cost £6000, we weren't going to argue. However, we hadn't reckoned on a chance encounter with Cambridge academic and adventure pilot Andy Hopper in an otherwise deserted Isfajordur airport. En route to Anchorage in his little Cessna, with a mate who was into climbing volcanoes, Andy offered to pass over the Lemon Mountains and phone our pilot with a weather report. Providing Andy with the GPS coordinates of our destination prevented any ambiguity and two hours later the answer was 'clear blue skies, sunny and stable'.

By 2pm we were on our way and after two flights all eight of us had landed on the edge of Greenland's Inland Sea. Originally, we had planned to make forays from a base camp by Cathedral but that now lay two days away and caused a reassessment of how we would operate. We split into three teams. Roy Ruddle and Robert Durran headed initially for new routes on Mitivagkat and Cathedral, while Dave Wilkinson and Geoff Cohen set out to try and find, reach and climb the highest peak in the unexplored North Lemons, Pt 2600m, according to the clearly error-prone map. In doing so, these pairs were also going to establish an Advanced Base Camp where their paths diverged, and stock that camp with half their food and the team's satellite phone. Meanwhile, the remaining pairs, Derek Buckle and Martin Scott, and Andy and Rachel Gallagher, mapped out a circular ski tour that would take in a number of unclimbed peaks stretching as far as the Lindbergh Mountains and Mitivagkat.

Although not originally planned, the expedition would not meet again as a whole until two days before its intended departure from Greenland. The next sections, therefore, tell the separate story of each of the three teams.

Durran and Ruddle

Packing our pulks with around 90kg each of gear and food for the next three and a half weeks, we watched the others head off for the Trillingerne peaks. Then we skied off into the twilight of the arctic night, heading for a proposed base camp site on the upper Frederiksborg Glacier. We soon realised how deceptive great distances are in the crystal clear air, and how slowly landmarks pass by on the vast glaciers. We never got used to it.
Eventually we camped, cold and tired, at 'Lake Camp', a mile or so short of a large melt pond at the junction of our side glacier with the Frederiksborg. Dave and Geoff joined us and, after a rest day and night enforced by steady snow, we moved in the heat of the midday sun to establish our base a couple of hours out onto the Frederiksborg. We immediately packed for a 10-day foray down the glacier towards one of our main objectives, Mitivagkat.

Saying our farewells to Dave and Geoff, who were heading off on their first attempt to reach the North Lemons, we set out for a long night's ski, taking hourly turns towing a single heavy pulk. This system broke up the toil nicely and allowed the unburdened one to stay ahead where necessary to find the best line through the crevassed areas. We finally set up our Bibler bivi tent close under the impressive twin peaks.

A recce that afternoon on 18 July convinced us that the rock on the lower half of their imposing north pillars was dangerously unstable. So we switched our attention to the North-east Ridge of the East Peak (c.2100m), which formed a fine, steeply-stepped skyline, with a small col at its foot accessed via a steep open ice slope. We set off for an attempt early next morning, but milder weather had set in, the snow was hardly frozen and we couldn't justify exposing ourselves to stonefall. A half-hearted attempt at a consolation rock climb on the neighbouring Wildspur was thwarted after a pitch by steep unstable rock and we returned to camp to await better conditions.
We waited for a frustrating four days. Continuing mild weather restricted us to short ski trips on the glacier in the brighter spells between periods of

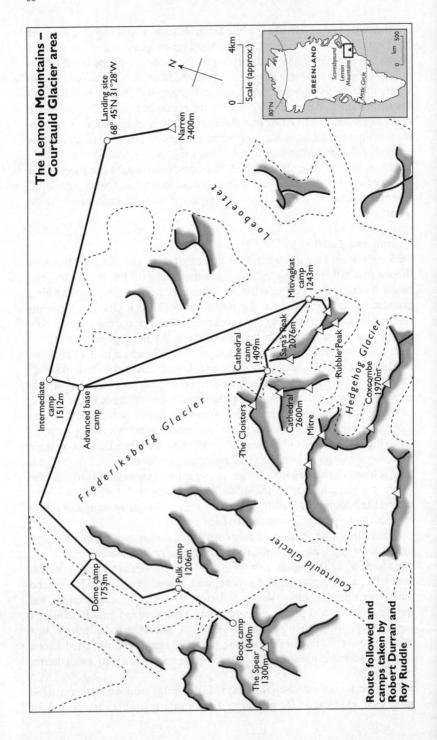

The Lemon Mountains –
Courtauld Glacier area

Landing site
68° 45'N 31°28'W

N

0   4km
Scale (approx.)

GREENLAND
Scoresbysund
Lemon
Mountains
Arctic Circle
80°N
0   km   500

Narren
2400m

Loeboelter

Mitivagkat
camp
1243m

Sara's Peak
2076m

Cathedral
camp
1409m

Rubble Peak

Hedgehog Glacier

Intermediate
camp
1512m

Advanced base
camp

The Cloisters

Cathedral
2600m
Mitre

Coxcombe
1970m

Frederiksborg Glacier

Dome camp
1753m

Pulk camp
1206m

Courtauld Glacier

Boot camp
1040m

The Spear
1300m

Route followed and
camps taken by
Robert Durran and
Roy Ruddle

rain or wet snow. Finally colder air arrived, the snow froze hard, and a 3am start on 24 July saw us quickly up the ice slope and onto the rock. The ridge gave a series of strenuous pitches in awkward chimneys and cracks, several of which would have achieved classic HVS status on Stanage, interspersed with easier slabby sections. The final step was steeper and more sustained. We investigated three lines in deteriorating weather but each turned into intimidating off-widths and we finally retreated probably within 50m of the summit. The abseil descent went smoothly as far as the ice slope, which, with the return of mild conditions, was being swept by rapidly worsening stonefall. Things became serious and scary so we were very relieved to find a good peg placement in the generally loose rock alongside the ice and make a final abseil over the bergschrund. It had been a 16-hour day, but the worst was still to come for Robert, when he suffered an excruciating cramp attack trying to get into his sleeping bag.

After a day's rest we decided to move overnight back up the glacier to the Cathedral group of peaks, where the unclimbed Cathedral East would be a major prize. Unfortunately Roy was feeling unwell the next day and after an afternoon recce of the glacial bay to the south of the peaks, Robert decided on a solo attempt on the minor but unclimbed peak of Cloisters West (2240m) to the north. He writes: 'Skiing to within 20 minutes of the col between the Cathedral and The Cloisters, I started up a 400m rock buttress at midnight. This gave interesting climbing on rock of variable quality, not sustained and never harder than about Severe, but I was very aware of the seriousness of the situation, alone in the vast wilderness spreading majestically below me. I lingered with satisfaction on the summit. The view was impressive of the north face of the Cathedral opposite and across the Courtauld glacier to the unvisited North Lemon peaks. Climbing and skiing carefully back down, I arrived back at the tent after an 8-hour round trip.'

Although Roy was now feeling much better, our supplies were running low, so we had to leave Cathedral East untried and the following night skied back up the glacier to base. An hour from the camp we crossed fairly fresh pulk tracks, the only sign we saw of Martin, Derek, Andy and Rachel in three weeks. They never spotted the speck of our camp on the vast undulating glacier.

A note in our tent from Dave and Geoff told us they had left only a couple of days earlier on a second attempt to reach the North Lemons. Since the weather was now excellent and they had not returned, we assumed they were making good progress and decided to follow their tracks. The following night (27/28 July) a long ski over the wonderfully easy glacial pass they had found, followed by a 7km descent that would have graced a top alpine ski resort, took us to 'Pulk Camp'. There, at 1206m, the snow gave way to dry glacier, with their route now open to some stunning peaks.

The next evening we shouldered heavy packs, descended onto an open glacier and headed for the most promising looking glacier-bay. Two hours later we ascended a short icefall and discovered Dave and Geoff's instincts had been the same. We stumbled upon their tent just as they were preparing for an ascent of The Spear. It was great to share a brew and catch up on their news before wishing them luck and heading off ourselves for an attempt on the nearby 'Nesthorn' (c.2200m). An interesting icefall and a steep ice slope led to a ridge of appalling rubble. We grovelled on up for as long as it was safe to do so, but the steeper summit rocks looked lethal and we retreated without regret some 200m below the summit.

The next day was spent checking up on Dave and Geoff's progress through our binoculars, and that night we walked up the glacier under their peak until we were below its stupendous North-west Face, an impregnable looking 1300m rock wall. They returned like jubilant zombies to our congratulations in the morning, but with our food again running low, we decided to leave them to their well-earned rest and head back towards base.

Having picked up the pulk and back on skis, we made our way laboriously in light snow back up to the pass where we camped in the hope of an improvement. By the next evening (1 August), glorious weather allowed us to make a wonderful ski tour over the three 'Dinosaur Domes' (2178m) to the west of the pass. In many ways this was the highlight of the whole trip: perfect snow conditions, magical light and amazing views stretching from the ice-bound fjord and the surrounding peaks to the distant Watkins Mountains and the vastness of the ice cap. On returning to the tent, we decided to keep the momentum going and pushed on back to base in deteriorating weather, arriving back at 6am just as the snowfall began.

This time it snowed for nearly eighty hours and we congratulated ourselves on having pushed on to the comfort of our large tent rather than the cramped Bibler. The time passed in a more or less random sequence of snacks, dozes and chapters from Jilly Cooper's latest novel. The most memorable incident was when a flight of about 40 ducks, apparently lost in the clag, passed over our tent in three different directions within 10 minutes. Apart from one snow bunting, a spider and two moths, this was the only wildlife we saw on the whole trip, but our hopes of finding the exhausted birds laid out in formation on the glacier ready for our pot came to nothing.

It cleared suddenly on the third day and, with only three days to go until the flight out was due, we decided to take the opportunity to return to the landing site. Setting off that night (5/6 August) in the deep fresh snow, we thought we were in for a long arduous uphill haul, but a bitterly cold and windy night soon scoured and hardened the surface and with little incentive to linger, we made rapid progress. Locating the small cache on the featureless plateau of the landing site, we used our GPS in anger for the first time. We pitched the tent and slept with satisfaction.

We were wakened around midday by the return of Martin, Derek, Andy and Rachel. Dave and Geoff made it back the following night. It was good to have the whole team safely together again after such an unintentionally diverse trip. The following day, Roy and I skied eight miles in a straight line to the foot of the prominent, but isolated and unclimbed, snow peak of

Narren (2400m), dug an avalanche test pit and skied straight back again –
all good, safe exercise! The route followed a mile-long slope that was clearly
lethal. One day of waiting for the plane and we were heading back to Iceland,
and limitless hot geothermal water.

Wilkinson and Cohen

The plane dropped us at the south end of the Lindbergh mountains. This
was not really a suitable base for climbing in the Lemons. Shortly after
10pm on the day we had landed, we left the landing site for our journey to
the Frederiksborg glacier, 19 miles away and a more suitable 'advanced
base'. Geoff's skiing experience was even more limited than mine. He had
never before used skis with skins, let alone pulled a pulk. But on these
wide-open spaces and scarcely noticeable gradients, that did not seem to
bother him. In spite of the late hour, the sun had not yet set, and even when
it did, the darkest it would get would be a light dusk, so a night walk was
fine. By the time we set off, Roy and Robert were tiny specks in the distance,
their size betraying the deceptive scale of this landscape. The specks were
to get even smaller.

Moving over this vast flat terrain required a detachment of mind, putting
one foot in front of the other in a seemingly endless sequence, with the
illusion of being on a treadmill, legs moving steadily, but no apparent
movement. After some two hours of this robotic action, progress was at
last evident, and we reached the vague edge of a plateau. The tracks we
followed plunged downwards in a slope of at least five degrees. The snow
was now getting firmer in the cool of evening and my pulk was pushing me
down from behind, so I resorted to big sweeping zigzags. After half an
hour of this descent, the angle eased, and we again followed the others'
tracks in a straight line. Their bodies were only just visible in the far distance
when they occasionally emerged from some indiscernible hollow. Moving
like automata, we plodded onwards, and by 4am, too tired to keep going
but too cold to rest, we finally stumbled across a tent pitched below a slope
leading to an icy blue lake.

After a rest day, we continued to our 'advanced base camp', which was,
in fact, to be little-used except as a gear and food dump. Our main objective
was to explore the North Lemon Mountains, the group to the north-west
of the Lemon Mountains proper, separated by the Courtauld Glacier. This
sub-range had never been visited, although Phil Bartlett and party had
previously climbed a small peak on the Frederiksborg glacier edge. We
intended to get into the heart of the region, but had yet to find a way. The
problem was that the area was relatively close to the sea. Consequently, the
glaciers were lower, steeper, and with less snow cover. All these factors
made them less suitable for travel with skis and pulks. The most obvious
approach was by the Courtauld Glacier, but we had heard from Phil that it
was quite crevassed and the snow cover did not extend very far. Our aerial
photo seemed to bear this out. Three alternative approaches were offered

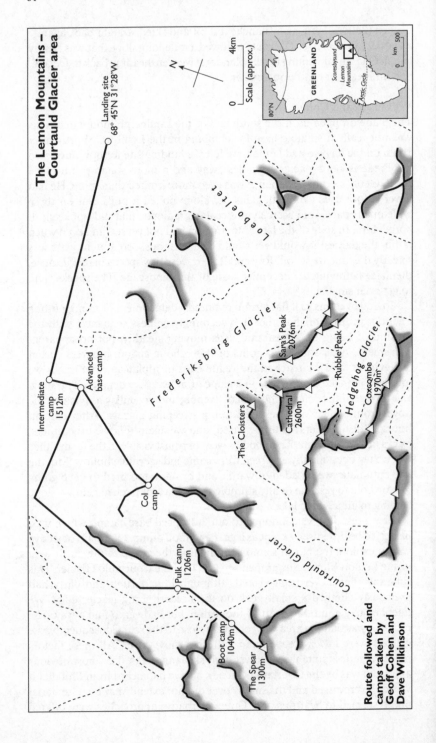

The Lemon Mountains –
Courtauld Glacier area

GREENLAND
Scoresbysund
Lemon Mountains
Arctic Circle
80°N
0   km   500

Scale (approx.)
0   4km
N

Landing site
68° 45'N 31°28'W

Loebøellet

Frederiksborg Glacier

Intermediate camp 1512m

Advanced base camp

Sara's Peak 2076m

Rubble Peak

The Cloisters

Cathedral 2600m

Hedgehog Glacier

Coxcombe 1970m

Col camp

Courtauld Glacier

Pulk camp 1206m

Boot camp 1040m

The Spear 1300m

Route followed and
camps taken by
Geoff Cohen and
Dave Wilkinson

up the next three glaciers to the north. In a spirit of laziness, we selected the first of these, which could be reached by heading immediately south-west from ABC. After a hurried repacking, we set off with 11 days' food supply, in the evening of the same day, while Roy and Robert headed south for their Mitivagkat objective.

The map was not accurate for access to our glacier, showing a direct descent from the Frederiksborg. In fact, there was a gentle rise for two or three kilometres to a shallow col before the descent started. Four hours after leaving ABC, we camped on this col. Next day we left all baggage at the col and did a short reconnaissance of the glacier beyond. A gentle descent for a kilometre led to crevasses, which got progressively worse, and an impressive icefall beyond. Better skiers could doubtless have got further, and the icefall might have been passable on foot, but not with pulks, so we gave up on that for access to the heart of the range.

For our first climbing, we decided on the mountain to the south of our 'Col Camp'. This mountain was in the form of a long ridge linking a number of peaks, running north-east to south-west, and marked 2010m on the Danish map. We had seen some of these from the previous day's reconnaissance, but it wasn't clear which was highest – and we're still not sure. Geoff thought we'd take about six hours, but he's a noted optimist in such matters.

Starting at around 4am on 19 July, we climbed easy snow directly above camp to a bergschrund, above which a steeper pitch led to a col on the ridge, just south-west of the very first peak, which is still unclimbed. We then turned west and traversed narrow snow ridges to a snowy summit. Inevitably, a higher one lay beyond. A steep descent led down to a col, the first of a series. In fact, this col was a complex of rocky pinnacles, which had to be climbed or turned. The route was never hard, but was long enough that pitching it would have taken several days. So we climbed unroped, crossing the tops of some towers – harder but better rock – and turning others on the flanks, which was easier but looser. The barrenness of the arctic environment was pleasantly relieved by colonies of flowers, apparently thriving in this harsh landscape. Several species were present, including something like a wonderfully translucent yellow celandine.

Eventually we reached the summit, or rather a summit, but like the buses, there was always another just behind. Another pinnacle-infested col intervened before the next summit. This gave a repeat performance of gendarme weaving, with an ice wall and a fine ice arête thrown in at the end. A scrambly section led to the top of a rock tower, the left of two, from which the snowy summit was easily gained. A long way beyond, past yet another pinnacle-bestrewn col, was yet another summit, but this one did not rise far, if at all, above our top. We looked long and hard, but could not tell which of the two was higher, nor did the map help. We named our mountain 'Switchback', due to the many undulations on its ridge, and gave it TD inf, with pitches of III and IV. We then had to reverse the whole route, in mild but deteriorating weather, a fine drizzle making the lichenous rocks slippery and even more time-consuming. Returning to camp in thick mist, it took us 20 minutes to find the tent at the end of a 20-hour day. The mountain's south-west summit appears to be about the same height, but is still unclimbed. This appears more easily approachable from the Courtauld Glacier. The far north-east summit, closest to the Frederiksborg glacier, is also unclimbed.

A few days of bad weather then gave a welcome rest. A clearer day on 24 July let us climb the huge whale-like mountain to the north of our col. From the camp, a short walk in a north-westerly direction led to a 45-degree névé slope which bypassed some ice cliffs on their right. Easier crevassed slopes then led to easy terrain, reminiscent of the Cairngorm plateau in a very snowy winter. A long gentle ascent, west then south-west, led us over twin domes of apparently similar height and the further summit gave us good views of our next objective. We then returned to camp untypically early, the round-trip taking a mere six hours.

Returning to ABC, 26 July proved a calmer day and we had no excuse for further procrastination. We set off with heavily loaded pulks bearing most of our remaining supplies, and skied north-west, then west, then south-west to the next glacier, the one on the far side of Humpback. This also had a long gentle rise to a col, contradicting the map. However, unlike the previous glacier, so similar-looking on map and aerial photo, this one gave a long easy descent for four or five kilometres on slopes which even we could ski down, pulks and all. All good things end, and this finally halted at midnight on a patch of dry glacier at 1100m, above a short icefall just before a major junction of glaciers. We camped here at our 'Pulk Camp', the furthest we could get with skis and sledges, which we left here for the next week and more. We were now at the heart of this little range and surrounded by unclimbed mountains. Further movement had to be on foot.

On our very first day's skiing down to the Frederiksborg Glacier, and again from Humpback, we had glimpsed two outstanding peaks in our area. The further one ('The Shield') had a big snowy north face, and was presumably the one shown as 2600m on the map. This was still rather inaccessible without a long slog on foot. Much closer was an apparently slightly lower but more impressive pointed mountain ('The Spear'), which dominated the view from Pulk Camp. This looked a fine challenge, but worryingly big and steep.

The Spear had a very impressive north face – an ice-smeared rock wall, and an inaccessible East Ridge on the left. Between the two was a mixed north-east facet, which looked long but climbable. Two possible lines seemed to give access to this facet from the glacier, a couloir on the right and a hanging glacier on the left, so the peak did look climbable. On the north side of this basin, several other mountains were queuing up to be climbed, should we decide against the main one, or have time for another. We left a small dump of food and gear at what we called 'Boot Camp', walked back to Pulk Camp, and returned the next day, with most of our gear and a week's food.

The weather was set fair, but the objective looked a serious one, so we made the following day a rest day, and started our route on the following evening of 29 July. It was at this point that Robert and Roy appeared, after reading our note.

Easy walking for an hour led to the route's foot, where we left ski poles. An avalanche chute on the left tempted us to take the left of our starting options. In the event, this choice came off, but only just. Frozen debris in the chute covered all crevasses, enabling rapid progress for 200m. A huge crevasse, not clearly visible from below, barred the way, and forced a long traverse right, using a sharp snow arête on the crevasse's edge, and losing some of our hard-earned height. An upward ice pitch then led to an equally long leftward traverse below another monster crevasse. This was crossed by a bridge of ice blocks, and above, past an icicle grotto, we made an even longer rightward traverse. This led to a break in the bergschrund at the foot of the mixed ground, and the start of the route's main section.

We pitched the rest of the route. The terrain was typical mixed ground at about 50 degrees. Most of the climbing was on ice overlain by a variable thickness of snow of variable texture, with occasional steps on rock. The climbing was never hard, but sustained, and with few resting-places, so the overall fatigue factor was out of proportion to the difficulty. But most of the belays were good rock ones. After 17 pitches of this, we reached a good ledge on the left-hand ridge, and took a ten-minute break.

The mountain became steeper and rockier. Towers barred the ridge ahead, so we traversed back onto the face. The next section had looked harder from below, but the going was made easier by a series of hidden terraces and snow gullies, which could be linked in a devious line so avoiding any difficulties. The angle eased, and we seemed to be nearing the top. A left traverse turned towers on the summit ridge, and a loose gully returned to the crest just short of a snowy peak. But this was just a fore-peak, a col lay beyond, then a rise to a higher summit.

Now tiring after 12 hours on the go, we traversed the fore-peak's snowy right face to the col. The narrow corniced crest was turned on the left via a rocky ledge with steep ice steps to a platform below the twin summit pinnacles. We took off our crampons for this one pitch, and reached the top – separately, because of the shortage of standing room – at about midday.

We had assumed that our mountain was not the mysterious 2600m one marked on the map, and looked forward to resolving this matter. But, although we had superb views of Cathedral and most of the other surrounding mountains, the view to the south was hidden by ghostly wreaths of sea-mist, drifting up on the breeze from the Courtauld Fjord.

We could wait no longer; we needed to descend. The cloudy wreaths had grown and multiplied, preventing a rest in the sun, and threatening a change in the weather. By now, we needed a break. We had decided to bring no bivouac gear, only a little spare clothing and food and a small stove and pan, so we stopped for an hour and a half of melting snow to rehydrate, shivering as we rested.

The cold forced us to get going. We considered abseiling, but although we had used good rock belays on the way up, it was really the wrong sort of rock and the wrong sort of angle for abseils. Steep enough to make climbing awkward, but not steep enough for clean rope retrieval. Ropes catching round blocks and jamming, or pulling loose blocks off, was not an appealing prospect. There were few spikes and flakes, so our abseil cord was no use. Most of the belays had been Friends and nuts in cracks. We didn't have enough of these to abseil anything like far enough. So we down-climbed the whole way, except for a single abseil over the bergschrund.

Fatigue, lack of rest and sleep-deprivation for two nights were taking their toll, as we struggled to maintain our concentration for pitch after pitch of descent. I battled to keep going in ten-minute shifts, separated by five-minute rests sitting on my rucksack.

Eventually we staggered onto the main glacier, where Roy and Robert had left us a welcome bottle of drink and a bag of sweets. It had started to snow, but we were only just aware of it. Stupefied with exhaustion, we tottered our devious way, as much sideways as forwards, back to camp, and 34 hours after setting off, collapsed into pits and oblivion. (The Spear c.2500m, 1300m NE Face, TD/mixed.)

Buckle and Scott, Andy and Rachel Gallagher

Faced with the closeness of the Trillingerne group we decided that these should be the first objective, even if they were technically in the Lindberghs. A short short spell with the pulks led to Camp 1 (1964m), where techniques learned by Andy Gallagher in Alaska led to impressive excavation and wall building activities. In a surprisingly short time the two tents were settled in their icy enclaves ready to face whatever the arctic climate had to offer.

We did not have long to find out since a marked deterioration overnight led to snow, wind and dismal visibility, seriously curtailing activities the next day. Still it did provide Martin and Derek with the opportunity to investigate the state of their day rations and to learn the hard way that pre-mixed aliquots of cheese and sausage impart a nice white coat to the former and an intriguing green hue to the latter. Andy and Rachel, on the other hand, were beginning to realise the disadvantages of transporting their food in large cardboard boxes, especially when they start to get wet.

With an improvement in the weather a recce was made of the surrounding mountains, identifying several potential routes on each of the three Trillingerne summits. This also provided an opportunity to look down on the vast Sorgenfri Glacier and for Andy and Rachel to climb the small peak between Trillingerne Central and South, an outcrop that they christened Bantam Point in recognition of its relative size. Armed with this knowledge, on 18 July all four of us skied to the prominent col between Trillingerne

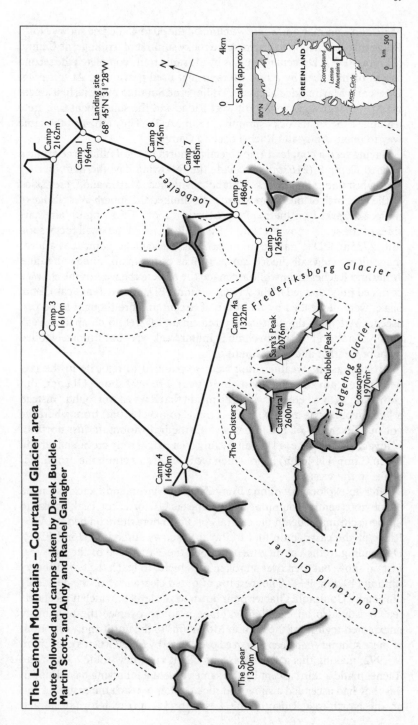

The Lemon Mountains – Courtauld Glacier area

Route followed and camps taken by Derek Buckle, Martin Scott, and Andy and Rachel Gallagher

GREENLAND
80°N
Scoresbysund
Lemon Mountains
Arctic Circle
0   km 500

N
0   4km
Scale (approx.)

Landing site
68° 45'N 31° 28'W

Camp 2
2162m

Camp 1
1964m

Camp 8
1745m

Camp 7
1485m

Camp 6
1486m

Loeboeltel

Camp 5
1245m

Camp 3
1610m

Camp 4a
1322m

Frederiksborg Glacier

Sara's Peak
2076m

Rubble Peak

Hedgehog Glacier

Coxcombe
1970m

The Cloisters

Cathedral
2600m

Camp 4
1460m

Courtauld Glacier

The Spear
1300m

Main and Central from where we climbed the 30 to 45-degree snowy North Ridge that gave access to an extended rocky summit of Trillingerne Central (2176m, PD+). Descent to the skis by the same route completed the second ascent of this peak by a new route to that used previously. At this point Derek and Martin skied across to Trillingerne South to make its first ascent via the 30-degree snowy North-west Ridge and the subsequent fine arête leading to the small rocky summit (2158m, AD). They returned the same way to rejoin Andy and Rachel back to Camp 1.

Having seen a couple of fine objectives north of the Trillingerne group a pulk to Camp 2 (2162m) was made the following day, the 8km journey taking just under four hours. Suitably positioned, Martin and Derek skied to the col north of the camp where they climbed the superb West Ridge of the peak marked on the map as 2610m on foot. Climbing on alternate sides of the sharp snow arête they eventually reached the small rocky summit (2735m, PD+, named Scimitar Peak), a vantage point that affords magnificent views of the ice cap, as well as of the main Lindbergh range. Andy and Rachel meanwhile ascended the peak to the west of the col *via* a corniced ridge that led to the 2479m summit (PD, named Tent Peak). Both peaks were descended by the route of ascent and are thought to be first ascents. Attempts the next day by Martin and Derek to climb Tent Peak and by Andy and Rachel to climb Scimitar Peak were unfortunately foiled by poor weather and snow conditions.

As soon as the weather improved we planned to relocate to the pre-designated advance base on the Upper Frederiksborg Glacier, but confusion as to where this would be meant that it was never found. Instead a 14.5km pulk was made to the interim Camp 3 (1610m) from where we got our first view of the impressive Cathedral Mountain just north of Mitivagkat. A further 11km on 24 July over extensively crevassed terrain led to Camp 4 (1460m) from which we intended to climb the prominent peaks to the west.

After an exploratory outing from Camp 4, Martin and Derek ascended the obvious central couloir of the twin peaks of Horseshoe Peak on skis to the bergschrund beneath the central col. From here they climbed the West Ridge of the east top on foot to the airy, snowy summit (1916m, PD+). Descending to the col they then climbed the East Ridge of the west top, first on snow, but then over a broken rock band, to reach the broad snowy summit (1928m, F+). The west top afforded clear views of the decidedly unfriendly Courtauld Glacier right down to the level at which it meets the sea. It was also an excellent vantage point to oversee the previously unexplored regions of the Lemon Mountains to the north and west. Both of these summits had been traversed previously by Phil Bartlett's expedition in 1992, making this a second ascent, albeit via a new route. Andy and Rachel made a third ascent by the same route the following day. Prior to this they had ascended a snow and rock couloir to reach the easterly knoll on the North-east Ridge of the west top (1810m) which they named

'Snowbunting Point' in memory of the bird of the same name that they saw there.

While Andy and Rachel were making their ascent of Horseshoe Peak, Martin and Derek skied up the shallow glacier to the south of the east top to the col leading back down to the Courtauld Glacier. From here they climbed on foot the steep (40° levelling to 25°), icy west ridge of the peak on the junction of the Courtauld and Frederiksborg glaciers to reach the broad snowy summit (1740m, PD+, named Sentinel Peak). This is believed to be a first ascent and the location gave commanding views of Cathedral Peak, Mitivagkat and the surrounding glaciers. Descent to the col was made the same way.

At this point we decided to complete a circular tour back to the drop-off site *via* the Lœbœltet Glacier, even though the junction between this glacier and the Frederiksborg Glacier was heavily crevassed. However, after about 9km of pulking wide crevasses and weakened snow bridges forced an interim stop at Camp 4A (1322m) to allow the temperature to cool. Shortly after midnight we proceeded as a rope of four through the glaciated minefield, awestruck by the size of the fissures *en route*, and were compelled to make a significant detour to reach the Lœbœltet Glacier. Camp 5 (1245m) was reached in the early hours of the morning. At mid-day (29 July) we moved again in order to establish Camp 6 (1486m) near the cirque of mountains bordering Point 2200m.

The following day Martin and Derek skied past the jagged central peaks (named Sawtooth Mountain) to ascend the most easterly of the northern couloirs, easily identified by the presence of a pronounced vertical intrusion in its central buttress. At the obvious col they continued on skis up the broad NW ridge leading to the snowy summit of what was subsequently named Whaleback Peak (1964m, F). Returning to the col they then continued NW to a second col that afforded access to the north ridge of the peak due east of Whaleback. This peak was ascended on skis until the final sharp arête, which was traversed on foot to the narrow summit (2100m, PD-, named Fin Peak). Return to Camp 6 was made by the same route. Later that evening Andy and Rachel also skied up to this second col and from there ascended the south ridge of the northerly peak to gain the corniced summit (2175m, PD, named Goblin Peak). All three routes are believed to be first ascents.

The next day Martin and Derek skied up to the col behind Sawtooth Mountain leading from the Lœbœltet Glacier to the Frederiksborg Glacier (1802m, named Sawtooth Col), but inclement weather prevented an ascent of the peak to its north, despite a clear route forward. Indeed, a period of bad weather then continued for several days, with low visibility and up to half a metre of snow. This prevented further exploration of this interesting cirque. Effectively confined to camp we sampled the delights of compo rations (especially treacle pudding) and continued the search for the coffee that Martin and Derek were sure had been packed prior to leaving the UK.

The decision to move camp nearer the drop-off site was delayed for as long as possible, but with time pressing on we were eventually forced to move camp in whiteout conditions and with the crevasses dangerously concealed. Moving in a rope of four we pulked to Camp 7 (1485m) on 4 August, arriving in a very sodden state. Fortunately the next day was considerably improved and a further pulk of 5.5km led to Camp 8 (1746m), which was a little over 5km from the drop-off site (Camp 9). This final distance was quickly accomplished and allowed us finally to rejoin Roy and Robert, and later Dave and Geoff.

With a few days to spare before being picked up and the snow reasonably consolidated, Martin and Derek decided to attempt the impressive south face of Trillingerne main peak. Leaving early they skied to the bergschrund just below the face and then climbed on foot through the frozen boulders lining the right-hand edge of the face. While steep (up to 45°) this route offered the least objective danger and afforded fast access to the summit ridge. Short, airy snow traverses then led to the true summit (2295m, AD–) and, a little further on, to a slightly lower subsidiary summit. This was the second ascent of this peak, but via a new route.

Summary:
The British Lemon Mountains Expedition 2002 attempted first ascents in the South Lemon Mountains, and the previously unvisited North Lemons from 13 July-12 August. Eighteen peaks were climbed, fourteen of which were first ascents and the remainder were by new routes. Three other major peaks were attempted. The most important ascent was the 1300m NE Face of The Spear, TD/mixed, in the North Lemons, by Dave Wilkinson and Geoff Cohen. We gratefully acknowledge the financial support of the BMC/ UK Sports Council, the Gino Watkins Memorial Fund, and the Mount Everest Foundation.

REFERENCES

Phil Bartlett, 'Kangerdlugssuaq'. *AJ104*, 91-96, 1999.
Phil Bartlett. 'British Mountaineering Expedition to East Greenland 1992'. (MEF Report 92/28).
Chris Bonington, 'A Greenland Adventure'. *AJ97*, 27-36, 1992/3.
Tom Chamberlain, 'Bishops, Actresses and Witches'. *AJ105*, 71-79, 2000.
Jim Gregson, 'Paradise Lost then Found; skiing and mountaineering in East Greenland'. *High* 200, 28-31, 1999.
Luke Hughes, 'Lindbergs and Lemons'. *AJ* 98, 147-151, 1993.
Graham Little, 'Gneiss and ice: Greenland on the rocks'. *AJ99*, 64-70, 1994.
Richard Pash, 'The Lemon Mountains of East Greenland'. *AJ106*, 31-36, 2001.
<www.wayupnorth.clara.co.uk>

NICK BULLOCK

Blind Date on Quitaraju

(Plates 10, 11)

Inside a steamy ski chalet in Chamonix, there were clothes hung on every available beam and the windows were running with condensation. It was crowded. Some were celebrating a successful ski trip, others mourning a washed-out winter climbing trip. Snowflakes swept against the window, stuck there for a moment, then slithered down the pane to be quickly replaced by others. This was the only time Al and I had met. We'd spoken a few times over the phone since, but that doesn't help much when it comes to recognising your future partner.

Now waiting at Manchester Airport, looking for a face that I recognised, I replayed my last phone conversation with Al, particularly his parting shot: 'This will be the ultimate blind date.' He wasn't wrong.

Spending the first week getting to know each other, we did the usual stuff that strangers do when together for the first time, carrying gigantic bags to base camp, arguing with taxi drivers, getting ill. We marvelled at the size of American climbers' rucksacks as we returned exhausted from climbs we were planning as warm-ups.

We acclimatised by going into the Parron Valley. Parron would be our first peak, at 5600m as good a starting point as any and a three-day round trip, according to the guidebook. We begged to differ. Setting off from base camp at 11pm, we returned successful at 10am next morning. A round trip of eleven hours. We were cruising.

The next peak was Artesonraju. The climbing this time was a little more sustained than on Parron, but still relatively straightforward. At 6000m, though, it tested our lungs. From the summit we had views of many of the Cordillera Blanca's finest, including the very thing we had come to Peru to climb: Quitaraju. Standing proud, the mountain threw down its gauntlet in the shape of its fantastic, massive South Face. There was only one existing line on this and plenty more room left to pop in another, play around, and enjoy our blind date.

Tucked up for the night, I stared at the roof of the tent, wondering about the next few days. Originally we'd planned a recce into the hanging valley beneath Quitaraju's South Face, but the hillside below was so steep we decided just to go for it. Al had scoped the face out the previous day and sounded suitably impressed: 'It's like several Galactic Hitchhikers stacked one on top of the other.' Secretly, I was pleased with his appraisal. It wouldn't do to bring someone all the way to Peru for a boring snow plod.

The following afternoon we flogged up the hillside, and then into the hidden, hanging valley of the Quebrada Quitacocha. It was a stunning place. The sun shone through the quenal trees covering both sides of the valley. Long marsh grass swayed in the wind. We descended onto the dry lake-bed where the sun beating down on the mud had dried the cracked surface into millions of herringbone lines. Following the crazy-paving at its edge, we picked our way to the end of the lake and, passing through quenal trees, started to climb to the head of the valley. Unfortunately we had other things than the scenery to occupy our thoughts: the massive, broken icefall spewing out from the bottom of Quitaraju's South Face for one.

During our MEF interview in London the panel of eminent mountaineers had dared to suggest that this icefall might explain why there had been so little action on this face. Al and I are quite similar in some respects. We are both driven, in a quiet way, although friends would probably describe us as just pigheaded and bloody-minded. At times though, such traits may be advantageous and the icefall looked like one of those times. The closer we got to it the more difficult it appeared – in fact, it looked impossible. This was the moment when any sensible party would have looked at other objectives, licked its wounds, laughed a little at how blind it had been, felt a little arrogant, perhaps, to have thought it could get through where others had failed; even, it has to be said, run away. Somehow that just wasn't an option for us.

After resting and eating the only proper food we had brought with us, we set off to try to find a way through the icefall. Our plan was good, but it depended on the ability to move quickly, continuously and lightly. The only food we took was to be eaten while we climbed: chocolate, biscuits, and sweets. There would be no food for cooking and so no fuel. We wouldn't be stopping so we didn't need sleeping bags or duvet jackets. We packed just one homemade Pertex bivvy sack. We'd sprint through the icefall, move together on the route using our recently gained acclimatisation, and reach the summit in no time at all. Then we'd abseil the opposite face which, as the standard route, was likely to be equipped. Once on that, we would endure a cold, hungry but safe bivvy, or more likely keep moving to reach base camp that night, exhausted but safe. It was a good plan.

Al started on the icefall, the beam of his head torch picking out small ice blocks he could hop between. But as we moved further into the icy maze, route-finding became more difficult and the blocks grew to monstrous proportions. Often, unable to go round towering séracs, we were forced off our line and had to tackle them head on, pitching hard and worrying ice and hoping the whole lot wouldn't tumble on our heads.

On the sharp end, I suddenly found myself beneath an overhanging ice wall. Getting started up the thing was desperate and the climbing was horribly steep from the first move. The ice was so hard it took two or three axe-swings to get a placement. Thuggery took over as Al surmounted the first obstacle and throwing in a cramponed heel-hook at the top, hauled his body ungraciously over the edge where even steeper ice awaited him.

Fortunately, the shelf Alf now found himself sprawled on followed a curving chimney. I placed an ice screw and began to follow this icy fault-line upwards. As the chimney increased to near vertical I started to bridge out over the dark void below. Nearing the top I noticed a large rounded block of ice wedged into the chimney. Moving onto the right wall to bypass the obstruction, I reckoned that a few more moves would put me on top of the sérac. Pulling level with the ice block, I took a breather. Then, planting the right axe as I leaned backwards, I began to move the left pick towards the top of the block. The pick touched and the block instantly fell away, plunging into the darkness below. My left axe had ripped free from the block's soft outer layer and I was left hanging from one axe. The freezing air stung my lungs as I panted. My sweat froze. The block bounced off the walls below, echoing down as tons of ice shattered in the blackness. Then it was still again. I did the only thing I could. I took a deep breath and pushed on. Reaching the top I quickly set up a belay and shouted: 'Safe!'

Safe?

The ice levelled out. Snow had settled, but not consolidated. Al now took over trying to find a way through. As his head torch swept from side to side, crystals sparkled. The snow deepened, first to our thighs and then to our shoulders. The ice creaked as the temperature dropped. Every so often the sound of a collapsing sérac detonated in the silence surrounding us. Slowly, carefully, we inched through. There was no respite. The water we had melted for the climb on the face had already been drunk. Our muscles ached and there was still more deep wading to come. The plan was ruined.

Finally, at 8am we finished crossing the icefall. Eight hours of continuous climbing and wading had made serious inroads into our reserves. We talked about traversing the base of the face, and so escaping. The most obvious line looked steep and hard. If it was covered in powder it would take for ever. After all the hard work getting through, we at least had to take a look at the face. If there was névé perhaps lost time could be clawed back. We would push it out, move together and reclaim everything that had been taken from us so unfairly.

I started off, dipping my toe in the water. The joint decision was made: if the ice was anything but perfect we would scuttle off to the left and escape. The steep, rocky bergschrund proved hard. More time was lost but I pushed on, climbing furiously up our chosen line. The snow was generally good – patches of névé mixed with water ice over bulging rock. Al climbed up to me, collected some gear, then climbed past. The decision was made. There would be no retreat. We were utterly committed.

Sweeping ice sheets of vertical sastrugi rippled over névé as far as the eye could see. Moving together we pushed upwards. The climbing was excellent Scottish IV with steeper sections of V. Our calves screamed, but there was nowhere to rest. We had been moving together now for a long time. Al had all the gear, putting even more pressure on his calves. He had to traverse from one side of the climb, teetering on front points, over to the opposite side recovering running-belays as he went. I pressed on urgently, the rope tugging at Al's waist.

'What the hell are you doing?' Al yelled, yanking at the rope. I knew what was happening below but the angle of the face and lack of anything solid to anchor to forced me on.

Stopping at the first available belay, an exceptionally poor spike with only axes as a back up, I waited hesitantly for Mr Powell to join me. Attached to the worst spike ever I waited to face the music. Al's anger was justifiable, perhaps – but with a great deal of climbing left, we were going to have to kiss and make up very quickly. The nature of the face changed. Thin, hollow ice now took the place of névé; powder snow thinly covered exposed rock. The angle of the face increased. I couldn't know it, but I was about to tackle the crux pitch. At least the confusion of the previous section was over. From here we would be pitching the climb.

A direct line would have been possible had the ice covering the near vertical slabs been good; but it wasn't. The slightly overhung corners might have gone, but for rotten ice. The whole pitch would certainly have been less scary with one or two good pieces of gear. By now I was twenty feet above my last piece, a shaky cam in loose rock. Rock poked through above and to either side where my picks had shattered the ice. I scrabbled at the ice but huge sheets peeled off. My forearms and shoulders burned, I needed a decent placement, a rest. Now. But upward motion was impossible. I could see a better-looking line to the left but reaching it would mean reversing to the cam. It was the only option. I started reversing, teetering down, expecting at any moment that my axes would rip. I fought to stop my limbs shaking while Al looked on, checking his belay. If the cam ripped, he would be holding a factor two fall. Come on, Nick, I told myself, stay with it.

I started the traverse. It was even more difficult but at least the cam had a better chance of holding and that gave me courage. The ice rang hollow as I tapped my picks into the thin skin covering rock with an inch of air between. Trusting it seemed madness but there was no other way. Putting all my weight onto my arms, I could find nothing for my frontpoints. I made a gentle kick but the ice peeled away revealing blank rock. Moving as quickly as I could, climbing on eggshells, I headed for an overhanging corner ahead where the ice looked thick and comforting. The trick is, I told myself, not to let the ice know I'm here. The trick worked. Al breathed out. Finally I pulled through the overhang on better ice.

The crux pitch was over, but that didn't mean the climbing was easy. Rope-length after rope-length we moved on. The climbing was superb, similar to the Orion Face on Ben Nevis. Finally the light faded. Al fixed an anchor while I dug out a snow ledge for us to spend the night. We huddled under Al's Pertex sack. My body cramped every time I moved, Al's eyes streamed with water. Avalanches poured down the face as cornices from the summit ridge high up collapsed. A cold night lay ahead. We were still only halfway up the face.

Climbing the first pitch of the morning Al shook the stiffness out of his legs. A steep, fluted snow-runnel led to a ridge and we followed more rocky runnels. Both of us looked up at the ridge, visible now, but so far away. Spindrift poured down and we screamed obscenities. The flurries slowed their pace. We crawled through a white wilderness. The runnels, on both sides, became fringed with bulbous mushrooms of ice. Al looked at them, weighing them up, wondering about a way off the top of the face. The idea of having to dig through some alien-shaped ice-monstrosity to escape appalled him.

Still alternating pitches, we continued to find consistently hard climbing, nothing quite as tenuous as the first day, but nothing easy enough to allow us to relax. Entering a large bay, Al set up an ice-screw belay. The summit looked very close now and continuing direct looked to be the best bet. Two or three pitches, perhaps, assuming the ridge we were looking at was the summit ridge and not a subsidiary top that led to more climbing. The next pitch should put us beneath the summit although climbing it was not going to be a breeze. Ahead the bay steepened to a rocky backwall with only one possible exit – an ice runnel guarded at the bottom by a rock overhang.

I placed three screws, more than on any other pitch so far. I knew how weak I had become. Steadying myself beneath the runnel, the effort required for this was going to be more than I wanted to make. Placing my left axe as high beneath the overhang as I could, I breathed deeply and closed my eyes. Forcing the air back out of my lungs, I stepped up. Locking off with my left arm I reached over and swung my right axe to get a placement. The ice was hard, too hard to get my pick in. I swung again. And again. Finally, I had a placement I could trust. But my body was empty. Muscle was being eaten by muscle to fuel movement. Pulling now on my right arm, I twisted the left and pulled the axe free. My upper body was past the overhang. The next placement needed to be as high as possible. The next placement needed to be good. I drew back my arm and swung. My feet stayed put while my left axe was driven home. Pulling now with both arms, I felt my feet cut loose. Quickly I drew my knees upwards towards my chest and carefully placed my front-points just above the lip of the overhang. I stood up, straightening my legs in a massive effort. I was established in the runnel and retched, my dry guts heaving.

Al watched as I set up the last belay on the route. Then he climbed up to meet me. We hardly spoke; there was nothing to say. We'd had enough. We deserved the summit. Wading, Al forced a trench through unconsolidated sugar for fifty metres. And then, finally, he was rewarded. The mountains all around were deep red as the sun dipped below the horizon. He looked on the whole of the range, re-born into the horizontal world. The sky turned dark and stars appeared. Al breathed deep. He was alive. The wind whipped up spindrift, stinging his face. The spell was broken. Time to belay.

We spent our third night out on the summit in a snow hole. The temperature plummeted. The night was shivered away. At dawn we quickly set off. Packing is a short affair when there is nothing to pack. By midday we'd reached the bottom of Quitaraju's North Face even though the fixed anchors hadn't materialised. We down-climbed all the way. We passed first Swiss climbers, who gallantly fed us tea and chocolate, and then a French team at the Alpamayo high camp who, magnificently, gave us all of their spare food. We dropped down to the very busy Alpamayo base camp, sneaking through without talking to anyone. Doggedly we pushed on, driven by the thought of food, flat ground and sleeping bags.

The meadows below our base camp were beautiful. Having just spent the last three days on a big, snowy, cold mountain we savoured the scene, our senses amplified. There were hundreds of lupins, forests of quenal, their bark peeling and their branches covered in damp thick moss. Mountain streams gushed down the steep slopes to join the swollen river running through the centre of the meadow. Even the dust, kicked up by our dragging feet as we headed back down to the Santa Cruz, was refreshing. A massive Condor swooped overhead, no doubt looking for tasty morsels. I don't imagine it saw anything worth picking from our bones.

At 8pm we reached the rock where we had stowed our kit three and a half days ago. The food bag was the first to be opened. It was time to dine.

A few days later, I leaned back in my seat and took a second drink from the flight attendant. I couldn't help but wonder what Cilla would have made of our blind date.

'Will I need my hat?' Cilla might ask.

'Oh, I don't think so. But we're going to stay in touch!'

ACKNOWLEDGEMENTS

Al Powell and Nick Bullock would like to thank the British Mountaineering Council and Mount Everest Foundation for grants, Joe Simpson for info and references and Jules Cartwright for matchmaking. Nick Bullock would like to thank Mark Goodwin for bringing some semblance of order to this article.

Exploration

TAMOTSU NAKAMURA

The Alps of Tibet – Part II

Revisiting the Nyenchentangla East

(*Plates 30–39*)

Three elderly members of the Japanese Alpine Club again visited the least-known parts of the Nyenchentangla East in Tibet during April and May, and October and November 2002. The object of these journeys was to explore the northern side of the range's central area and to reconnoitre the highest unclimbed peak Nenang (6870m).

Part 1: In the heart of eastern Tibet

Travel to less frequented regions of Tibet is always unpredictable, even these days. The hazards are various, partly to do with having a permit to a restricted area, partly to do with unstable weather, dangerous roads, dreadful landslides, trouble with local people and lack of information. However, we persevered, bearing in mind that anything can happen but nothing is impossible in China. An important key to success is the ability to cope with any situation in a flexible manner and to change route without hesitation depending on circumstances. We were forced to abandon our original plan to enter Yigong Tsangpo and to cross Shargung La on the Tsangpo–Salween Divide to the north since a section of the gorge on the way was impassable.

Between 24 April and 17 May we drove 3600km. There were five of us, myself, aged 67, Tsuyoshi Nagai, 69, Eichiro Kasai, a mere 60, and two Tibetans, Tashi our guide and Tsering, the cook. We flew to Lhasa on 22 April and by 27 April we were standing on Jiayu Bridge (3295m). This is where the old China road – 'Gya Lam' – from Peking to Lhasa crossed the Salween or Nu Jiang. A pundit dispatched by the Survey of India reached this bridge on 2 September, 1882. (See Map 'To the Alps of Tibet' on page 82.) Immediately after the bridge, the road went along the deep gorge of a small tributary to the west along the old China road until soon afterwards the valley opened up. We passed through Kansa (4100m) and Old Lhorong where the ruins of a large monastery, destroyed by the Red Army at the time of the Cultural Revolution, are strikingly dominant on the hill looking over Kansa village. After crossing a final pass (4500m) we arrived at Lhorong (3680m).

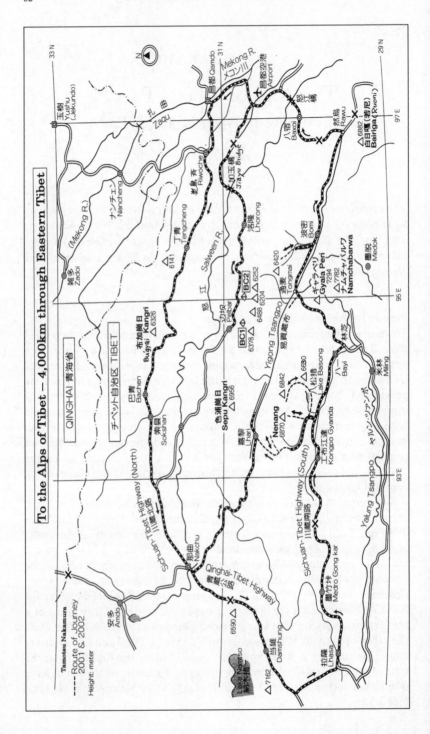

To the Alps of Tibet – 4,000km through Eastern Tibet

Sky burial and the least-known valley

Before moving on, we visited the Zudo monastery of the Gelupka sect which at present has 125 monks. One of the monks was kind enough to take us to the place used for sky burials not far from Lhorong township. When we came to the place at about 11am, the ceremony had already finished but a hundred vultures was still gathered there, on the ground and in the sky too. The vultures were being fed with dumplings made of *tsampa* and smashed human bones.

Next day, 29 April, we continued. The current road runs westwards from Lhorong to Pelbar almost along the old China road, Gya Lam, in the northern foothills of the main Tsangpo-Salween Divide. We left Lhorong at 8.20am and stopped at Shopando (3400m) to ask villagers about the traffic southward to Bomi, but the trade footpath which crosses a high pass over 5000m was closed due to heavy snow. At 10:20am we crossed a pass (4440m) and at noon again asked villagers in Parirang (4080m) about the trail to Bomi. Their answer was the same. Nobody could cross Tungla La (5262) down to Bomi in May because of snow but a three-day horse caravan would possibly carry us to Bomi between mid-June and early October. Ronald Kaulback and John Hanbury-Tracy crossed this pass in 1935.

We crossed the highest pass (4760m) down to the village of Lhatsa (4135m), crossed another pass (4490m) and then entered a wide open riverbed in Puyu valley to the south-west. The road was only a track, which at times crossed river streams and was non-existent here and there. In the rainy season no vehicle would be able to drive up the valley because of the higher water levels of the streams.

After an hour's drive in the mist, one of Landcruisers became stuck in the stream. It was like a sudden death. Villagers in the vicinity kindly worked till dark to pull out the car from the stream and a truck also came to help. In spite of the villagers' help, however, all the efforts were in vain. We pitched tents (4080m) near the stream. It snowed all night.

In the morning, ten horses and eight porters from Shel Shep village arrived and leaving the vehicle stuck in the stream we trekked up the valley and arrived at Shel Shep village (4110m) after lunch, where we lodged in the shed of a Tibetan house. Shel Shep is the last point that foreigners have reached in this direction. Many caterpillar fungi, known as yarchagamba, which are an important source of the villagers' income, grow around there. Just one can cost 40p. Trees and bushes for fuel are abundant in the lower valley but they use yak dung for fuel in the upper pasture.

On the morning of 1 May the weather was wonderful; the magnificent snow peaks of Kona I, II, III appeared for the first time above the headwaters of the valley to the south-west. (See also Map 'Nyaiqentanglha East – Central Part on page 84.) Just before 10am our caravan departed from Shel Shep and marched up the right bank of the wide open riverbed toward the headwaters. We soon passed nearby the primary school of Puyu village. The Puyu valley separates to two principal glacier valleys at the end.

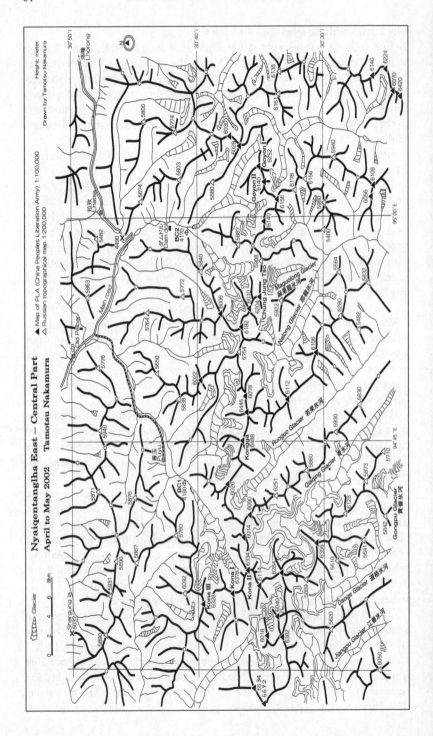

Nyaiqentanglha East – Central Part

April to May 2002   Tamotsu Nakamura

Map of PLA (China Peoples Liberation Army) 1:100,000

Russian topographical map 1:200,000

Height: meter

Drawn by Tamotsu Nakamura

4. Nawang Gombu is introduced to HM The Queen by Charles Clarke while George Band looks on. Mike Westmacott and George Lowe are also visible. (*Pic Photos*) (p3)

5. All the Everest men, minus Westmacott, photographed in the Western Cwm in 1953. Gombu, Tenzing Norgay's nephew, is seated ninth from the left, wearing goggles. (© *Royal Geographical Society*)

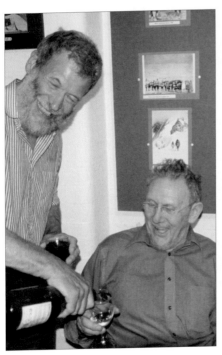

16. John Temple and Bill Ruthven sharing a champagne moment.

17. Nick Clinch, leader of the first successful expedition to Gasherbrum I in 1958, with Mike Westmacott.

18. Eliza Moran of the UIAA's Alpinism Commission and AC President Alan Blackshaw.

19. Chris Fitzhugh, *right*, listens carefully to Brad Washburn as Charles Wylie looks on.

20. Markus Schmuck, member of the four-man expedition to make the first ascent of Broad Peak, with his family.

21. HM The Queen accepts a bouquet from Hannah Nicol, grand-daughter of Hamish Nicol and George Band.

22. Chris Bonington and David Attenborough raise their glasses.

23. Jean-Jacques Asper and Ernest Hofstetter with his family, both from the Spring 1952 Swiss Everest Expedition, together with Tenzing's Norgay's eldest daughter Pem Pem Tshering and Sally Hunt.

4. Grant Piper on Sladden Saddle (2344m) with Aoraki/Mount Cook behind. (*Paul Knott*) (p116)

5. Fox Glacier from Chancellor Hut. (*Paul Knott*) (p116)

26. The stupendous SE Face of Kyzyl Asker (5878m) with the curved gully climbed by Robertson and Tressider clearly seen reaching towards the summit. (*Guy Robertson*) (p43)

27. Nevado Chácua Grande (5350m) in Peru's Cordillera Jatún Chácua, seen from the NW, upper Jancapata valley. (*Evelio Echevarría*) (p111)

28. The north end of the Cordillera Jatún Chácua, with the Rumicruz seen from the SSW. (*Evelio Echevarría*) (p111)

29. Steve Sustad starting up the central chimneys on day one of the first ascent of
    Misión Improbable on Los Gigantes, the vast sea cliff off the Canaries. (*Pat Littlejohn*) (p49)

The left, to the east, is a glacier valley towards one of the most impressive peaks, Kongga (6488m) and the right, to the west, is a valley towards Kona I, II and III, exceeding 6300m. At about noon we set up our base camp – BC1 – (4180m) at a point near the confluence of two streams beyond old glacier moraines and close to a stream flowing from the west valley. There are summer lodges for pasturage of Puyu villagers.

Puyu valley
In the afternoon we entered the west valley and attempted to reach the ice falls in the lower part of the glacier surrounded by the three peaks of Kona. We trekked a yak trail from BC1 to the southwest along the right bank of an infant glacier lake, a third of which was still frozen. Apparently the retreat of the glacier was forming the lake. The trail was exposed to frequent rock avalanches that fell down from precipitous slopes above the right bank of the lake, threatening us all the time. In an hour we reached the glacier tongue, and then ascended yak trails on the lowest part of glacier from the end, the surface of which was covered with debris. At 3.30pm we got to the foot (4300m) of the icefalls and returned to BC1 that evening. The weather changed and it began to snow.

BC1 is at 30°40.266'N and 94°41.482'E. On both sides of the two valleys, west and east, a mark of erosion made by glaciers is clearly observed. The mark runs in ten to a hundred metre high strips along the foot of the mountain. It tells us of the retreat of the glaciers. Similar erosion is also seen in the Dam Dol valley. According to the Russian Topographical Map (RTM) of 1:200,000, the glacier surrounded by Kona peaks has an overall length of about 8km from the farthest glacier head down to the glacier tongue. Beyond the watershed that the range of Kona and other 6000m peaks form, Qiaqing Glacier, the largest glacier in the basin of Yigong Tsangpo, 35km in length, flows down to the south-east.

On 3 May, we entered the eastern valley traversing up and down yak trails on undulating old moraines covered with low conifer trees and shrubs to the flat riverbed. We went up to the glacier end where no glacier lake yet exists. The lower part of the glacier was covered with debris. We could have had a glimpse of the magnificent profile of Kongga (6488m) if it had been fine. The upper north face of Kongga was beautifully adorned with fluted snow and ice and the summit ridge was guarded with huge overhanging cornices.

The sight of the east valley from BC1 is narrow, but RTM indicates that the glacier of the east valley separates to two streams at about 4km from the glacier end. The left one stretching to the east is the main stream, being about 6km long, whilst the right one going up southwards to the foot of the north face of Kongga and then westwards is only 2km long. The glacier width is about 2km at the confluence where ice falls are viewed from Puyu valley. Behind Kongga to the east, a 6445m peak exists on the main watershed between the Salween and Tsangpo according to the 1:100,000 topographical map of the China People's Liberation Army (the PLA map). But this peak cannot be seen, being hidden by Kongga. On the southern side of the watershed two glaciers flow down to Yigong Tsangpo. The one in the west is Ruoguo Glacier, 14km in length and the other in the east is Nalong Glacier, 18km in length.

By 4 May, the Landcruiser had been repaired and collected us at BC1 so next day we moved to the new township of Pelbar. It was experiencing a construction boom, which government policy is accelerating. Many new houses were being built. Tibetan villagers of Puyu were working there together with Chinese migrant workers. Recently a new road has connected Pelbar to Biru County in the upper Salween basin. Now you can drive from Pelbar to Lhasa via Nakchu in three days.

Dam Dol valley

On 6 May , we left Pelbar for Base Camp 2 – BC2. We drove back along the desolate valley and saw another sky burial site near old Pelbar village. Before reaching a high pass near Lhatsa we entered the open valley of Dam Dol, accessible by Landcruisers. The topography and river conditions of the valley are very similar to Puyu valley.

Having passed Dam Dol village on the left bank, we set up BC2 (4170m) on a small pasture near a confluence of two streams, where Dam Dol valley separates into two glacier valleys. The west valley leads upwards to the south-west and the mighty white peaks of the Chung Jung Tso (6204m). The east valley leads to a pair of enchanting peaks, Goyon I (6252m) and II (6140m), separating the glacier to the east and south. From BC2 directly to the south there is a view of beautiful Goyon II and prominent erosions by glaciers that closely resembled the Puyu valley.

The main glacier of the east valley flows down from the south-east to the north-west, and a branch glacier runs from the south and merges with the main glacier at a confluence about 6km from the glacier end. The main glacier is about 7km in length from the confluence to the glacier head, whilst the branch glacier is about 3.5km in length to the south. The main glacier has an overall length of 13km. Beyond the watershed to the south there is Maguolong Glacier, 14km long, that flows down to Yigong Tsangpo. Six 6000m peaks are ranged on the Tsangpo-Salween divide above both glacier-heads.

In the west valley the glacier flows down south-west to north-east. It is about 4km from the glacier end to the confluence of two glaciers; one leads south and the other south-west. The former is about 4km to the glacier head and the latter is about 3km. Beyond the watershed to the south there is a branch glacier of the Nalong Glacier and other nameless glaciers. Four 6000m peaks on the Tsangpo-Salween Divide encircle the glacier heads. Old moraines of the east valley reach a confluence of the two valleys and they block a stream from the west valley.

On 7 May, we left BC2 to reconnoitre the west valley. We trekked a yak trail along the left bank of the stream. On the way we had a wonderful view of Goyon I and II with a glacier lake to the southeast. In an hour we entered a wide-open flat riverbed going beyond the moraines of the east valley. A panorama of snow-white glittering Chung Jung Tso (6204m) suddenly came into sight. There was a small Tibetan village of only two houses. A Tibetan woman of the village kindly guided us to the upper glacier valley along a yak trail on the left bank making a detour to the upper pasture. At about noon we reached an ideal vantage-point at 4450m. We saw Chung Jung Tso and 6000m snow peaks ranging to west, a profile of the glacier flowing down in an S curve and an infant glacier partly covered with ice. On the way back the villagers received us very warmly, offering yogurt and butter tea. A girl and young woman made themselves up painting colored dots on their faces.

We wanted to explore to the east next day, but landslides blocked our path and we contented ourselves by visiting the ruined gompa of Dantseden. Next day we were forced to return to Lhasa, a journey of almost a week.

Part 2. The holy mountain and north of Bomi
Early snowfalls in eastern Tibet jeopardized our original plan for the autumn of 2002. We had the ambitious plan of crossing the heart of the Nyenchentangla East from south to north. As things worked out, we couldn't have asked for a better trip. First we made a complete exploration of the holy mountain of Nenang (6870m) and afterwards we visited the Jalong glaciers and peaks in the upper valley of Botoi Tsangpo north of Bomi.

Nenang unveiled
On 20 October we arrived in Lhasa and three days later we were in the town of Jula. (See Map: Holy Mountain "Nenang" on page 89.) On the morning of 24 October we organised a caravan with three horses for riding, five yaks to ferry loads and five muleteers at Bela village a little north of Jula and departed for Nenang. The caravan passed through Sebu village (3630m) and turned westwards to the Renbu valley with beautiful gorges covered by dense conifer forests. We set up the first camp at a small pasture called Pama (3790m), at a junction with the Nenang valley.

Trekking northwards up the trail through primeval forest on the right bank of Nenang valley, we camped at the pasture of Zhonggo (4100m) where we could catch a glimpse of the upper part of Nenang's south face. According to our Tibetan muleteers we were the first foreigners to look upon their holy mountain Nenang.

In the morning, we followed a yak trail across the main stream to the left bank before a large waterfall and ascended in zigzags through steep conifer forest to a small pass. With no prior warning a breathtakingly magnificent panorama of Nenang came into view beyond two glacier lakes. The pass is an ideal lookout point. Below the treacherous ridge and the precipitous south face, guarded and beautifully adorned with fluted mixed ice, a harsh wave of glacier icefalls streamed down into the lake in the form of a huge white dragon. The sky was cobalt blue. A leader of the muleteers told us that we had good fortune as the god of Nenang would scarcely allow visitors to see the holy mountain. The muleteer explained that 'Ne' meant holy thing, 'nang' meant inside and therefore Nenang was interpreted as a holy mountain hidden inside of the valley. After two hours we descended to Pama pasture. On 27 October we left Pama and returned to Jula. The holy mountain Nenang (6870m) is now, with the ascent of Sepu Kangri, the highest unclimbed peak in Nyenchentangla East.

Attempt to cross Laqin La
We moved from Jula to Punkar (3760m) by truck and on 29 October made one day's trek to the beautiful Lawa valley to the east of Punkar with a view of the profile of Birutaso (6691m). Lawa is surrounded by high peaks like Chuchepo (6550m), a nameless snow pyramid of 6620m and Birutaso. We walked up to Kangpu Monastery and Lake Kangpu north of Birutaso. But we failed to see Birutaso.

In Punkar we arranged for animals to cross the Laqin La (5300m) to Niwu on the right bank of the Yigong Tsangpo. According to the villagers there are three high passes over 5000m to Niwu Qu, a valley north of Nenang down to Yigong Tsangpo, but pack animals can only cross the Laquin La.

The plant-hunter, Frank Kingdon-Ward stayed at Punkar in 1924 on the way to cross Keng La to Lhari. For three-quarters of a century this remote village had been calm and quite. However in recent years the circumstances have been changing as rapidly as in the other isolated areas. Roads suitable for vehicles are under repair. Some Tibetan houses make use of a solar battery unit for lighting and also kerosene engines to generate electricity. They enjoy videos. Villagers gain a substantial income from caterpillar fungi for Chinese traditional medicines and Matsutake, mushrooms which are exported solely to Japan.

There was much difficulty in organizing the caravan to cross Laqin La for two reasons. First because this autumn snow had fallen earlier than in a normal year, the caravan leader and some of muleteers were afraid of snow on the pass and were unwilling to go to Niwu. In particular they worried that heavy snowfalls would prevent their return journey. Second, one of the horse owners demanded compensation for the death or injury of his horses should this occur on the way. Discussions lasted a long time. In the end, they finally agreed to arrange for a large caravan to carry us to Niwu with 11 horses and five muleteers. It snowed that night.

It was a late departure from Punkar. The caravan followed a trade path through Jiagongna valley toward Lhari and camped at a small pasture at 4040m alongside the stream. The weather remained snowy and on

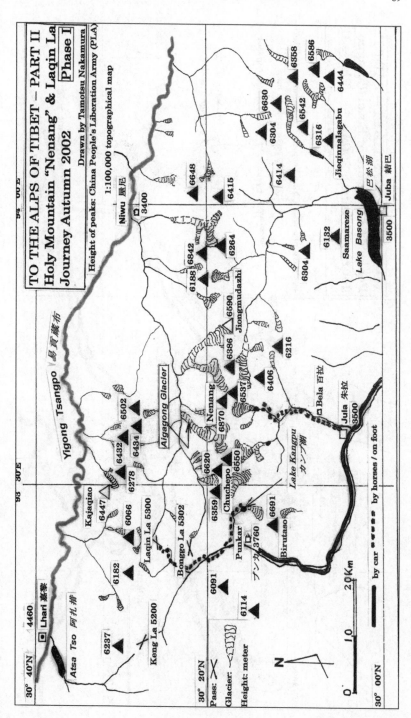

TO THE ALPS OF TIBET – PART II
Holy Mountain "Nenang" & Laqin La
Journey Autumn 2002 Phase I

Drawn by Tamotsu Nakamura

Height of peaks: China People's Liberation Army (PLA)

1:100,000 topographical map

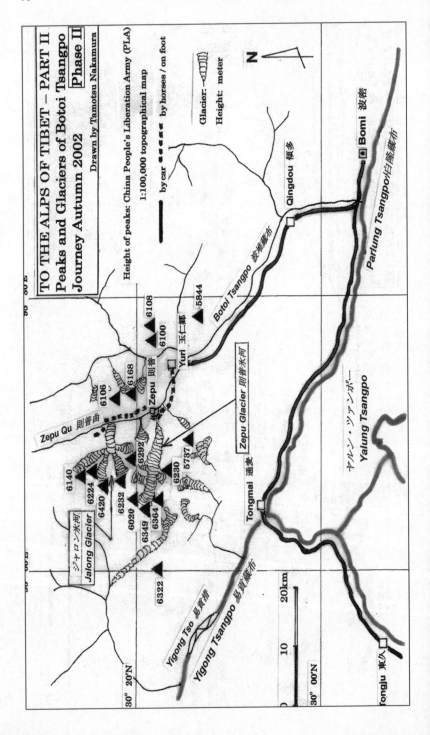

TO THE ALPS OF TIBET – PART II
Peaks and Glaciers of Botoi Tsangpo
Journey Autumn 2002   **Phase II**

Drawn by Tamotsu Nakamura

Height of peaks: China People's Liberation Army (PLA)
              1:100,000 topographical map

━━━ by car   ᐸᐸᐸᐸ by horses / on foot

N

Glacier: ⟨⟨⟨⟨⟩
Height: meter

Qingdou 傾多
Bomi 波密

Botoi Tsangpo 波堆藏布
Parlung Tsangpo 白隆藏布

6108
6100
Yuri 玉仁鄉
5844

6168
6106
Zepu 則普
Zepu Qu 則普曲
Zepu Glacier 則普米河

6140
6224
6420
6232
6020
6349
6292
6364
6230
5787
Jalong Glacier
ジャロン米河

Tongmal 通麦
ヤルン・ツァンポー
Yalung Tsangpo

6322
Yigong Tso 易貢措
Yigong Tsangpo 易貢藏布

20km
10

30° 20'N
30° 00'N

Tongju 東久

31 October 15cm of snow fell. The caravan entered a branch valley to Laqin La and after two hours' march up the valley we arrived at a wide-open pasture at 4480m where the valley divided to the northwest and to the northeast. The latter led to Laqin La.

Next morning, 1 November, the weather was fine and cold. The caravan climbed the branch valley toward Laqin La. When we reached the last pasture at 4870, the muleteers suddenly refused to cross and go down to Niwu. They emphasised the difficulty and danger of crossing the pass judging from the conditions of the heavily snow-covered northern side of mountains that surrounded the valley. No option was given to us. We had to abandon our original plan. We set up the tents at the pasture and searched for a trail to the Laqin La. We had to ascend the following day to at least the pass before retreating.

As we ascended next morning, the path not only became steeper but was entirely buried under the snow. Route finding was not easy. The conditions were obviously too dangerous for pack animals to follow the trail safely. We stood atop Laqin La (5300m) at noon. I had greatly anticipated a grand panorama from the pass of shining 6000m peaks and glaciers north of Niwu valley. To my disappointment, however, what appeared in front of me to the north was not so alluring or fascinating. Only a spiky rock peak of 6060m towering in the north-west was attractive.

No Kajaqiao 6447m was visible, and other 6500m high peaks were also out of sight, being hidden by lesser ranges on the southern side. We descended to a camp at 4390m and decided to return to Punkar as soon as possible in order to carry on Phase II to the unknown mountains of Botoi Tsangpo, a tributary of Parlung Tsangpo north of Bomi.

Unknown peaks and glaciers north of Bomi

Leaving Punkar, we travelled to Xueka and then Lake Basong. The weather became stable and the scenery of Lake Basong, with autumn leaves and surrounding peaks soaring into a blue sky, was nothing short of spectacular. These were indeed the Alps of Tibet. On 7 November we left Bayi and crossed the Seti La (5410m) before descending to Tongmai (2150m). (See Map 'Peaks and Glaciers of Botoi Tsangpo' on page 90.) From the Seti La we had views of Namchabarwa, Gyala Peri and other 6800m unclimbed peaks near the Tsangpo Great Bend. The road from Bayi to Tongmai is now being paved for its whole length.

On 8 November we left Bomi and entered the Botoi Tsangpo from Bomi to Yuri and Zepu via Qingdou by Landcruiser. The valley is open and populated. It was surprising to find a large jail in such a small village. Now there was a breath of winter in the air. Tempting and challenging rock and snow peaks came into sight and we arrived at Yuri. Ronald Kaulback and John Hanbury-Tracy passed this valley to the north in early October of 1935 on their journey to seek the upper Salween. We spent overnight in a shabby rest house at Yuri and organized a caravan.

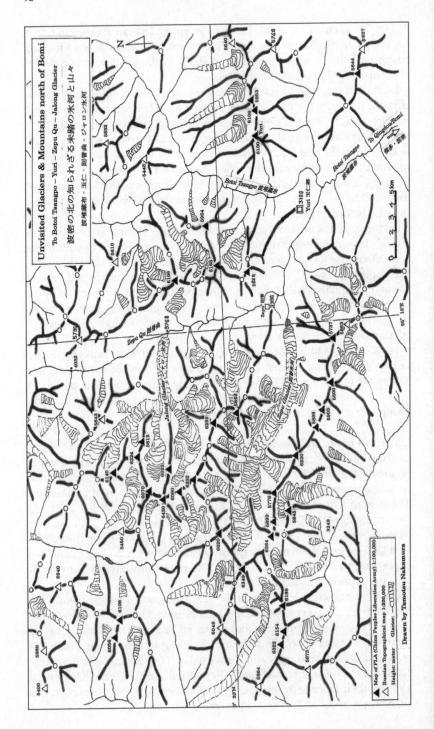

Unvisited Glaciers & Mountains north of Bomi
To Botoi Tsangpo – Yuri – Zepu Qu – Jalong Glacier
波密の北の知られざる未踏の氷河と山々
波堆藏布 – 玉仁 – 則曲曲 – ジャロン氷河

Drawn by Tamotsu Nakamura

Yuri has a primary school, hospital, bank, shops and power station with a diesel engine generator. It is located at the confluence of Zepu Qu north-westward and Botoi Tsangpo to the north. This valley leads to the Tungla La (5267m) on the Tsangpo-Salween Divide that Kaulback and Hanbury-Tracy crossed. We were able to have a view of the range of snow-white peaks surrounding Zepu Glacier from Yuri to the north-west. Zepu Glacier is the third biggest glacier in the Nyenchentangla East with an area of 66 sq km.

To the unknown Jalong Glacier
Zepu Glacier was considered very attractive, but had previously been studied, so we narrowed the target of our exploration to Jalong Glacier and the veiled peaks in its vicinity. (See Map 'Unvisited Glaciers & Mountains north of Bomi' on page 92.) We left on 10 November, through a broad valley and then into dense forests of large conifers and we had no view until we crossed the Zepu.

Then the Jalong Glacier appeared. The terminal part of several kilometers was covered with sediment. The slope was very gentle but the surface looked rough and complicated. It would be similar to the other glaciers in this mountain range. We set up tents near the bridge at 3760m and the muleteers lit large fires to protect us from bears and snow leopards.

I rose early next morning to climb up to a vantage point we had discovered the day before, looking west down the Jalong glacier. We had to take advantage of the slim chance of taking photos of Jalong and its peaks. Morning mists and clouds were gradually moving away and fading as the sun rose. From the south to north-west a spectacular panorama of the most alluring peaks – Jalong I (6292m), the highest Jalong II (6420m), Jalong III (6070m) and Jalong IV (6224m) was unveiled in one hour. The glacier between Jalong II and III seen before me flowed eastward forming terraces and icefalls one after another. Phase 2 was complete.

BIBLIOGRAPHY AND MAPS

In English:
The Alpine Journal, 1998, 1999.
Chris Bonington and Charles Clarke, *Tibet's Secret Mountain – The Triumph of Sepu Kangri*, 1999.
Ronald Kaulback, *Salween*, 1936.
John Hanbury-Tracy, *Black River of Tibet* 1940.
Frank Kingdon-Ward, *The Riddle of the Tsangpo Gorges*, 1926.
Francis Younghusband, *Peking to Lhasa* (Journey made by Brigadier-General George Pereira), 1925.
J B N Hennessey, *Exploration in Great Tibet and Mongolia, 'By AK, 1879 - 1882, made in connection with the Trigonometrical Branch, Survey of India,'* 1884.

In Chinese
Chinese Academy of Sciences, *Glaciers of Tibet*, 1986 Beijing.
Chinese Academy of Sciences, *Glaciers of China*, 1986 Beijing.
Science Publishers, *Japan-China Joint Research of the Glaciers in Qinghai-Tibetan Plateau 1988*. Beijing, 1993.
CMA & TCMA, *Immortal Mountains in the Snow Region*, 1995.

Maps
Mapping Agency of Tibetan Autonomous Region, *Maps of Tibetan Autonomous Region 1:950,000 - 1:1,500,000.*
Chinese Research Institute of Surveying and Mapping & CMA, *Map of Mountain Peaks on the Qinghai-Xizang Plateau 1:2,500,000*, 1989.
China People's Liberation Army, *Topographical Map 1:100,000*
Russia, *Topographical Map* 1:500,000 & 1:200,000.

JOHN TOWN
Nyenang and the Nye Chu

(Plates 35, 40)

In September 2001 Derek Buckle and I explored the mountains at the head of the Wortse Chu, to the north of the Draksum lake, in the Kongpo province of east central Tibet. Despite finding a wealth of beautiful unclimbed peaks, we failed to reach the two highest peaks of the range. The first, N69, unnamed and marked as 6842m on Chinese maps and 6920m on detailed Russian maps, lay out of sight behind the headwall of the He Chu. The trackless upper gorge of the Wortse barred access to the second peak, Nyenang, 6870m or 6730m.

In 2002 I teamed up with Nicky Hart to take another look. I was determined to reach and explore these two mysterious giants and, since the southern approach had yielded little result, thought that a route from the north might hold the key. The watershed of the range forms the boundary between Kongpo and the province of Lhari. On the northern side the rivers and glaciers run down to the Nye Chu, which runs for 70km from its source below the Lochen La to its junction with the Sung Chu. A few kilometres further east the river joins the Alado (Dakson) Chu to become the Po-Yigrong, which continues eastward into a series of savage gorges. Frank Kingdon Ward had come this way in 1936, travelling west up the gorges from Tongkyuk to Rigongka (Ragoonka), on through Nye and over the Lochen La. The weather was bad and he had only a few glimpses of the spectacular main range as he made his way over the pass. This route took several months and was plainly not a starter for anybody with a steady job, even with employers as understanding as ours. In any case Kingdon Ward's hair-raising accounts of the gorge were not encouraging.

Some Chinese maps showed another approach to Nye, via a road running south-west from the city of Nakchu to the town of Atsa, on the old Gya Lam caravan route from Lhasa into China, and then down the gorge of the Sung Chu. Chris Bonington and Charles Clarke had travelled this route in 1996 as far as Lhari, the former provincial capital, about 20km east of Atsa and had various unkind things to say about the road, but I could not find any accounts of anyone traversing the final 60km down the lower part of the gorge to Nye. Charles' most recent expedition report said that it was unlikely that permission could be gained for travel in this area. The sensitivity arises from continuing controversy over the Panchen Lama, with both the Chinese and Dalai Lama's candidates having been found in Lhari province, in the town of Chiali, just north of Atsa.

Rather than becoming too discouraged I took courage from Kingdon Ward. At Temo Chamna he flourished his 'permit' to Tibetan officials, before heading up the Po-Yigrong gorge. At a later stage he learnt that the 'permit' was in fact a letter denying him permission to go any further. In our case I followed my usual practice of faxing to the ever-reliable Bikrum Pandey in Kathmandu a map of where I wanted to go and not asking too many questions when I was told it could be arranged.

The MEF supported us with a grant and Loughborough University was generous enough to release me for four weeks over Easter. On Thursday, 21 March 2002 we reached Kathmandu unusually refreshed; there had been no economy seats left, so we had travelled business class and been upgraded to first on the last leg.

Two days later we flew to Lhasa and were greeted by our guide and translator Dawa and his companion 'The Driver'. It was immediately apparent that these were two very sound men, even by Tibetan standards. I was particularly impressed by The Driver's beaming smile and white gloves. In Lhasa we met their boss Mingma, a man who was willing to go out of his way to make our trip a good one; just how far would become apparent later in the trip.

On 25 March we set out from Lhasa, taking the tarmac main road north through Yangpachen and reaching the outskirts of Nakchu in about six hours. We didn't enter the city but refuelled and then doubled back a few kilometres to the Atsa turning, crossing the frozen Nakchu river on the way. Conditions up here were tough. Anybody outside the warmth of a vehicle had their faces wrapped against the wind. It was a lonely business as we headed away from the traffic of the main road and into the gathering darkness of the late afternoon. The deserted dirt road was in poor condition and at times the way was far from clear.

Road maps of this area are vague as to place names and distances, but it gradually became apparent that there really isn't much worth marking on a map anyway. Somewhere in this snow-bound wilderness of endless plateau and low hills were two 5100m passes, the Shilok and Apa La, the highest on our route. We both assumed that long before crossing these some homely truck-stop would duly appear over the horizon, with a warm fire and plenty of tea. Instead it started to snow. We struggled on into the darkness. There was no opportunity to discuss whether it was time to call a halt, since there was nowhere to do so. We climbed gradually, the air became thinner and the road gradually disappeared. Just before things became impossible the road levelled out and dipped down to a storm-bound hovel. On the way back the Tibetans had to walk this section, to guide the vehicle through the whiteout. The inhabitants suggested we cross the second pass, which lay just ahead of us, and try to find shelter lower down. Given the weather and the state of their accommodation, I thought they might want to come with us.

We pressed on, crossed the second pass and stopped at the first house we could find. Relief at finding somewhere warm and dry was fast tempered by the realisation that we had not descended very far and were in for an unplanned night at 5000m, with prior acclimatisation limited to one day in Lhasa at 3500m. An appalling night duly followed, lightened only by the opportunity to practise a little amateur medicine. Mingma had trapped The Driver's thumb in the car door in Lhasa and Dawa requested the most powerful painkiller we had. We duly administered the second best and The Driver quietened remarkably. He had, we were told on enquiry, lost all feeling in his tongue.

The next day we pressed on, across high featureless plains and low hills, with the occasional group of houses huddled against the elements. On an icy section the Landcruiser broke through the crust and sank to the axle. Eventually a tanker passed and hauled us out. Shortly afterwards we took a wrong turn, then doubled back, only to find the tanker bogged down in front of us. Figures and vehicles gradually appeared out of the snow to pitch in and two hours later we were on our way again. Towards mid-afternoon the road started to descend into a shallow valley system, which led to the town of Atsa, at the northern end of the Atsa Lake, also known as Lhari, in its role as capital of that province. Official outposts, however bleak, usually provide good Chinese cooking and we feasted gratefully in a sub-zero dining room.

We drove onwards, first over a low pass and hydro scheme, where the road to Chiali branched off to the north, and on into the gentle beginnings of the Sung Chu valley. A beautiful snow peak was lit by the sunset as we wondered, as so often travelling in Tibet, whether we were ever going to stop. Relief came in the shape of a small village, with a picturesque gompa, whose headman was kind enough to give us shelter and whose population found us endlessly fascinating. Foreigners were rare here, though there had been Japanese some years ago, attempting the snow peak. A light snow fell overnight and dusted a bald section of the road just below the village. The vehicle slipped gently sideways here next morning prompting a speedy exodus by all but the man at the wheel.

The gorge grew deeper and deeper and we began to be able to plot our progress in detail, using GPS points inputted from Russian maps in the UK. As we descended the air became warmer and the road more and more difficult. Landslides and rockfall were obviously a regular occurrence and it was often necessary to get out and remake the road before we could proceed. As the gorge closed in, houses gradually disappeared and dense forest crowded the slopes above. It is said that fewer than 100 vehicles a year make it down this road and it is easy to see why. After eight hours of painstaking driving, we crossed to the right bank by a concrete bridge. Its mangled predecessor could be seen in pieces some way down stream. But despite the rock walls on either side, we knew the end was in sight.

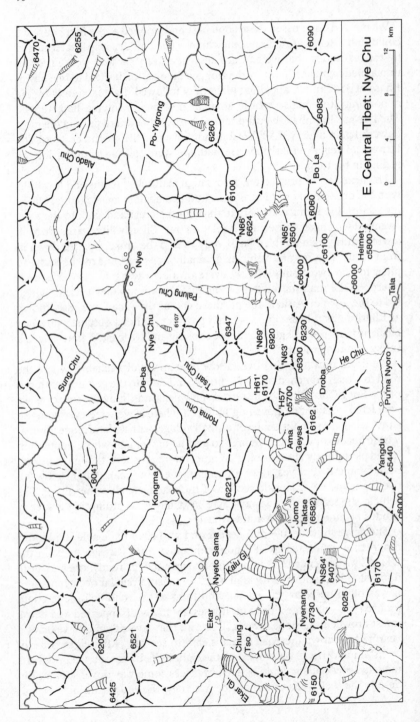

E. Central Tibet: Nye Chu

Shortly afterwards the gorge suddenly opened into the wide sunlit Nye valley, surrounded by high mountains, where a series of substantial villages nestled amongst extensive fields of barley and potatoes. The eastern end of the valley framed some impressive snow peaks, which rise to the north of the Po Yigrong Gorge. Nicky later visited this eastern end, where the Alado Chu issues from a massive cleft to join the Nye Chu, and then, as the Po Yigrong, falls eastwards into an even more impressive gorge.

At Nye the road ended and we would continue our explorations on foot. The mayor provided us with a room with electric light courtesy of the valley's hydro station, and we set about finding horses. The next day Nicky and I explored the approaches to the Palung Valley, which runs seven kilometres south from Nye to the Palung Glacier, and then a further ten kilometres to the main watershed and a possible view of the elusive N69. The Palung Gorge was not for the faint-hearted. There may be a route to the glacier but it would need local help to find it. We became hopelessly lost in the dense bamboo forest clothing the side of the gorge and retired in disarray.

Our main hope was that we would gain a view of N69 by a relatively modest climb up the Tsari valley, which branched south from the Nye Chu at De-ba, about a day's journey west. We would then continue on up the main valley to the villages of Kongma and Nyeto Sama, which promised access to Nyenang and other major peaks.

As our horses and horsemen assembled it was clear that they had little or no experience of expedition transport (or any other kind, one is tempted to say). After an hour, a leisurely lunch was taken, together with the opportunity to shoe a horse or two. The mules in the party did not like the airy and precarious cliff-track which followed, and an extended traffic jam ensued. We left them to it and were rewarded by a peaceful stroll through idyllic woods of oak and pine to De-ba.

The two of us set off with determination before dawn the next day into the Tsari Gorge. After being misdirected by two locals through the thorn bushes of the river banks, we eventually found the path and began to experience what it had to offer. For a while it climbed pleasantly enough up and along the valley side, but then hit the remains of a massive landslide. The path disappeared amidst a chaos of brambles and smashed trees from which we eventually emerged an hour later. When we regained the path far above, it had been so undercut by the landslide that anyone coming the other way would have plunged unwittingly to their doom. Beyond was another landslide, this time barred at the far side by a continuous line of cliff. More in hope than expectation I aimed for a tree which had fallen diagonally across part of the cliff face. On inspection it appeared that one balanced out along the trunk until a lunge gained access to the relative security of a turf ledge. Nicky seemed impressed I had spotted this and so was I.

The landslides seemed to be at an end but we now started to encounter a series of frozen streams, which proved time consuming without axes or crampons. Finally a larger torrent blocked the way. It had cut a deep trench whose sides slipped away at the first attempt to descend. At the second try a large boulder gave way leaving me hanging by my hands. After 8½ hours and just three kilometres of horizontal progress, it was time to give up on 'Nightmare Valley' and hope we made it back to camp without serious injury. This ended our hopes of seeing N69, but on a clear day on our return journey down the Nye Chu, we had spectacular views of the north faces of N63 and Peak 6170 glittering above the far end of the 17km gorge.

The following morning we continued on up the main valley, climbing gradually through unspoilt woodland to camp at the point where the valley narrows before turning south-west towards Kongma. This was the poorest of the hamlets we had encountered, with the inhabitants eking out a meagre existence in the perpetual shadow of the peaks towering above. We had reason later to be grateful to these people.

From Kongma the valley begins to open out, houses reappear and the path ascends to a whitewashed shrine marking the boundary of the upper valley. Nyeto Sama lies in the centre of a plain about ten kilometres long. Another large village lies at its near end and the hamlet of Ekar marks its western boundary. Beyond Ekar a large glacier spills directly across the main valley, blocking it entirely and forcing the track onto its northern slopes. The route to the west follows the headwaters of the Nye Chu up to the Lochen La (5300m), giving access to Pungkar and the upper part of the Drukla Chu, and on over the Tse La to the Gya Lam. This was the route followed by Kingdon Ward in 1936.

As we approached Nyeto Sama, a dazzling area of snow peaks appeared to the south above the broken terraces of the Kalu Glacier. Most spectacular of these was a blade of ice and snow and I gradually realised, with some incredulity, that this must be the northern aspect of Jomo Taktse (6582m), which we had seen from Kongpo the previous September. Seldom can a mountain have been blessed with two such spectacular and contrasting aspects.

A series of other unnamed peaks ran south from Jomo Taktse down the eastern side of the 'Y'-shaped Kalu Glacier, which has such a characteristic appearance on maps and satellite photos. No doubt there were others bounding the western side, but time prevented us from exploring. Our main aim now was to explore the northern approaches to Nyenang, called Kangla Karpo by the local people, where a high lake, the Chung Tso, promised to offer a grandstand view. We therefore hurried on to Ekar and pitched camp just beyond the village.

The weather closed in for the next two days but on 4 April, after early morning snowfall, we made a damp crossing of the main river. A group of wood-cutters showed us onto a good path which climbed steeply for 600m up through the woods. Fresh snow had filled in the line of the path making it hard going as it zigzagged precipitously high above the Chung Chu and onto the shoulder above. From here it was a short descent into the upper valley and then a flog through new snow towards its head. Nicky ploughed a heroic trough through waist-deep powder up onto the moraine and we could then look down onto the lake itself. The 2500m north face of Nyenang or Kangla Karpo was laid out before us in a stunning panorama. The main peak rose sheer above us, dropping westwards to an icy comb whose flutings formed the headwall of the glacier basin. From its foot the Chung Glacier fell in a series of icefalls into the waters of the lake. The north peak and north ridge fell vertically towards us in an angry series of rock walls and séracs.

It was too cold to stay long but these few moments made all the efforts of the previous days and weeks worthwhile. On our journey back our guides and pack train managed to lose us entirely and, but for the good people of Kongma finally understanding our predicament, we would have spent a cold and hungry night out. The police discovered us in Atsa and assigned a nice young man to accompany us to the Public Security Bureau office in Nakchu. Sensitivities over the Panchen Lama had been heightened by a recent visit to Chiali by his parents. We received an hour's lecture in Chinese on the evils of travelling without a permit – we thought we had one – followed by a promise in English that we were nevertheless very welcome in Tibet and would be provided with an escort to 'the best hotel in Nakchu'. The Nakchu Hotel desk-staff wear down jackets in April and the restaurant is the only one I know where they give butter tea to tourists. Mingma appeared out of nowhere. He had driven the six hours from Lhasa that morning and had taken tea with the police inspector before we arrived. Apart from the odd car wreck passed on the road to Lhasa it was all down-hill from there.

JULIAN FREEMAN–ATTWOOD

The Mountains of the Gangdise or Transhimalaya of Tibet

(*Plates 41–43*)

Sven Hedin the Swedish explorer, was probably the first to coin the term 'Transhimalaya'. He was referring to the broken series of ranges, mostly with a north-west to south-east orientation, which form the Gangdise Shan. Because all the north-flowing water of the main Himalaya ends up back in the south, Hedin argued, these mountains are the true watershed of the Himalaya, well to the north of the Tsangpo valley where north-flowing water remains in Tibet. Since the highest points are in isolated massifs, a definable drainage system was hard to pinpoint.

It's important to understand the hydrology of the Transhimalaya before moving on to the geography of the ranges. Bear in mind that 47 per cent of the world's population live downstream from one or other of Tibet's rivers. That percentage is set to increase with rising populations in China, Bangladesh, Nepal, India and Pakistan.

The rivers that make up this figure and which rise in east Tibet – not Gangdise – are the Yellow River, the Yangtse, the Salween, the Irrawaddy and the Mekong. The main streams rising in the western Gangdise are the Yalung Tsangpo, which becomes the Brahmaputra, the Indus, the Sutlej and the Karnali, this latter being a tributary of the Ganges.

All these latter four rise within 60 miles of each other around the area of 31°N 81°E. The source of the Sutlej is just to the south-east of Lake Manasarovar and known at that point as the Lang-chu. It eventually joins the Indus. The source of the Karnali is just south of the mighty Gurla Mandata. The Tsangpo itself rises 30 miles to the south-east of the Sutlej, in a range known as the Kubi Kangri, containing peaks between 6400m and 6700m and positioned on the Nepalese frontier north of Api. It then heads off east, failing to break through the main Himalaya until the gorges around Namche Barwa. The opposite is true of the Indus, the only one of these four whose source is Transhimalayan. It rises north of that most holy of peaks, Kailas, in a minor range named the Yalungselung Rigyu. Not only is Kailas firmly in the Gangdise but the entire range is sometimes marked on maps as the Kailas range. The Indus flows off north-west and out of our story but not before it has picked up waters from Nganglong Kangri or Aling Kangri (6450m) which is to me the most westerly massif you could claim to be Transhimalayan. This is about 80°E and just north of Tibet's principal far-west town, Ali Shiquane, beyond which you enter the Aksai Chin.

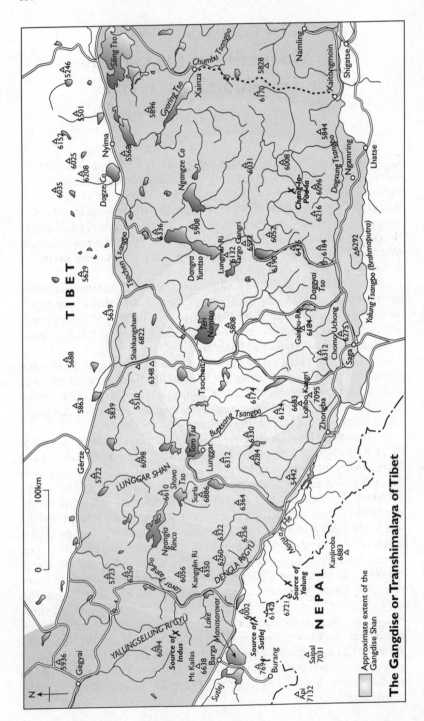

The Gangdise or Transhimalaya of Tibet

The southern boundary of the range is easier to define. It is the Tsangpo which begins life as the Maquan He. This remains the southern extent of the Gangdise until approximately 88°E, or a point between Lhatse and Shigatse. I say approximately, as it remains indistinct where the Gangdise end and the Nyenchentangla ranges begin. Some would claim the range to continue to the longitude of Shigatse. We thus have a minimum Gangdise length of 480 miles. Finally the northern extent of the range runs to approximately 32°N where it blends into the southern Chang Tang plateau, that area of north-western Tibet which runs eventually up to the Kun Lun ranges. Therefore, from the Tsangpo up to 32°N is about three degrees of latitude, or 200 statute miles.

If this does not sound extensive to the reader, it may help as a comparison that the Gangdise, at 96,000 square miles is slightly larger than the United Kingdom and Northern Ireland. The highest peak in the range as a whole is Loinbo Kangri (7095m), the only peak over 7000m the Gangdise can boast.

Linking this ill-defined watershed to the Tsangpo are various south-flowing streams. These mostly do not emanate from one or other of the great Transhimalayan lakes. Usually, and this is where the true watershed lies, the rivers cannot break south and instead flow into one or other of these lakes. The water is dissipated not by any great further north-flowing streams out of them but by evaporation and probably complex underground water systems which may resurface as springs great distances away and down. I suspect evaporation by sun on these lakes is amply assisted by the frequent strong winds, associated with the central plateau and Chang Tang, and these blowing over great lake surfaces must take their toll especially when the amount of water entering the lakes is not necessarily vast.

Starting in the west, Ngangla Rinco, 30 by 12 miles, is on the north side of the watershed. The two rivers feeding it, which merge 30 miles from the lake's west end, are the Aong Tsangpo emanating from the northern slopes of the Surnge La not far from Kailas and the Lavar Tsangpo, originating from the Lavar Kangri range.

Water from the Lunggar range also enters the northern shore. Heading a little east, the watershed of the Surla range is marked by the east-west Surla La (5833m). The north part of the range drains by way of the Pedang Tsangpo into Shovo Tso which is therefore north side. To the south of Surla (6886m) runs the Tsachu Tsangpo eventually merging with the Yalung Tsangpo or Brahmaputra.

The next lake to the east is Taro Tso, 25 by 12 miles, which is to the north of the watershed and fed by a great stream the Buptsang Tsangpo. This runs up from the Loinbo Kangri range 29.5°N 84.5°E for a hundred miles through what is arguably the highest inhabited area in Tibet. The nomads hereabouts live all year at over 5000m, greatly exceeding anything in South America. Hedin visited here in 1906 and noted, as there is today, a great variety of wildlife.

Between 85°E and 86°E and again in the north watershed is Lake Zhari or Teri Namtso, 35 by 15 miles. This is fed by the Tsochen Tsangpo which runs north from the Sangmo Bertik La, a 5550m pass which Hedin also crossed.

A degree further east is the great Bonpo holy lake, Dangra Yumtso, some 45 by 12 miles, with the remote Sezhik monastery on its southern shore. The lake is in the north watershed and fed by the Targo Tsangpo from a point north of Hedin's Chang-La-pod-La, which is the high point between it and the Yarlung Tsangpo. Hedin was told there were many passes called Chang-La-pod-La. Chang signifies 'north' or 'north country'; Pod or Po is Tibet, or at least central Tibet, chiefly inhabited by a settled population. Chang-La-pod-La is therefore 'the pass between the northern tableland of the nomads and the country to the south having drainage to the sea'. Hedin was often told that, whatever the name of a pass, it was always a *Chang-La-pod-La* when it lay on the great watershed between the inland drainage of the north and the river basin of the Tsangpo to the south.

Dangra Yumtso and nearby Shuru Tso, both have a north-south orientation which, unlike the mountain ranges, is rare for lakes of the Transhimalaya. The final two great lakes are Siling Tso which is arguably not in the Gangdise and Nam Tso which is firmly in the Nyenchentangla ranges. There are of course innumerable lesser lakes.

One of the earliest explorers of the Gangdise was the pundit Nain Singh followed by British officers Rawling and Ryder who were accompanied by Lt F M Bailey returning from Younghusband's 1904 mission to Lhasa. They followed Nain Singh's route to Lake Manasarovar, south of Kailas, and confirmed much of his work.

But it is the name of Sven Hedin that will always be linked with the ranges due to his four years of travel within it at the turn of the twentieth century. He was much admired by Lord Curzon, the viceroy of the time, but his German sympathies in the First World War and Nazi sympathies in Second World War brought him into sharp conflict with those who had previously admired his work.

Although Hedin had broken the veil hanging over the region, no mountaineering was accomplished until very recent times. This is not altogether surprising given the difficulty until recently of gaining permission for even the more accessible areas of the main Himalaya. Anyway, most climbers were interested in bigger fish than the Gangdise had to offer.

Having said that and although it is true that the geology of the ranges gives rise to peaks of less steepness than those of the Himalaya, there are nevertheless more than just a few exceptions to be found which give hard complex face and ridge climbs. On the plus side, the weather in general can be much more stable for longer periods than in the Himalaya or eastern Tibet. That is if you discount quite marked diurnal temperature fluctuations and vicious dry winds. At least they often blow out of a clear blue sky. As with any area there are bad years, especially in times of global warming when the seasons seem to become jumbled around into disorder. In winter the nomads will tell you that there is not much depth of snow, roughly knee deep, but that it remains lying for months with very low temperatures and dry air. If seen from the air in winter, the sheer scale in area of snow cover has given rise to Tibet being termed the third pole.

With regard to the mountain ranges of the Gangdise and in an attempt not to complicate matters, we will start again, as with the rivers, from west to east. Most of the ranges are between 20 and 45 miles in length and between five and 12 miles in width. The most westerly is Nganglong Kangri (6596m), which lies just north of the infant Indus and can be viewed as a relatively small group. It was first seen, named and given its location by the pundit Nain Singh in 1867. The height was entered in his record as 'exceeding 23,000ft and possibly 24,000ft'.

Next, there is the group around Kailas itself. The spiritual significance of this mountain for both Buddhists and Hindus is well known. The kora path around it is a gruelling affair of 33 miles taking some three days, and much longer than that for devotees who prostrate themselves the entire way including a crossing of the Drolma La (5630m).

Kailas is often quoted as over 6700m but all the Chinese maps put it at 6638m and they are probably correct. Happily, it has never been climbed and nor should it be although the Chinese, possibly in an attempt to outrage the Tibetans, gave permission to the Spanish to climb it quite recently. Many in the West, as well as in Tibet, put pressure on the climbers, who eventually backed down. It was pointed out that nobody would be much impressed by the mountaineering feat and that, for them, it might mean a one way ticket to the everlasting depths and darkness.*

Some 70 miles to the east and centred on 82°E to 83°E is the Dengla Rigyu range with the highest peak Kangqen Ri (6350m) standing at the northern end. I have not come across any photographs of it or the rest of the 35-mile-long massif. Just 30 miles to the east again, we come to the Surla Range, which was well documented by Hedin in 1906 to 1908 and of which he executed some very fine drawings.

The highest peak is Pt.6886m in the north of the range, and when I accessed the area some years ago from Taro Tso, I was met by a wall of fog which persisted for several days. Time ran out, it being late October, and snow was beginning to fall. I was therefore unable to get any photographs although I was undoubtedly at the point 31°N 83.5°E where Hedin sketched a great east-flowing glacier from the range. The nomads here build wide stone circles, rather Celtic-like, around their tents to keep away the evil one.

The only township hereabouts is Lunggar, which stands quite near Taro Tso with salt mines to the north. The wild men of this place had changed

* Editor's note: The circumstances surrounding this proposed expedition remain confused and controversial. But it was not the first time the Chinese had offered Western climbers the opportunity to climb Kailas.

little in 90 years according to the faces in Hedin's photographs. There is a monastery still existing which, as with many in Tibet, was destroyed in the Cultural Revolution and recently rebuilt. We had a copy of Hedin's drawing of it and we also knew it was the monastery that the red-hat monk came from in Kipling's book *Kim*, and whom Kim met outside the museum in Lahore. The monastery, and this is common to rebuilt ones, is permitted usually less than 12 monks, the authorities being wary of too many of the church gathered in one place. Seven monks and one nun lived in caves behind the monastery. You get a strong feeling there that the strength of their faith will never be squashed by such petty government edicts and rules.

Another equally long and significant range lies just to the north of the Surla across Ngangla Rinco, the lake mentioned earlier. It is named Lunggar and has as its highest peak Pt.6610 in the south of the range. In fact the highest peaks often lie close to the lakes. I suspect this was the peak incorrectly positioned by Nain Singh, historically put at 7216m and named Kuhanbokang.

Looking south, upstream along the Buptsang Tsangpo river, is the Loinbo Kangri range. (Hedin: Lunpo Gangri). The highest peak, Loinbo, is the highest in all the Gangdise at 7095m and corresponds to Pk.W134 of the Ryder and Wood survey of 1904. The mountains are of granite and the southern half of the range contains some very fine looking rock peaks although the rock is somewhat flaky. The main ice mountains are Talha Zhenggo (6317m), Gopalho (6453m), a beautiful pyramid, and Phola Kyang (6530m). Then north of Loinbo, which itself has a rocky and technical looking Pt.6645m, is the Nyidokang La and beyond that Kangbulu (6603m), this latter peak of less interest.

Some 55 miles to the south-east of Loinbo and centred around the Chinese military garrison town of Saga lies the Kanchung Gangri ranges (Hedin: Chomo Uchong). The highest peak Pt.6450m (possibly only 6312m) is in view from near the town and looks quite complex to access. Sven Hedin spent a considerable time surveying and drawing the range.

If you were to travel north from Chomo Uchong you would pass hot springs and geysers en route to Daggyai Tso. On the left is a significant range with a peak marked on Chinese maps as Gainbu-Ri (6184m). If you go on 150 miles, crossing the Lapchung and Nakbo ranges, past Tsochen and the Teri Namtso lake, you end up at a massif called Shahkangsham, some 18 miles in length and way up at 31°40'N. Nain Singh was the discoverer of this range on his 1873-75 journey from Leh to Lhasa. He gave it a height of 7660m; the range was marked at 25,000ft by Hedin, who referred to it as Nain Singh's Shahkangsham. I ascertained the height of this peak to be over 6800m, which correlates with the RGS map measurement of 6815m and the Chinese height of 6822m. There are a dozen good-looking 6000m peaks in the north sector of the range including the south summit Pk.6600m. A large rocky south face dominates the mid-range, soaring up to a peak of around 6500m.

As you approach the northern Gangdise the wildlife is spectacular. You can see in just a few days Tibetan wolf, antelope, gazelle, marmot, foxes, hares, bharal sheep, wild ass, eagles, ducks and geese, black-necked cranes and even lizards. There were flocks of small birds in some numbers, most of which I was unable to identify. Partridges and ram chikor can also be seen. Conversely the amount of human habitation decreases with the aridity found in these regions.

South-east of Shahkangsham and visible from it in clear weather at 120 miles distant is the Targo Gangri range. This is a fascinating area, south of Lake Dangra Yumtso at 31°N 86.5°E and, as mentioned before, holds the main Bonpo monastery in the Gangdise. Their holy mountain is Targo-ri, sometimes known as Lungma Ri. The lake, like Shakangsham, lies on the edge of the windy Chang Tang and at the northern limits of our definition of the Gangdise.

There are only a handful of Bonpo monasteries in Tibet and just three per cent of the country's inhabitants profess to be of that faith. Hedin was refused entry to this one or indeed from travelling beyond 'by a troop of twenty horsemen armed to the teeth who had been sent by the governor of Naktsang with orders to stop us in case we should attempt to advance to the holy lake'.

Three other Bonpo places of worship in Tibet are Chorten Nyima on the northern Sikkim border, Laya on the Bhutan border and Takpa Shiri on the Arunachal Pradesh border. Flying from the monastery's roof was the black trident symbolising the land of the gods (of a white colour), land of men (red) and land of the water spirits of the lower world (blue). A king reigns in heaven as well as in the lower world but the greatest in power on Earth is the 'earth mother'. This worship of the natural world is also associated with animistic and ancestor worship. Circumnambulations are undertaken in an anti-clockwise direction, the opposite to Buddhist practice, although the two religions have huge amounts in common.

The approach to the lake can be made from the west but also from the township of Sangsang to the south by way of following a tributary of the Dogxung Tsangpo. This takes you over 5500m passes and on to a good-looking peak of 6436m called Dobzebo with a monastery 1500m below its castellated top. Hedin was forced out this way in 1906. The first township you come to is Tsatse at the southern end of the turquoise lake Xuru Tso, some 15 miles in length, complete with its own quite extensive range to the west. From here you can see Targo. There is a great red gash to the side of Targo Gangri's south face where the nomads say that in a battle Dobzebo fired an arrow at the mountain's knee. On Dobzebo you can see where a returning arrow from Targo was said to hit him in the stomach.

The Targo range comprises about 16 peaks over 6000m with the highest and most prominent, although not the steepest, being Targo Gangri itself at the southern end. These highest peaks used to form a massive peninsula eastwards, jutting into Dangra Yumtso in days when the lake was much larger than in present times. Again Nain Singh noted the peaks on his 1873-75 journey and Hedin was arguably the next to go there. A height of 7400m for Targo Kangri was revised down to 7100m and then 6572m. The latter height I can confirm is accurate. The central part of the range contains some of the most interesting mountains of all the Gangdise, and like Loinbo, is composed of granite.

Some 140 miles east of Targo is a peak as good a candidate as any to mark the far eastern end of the Gangdise. That mountain lies south of Gyaring Tso, another 35-mile-long lake, and is named Gyagang (6444m). Its position is at 88°40'E, nearly that of Shigatse.

There are, of course, many other sub-ranges not mentioned above, that may be seen through extensive travel in the Transhimalaya. For now they are too numerous to mention.

EVELIO ECHEVARRÍA
Cordillera Jatún Chácua, Peru

(*Plates 27, 28*)

It was the 1971 Polish expedition to Peru that drew attention to this almost wholly unknown Andean range. Before, and also after the year of 1971, the very few parties that had visited it referred to it as a part of the Cordillera Raura, which belongs to the north-central Peruvian Andes. But the Jatún Chácua is a different range, with an established and well-known local name and is separated from the Raura by the 30km-wide hilly moors of the Oyón basin. This contribution briefly introduces a range that offers a challenge of an almost unique kind: long walls of steep, black rock with smooth slabs ranging between 200m and 500m high. But it is not a range for everybody. When I visited it in June 2002, I learned that the local highlanders commonly refer to it as the Cordillera Chácua. The real, unabbreviated name is Cordillera Jatún Chácua (Quichua: 'the big birds'). Anyone would be inclined to think that this name is meant for the Andean bird par excellence, the condor. But in the area, there are places that bear the name *luli*, for example, Lulicocha, or 'lake of the lulis'. Within Inca mythology, the lulis were giant birds that flew at summit level, touching the summits with their wings. Thus the name of this range simply means: 'Of the giant birds.'

Location and access
From Lima, a bus-ride over a well travelled, second-class road leads to the towns of Churín – thermal baths! – and Oyón. The latter is the obvious starting place for this range. Oyón (Quichua: 'barren') is located some 190km north of Lima, has a population of 5000 people and is probably 3000m above sea level. It has a hostel, two basic hotels and a number of restaurants and small grocery shops. Through Oyón flow the waters of the Pucayacu River (Quichua: 'red waters'), which is born in the heart of the Jatún Chácua. In Oyón, one can take a van that runs daily along the Pucayacu valley, servicing small hamlets and local mining operations for coal and copper. The van, locally called a combi, does not usually go higher than the last Pucayacu mines, located halfway up the long valley. But drivers are quite willing to accept an extra sum to reach the mouth of any of the several higher, lateral valleys running into the Pucayacu (see map on following page). This additional ride is done over a rough road. In my case, for his extra trouble, the driver left me at the very end of the mining road for an equivalent of US$15.

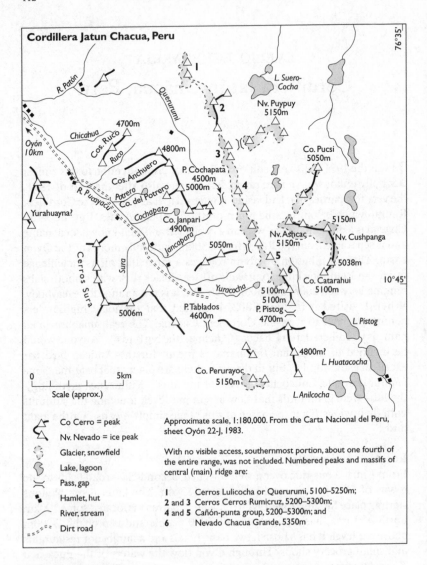

Cordillera Jatun Chacua, Peru

Co Cerro = peak
Nv. Nevado = ice peak
Glacier, snowfield
Lake, lagoon
Pass, gap
Hamlet, hut
River, stream
Dirt road

Approximate scale, 1:180,000. From the Carta Nacional del Peru, sheet Oyón 22-J, 1983.

With no visible access, southernmost portion, about one fourth of the entire range, was not included. Numbered peaks and massifs of central (main) ridge are:

1   Cerros Lulicocha or Quererumi, 5100–5250m;
2 and 3 Cerros Cerros Rumicruz, 5200–5300m;
4 and 5 Cañón-punta group, 5200–5300m; and
6   Nevado Chacua Grande, 5350m

The range and the highlands

The Jatún Chácua is composed of three parallel ridges running north to south for some 30km. The Pucayacu River and its parallel mining road run between the west and the central ridges. Lateral valleys leading to the peaks of those ridges are short, but to reach the eastern ridge, which offers some pleasant glaciated domes, there seems to be no direct access. It may be necessary to ascend to the Pistag Pass and descend into the Pistag and Huatacocha basins of lakes and moors to reach the base of these little-known mountains.

This range is typical of central northern Peru – rock and ice peaks over 5000m, rising over moorlands populated by sheep and llama herds. There are, however, a few lower valleys with healthy vegetation. Their rocky sides have forests of *quenua* (Q: polylepis), a small Andean, red-barked tree that prefers steep slopes. They seem to reach as high as 4600m above sea level. Are these the highest forests in the world? Fringing the local meadows are also blue lupins and yellow daisies. Human population in the highlands is extremely reduced, with barely a clan established at the entrance of each valley descending into the Pucayacu. Climate is typically Andean Peruvian. In normal years, a dry winter from April to September is followed by a wet tropical summer. Water is found in every valley, but somewhat polluted by grazing animals.

The peaks and the icefields
This range offers no other attraction than mountain climbing. It is a peculiar one. The western ridge is composed of rock and scree mountains rising to some 5150m. Only their north-east flanks are visible from the Pucayacu road. The main or central ridge is by far the chief attraction of this range. It is a continuous wall of exceedingly steep domes, peaks, towers and needles, composed of a remarkable black rock, perched above a fairly even icefield. Western sides are long slabs rising in some parts to some 500m of unyielding smoothness. Since this ridge is long, rugged and spiky, it is not easy to determine which its individual peaks are. According to the Carta National del Peru (1981, 1:50 000), the central ridge begins with the Lulicocha massif at the sources of the Paton and Quererumi streams and continues south unabated, all the way to the Pistag Pass. South of that pass, there are rows of rock and scree mountains, some 4800m to 5150m high.

The western ridge is lower, and judging from the little I was able to see of it from Pistag Pass, also tamer. But it has several rock peaks and rounded ice domes that seem to promise pleasant exploratory work.

The Oyón sheet of the chart just quoted, encompassing almost the entire Jatún Chácua range, shows 30 peaks worth that name, between 4800m and 5000m and 42 others, between 5000m and 5350m. It is not known which is the highest point in the range. Besides the imposing Chácua Grande (5350m), the map shows at least six other peaks of the central ridge attaining at least 5300m. At the southernmost end of the range, there is also a Nevado Chururuyo, 5350m high. There is no obvious approach to the Chururuyo section.

Exploration and climbing
The modern history of this range is brief. In 1927, a surveying party of the American Geographical Society, New York singled out and measured four peaks here and there, leaving vast tracts of uncharted spaces between them. Thus, we cannot locate the four peaks this party listed: south to north, Peak 1, 5412m, Peak 2, 5390m, Peak 3, 5356m, and Peak 4, 5229m.

About 1966, a preliminary chart, the Pre-Carta, was issued in Lima. It continued in use until 1981, when the Carta Nacional, 1:50 000, with its Oyón sheet properly surveying the entire Jatún Chácua, appeared. Unfortunately, few peaks on this last chart were listed with exact heights. Most of 70-odd high elevations over 4800m needed to be identified according to their contour intervals. Besides, many local peak names, not on this chart, seem to exist, but the absence of local inhabitants in the highlands will make their collection difficult. The search for local mountain names and the determination of the very highest peak in this range remain a geographical task yet to be accomplished.

The history of climbing is also brief. In the 1960s, Peruvian parties, apparently from the large town of Churín, ascended four peaks in the Yurahuayna massif, in the north-west periphery of the range, from 5000m to 5190m. In 1971, an enterprising Polish expedition led by Henryk Furmanik, climbed the difficult Nevado Chácua Grande (5350m) and a couple of lesser peaks. The good reports produced by the Poles were under the proper heading of the Jatún Chácua range. As to heights, the Poles quoted the accurate Pre-Carta of 1966. In the year 2000, however, a German expedition from Saxony, led by Markus Walter, reclimbed Chácua Grande and ascended other lower, nearby peaks. In spite of the existence of the good 1981 Peruvian chart, the Saxons quoted higher elevations and referred to the area as a part of the Cordillera Raura, whose nearer peaks are not to be found until one travels some 25 km north of the Oyón basin.

Future parties to this range will then have to choose between extremely exposed rock-work on the central ridge, or less difficult mixed work on the eastern ridge. Small parties are advisable because there are no resources in the higher valleys. Logistics are simple, since Oyón is served by several bus lines from Lima, an eight-hour ride costing about US$5. Then, in Oyón, a van is hired to the entrance of some higher valley, a ride some three hours long costing about US$15. Spanish is an absolute necessity for all forms of communication. Those who may seek new ground are advised to avoid the Yuracocha and the southern rim of the Jancapata valleys, which have been explored already by the Poles and Germans.

In June 2001, I travelled alone to this range. Bad weather was my constant companion (the same type of weather that caused several deaths in the Cordillera Blanca). I first ascended the Pistag pass, but the typical unstable weather of the Peruvian eastern slopes forced me to head back to the west side of the main ridge. I finally camped on the Cochapata pass. Visibility had been poor for an entire week. I set out, all the same, for an attempt on some of the southern Rumicruz peaks, shown on the chart at 5300m. But when the mists dispersed, the black, smooth walls of those mountains appeared so wicked and sinister that I recoiled in fear back to my tent. In another valley, still under bad weather, I climbed the pleasant west rock face of the unnamed, serrated mountain of 5000m, rising west of the

Cochapata pass. On the summit (probably no higher than 4900m), I found a cairn, no doubt erected by local highlanders, since there was an easy route on the north side of the mountain. I christened it Cerro 'Janpari' (Quichua: 'many points').

In all, in the Range of the Giant Birds, I spent thirteen days, ten of which were in bad weather. I was not to see blue skies again until I finally arrived back in bleak Oyón.

BIBLIOGRAPHY

O M Miller, 'The 1927-1928 Peruvian Expedition of the American Geographical Society.' in *Geographical Review XIX*, 1, pp1-37, 1929.

W Henryk Furmanik, *Peruwianskich Kordylierach*. Katowice, Poland: Slask, pp155-173, 1975.

Two brief notes in *American Alpine Journal* 1972, p167 (Polish expedition) and 2001, p283 (German expedition).

MAPS

Carta Nacional del Perú, sheet Oyón 22-J, 1:50 000, 1983.

PAUL KNOTT

A Mountaineer's New Zealand

(*Plates 12, 13, 24, 25*)

New Zealand: green, clean and wild, a land of adventure sports and famous walking trails through wild country, an Antipodean version of Britain but with bigger mountains. These are some popular images of the country I have come to know over the past four years. Though they hold some truth, there is much more here for the mountaineer than the photogenic scenery and packaged wilderness attractions. Most importantly, nearly all the wilderness is untamed and well beyond the reach of popular tourism.

The wildness of New Zealand contrasts strikingly with the picture in most of Britain and Europe, where it seems human activity has long since tamed nature and even seems set to banish it entirely. Here, nature is often still in control. Sometimes mountain access has become harder over time, not easier. The Ball Hut road near Mount Cook is steadily disappearing as the moraine erodes with glacial recession. Huts often have to be moved before the land they stand on collapses. Mount Cook itself lost a huge mass and ten metres in height in a landslide in 1991. On the drive to the mountains, if the roads are blocked it is by landslip, flood or snow, not by traffic, even where both road and rail in both directions share a single-lane bridge. Once at the road-head, the typical walk-in covers many miles and involves multiple river crossings. Bridges are an occasional luxury. For me, all this is somehow appealing.

With this wildness goes a culture that understands the outdoors and adventure. With broad support, a number of Wilderness Areas have been designated, the Olivines, for example, and the Adams Wilderness. These are true wilderness, with no maintained tracks, no huts or facilities of any kind, and no aircraft landings. One must approach them over several days, heavily laden, over wild and often difficult terrain.

In New Zealand this level of effort and adventure is downplayed as the norm. Naturally, one seldom meets others in the hills, and perhaps because of such infrequent visits the guidebooks have a refreshing simplicity about them, with exquisite understatement and sometimes even a reluctance to give grades. Again, for me this only adds to the experience.

In this article I try to give an impression of the available potential by describing some of the trips I have made to date. Starting from the south, the first of the major massifs is the Darran Mountains, a huge wilderness that would be practically inaccessible were it not for the thin line of tarmac of the Milford Road. Above the road are huge, steep granite walls revealing extensive climbing potential within easy reach. The crux of the journey, the Homer Tunnel, adds to the sense of awe with its irregular rock walls, gushing water and narrow width. There are excellent ice routes in the area in winter, although the terrain and an incredibly high precipitation rate often lead to extreme avalanche risk even on the main road.

The steep and complex terrain here makes the mountains much grander than their heights would suggest. On my first visit, ignorant of its reputation, Graham Holden and I had a naive plan to climb the SE Ridge of the highest peak, Tutoko (2746m). In perfect January weather we drove directly to Milford Airport, and within a short space of time found ourselves alone and committed in the middle of intimidating alpine terrain. Stunned by our surroundings, we spent a good while looking around, orienting ourselves and working out how we might get to the mountain. We also wondered how we would find our way out, but left that problem until later.

We elected to walk along an obvious rocky ledge to a bivi closer to the start of our route. After four hours of traversing ice pinnacles and repeatedly re-ascending to higher glaciers, we finally overcame all the hidden obstacles and reached the chosen flat piece of rock. The reascents continued in the dark the next morning, along with some down-climbing of glacier ice, until we entered the couloir leading to Turner's Pass, which we found poorly frozen. From its top we also had to negotiate an airy ridge traverse and make a steep abseil before at last reaching the start of the route proper.

We climbed the ridge's three rock steps without problems, though some of the snow between them was rather insecure. Our progress slowed on the sharp arête above, as we had to meticulously consolidate every footstep while watching in horror the gathering wet snow slides we were setting off. Finally a section forcing us onto a steep face made us concede to the poor conditions. Despite turning back below the summit, we were late reaching the bottom of the first rock step and elected to bivi.

For our descent the next day we decided to avoid the discontinuous ledges we had used on the ascent by continuing down the Age Glacier. Finding no exit at its bottom we had to climb up a glacier-worn side-wall, which although easy angled took us several hours to surmount with some marginal climbing and sparse protection. When we eventually made it back to our gear stash we were fortunate to meet some people, who solved several problems for us by showing us the way to Turner's Bivi, describing the descent route, and even giving us a can of beer.

The descent involved two long abseils off small shrubs, much bush bashing and wading, and finally a long descent on a trail through rainforest full of ferns and lichens that seemed to go mostly uphill. The first signal we might be nearing civilization was a faint whiff of diesel. A few metres on we stepped disbelievingly onto the road.

The next major massif along the main alpine chain is the Mt Aspiring region. An ascent of Mt Aspiring was described in AJ106; here I will briefly describe my early December ascent of the classic South Face. We approached by walking in to French Ridge – a way I would also recommend for accessing the soaring South-west Ridge of the mountain. As is typical, the walk was almost level for some hours then climbed abruptly and brutally up what seemed like vertical rainforest. Eventually the angle eased a little and the forest gave way to scrub and grass leading to French Ridge Hut. The tattered rubber door seal indicated an active kea population; later we heard them sliding down the steel roof and peering in upside-down from the gutters to watch our reaction.

We waited out three days of cloud, wind and warmth, making the ascent on our last available day. We were lucky. Often north-westerlies can bring storm conditions to the mountains for a week or more. Starting soon after midnight we made rapid progress up the 700m ascent to the 'Quarterdeck' and across the névé to the face, where pre-dawn light helped us find a way across the bergschrund. On the route itself we made slower progress, pitching the 500m main section on strength-sapping water ice. Right-slanting ramps kept the climbing angle low, but took us over fantastic terrain. Retreat would have been difficult and I was glad of Graham's steadiness at the sharp end.

We finally reached the summit at 3.30pm, finding the snow on the west side of the mountain softened by the sun and enveloped in transpiration cloud. Playing safe, we took the long way down via the standard route on the North-west Ridge. From here our return to French Ridge involved several hundred metres of reascent up heavy snow on the Bonar Glacier. Exhausted and dehydrated, we finally staggered back to the hut at 9.30pm.

As well as ice and mixed alpine routes, New Zealand also offers plenty of mountain rock climbs. These can be on good rock, in spite of the often deserved reputation for looseness in the mountains. Highlights include sub-alpine rock to a high standard at Twin Streams near Mount Cook and high alpine rock in several areas including the Balfour and Fox Glaciers. There is much unexplored terrain.

Nearer to Christchurch is Cloudy Peak, another subalpine venue. The wonderful ambience here is established even on the drive in, over a gravel road with tantalising views to the isolated Mt d'Archiac, ending at the pretty Erehwon ('nowhere' backwards) high country station. From here the four to five-hour walk-in starts with a crossing of the Clyde River, and continues up the stones and braided channels of the Havelock. This terrain rewards skill at finding the least foot-turning gravel and picking shallow crossing points, as well as a go-for-it attitude to wet feet. On one visit we were forced to link up for the crossings and in flood the rivers cannot be crossed except by aircraft. Above, the route involves climbing the steep scrubby hillside. This is another energy-sapping activity, the 'scrub' being a dense blanket of exotic and often spine-covered vegetation.

The climbing itself is up to 400m, with several different crags and a high ratio of rock to existing routes. So far, I have only touched its potential with an ascent of the modest but pleasant South-west Ridge in windy conditions. For me, the rock quality and situation more than compensated for the effort involved in accessing the area.

A more accessible destination is Mt Somers, where the attraction is a vast array of crags consisting mostly of rhyolite columns, many of them directly above the conveniently sited Pinnacles Hut. This is a mere two hours' walk from the road on an undulating forest trail. The routes are a full rope-length, sometimes with infrequent protection, but with great views out across the Canterbury Plains. Despite its obvious attraction the area is only moderately popular, and potential new routes can be seen even from the hut. On one visit aimed at scoping these out a mist from the plains sent us to the far side of the mountain where we were presented with a promising-looking but untouched red buttress. We climbed two nice routes (around VS-HVS) with good friction and gear, and the added bonus of some spectacular trundles, although at the price of one of the ropes. Another trip, also chancing a mediocre weather forecast, worked less well. After some warm spring afternoon climbing near the hut, the trip ended prematurely when we woke the next morning to a white landscape of late spring snow.

The rainforests of the West Coast embody all that is real about the New Zealand outdoors. My first real exposure to them was on a Christmas attempt on Mt Whitcombe, an experience that was also enhanced by being for once the sole 'international' on a real Kiwi trip. We drove for two hours from Christchurch and stopped as arranged by a small plane sitting in an open barn. The plane's dulled paint-work and general rustic appearance fitted the setting perfectly. The farmer turned up in his pickup, and soon we took off through the uncut grass of his paddock. The landing strip was a narrow thread of gravel someone had levelled many years earlier. We landed fast with the breeze behind us.

It was a short walk up onto the Ramsey Glacier, then up to a 'slate quarry' campsite. To our surprise it was a starry night and we made rapid progress on the frozen névé, to reach Erehwon Col in two hours. Here we surveyed the options for climbing Mts Whitcombe and Evans. We had only limited information available. Neither mountain features in a guidebook although Mt Whitcombe features in Hugh Logan's excellent *Classic Peaks of New Zealand*. Nor are they frequently climbed.

We opted for an indirect route to Mt Whitcombe via Snowdome. This involved a 300m descent and reascent on the wild West-Coast side, thus exposing us to the storms that come from this direction. Out in the Tasman Sea there was indeed a line of black cloud, but we ignored it. Arriving at the final slopes of Snowdome in wet snow and thick mist, we elected to forego the 1km ridge leading to Mt Whitcombe and descended before conditions worsened further. Our return involved stonefall, an exhausting trudge through heavy wet snow, and a crevasse fall.

Christmas Day dawned murky and dull. We descended to the landing strip, giving up on climbing in favour of our stash of wine and goodies. Shortly afterwards rain gave us the excuse we needed to indulge in the usual Christmas gluttony, but not before we had made a start on the sporting way out via Whitcombe Pass to the West Coast. The next morning we soon began to encounter some more scrub, which in this case meant thick head-high vegetation covering bouldery ground. Prolonged close combat was required, unassisted by any signs of a trail in spite of the fact that we were on one of the better known, and easier, of the trans-alpine routes.

A few kilometres beyond the pass we started to see trail markers, but this did not herald the start of any discernible track. We spent much time negotiating river boulders, thick scrub, and unstable landslips. This was fun in its own way – rather like a Lake District ghyll scramble or a moderate canyoning trip – but many of the boulders were liberally covered in wet moss, and on this unrelenting terrain some slips and falls were inevitable.

Periodically this primeval wilderness would be relieved by a small grassy oasis with a neat little hut equipped with bunks, fireplace and much-needed sandfly screens. Our arrival at the Wilkinson Hut was marked by torrential rain and intense thunder, which continued for another 15 hours. The following day our concerns about our passage being blocked by raging torrents, landslips and fallen trees turned out to be well founded. We spent two hours crossing the first side stream, then another four on steep descents and exhausting reascents, ducking, weaving, slipping and splashing to reach the next hut. We had covered five kilometres on the map. Fortunately, after this the terrain relented a little.

On the third walking day we winched one another over a final cable-way across the main river to join a rough vehicle track and a gradual transition to civilisation. News reports about flooding suggested it had been wet even by West Coast standards, yet my companions talked of trips with wetter, harder and slower going. I have no desire to test their claims; to a degree this activity reminds me of the 'mountain tourist' scene in Russia, with which it seems to share a certain sense of masochism. That said, the trip overall was both memorable and surprisingly enjoyable.

Ski touring is another mainstream mountain activity in New Zealand, since there is a natural transition to touring from the ski fields, which provide starting points for ridge traverses, back bowls, and even ski-lodge to ski-lodge touring. Another alternative, which worked in early season 2001 and 2002, is the Lewis Pass. This has the added advantage of nearby Maruia hot springs; there are also secret 'wild' springs. Chilled by the frosty midwinter air and teetering barefoot over the verglas-covered rock I couldn't help feeling dubious as I approached them, but once in it was a great pleasure to be so warm in the open air under the stars and snowy hills.

My introductory ski tour in the higher mountains started with a spectacular flight around and amongst the cloud to the tiny Barron Saddle Hut. From here we followed a pleasant and mostly downhill ski route along a shelf and over Sladden Saddle to the beautifully situated Mueller Hut. As the cloud cleared, our mild exertions were rewarded by inspiring views of Mount Cook and the sérac-torn face of Mt Sefton.

A more energetic venture is the nearest New Zealand has to the European Haute Route, sometimes known as Symphony on Skis. Starting in the Rutherford Stream above the Godley Valley, and finishing down the Fox Glacier on the West Coast, this was first traversed on a single day in 1985. Most parties take up to a week to allow for a more leisurely pace and time for bad weather and side trips. In August 2002 I undertook a slightly truncated version of this by flying into the Murchison Glacier. After a bumpy landing on scoured glacier ice we skinned up to Tasman Saddle in a strengthening southerly wind that was loading the headwall with windblown snow. We stopped in the Kelman Hut to shelter and ate the fresh eggs someone had left, then went over to the busier but warmer Tasman Saddle Hut.

The next day was the crux of the journey, the crossing of the main divide, and as we had planned, this was the best weather day with blue skies and little wind. We skied down the Tasman Glacier to an alarmingly low 1250m, then crossed some moraine to commence skinning up the Rudolf Glacier. The headwall here can be problematic, and we were a little concerned by the sight of fresh avalanche debris. We took the safest-looking line, cramponning up the broad and somewhat icy couloir to the right of the main icefall. At its top we crossed back onto the upper glacier for a weary final pull up to the 2635m Graham Saddle. Approaching its crest, teetering on scoured ice, we were rewarded for the long climb by what felt like the climax of a symphony. A wonderful evening winter sun was glinting on the Tasman Sea, far below and only 30km distant, and the peaks around the Franz Joseph névé were subtly tinged with its warmth.

We descended on the western side to the névés of the Franz Joseph Glacier, then traversed across to Centennial Hut. The scenery and situation were wonderful, but as is apparently quite common there were big sastrugi everywhere, so our skiing was not wonderful. The hut was full of people who had flown in, many of them discovering the limitations of snowboards for traversing glaciers. After a night there we crossed our final pass, the Newton Pass, to the Fox Glacier. Here too there is a useful hut, Pioneer Hut, which gives easy access to some excellent alpine ice routes and rock climbs. We continued down the glacier, finally managing some proper turns in the spring snow, to Chancellor Hut overlooking the spectacular icefall of the Fox Glacier. The walk out from here involves crossing the lower glacier, whose difficulty and feasibility changes rapidly. Unenthusiastic about walking out in ski boots, we elected to finish the trip with a short helicopter ride.

As I conclude this article I realise that I have covered only a fraction of New Zealand's mountain opportunities. I could certainly write as much again based on my unrealised projects. As with other adventurous locations, climbs here require dedication, energy and time. They also require the right conditions, a good window in the typically unsettled weather, and often more than one attempt. My attempt on Mt d'Archiac last spring was a case in point. On the second day walking in we found ourselves repulsed by a prolonged and rather alarming display of wet snow avalanches before even reaching the mountain. It would not be too wide of the mark to talk of Scottish weather in alpine mountains with greater ranges approaches. Nonetheless, given a willingness to adapt the activity to the season, conditions and weather, fulfilling mountain adventures can be found at any time of year. For the best of these it still helps to be, as R L G Irving put it in his 1955 *History of British Mountaineering*, 'undaunted by heavy swags, by constant and prolonged spells of vile weather and trained to deal with all sorts of conditions and formations of snow and ice'.

JAMES HARRIS

Sailing and Mountaineering on the Antarctic Peninsula

British Army Antarctic Expedition 2001-2002

In early November 1991 a small band of mountaineers huddled in their two remaining storm-lashed tents on the beach of Molke Harbour, South Georgia. They had been ashore for nearly fifty days, frustrated by the notorious South Georgia weather after landing on the wrong beach. Now at the eleventh hour they were having to wait for a pick-up by boat while their base camp was slowly torn apart by a week-long storm.

I was last off the beach the morning we were picked up and the inflatable capsized in the surf. Later, warming up in the engine room of our pick-up vessel, I mused on our experiences. It seemed obvious to me so I turned to Dick Pattison, my climbing partner, and said: 'Next time we'll bring our own bloody boat!' And so the British Army Antarctic Expedition was born.

These things are never quite as easy as they first seem. It was to be another ten years before we achieved our ambition to return south in our own vessel. Finding a suitable yacht, getting the Army to agree to the time off, selecting a team and – the hardest part – raising the money, all took time. The Services did not own a yacht that was large or tough enough for our needs, so after a number of false starts we ended up with a 72ft steel ketch called *John Laing*, chartered from the Ocean Youth Trust, a sail-training charity. She was sailed to the Falklands Islands by three Army crews, at which point a team of 16 mountaineers and sailors took her over for the final ten-week leg of the voyage.

We sailed from the Falklands at the end of November 2001 into the depths of the notorious Drakes Passage. The trip across to the Antarctic Peninsula took six days, during which some of the landlubber mountaineering team decided to take up a routine of dieting and hanging over the side rail to get a closer view of the sea. The first port of call for the team was Deception Island where we sought refuge from an approaching storm. The expedition had a number of aims, mountain exploration being but one. We also planned to conduct survey work for the Hydrographic Office, undertake a heritage and historical site survey for the Scott Polar Research Institute, record various wildlife details for the British Antarctic Survey and collect geological samples for Brighton University. Deception Island offers little by the way of mountaineering challenges, so while we were at anchor many of the non-mountaineering projects started in earnest. And the skipper amused himself untangling a rope from around the prop.

The storm passed and we headed further south to our target of the Danco Coast. In 1957 Sir Wally Herbert had led a dog-sled team down the spine of the Antarctic Peninsular from Hope Bay in the north, to the Reclus Peninsula where the team were picked up from Portal Point. Sir Wally had been supported by a team which had over-wintered at Portal Point. They pioneered a route up the Reclus Peninsula to the Peninsula Plateau. It had taken them six weeks. Once on the Peninsula Plateau the support team made the first ascent of Mount Johnston, at 7580ft one of the highest points on the Peninsula. Sir Wally had been very helpful to the expedition and our first target was to make the second ascent of Mount Johnston.

On 10 December 2001, a recce team of three was landed at Portal Point, the yacht was secured at the nearby anchorage of Enterprise Island and the balance of the mountaineers prepared loads to follow on the next day. The aim was to identify the 1957 route and cache sufficient food on the Reclus Peninsula to support a three-week trip up onto the Plateau and an ascent of Mount Johnston. From Mount Johnston it was hoped we would be able to push on further along the Forbidden Plateau and make the first ascent of Mount Walker lying about 10km to the west. The recce went well until I carelessly fell into a rather large crevasse. The rope held but I didn't dwell on the view down for too long. Because of the very deep snow it took some two hours to extract myself, having in the end to tunnel up through the side wall of the crevasse. To add insult to injury, I lost a ski down the crevasse and was forced to wade through deep snow for four hours back to our tent.

Having survived this minor drama and successfully identified the 1957 route, we left a cache to sustain a future attempt and retired to the yacht to contemplate our next move. After dinner our 'tame' accompanying journalist, Sam Greenhill from the Press Association, approached me and asked if I minded if he penned a piece on my crevasse fall. I agreed saying that I thought there would be little interest as crevasse falls were an occupational hazard of mountaineering. Needless to say, thanks to satellite phones and e-mail, within 24 hours the story had made headlines in most of the national papers. The phone started to ring with endless requests for interviews from radio and television stations. The hits on our website rose from 150 a day to 7000. The sponsors and Army PR were happy. It seemed my 'publicity stunt' had worked.

We sailed further south into Paradise Harbour to try to identify an exit from the Plateau that would allow a round trip of Reclus Peninsula, Mount Johnston and Paradise Harbour. Unfortunately, very dense ice stopped the yacht where, like Shackleton, we became stuck albeit for only a few days. Because of the ice in Paradise Harbour, landing proved difficult so we decided to cut our losses and head back to the Reclus and start the ascent to the Plateau and Mount Johnston.

Setting off on 22 December in beautiful conditions, we reached our high cache late that evening and established a base. The following two days were spent moving the cache up steep ground onto the shoulder of Harris

Peak (3287ft) but deteriorating weather meant we were forced to return to our Base Camp. Christmas Day was spent confined to tents as the weather had become unworkable. As we set off on Boxing Day morning the weather was beginning to clear and by the time we came to undertake a difficult exposed traverse under the summit of Harris Peak the weather had cleared completely. One of the ropes took the opportunity to climb Harris Peak and take some photos while the rest of us pushed on, reaching the Bayly Glacier above the first icefall, where I had previously fallen into the crevasse.

Once onto the Bayly Glacier the route up was straightforward with a steady ascent in good firm snow conditions. We paused regularly as we skied, trying to take in the scale of the magnificent vista around us. It was simply breathtaking; mountains and glaciers as far as we could see were all covered in snow and ice with no exposed rock. We finished the day camped below the second icefall on the Bayly Glacier.

Unfortunately, the following day the visibility had once again reduced dramatically and it was almost impossible to find the route. We had a couple of crevasse falls trying to negotiate our way through the second icefall and so decided to camp and wait for the weather to clear. After 24 hours or so visibility began to improve and it was possible to pick our way through the icefall onto the long and gently-sloping final section of the Bayly Glacier which led to the Foster Plateau, named after Dick Foster who had led Sir Wally Herbert's support team. We skied along the Plateau to the base of Mount Johnston where we quickly established camp and grabbed some food before immediately setting off to climb the mountain. We had learnt by now that as the weather in Antarctica was so fickle, you had to take your chances as they arose. The joy of 24-hour daylight meant that could be anytime.

By now it was late on 28 December and we had been on the go for over 16 hours but the prospect of reaching the summit renewed our vigour. The climb was easy with only a bit of grade 2 ice on the final summit pitch. All nine members of the mountaineering team reached the top around 1am on 29 December. Unfortunately, as we approached the summit the cloud once again closed in and we were robbed of the magnificent views looking out across the top of the Antarctic Peninsula.

The next few days were frustrating as once again we were confined to our tents waiting for yet another storm to break. By now our rations were beginning to run low and as there was no sign of an improvement in the weather, I reluctantly decided that it was time to cut and run. The route down the hill was more straightforward than the ascent as we were able to accurately retrace our steps using marker wands and GPS. Two days later, on the 4 January 2002, we were back on the yacht celebrating a belated Christmas and New Year in some style, complete with morning swim.

Once the hangovers had given way we set sail and headed to Port Lockroy where there is a small UK heritage site in the old base, manned for the summer by three Brits. This stop-over allowed us to get the sailors out for a day on skis and to try their hand at a spot of mountaineering on the lower peaks on Weincke Island. The minor summit of Jabet Peak was climbed several times and the more notable peak of Mount Luigi (4708ft) was scaled on the night of the 9 and 10 January in fabulous twilight conditions. It was during our time on Weincke Island that Sarah Piesse, the lone female member of the team, fell during a roped descent, fracturing her thumb. Fortunately this was the most serious injury of the trip and our doctor was able to spend his time climbing.

From Port Lockroy we moved back to Paradise Harbour which was by now mostly clear of ice. We anchored in a little bay called Skontorp Cove. From here we mounted a number of mountaineering forays using our two inflatable boats. The first was to climb Mount Banck (2208ft) which guards the southern entrance to Paradise Harbour. The climb was straightforward with a need only to put on crampons and pitch the last 200ft or so. Nevertheless, from our research it appears that the climb was probably the first ascent. Inevitably the summit was once again enveloped in cloud and snow as we arrived.

The next few days were spent trying to outwit the weather and establish a route up Mount Heogh (890m), which lies at the northern end of Paradise Harbour rising above Waterboat Point. Our first attempt along the western ridge failed in deteriorating weather when we came up against large over-hanging ice blocks. For our second attempt on the mountain we teamed up with the 'Endless Summer' expedition who were also climbing and conducting glacial research in and around Paradise Harbour.

This time we attacked the eastern ridge. The route involved skiing round and up through an icefall. To gain the summit ridge we abandoned our skis and pitched 300ft of exposed grade 3 ice under some overhanging séracs. Once on the ridge, snow plodding for a few hundred metres brought us to the summit and this time we beat the clouds and were treated to the most fantastic panorama of Paradise Harbour as the sun was just setting below the horizon. This was followed by an equally memorable descent through some fantastic powder in eerie grey light.

As the yacht had to be back in England by mid-May, time was now beginning to press, but we wanted to make a final port of call at Elephant Island before heading back to the Falklands. The expedition had agreed to undertake some geological sampling in and around Elephant Island, as well as examine a possible heritage site and conduct a wildlife survey. Our first sight of the Island was bleak and grey, the sea was rough and a large swell was adding to the general discomfort on board the yacht. The conditions meant we were unable to put parties ashore for 24 hours but by late morning on 27 January conditions had calmed enough to land two parties. One put ashore at Hut Point to cross the Island to Stinker Point where various surveys would be carried out. The second party were landed on the southern end of the island at Cape Lookout from where they planned to climb the highest mountain on Elephant Island – Mt Pendragon (973m). Meanwhile the yacht circumnavigated the island collecting geological samples from various points, including visiting Point Wild where Shackleton's crew had been stranded.

Crossing the island, a distance of about 15km, appeared to be fairly straightforward; the day was sunny with interspersed low cloud. All was going well as we descended from the high point of the route (737m) down towards Stinker Point until about three kilometres from our destination when we hit a series of well-hidden crevasse fields. The snow gave very little indication of where the crevasses lay and the next two hours were spent nervously picking our way through this very difficult terrain with countless holes opening below our skis. Fortunately there were no serious falls but the team were very glad to reach the safety of the moraine leading down to Stinker Point.

Meanwhile the Mount Pendragon team was enjoying a spectacular climb through the cloud into the sunshine and onto the summit of Mount Pendragon, just as the sun was setting. The whole of the summit dome was covered in a series of vast ice mushrooms, which had to be overcome by various orthodox and unorthodox means to claim the prize.

After a further three days ashore collecting various samples, the land teams were picked up and the expedition sailed north for the Falklands. We arrived at Mere Harbour in the teeth of a gale, which made coming into harbour the most challenging sailing of the trip. And so came to an end the Antarctic leg of the expedition. It had been all those things Service expeditions should be: challenging, demanding, productive but very enjoyable and rewarding. Out of the team of 16, five of the participants were relative novices who were selected on merit. It is hoped that the experience will encourage them to undertake expeditions of their own, perhaps even back to Antarctica where there is still plenty to do.

Issues

ED DOUGLAS

The Evolution of Exploration

I'm not sure how many climbers still read the books of the botanist and explorer Frank Kingdon-Ward. He was a prolific writer, particularly about the Himalaya, publishing 25 books in 50 years, the last of them appearing in 1960, two years after his death. The best known is probably the description of his greatest piece of exploration *The Riddle of the Tsangpo Gorges*, published in 1926. The recent flurry of exploration in this region has reawakened some level of interest in Kingdon-Ward among the public. But, for the most part, he is known mostly to those with an interest in plant-hunting.

Kingdon-Ward was a great intellectual speculator but some of his ideas about the origins of man are engagingly loopy. In the autumn of 1940 he argued in the *Daily Telegraph* that the war had been caused by a resurgence of the Neanderthal strain in the blood not just of the German nation but the Russians too. Far from being wiped out by *Homo sapiens*, Neanderthals had interbred, particularly in Northern Europe, where their lumpen character had survived: 'We cannot get away from the horrible truth that behind the immense glittering façade of Western culture lurks the black shadow of Neanderthal man. The cold ferocity, the snarling rage, the sterile sadism, the grunting sensuality we see all around in Central Europe today are, in the literal meaning of the words, brutal and inhuman.'

The Teuton and the Slav, Kingdon-Ward argued, preferred ideals that are 'always animal' and he saw the struggle of the Allies to defeat Germany as the opportunity to 'cleanse the Earth of this foul taint'. (Of course, the Nazis were writing similar things about the Jews. Empathy with a fellow human is strong, even among soldiers during a war, so those prosecuting aggression dehumanise the enemy, make them subhuman and therefore easier to annihilate. We are all capable of racism, unless we talk ourselves out of it.)

Kingdon-Ward was echoing views widely held at that time about the Neanderthals, who have shared the Philistine's poor reputation. But Neanderthal 'cold ferocity' and 'snarling rage' are no more than stories, narratives spun from scanty evidence to convince ourselves that *Homo sapiens* is an improvement, that we are in fact nature's ultimate achievement. There is still much to discover about Neanderthals, but we know more now than we did in 1940. For instance, their brains were bigger than ours, and far from being brutish, current academic opinion holds that they were largely peaceful. Humans and Neanderthals coexisted for millennia before the latter died out, as they surely did. There is little evidence that these two hominids interbred.

I don't wish to mock Kingdon-Ward's ideas, because at least he was thinking widely, and that is what I want to do now, in attempting to offer an evolutionary explanation for why someone might want to go climbing. I imagine more pragmatic readers who get this far will be grinding their teeth at the prospect of another essay about the 'why', preferring the 'how' and 'what'. Climbing, they will argue, is a personal choice made for a million different reasons and to analyse why someone should do it is to deny our basic individuality. Besides, they say, we have better things to do with our time. All I can do in response is wave them a fond farewell.

The origins of climbing are often explained as a confluence of several strands in economic and intellectual change in Europe in the nineteenth century. Romanticism and the sense of the sublime, for example, put mountains back on the map as a landscape worthy of intellectual consideration. Improved communications and disposable income allowed the English upper-middle class to take extended holidays in the Alps. The growing culture of scientific enquiry saw the mountains as an opportunity to explore new worlds of understanding like geology and geography.

That conventional view is not incorrect, and was most recently explained in Robert Macfarlane's new book *Mountains of the Mind*. But for me, these are proximate causes of how climbing came about, not the deeper, underlying roots within human nature itself that drive some of us to do these things. You could argue that new conditions in society led to a new activity – mountain climbing – and that is all the explanation you need. But for me that argument is woefully inadequate. It's like explaining how a car works when you're attempting to describe the excitement of driving fast.

For most people, mountaineering is a nonsensical activity, which is why we often find ourselves explaining why we do it. It's dangerous, physically demanding and apparently without reward. What's the appeal? In response, I usually ask people what is the point of opera, or *haute cuisine*, or clubbing.

'But those things are fun!' they argue, before getting the point and thinking us weird for finding risk and discomfort enjoyable.

George Mallory made the same point more forcibly. 'What we get from this adventure is just sheer joy. And joy is, after all, the end of life. We do not live to eat and make money. We eat and make money to be able to enjoy life. That is what life means and what life is for.'

Climbing, Mallory seems to be saying in his passionate, impulsive response, is just another part of human culture, which is as various and complex as anything we can imagine. The human brain is the most complex thing in the universe we've yet discovered. But human history is much more than the activity of one mind in isolation. The confluence of many human brains with apparently limitless combinations over a long period of time has produced activities spanning meditation to wild excess, from Bach to Jane's Addiction, from Mrs Tiggywinkle to Genghis Khan and everything in between. (One thing we know about Neanderthals is that their 'culture' barely changed in tens of thousands of years. We may have lived next door to them, but I doubt I would have gone round for dinner more than once.)

But while all this reveals the diversity of human culture, it doesn't explain why mountain climbing *per se* should be attractive to some human minds. To begin my explanation of that, I'm going to turn back to Kingdon-Ward and his vagrant mind. Among his literary output was a slim volume called *Modern Exploration*, which was an attempt to explain and analyse the history and future of our slow spread over the planet's surface, and by analogy the growth of human knowledge. I was most attracted by his chapter 'The Evolution of Exploration', not because of what it contained, but simply for the idea itself.

In this chapter, Kingdon-Ward never questions the supremacy of Western civilisation and believes that exploration only really started after the rise of urban culture, which in the 1920s was thought to have begun exclusively in the Middle East several millennia before the birth of Christ. Other 'races', he says, have been colonised by Western cultures because their 'civilisations' are not as developed; it has been left largely to Christians and Muslims to explore our world because we are superior.

That view was typical of a man of his class and upbringing, but it has been more or less discounted and quite rightly so. I am not going to rehearse the arguments now, but Jared Diamond's sweeping overview of human development *Guns, Germs and Steel* is the best explanation of how, largely by chance, one group of humans has come to dominate economically the rest of the world.

What appealed to me about the phrase 'Evolution of Exploration' was its acknowledgement that exploration had adapted over the years to meet different circumstances at different moments in history. All human culture has done this: religion, philosophy, music and so on. Why should exploration be any different? Richard Dawkins introduced the idea of the 'meme' in his book *The Selfish Gene*, a meme being a package of cultural information that thrives and mutates in the same way that an organism does. Exploration is simply another meme.

Kingdon-Ward believed that 'mountaineering is not exploration' and so devoted little attention to it in his book. In a way he was right. We typically see exploration as the discovery of previously unknown country for economic, political or religious benefit. Biologists may see it as the acquisition of resources. Successful groups of humans, whether these are nations or religious institutions, are resource vacuums. South American Indians understood that intimately, even as they were annihilated.

Climbing, surely, has little to do with these great currents of history. What does the colonisation of the Americas have to do with an eccentric, little-known sport in nineteenth-century Europe? What 'resources' are gained from climbing a mountain? Later, I shall argue that the 'resources' are often more connected to our self-esteem and appeal as individuals – although money does come into it. But first, it's worth reviewing just how old our sport is.

Go back further than the rise of urban culture to before recorded history. Imagine the slow spread of humanity, from its source in the Rift Valley along the coastlines of the Earth's landmass. Within the period of a few tens of millennia, a species, which had faced near extinction, reduced at one stage to a small band of perhaps a few hundred individuals by disease and predation, managed to colonise the entire planet.

Language, the ability to communicate learning, must lie at the heart of our success. But our long journey required considerable exploratory skill as well. Each desert was new, every jungle held unknown dangers. Long before the rise of the nation state, or of cities, or of agriculture, small bands of humans were spreading down the coasts of the Americas, the last Continent to be reached. They would have met threats they barely understood and would have needed to adapt their way of life faster than the usual mechanisms of evolution could allow.

Consider the difference in technological ability between, for example, Arctic Inuit and Aborigines in Australia. And yet the genetic difference between them is minuscule. Our adaptability to circumstance lies in the way our brains work. Over hundreds of thousands of years, we have learned how to create an environment in which we can survive and then thrive. We do not rely on a particular niche, like a lion or an ant, we use our brains to make it how we like it. As long as there is enough to drink and eat, then we can live there.

All kinds of physical environments have been exploited for their resources, including cliffs and mountains. We think of climbing as being a thoroughly modern invention, but in fact we must acknowledge that the activity is much older than the sport, and has been used to exploit untapped resources by people who had no other option.

Let me give you a couple of examples. Last year I explored the coast around the Spanish port of Javea, at Cape Nao. The neighbourhood at Cape Nao is the wealthiest on this part of the coast, a kind of Costa Blancan Marbella. It's hard to conceive, barrelling up the A7 from Alicante, that this was once one of Europe's most economically deprived regions. (Now it is simply one of the ugliest.) For those without access to capital, making a living was a desperate struggle.

Access to the sea was restricted to those who could afford a boat, so those without capital chose to fish instead from the cliffs around Cape Nao, a small niche that no one had yet claimed as their own. The closest climbing these days is on the Peñon d'Ifach at Calpe a few miles south. But while the Peñon is bigger, the cliffs at Cape Nao are still 300ft high and very steep. I imagine the rock is too loose to attract many climbers – think Gogarth on a bad-hair day. Yet this was where Javea's poorest went to work. Using wood and bamboo, ropes woven from the dried leaves of a local date palm and big metal pegs hammered into cracks the fishermen produced the ultimate artificial routes. Most of them have now rotted away but from the belvedere on Cape Nao you can still see the odd ladder. Tourists must wonder what they are doing perched in the middle of gigantic cliffs.

The Spanish historian Toni Barber has maintained one of these fishing 'routes' as a kind of a museum to this remarkable industry. His friend José Miguel García, a climbing guide from Sella, took us to a less developed stretch of the coast and we bushwhacked across steep slopes of loose limestone to a cave perched above another colossal drop. This was where the fishermen would pause before starting down.

A thick iron spike marked the top of the line and José swung onto it and climbed down, perched on little globs of cement stuck to the rock, clipping his rope into the rusting garbage buried in the cracks. The cliff dropped away below his feet to the sea, which sucked and blew around its base. A short ladder had been lain across an overhang. It creaked and shifted as José settled his weight onto each rung. Then it was my turn.

It was quite a trip. Although I was clipped into José's line I still felt horribly frightened. Nothing seemed solid and I gripped the bizarre collection of electrical flexes and bits of wood and wire with complete trepidation. Little nicks had been chipped out of the rock or else I tiptoed on lumps of hastily spread cement. Below was nothing but the salt air. When I reached the broad ledge, José set off down the next vertical section of cliff to a longer and even more wretched ladder.

'Oh God,' I moaned to myself, 'this is turning into something monstrous.' Then José's rope ran out and soon after we were reduced to down-climbing slabs of friable rock, clinging to the rotten strands of line that hung from the cliff, still a hundred feet above the sea.

The fisherman who worked this route would climb down it each evening – alone. He would spend the whole night at the base of the cliff on a ledge built from bamboo and wood, hung from big iron hooks driven into the cliff. In the morning he would stow his ledge and climb back up with his catch before walking to market, some ten miles away. All along the cliff here and elsewhere on the coast were pitches like this, each one controlled, maintained, sometimes rented out to those too poor to equip routes for themselves. All the fishermen knew who worked which route.

The practice went on for generations – I still haven't found out how many – and ended only fifty or so years ago. It's likely that long before Haskett-Smith climbed Napes Needle, fishermen were descending these cliffs at harder grades out of economic necessity. And yet this world is now almost forgotten and without Toni Barber's interest and scholarship would have been completely so.

This experience made me recall a climbing trip I took to Mali and the huge sandstone towers near Hombori called collectively the Hand of Fatima. Villagers recounted the story of two brothers Ousmane and Maliki Zindo who, around 1900, scaled the cliffs solo collecting vulture eggs and marabou chicks. Both brothers ultimately fell to their deaths. The broken body of one was found beneath Kaga Tondo with a bounty of eggs in the leather bag around his neck. He had reached the nests close to the summit, most likely through a combination of the west face and north pillar, climbing up to V+ in grade, unroped and barefoot. When the first Western climbers reached the summit, they found potsherds left by previous, forgotten generations.

You may argue that these men – 'Known Unto God', to coin a phrase – weren't climbing for the same reasons as we do but I don't accept that. Virginia Woolf might once have claimed that human nature changes, but it doesn't, at least, not overnight. Only our own personal perspectives do. I felt, climbing down that cliff in Spain, a powerful connection to whoever it was that first came this way, just as I do on a route on Cloggy. (Where, of course, the botanist clergymen Williams and Bingley were climbing in 1798.)

If you can accept that the fishermen on the coast near Javea, or the young men of the Sahel, or the copper miners in Snowdonia were pioneers too, then you really do begin to see climbing as something deep and rich and very, very old. Because adapting to new environments is something humans have done throughout history, just to survive. Those Spanish fishermen were never in a guidebook, and were illiterate, so never wrote a journal of their exploits. But what they did was every bit as impressive as a thousand Napes Needles.

Of course, those forgotten adventurers quit that tough work as soon as something easier and better paid came along, whereas we actually pay to suffer in this way. Doesn't that signal a major difference in motivation? I'm not sure. John Amatt, who made the first ascent of the Troll Wall in 1965, has said: 'It is one of the great paradoxes of human existence that by nature we seek out comfort and predictability, using all of our financial resources and intellectual power to devise technologies that will make our lives easier and less stressful. The paradox is that once we have created the comfort we desire, we must leave it all behind if we are to move forward toward future opportunity.'

I think evolution solves this conundrum rather easily. We have an innate desire to seek security, both in terms of the resources we can draw on to survive and, critically, bring up children, and in security from threat. But we also have the tools to face an environment that is more dangerous than the one we have created for ourselves. Solving problems, facing risk and working as a team make us happy as individuals. They are their own reward. It is under these circumstances that our brains are doing what they are designed for. Take away risk and adventure – in their broadest meanings – and the kind of boredom that leads to drug abuse and joy-riding becomes a threat. But no one *wants* to live in a dangerous environment, at least not for long. Both Reinhold Messner and Doug Scott have written that the sweetest moment in an expedition is the moment just before you reach base camp, when the climb is almost over.

I remember interviewing the psychologist Steven Pinker and discussing with him the alleged crisis among men in modern Western society. He described to me the circumstances of our social groupings, under which we evolved. 'Small groups of men,' he said, 'working together in a risky environment to solve problems. That's what makes us happy.' It did sound remarkably familiar.

Think of Coleridge on Scafell in 1802. (Kubla Khan, rock climbing *and* a laudanum habit – that's my kind of man.) 'There is one sort of Gambling, to which I am much addicted;' he wrote to his lover Sara Hutchinson after his experience on Broad Stand. 'When I find it convenient to descend from a mountain, I am too confident and too indolent to look round about and wind about 'till I find a track or other symptom of safety; but I wander on, and where it is first *possible* to descend, there I go – relying upon fortune for how far down this possibility will continue.'

In other words, Coleridge delights in being reckless. (I love the phrase 'symptom of safety', treating security as though it were a disease.) He is caught up in emotion, half thrilled, half terrified, as he contemplates climbing and jumping between each terrace and ledge. Finally, the prospect of the next hard move is too much and he is forced to lie down to recover his equilibrium. 'O God, I exclaimed aloud – how calm, how blessed am I now – I know not how to proceed, how to return, but I am calm and fearless and confident.' This emotional state will be familiar to anyone who ever pushed their grade on a rock climb or on a mountain.

There remains one hole in this argument that I have yet to close. You might be persuaded that the activity of climbing matches some atavistic urge that our evolution has left instilled in each of us. But our lives are about much more than the acquisition and management of resources, aren't they? Isn't it rather dehumanising to see things in such general, reductionist terms? We feel more self-aware and happier as individuals from climbing. Why can't we leave it there?

I've avoided discussing philosophy so far, partly because I have read very little, and partly because I don't trust its value. The evolutionary biologist Edward O. Wilson once described philosophy as 'a series of failed models of the mind'. But philosophy is for many of us the first port of call when dealing with our psychology. After all, what else is there?

For most arts graduates of my generation, any discussion of psychology usually involves Freud and sometimes Jung, but as Gore Vidal once said of Freud, anyone who gets the Oedipus myth wrong can't be trusted to explain how our minds work. His obvious contribution was to make us consider how our subconscious mind, particularly with regard to sexual desire, underpins a great part of our behaviour and by extension our culture.

Far more persuasive for me on the subject of how our psychology is constructed are modern neuroscientists and philosophers like Michael S Gazzaniga and Daniel Dennett. The brain, they argue, is an organ shaped by evolution and should be studied in that context. Their attempts, and the attempts of others like them, to explain the brain's function, which is the mind, are more rooted in evidence and experiment than that of traditional philosophy. They reveal us to be creatures not just concerned with having enough to eat, as Mallory agreed, but creating an identity for ourselves, telling the story of our own lives.

As humans we are caught between two opposing forces, the desire to be innovative and the desire to conform. If we are innovative, then we seem more attractive to potential mates, but we also risk the ridicule of the group, which can leave us isolated from the social support we need. Most of us play safe and choose the group. The truth is that very few humans are original. Rather, we are fast-followers, quick to capitalise on someone else's good idea, once we are sure it will work. ('The human mind,' Dennett once wrote rather cheerlessly, 'is a dunghill in which the larvae of other people's ideas thrive.' But then again, watching the fashion industry, perhaps he has a point.)

Climbing's image is of an exciting but dangerous enterprise that adds lustre to an individual's reputation as a risk-taker, someone who is determined to live life to the full. So many of us start in adolescence and young adulthood, looking for a sharply defined world in which we ourselves can be defined, a world that is brighter than the one we grew up in. Mountains become arenas in which we learn and tell our own stories.

The greatest climbers are those who are truly original, who climb new mountains or hard new routes in a pure style. But climbing is a little world, and ultimately a small but satisfying glimpse of heaven. I think George Mallory understood that, even as he created mountaineering's most enduring myth. Knowing John Maynard Keynes and the Bloomsbury set left him with the sense that the world he had chosen was too small to realise his ambition. Because the greatest explorers of all were never men seeking new shores or hacking through jungles. They were those with minds agile enough to discover what is both true and unknown, about both ourselves and the world we live in.

ALAN MULLIN

Commitment and Bolts in Patagonia

Kevin Thaw, a friend I'd met four years earlier at an international climbing meet, invited me to climb in Patagonia. I jumped at the chance. Like many aspiring alpinists I had read tales of Patagonian climbing hardships and conquests and been intrigued by this inspiring mountain paradise.

Kevin had one route in mind, the Czech Route on the West Face of Fitzroy. The route, 7000ft long, had been climbed siege style over two seasons with much fixed rope and aid climbing. Kevin's ambition was to climb it in a lightweight alpine-style push. This would be a two-man job with a rack and a rope, no sleeping bags, and no back-up. We did the route, alpine style, in February 2000 in a 25-hour single push with one cold bivvy, albeit not to the summit as we were beaten back 250m short by horrendous weather. The choice had been easy. Either we went down and lived, or tried to continue and likely die. We had no regrets about making our choice. I just didn't care that I hadn't reached the top, as I'd survived the most eye-opening climbing experience of my life. I had only been climbing for three years and had never climbed any alpine route before. The possibilities of using lightweight style in Patagonia seemed limitless. I felt I was at the start of something.

At the end of that same season Kevin had suggested returning for the ultimate alpine route, the Maestri-Egger on the East Face of Cerro Torre. It had reportedly been climbed in lightweight alpine style but no modern team had repeated the ascent. Despite over 20 known attempts by some of the foremost alpine climbers of their generations, the route had still held out. So Kevin and I had returned for the 2002 season, but as bad luck often has it, our friend Leo Houlding broke his ankle 300m up on the route and we descended for the season.

Kevin and I had both believed that the 2003 season would be the right one and so we arrived hoping to indulge ourselves in our own alpine-style heaven. We would take no sleeping bags, a little food, two ropes and a rack. These were our only requirements. However, bad weather for well over 40 days put paid to that plan. Next season may be the right one, but only time and the Patagonian weather will tell.

Patagonia in1959 was – arguably – the time and place where the alpine-style ascent of the century occured, with Cesare Maestri and Toni Egger climbing their route on Cerro Torre. Maestri was an Italian climber who had specialised in high-risk solos in the Dolomites and obviously knew about all-out climbing commitment. He had been to Patagonia in 1958 but his expedition had been called off when the leader viewed the mountain for the first time and declared it impossible.

Maestri vowed to return the next year, and his partner for that trip was a formidable Austrian ice climber by the name of Toni Egger, who had a creditable list of hard ascents in the Alps and was known to be amongst the best ice climbers in Europe. On his return in 1959 Maestri opted for the line on the right-hand side of the East Face. After fixing ropes on the first 300m the two climbers opted for an all out alpine-style push on the remaining 1000m upper wall. They lacked most of the gear modern climbers now take for granted. They had no cams, no nuts, no jumars or hawser-laid ropes. Both climbers were leading and seconding carrying 50lb sacks. It took them a mere five days to climb the route and descend. They had a little food, one rope, one long-shafted ice axe each and, of course, nerves of steel. Unfortunately, on the last section of the descent, Egger was killed by falling ice which frequently sweeps down the East Face.

Forty-four years after this ascent the Maestri-Egger still strikes fear into the hearts of modern climbers. It is widely respected as perhaps technically the hardest and most objectively hazardous mountain route in Patagonia. The climbing is very intense even by modern standards. Added to that is the fierce Patagonian weather and a lack of back-up should things go wrong. Being rescued there in bad weather is not an option.

It may not be popular for me to say so, but climbing commitment in Patagonia has not advanced as much as gear. I know that modern equipment and knowledge have meant fierce technical and physical advances in the mountains. But what if we have neglected the psychological advances that should have developed alongside the technical ones? Mental breakthroughs were notably more evident in the late 1950s.

If I am wrong, then why has the Maestri-Egger not been equalled, never mind surpassed, in terms of commitment to the essence of alpine-style climbing? Could a lack of psychological development be the reason? I had the pleasure of discussing the Maestri-Egger climb with some of the most experienced practitioners of Patagonian mountaineering during my last trip. Slovenians, Spanish, Austrians, Italians, and Argentinean climbers all agreed on one thing. If the route was indeed climbed – and that is a matter of doubt among many climbers – then Maestri and Egger put up a route that goes beyond any subsequent Patagonian ascent. Four decades have passed and not one modern ascent in Patagonia has come close to it in terms of the style and the commitment they used on Cerro Torre in an era when climbers were limited to the most basic climbing equipment.

Despite their lesson in style, few climbers have learned from their lesson. Most routes climbed in Patagonia have been put up using fixed ropes, bolts, and hard aid climbing, which is perhaps understandable when you look at the time-scale in which many of them were climbed. However, even now, modern teams who go to Patagonia in the 21st century still aspire to fix ropes and use bolts. All this has happened in an era when style has supposedly advanced far beyond that of the late 1950s.

I was unsure if the use of bolts in Patagonia was still relevant. So you can imagine my surprise when I was told about an Italian expedition, led by Mauro 'Bubu' Bole, that planned to climb a new route on the South Face of Cerro Torre. Allegedly, they were planning to use 300 bolts to fix a portable sleeping box and all the belays on the route. I nearly died of shock. By anyone's reckoning, 300 bolts is excessive. It was a struggled to believe that I was hearing this about a world-class climber on one of the world's most inspirational peaks.

I questioned Bubu on his proposed use of 300 bolts on Cerro Torre. His answer? 'Safety is important and the safety and comfort of my team is important.'

'Well!' I responded. 'If it's safety and comfort you want, perhaps you should have stayed at home?'

This brought much laughter from the other British climbers around, and from Bubu himself. We then passionately debated the use of bolts for quite some time before he rather dejectedly left our company.

I personally thought siege style in Patagonia had died out long ago. Surely climbers who choose this style know they can beat mountains into submission and succeed on most objectives, given the right quantity of bolts, gear, time and fixed rope. I often wonder what climbers get in return for this approach. Is it really personal satisfaction? Or does it come down to conquest and celebrity? Whatever the reasons, surely this approach brings neither long-term satisfaction nor a decent respect for the future of mountains and mountaineering? As Messner put it, the use of bolts in the mountains is just 'the murder of the impossible'.

You might ask, what right did I or anyone else have to question Bubu on his intended use of bolts? The same right as anyone who is passionate about the mountains and the long-term implications of bolting on them – it's our future too. It's that simple. I knew he wasn't going to change his approach on the strength of some British climber's opinion, but it's important to exercise our freedom of speech!

I wonder whether Bubu's alleged use of 300 bolts to climb his route in Patagonia would have been forgotten in the frenzy of success. More to the point, if he had summited Cerro Torre by a new line, would it have mattered to others how he had got there? I know my own opinion would not have been popular if he had succeeded. Luckily the weather put paid to his proposed plan.

However, this story illustrates how in the 21st century there are climbers who don't think twice about this bolting issue – or even care. Planning to climb in Patagonia with 300 bolts and other artificial equipment surely eliminates the real essence of all-out climbing commitment. If the desire by these climbers to conquer the mountains at any cost, using all available means, is acceptable, then the question must be asked: what point is there in looking towards the mountains for our future climbing challenges, especially if they are based on nothing more than the plethora of materials climbers have to hand? Why not just stay on local sport crags?

Bubu's plan to bolt all the belays on the South Face of Cerro Torre, which is 1500 metres high, would have removed any real value in climbing it; for it is only the style in which we climb a mountain that gives lasting satisfaction. Surely the essence of climbing in good style is for the climber to use his or her own natural skills and cunning? That surely must mean placing natural gear and not drilling protection on the lead. The natural method should be the favoured style of climbing in Patagonia, as only that approach will allow this beautiful resource to be used by future generations.

Success, safety, security – these are not the reasons that should motivate climbers to climb in Patagonia, or any other mountains for that matter. I know from experience that these aspects cannot be guaranteed. Maybe relying on overall ability more than on bolts and fixed ropes means that it will take more than one season to climb a Patagonian objective in good alpine style. However, it should be acknowledged that this is obviously not an acceptable risk for certain climbers. In which case, they shouldn't travel to Patagonia.

The style and commitment in which Kevin and I chose to attempt to climb the Maestri-Egger meant that no matter how uncomfortable and uncertain the journey and its outcome might be, we were really only interested in meeting the mountain and route on its own terms. We were good enough to have excelled there previously without bolts or fixed ropes, and we climbed well, with knowledge acquired through our combined experience. When Kevin and I return we might even find out whether our combined abilities and commitment count for more as climbing aids than just the modern hardware we have to hand.

Thus we hope to overcome the route using the above experience and of course a few of the gifts that nature bestowed upon us, these being mainly our brains and, as the Argentinians would say, our cajones. I know for a fact that these qualities are of real value in climbing in Patagonia and nothing less than all-out commitment will help overcome this 44-year-old route. This is surely the route which will ultimately define the future of Patagonian alpine-style climbing. Have Maestri and Egger defined the climbing style for future generations in Patagonia? For some they certainly have, but for others the alpine-style ascent has never even existed.

WALTER BONATTI
Men, Mountains and Adventure
Translated from the Italian by Robert Marshall

I have only one aim when I talk about my experiences, to remind you what wise men have always pointed out as the correct path to follow. They say that each of us must be the author of his own story as it unfolds throughout the course of his life. From this idea it is easy to conclude that, if you wish to build your own spiritual identity, your basic need, your only goal, should be to assert yourself and grow. This calls for commitment, which demands passion, perseverance and integrity. This will have excellent results – you will feel stronger and more resolute and as a result will feel like a winner. We therefore should never wait for anything to come as a gift from others, and still less for so-called 'luck'. Our 'lucky stars' are merely what we manage to create for ourselves, step by step, year after year, experience after experience. Everything must be paid for with our own hides. This then is not luck, but continuing growth. To reaffirm what I have just said, I offer the experience of an entire lifetime – my own life.

I am not a mountain man by birth, but became wedded to the mountains by pure passion after growing up in the flattest part of Italy, the plain of the Po valley. I will say at once that my adventurous instincts, which were to become the driving force of my life, were undoubtedly produced by curiosity, an abiding curiosity which little by little became ever more associated with dreams and an insuppressible need to give concrete reality to all this.

A difficult adolescence also contributed a great deal to the development of my character. I reached this rite of passage during the defeat of Italy in the Second World War and by the resultant sudden collapse of human values and the lack of any real prospects, which were totally absent in my country at that time. This happened to a lad who was just then facing the realities of life. The consequence of this environment could drive a man two ways, into moral degradation for the poor in spirit, or to the exact opposite in those with positive potential. Fortunately, this latter alternative was what happened to me.

While still young – only eighteen years old – I began mountaineering at the highest level, and this led me in less than a year to repeat the most difficult climbs achieved up until then by my predecessors. But doing extreme climbs was for me not so much a flight from the daily round, however understandable that might have been, nor rebellion against the misery of a dull world, as Italy was at that time. It was rather an obstinate and irrepressible need to succeed over and over again.

For the next sixteen years, I travelled in the Alps and the other mountains of the world, following my dreams as a means of fulfillment, going always a little further. I believe that only when you dream with your eyes open can you conceive things that represent the limits of your sensitivity.

In fact, my achievements existed for me from the very moment they took form in my mind. To transform them into reality was no more than a logical consequence of that thought. When I first imagined what would eventually become my most significant ascents, I found myself in a peculiar state of mind in which anything seemed possible, even normal. Doing the climb, making it a reality, was no more than the natural and inevitable outcome of that idea, and certainly no more real than it had been at its conception. It is when you are imagining things that you live intensely, and it is only when you believe in yourself that you are able to really develop concepts. So, up there, as exploit followed exploit, I felt more and more alive, free, and true to myself. I was able to satisfy that innate need of every man to test and prove himself – to know and to understand. I have always followed my emotions as well as my creative and contemplative impulses.

From the start, mountaineering for me was an adventure. It could not have been otherwise. I always wished to live adventurously, but with due respect for tradition. Soon, however, this became a fascinating way of living and knowing myself, and it was also helpful to my physical and mental wellbeing. I have always admired mountaineers of every epoch, but I have never regarded any of them as a model. So I read their books, saw, heard and evaluated them, but only to create my own self, not to copy them. I am convinced that mountaineering improves only those who improve themselves. It certainly doesn't improve the apathetic or the arrogant. It isn't being a mountaineer that enriches a man – indeed, as I have already said, what he carries inside himself grows in a particular way if he has integrity.

All my climbs have been equally important to me, leaving aside the difficulty and commitment they demanded. I remember them all in the same way, with satisfaction, because they were all imagined, wanted, sought after, experienced, delighted in, and they have all been cut to my measure and so were right for me at the moment they happened. Everyone knows that great trials either toughen you or annihilate you. This is the story of life. It follows from this that each of us is the sum, the end result, of his own experiences. Mine have made me grow, and so my limits have expanded.

It was by practising traditional alpinism that I was able to enter into harmony with mother nature, but it was only solo climbing at the highest level that released the deepest inborn energy of my being. In this way I was better able to know my motivation and my limitations. Moreover, I learned how to make crucial decisions for myself, to judge them by my own measure and, naturally enough, pay for them with my own hide. In brief, solo climbing was an effective, formative school for me, a precious condition, even a necessity at times.

So I reaffirm my conviction that in a climb there is nothing more profitable than solitude and isolation to sharpen your sensations and amplify your emotions. It was thanks to these guiding principles that I was able to complete a fascinating internal voyage of discovery, to examine and understand myself, other people and the world around me. I can say now that I know myself better, know what I have achieved and what I want from myself and others. Naturally I fight against ill-will if it arises, but I can accept criticism. It can be helpful if it is constructive; whereas destructive criticism is like the air to me, it doesn't affect me.

One could say I have been lucky, but I don't believe in luck, nor in fate. Fate is what we knowingly create for ourselves with the sole limitation of the unforeseeable. Many years have passed since the time of my climbs, but the mountains have left within me, still vital and indelible, the imposing images of their architecture, of their superb, severe outlines suspended in the sky – alien at times to the measure of man and certainly far beyond his limitations. With the eyes of the mind I can still recall those freezing, silent heights in every detail and, as before, my thoughts fly in a constant circuit from things to imagination and back again, liberating new perceptions, unknown dimensions which constantly slide away from any attempt to explain them. How true it is that only by understanding beauty do we possess it.

This, and more besides, is what I described in my book *Mountains of My Life* about my experiences, up to the day of my winter ascent of the North Face of the Matterhorn in 1965. It was really then that I concluded my climbing career. I realized that after this adventure of mine, achieved by classical, fair means, I would not have been able to push on further without accepting the compromises inherent in the new climbing techniques, with their battery of artificial aids that I had always disdained.

And now, even so many years after the epilogue of my mountaineering career, I wish to set out some concepts drawn from my motivations in mountaineering. What makes me speak of them is the ever more obvious corruption which undermines mountaineering ethics, making orphans of the values it regards as outmoded, while at the same time persisting in a laboured search for other motivations in which to believe.

Granted, we all are free to believe whatever we wish, to adopt whatever rules we find are most convenient for our aspirations. We are free to climb in our own way. I too, for the same reasons, chose a mountaineering philosophy consistent with my ideology. It was traditional methods that inspired me right from the start. This classical way of climbing is an alpinism that, in the act of measuring your limits against the great mountains, puts your whole being to the test: physical endurance, principles and moral values, with nothing whatever held back. And this, which I define as 'greater mountaineering', becomes especially austere and demanding precisely because of the limitations put on the technical means we choose to accept in confronting the mountains.

But greater mountaineering is even more fascinating and gratifying if we keep in mind its historic and ethical values, quite apart from aesthetics. Personally I have never been able to separate these three elements nor choose between them, since for me they are fundamental. To this end, I committed myself and conformed to the mountaineering methods of the 1930s, obviously adopting the essentials, not to mention the elementary and limited equipment used in those times.

But why would I have chosen limitations so anachronistic in my own era? Certainly not because of masochistic perversion, but so I could preserve an unchangeable measuring stick, a sort of Greenwich Meridian, unalterable by time or conditions, a reliable constant that would allow me to reach an impartial judgment about things and also about myself.

I chose what I believed to be the just, fair rules of the game I had chosen. These rules I imposed on myself right from the beginning, and I would still choose them today, to guarantee myself a bond and a sure means of comparison with the past to which I had always referred. By committing myself in this way, I have been able to test myself to the depths against those who went before me. I have also been able to remain in harmony with the physical and psychological conditions involved in the exploits of the past. I have also been able to evaluate objectively the importance of what I had achieved.

If we ignore the past and refer only to the present in making judgments about mountaineering, I believe we will never be able to formulate just and clear criteria, which allow us to understand what mountaineering really is. The present is increasingly technological, ever more liable to remove from a climb its peculiar difficulties, its unknown problems, even its impossibility. It's a world in which a mountaineering exploit often has the sole merit of confirming the success of technical equipment used. This is the future we face if we have never understood what mountaineering's limits and motivations were in the past.

Learning in this way, the mountains have given me more than I could ever have hoped for. This was despite the fact that I eventually realised I wasn't just a mountaineer. As the years passed I came to understand that my true character was driving me always more to experience adventure in its widest universal expression. So I had to broaden my horizons. I was then transferring my extreme mountaineering, with all its psychological components, out of its vertical surroundings and putting it into an adventurous context which was just as extreme but, for the most part, as yet unknown.

I had to trust the instincts of my life in an even vaster multi-dimensional cultural world, where the real space in which I was travelling would be, above all, that of the mind. In short, I felt that I was embarking on a period of personal growth. After the great mountains, a huge world now awaited me. From then on I went everywhere, and came to grips with forests, deserts, lost islands, the depths of the sea, volcanoes, icy and tropical latitudes, not to mention primitive peoples, wild animals, the remains of ancient civilizations. But everything I did provided me with the most beautiful, significant and richest of sensations because, as before, I used to intensely long for every one of these experiences before living through them.

I had the chance to become a journalist, a special correspondent of the then great Italian weekly journal *Epoca*, published by Mondadori, and had *carte blanche* to produce, where and when I wished, my 'extreme journalism' and 'introspections'. But how did it start, this new adventure?

First of all, I revisited my childish fantasies and the books I had read as a boy concerning the things I used to dream about so much. At a certain age we all dream about what we read. I was now able to give life to these dreams and make from them the motive for my travels. At that time, in the 1960s and 1970s, there were almost always difficulties. Very few people had been to such places and few even knew anything about them. In the journeys I made, I tried never to fight with anyone or anything. I was seeking a point of contact with the savage world in order to know it better, assimilate it and transmit this world to others by means of words and pictures. This is what I wanted to do, developing my own variety of journalism, making the reader understand that behind the notebook and camera was a mere man, full of curiosity and alone with his emotions.

It is now clear to everyone that I am instinctively attracted to and fascinated by primordial nature. Because of this I climbed down into active volcanoes and I went into those smoking craters above all to see how the world was made when it began, to imagine how things would have looked the day after its creation if anyone had been there to see. One can therefore imagine how much emotion, surprise and admiration was aroused in me by an episode of that sort.

What drove me on and sustained me in all those situations I lived through, in every experience I had after I had given up mountaineering, were the same forces which had driven me up 'impossible' mountains. Nothing had changed. But in all this, my intention was always to know and to consider, to test myself, entering as far as possible into conditions that were able to awaken long-buried ways of being, inherited through the generations, but now dormant in most of us.

I wanted to experience to the full the freedom of knowing myself to be absolutely detached from any sort of technical, organised support which if necessary would have helped me, supplied me with provisions or even saved me if I got into trouble. Naturally the places and situations I chose offered all those ingredients which could give life and logical sense to my adventure as I envisaged it.

In this way, detached and far away from all that one might regard as the developed world, I can say that on most occasions I came to know a world still untouched from the time of its origin. On my travels I encountered all manner of wild animals, and also primitive tribes whose mode of dress had remained unchanged for millennia. In those places sun and rain, birth and death remained the only reality, which regulated their lives. Their survival was torn tenaciously from a difficult environment hostile to life. They were ignorant of the rest of the world, which ignored them in its turn. But then, in those far-off lands, huge and without history, where nothing changes, everything repeats itself in an endless cycle. I experienced fears and hopes, discomfort and exaltation. I listened to absolute silence, to hurricanes. I inhaled the vapour of volcanoes, the smells of the jungle. During dark nights my merest glance encompassed a plethora of stars. With my mind floating I have wandered, dreaming of impossible horizons, giving human proportions to the infinite, until I have lost myself in the universe. Now more than ever I am convinced that a man's life makes sense only if it encompasses everything he has within his being. It is there, in the mind, that real spaces are created.

However, although on my new travels in the six continents there was no lack of great mountains, Mont Blanc has remained the one I have most assiduously explored again and again by all its ridges and valleys. I have done this much as a man returns to his own father, to converse together with all the affection and memories a son looks for in a parent.

This essay was presented as a lecture at the Festival of Mountaineering Literature. The Alpine Journal is grateful to Dr Terry Gifford, Director of the Festival, for his assistance in its publication here.

0. The magnificent Kongga (6488m), its N Face towering above the headwaters of the Puyu valley. (*Tamotsu Nakamura*) (p81)

1. Kona I (6378m) on the right and Kona II (6344m) towering above the Puyu valley, viewed towards the SW. (*Tamotsu Nakamura*) (p81)

32. Goyon I (6252m) *left* and Goyon II (6140m), which drain into the Dam Dol valley. (*Tamotsu Nakamura*) (p81)

33. A closer view of Goyon II. (*Tamotsu Nakamura*) (p81)

34. The southern side of the holy mountain of Nenang (6870m), the highest unclimbed peak in Nyenchentangla East. (*Tamotsu Nakamura*) (p81)

35. The same mountain from the north, viewed during John Town's expedition. (*John Town*) (p95)

36. Above Basong Lake to the east. (*Tamotsu Nakamura*) (p81)

37. A close-up from the same viewpoint.
(*Tamotsu Nakamura*) (p81)

88. A stunning nameless and unclimbed peak (5844m) SE of Yuri village. (*Tamotsu Nakamura*) (p81)

89. The equally stunning Jalong I (6292m), taken from near the terminal of the Jalong glacier to the SW. (*Tamotsu Nakamura*) (p81)

40. Jomo Taktse (6582m), from the north. (*John Town*) (p95)

1. Nomad woman and children of the Surla Range, in the Transhimalaya of Tibet. (*Julian Freeman-Attwood*) (p103)

2. Pk 6530m seen across the Qulunggam Glacier in the Loinbo Kangri Range of the Transhimalaya. (*Julian Freeman-Attwood*) (p103)

43. Tibetan antelope in front of the E Face of Targo Gangri (6572m). *(Julian Freeman-Attwood)* (p103)

Art, Science & Nature

ELAINE ASTILL

Elijah Walton: His Life and Work

(*Plate 49*)

The artistic representation of mountain landscapes is still close to the hearts of all mountain-lovers, just as it has been in the last two centuries. That appreciation can be for an accurate imitation of a contour against the skyline or for the subjective expression of the emotional state that mountains provoke. The horror and thrill of soaring peaks or black abysses has changed to a form of celebration over the years, as interpretation follows the prevailing philosophy of the time. *Conquistadors of the Useless,* the recent exhibition of contemporary art at the Alpine Club, showed just how far down the artistic road self-expression has roamed.

Elijah Walton was an artist whose work was a familiar feature at Alpine Club exhibitions in the late 19th century and whose skill encompassed fine geological accuracy and a supreme Romantic vision. Very little has been written about this Birmingham-born artist[1] who is best known today for his watercolour views of the Alps and his illustrated books. It was the recognition of his representation of the mountains that qualified him for early membership of the Alpine Club. The handwritten entry for February 1863 in the minutes of the first *Alpine Club Journal* [2] cites Walton's election as a member but makes no note of his qualification. However, the point is recorded in *The Alpine Club Register* [3] which clarifies that he was the first member to qualify purely on artistic grounds. Edward William Cooke, RA, preceded him in 1859, qualifying on both his mountaineering and artistic skills, and George Barnard's election on artistic grounds followed Walton in December 1863. Fom its early days the precedent was set to open membership of the Club beyond those with high qualifications in the sport to those judged 'to have made significant contributions to mountain science, and literature and art'.[4] Walton was the first of many eminent figures included in the *Register,* such as Mathew Arnold, Theodore Duret, and John Ruskin.

Walton's friendships with two founder members and later presidents of the Alpine Club, William Mathews (1828-1901)[5] and the Reverend T G Bonney FGS (1833-1923),[6] were of great relevance to and of enormous personal influence on Walton's artistic career. Their combined passions for the mountains, love of nature, and scientific and spiritual backgrounds reflected Ruskin's ideals and neatly dovetailed with Walton's artistic nature. His friendship with Mathews was indeed fortunate, for besides turning his attention to the Alps for subject matter[7] he also introduced Walton to the

Reverend Bonney, resulting in their lifelong friendship and successful artistic and literary collaboration. Mathews' love of the Alps and his natural climbing ability had led to his idea for the formation of the Alpine Club in 1857. He wrote of 'an Alpine Club, the members of which might dine together once a year, say in London, and give each other what information they could'.[8] As an amateur painter himself, he was naturally interested in channelling Walton's talent and became a principal patron.[9] Bonney wrote of Walton's change of genre:

> ... the impulse for this change came from Mr William Mathews, who had employed him to make a drawing of one of his own sketches, and had been so struck with the vigour and originality of treatment, that he urged him to undertake a sketching tour, and offered him a tempting commission.[10]

In a period when the exploration of the Alps provided fresh inspiration for artists and a popular destination for the newly enfranchised middle-class tourists, Walton's change of subject matter from his early stilted Victorian scenes to Alpine landscapes held a contemporary relevance and was eagerly received.

The Rev T G Bonney, who published prolifically, was a fellow of St John's College, Cambridge, a Doctor of Science and a practising clergyman at different times in his career.[11] There is no doubt as to his standing as an eminent and learned member of society, and Walton later referred to him as 'my learned friend'.[12] Bonney combined his formidable career with his love of nature and the Alps. He often wrote of the numerous excursions to the Alps that the three friends shared, where Walton was often left to sketch in lower regions whilst he and Mathews continued with their high level climbs. Of an ascent of the Grivola from Cogne in August 1862 with William Mathews, Bonney wrote: 'We reached the arête of the Poussets at 2.45pm where we found our artist friend Elijah Walton hard at work upon a sketch of the Grivola.'[13] It appears that the friendship between the three men was very strong and that the combination of their talents was of mutual benefit. The texts that Bonney wrote for seven of Walton's ten illustrated books give a clear indication of their shared interests which were representative of the empirical mood of culture and society in mid-19th century Britain.

Mathews's patronage allowed Walton a continuity of support from his initial and unknown patroness who had funded his education from the age of eight at the Birmingham Art School and at the Royal Academy.[14] Following his marriage to Mary Neale in 1860, Walton combined his honeymoon with a painting excursion abroad and was totally inspired by the transcendental beauty of the Alps and the light and culture of the Middle East. His painting style altered dramatically and it is clear that the benefits of patronage enjoyed by Walton were instrumental in enabling him to embrace a wider world and develop his artistic and social aspirations.

Walton was born into a working-class family in Bromsgrove in November 1832, and died insolvent in the same town forty-eight years later. His life represented a realisation of the Victorian ethic of the value of work to accomplishment. With his personal qualities of perseverance, determination and aspiration to achieve, he overcame personal tragedy – being twice widowed – and forged his career, embracing the new technologies of photography and chromolithography in the presentation of his work to a wider market. With his illustrated books and paintings inspired by his travels Walton sought to adorn the drawing rooms of the prosperous middle classes. In middle age Walton exhibited pride in his achievement and a spirit of civic philanthropy and altruism by the gift of three paintings to the newly opened Birmingham Art Gallery that was noted in *The Art Journal*:

> By the generosity of Mr Elijah Walton who is so well known for his transcripts of alpine scenery ... the gallery has been put in possession of three grand pictures ... We trust Mr. Walton's example will be imitated by others whose early life has been spent in the midland metropolis.[15]

Only one painting from the gift remains in the Birmingham Art Gallery. It would appear from the grand scale of this work that Walton painted *Monte Marmorolo, Italy* expressly for this particular public gallery.[16] Later as President of the Bromsgrove School of Art[17] he established the library with gifts of three of his works that he had written specifically with the intention of aiding students of art.[18]

Walton appears to have presented himself in a somewhat eccentric idiom and a rare and charming profile of his aesthetic appearance and manner exists in the memoirs of Charlotte, the sister of early AC member Francis Fox Tuckett, whom Walton often visited at the family home.[19] Charlotte provides a visual description of Walton that represents the only known observation of the artist, and as such is worthy of quoting in full:

> One of our rather frequent visitors was Elijah Walton the artist whose drawings of Switzerland and Egypt are a joy to many. He had lost his wife in Egypt and was rather lonely and very eccentric. He affected a peculiar dress and ways, wearing his hair in little curls all over his head and a tunic of black velvet, with the sleeves slashed at the shoulders with some very bright colour. Yellow Turkish slippers completed this indoor costume. He liked to make effects and to call out sympathy, would push away his untasted food and when anxious enquiry was made as to the cause, would murmur 'one of my moods'. We soon found the best cure was to take no notice and then the knife and fork were resumed. He used to bring a great portfolio with his season's work and give us the delight of looking through them before they were exhibited to the public. His little ways were very funny but we got to like him very much. He was very short and used to gaze with adoring eyes at my tall sister and say piteously,

'What a pity that you are so tall,' and I remember how he retired into a corner and sulked for a whole evening when a very charming and talkative guest arrived to spend the night.[20]

Walton's frequent travels inspired him, and his prolific output was aimed at differing levels of the art market. He produced images of the splendours of the Alps and Norway, of the exotic Middle East and closer to home of the Lake District, Scotland, Wales and the Isle of Wight. The democratisation of culture so prevalent in the Victorian period was fuelled by the diminishing costs of printing technologies, and news periodicals and a plethora of exhibition venues fed the appetite for images by the growing middle-class market. Walton catered for this market with his watercolours and oils that ranged in size and price to suit all pockets, frequently exhibiting in the Pall Mall gallery of his publisher W M Thompson and in his own gallery at 4 Westminster Chambers. Catalogues to two of his exhibitions exist and give a rare insight into his marketing strategy.[21]

A review of Walton's work would not be complete without reference to his Egyptian *oeuvre*. He enjoyed a protracted stay in Egypt in 1863-64 and kept a sketch record of his experiences in the Bedouin desert encampment in which he stayed. Many of his drawings and watercolours of almost impressionist Egyptian landscapes, indigenous portraiture in mixed media and studies of the anatomy of the camel are well represented in the archives of the Victoria and Albert Museum.[22] Among these sketches is a self-portrait, the only known image of the artist.[23] A work of this *oeuvre* worthy of discussion is a large oil painting held at the Fitzwilliam Museum: *The Tombs of the Sultans' near Cairo, Sunset* (1865), which was given a scathing contemporary review when exhibited at the Summer Exhibition at the Royal Academy.[24] Given the vitriolic nature of the committee's view – that the painting was 'fortunately hung in a place of safety over the door, so that should absolute flames burst from the picture, nothing more than the ceiling will be consumed'[25] – it is not surprising that Walton preferred to use private exhibition space after this date. However, the review is representative of the criticism directed at the visionary and radical atmospheric effects that Turner had produced, that must have inspired Walton. The work is highly focused and skilfully draws the eye towards the distant tombs that are silhouetted by the setting sun, and the minute observation in the foreground is comparable with Pre-Raphaelite landscapes. The huge scale, emblematic and vibrantly expressive colouration of the setting sun and the cast shadows create a desolate beauty that sets this work apart from the rest of Walton's work up to this date.[26]

Walton's initial publishing venture *The Camel, Its Anatomy, Proportions and Paces* (1865) is a triumph of his considerable skill and personal dedication to the integrity of artistic and anatomical correctness, equivalent to Edward Lear's in *Illustrations of the Family of Psittacidae* (1830-32). Like Lear, Walton prepared the lithographic stones himself. So compelled was he to study accurately the anatomy of the camel that he purchased an animal and studied it in life and death. He executed sensitive pencil drawings of many positions of the camel in movement and at rest, indicating the proportions of the body, and also the differing ratios of the distances between the animal's footprints at differing speeds of travel. Walton's drawings show a masterly control of the pencil and their detail and accuracy has been compared by a contemporary,[27] and a recent scholar,[28] to Stubbs's study of the anatomy of the horse, a century earlier.

Of his seven topographical publications in collaboration with Bonney, *Peaks and Valleys of the Alps* (1867) has become a cornerstone in mountaineering literature. The list of owners of Walton's original paintings (that were reproduced for the chromolithographic plates) clarifies that the core of Walton's patrons for his alpine work were among the small circle that surrounded the founder members of The Alpine Club. *Peaks and Valleys* was Walton's initial literary collaboration with the Rev Bonney, whose accompanying text reveals their deep friendship, Walton's development as an alpine artist and their Ruskinian inspiration. With frequent reference to Volume IV of *Modern Painters,* Bonney praised Ruskin's great understanding of the Alps:

> ... no one whose writings are known to me understands the Alps better than he. ... If his fourth volume of 'Modern Painters' were more studied, we should have fewer of those caricatures of nature which, now under the names of 'Scenes in the Alps', too often disfigure our Exhibitions.[29]

Ruskin's proclamation '*Of Mountain Beauty*',[30] in which he discourses on the structure and formation of the mountain landscape and its perception by the artist, appears to be Bonney's touchstone in his communication to the reader. Ruskin used the work of Turner as a 'distinguished representative of modern, as opposed to ancient practice',[31] and it appears that Walton was a disciple of both the Ruskinian principles of truth to nature and Turner's freedom of artistic expression. It was Turner's combination of minute observation and Romantic expression that was Walton's greatest influence. An interesting example of Walton's emulation of Turner is found in an account Bonney wrote of their Norwegian tour of 1869, in which he referred to 'the weird beauty of the scenery', and 'the Turnerian mystery always present'.[32] He continued with a description of how, on a squally evening, when he and Walton were aboard a steamer, the heavy storms and cutting wind drove him below the deck:

> My companion E Walton, whose enthusiasm for his art renders him proof to most of the minor miseries of life, could not find it in his heart to leave such studies of storm-cloud, sea and mountain, and even succeeded, by propping himself against the funnel, in making some useful pencil sketches.[33]

Turner had painted *Snowstorm* (1842), following his visualisation of it while lashed to the mast of the *Ariel*, the unjust criticism of which inspired Ruskin to defend the artist in *Modern Painters*.

A letter to the editor of the *Alpine Journal* by a 'Lover of High Alps', in 1865, reviewed the picturesque view of the Alps represented in current exhibitions. The writer was critical of the representations of Alpine scenery in the Academy and 'the two watercolour galleries'. The author continued:

> ... if other artists were as truthful in representing nature ... we might shortly hope to find among them a worthy rival to Mr Elijah Walton, whose exquisite drawings [are] now on view at the German Gallery in Bond Street. ... Those ... who desire to see the Alps rendered truthfully and beautifully, should certainly visit this gallery. 'Sunset on the Aiguille and the Glacier de Trient' would amply repay a visit by every lover of the High Alps.[34]

Glacier de Trient appears as Plate 21 in *Peaks and Valleys of the Alps* and was loaned for chromolithographic reproduction by Francis Fox Tuckett. Walton published a further eight books, writing the text for *Clouds and Their Combinations* (1868) and collaborating with Bonney for *Flowers from the Upper Alps* (1869), *The Coast of Norway* (1871), *Peaks in Pen and Pencil* (1872), *Vignettes Alpine and Eastern* (1873), *The Bernese Oberland* (1874), *Welsh Scenery* (1875) and *English Lake Scenery* (1876).

At this point it is relevant to note Walton's exploits in the Alps beyond those of the artistic kind, notably his achievement in making the first passage of the *Col de Planaval* in 1865, his account of which was published in the *Alpine Journal*.[35] Walton described his expedition with the guide Jean Tairraz, and his comments on the view from the col recall Ruskin's exhortation on the 'tone of landscape colour' in *The Mountain Glory*.[36]

The *Alpine Journal* also published Walton's account of being the first Englishman to enter the *Gouffre du Busserailles* in January 1866.[37] The Club's picture collection holds a sketch and hand-drawn map of the caves that Walton made during his visit. This is a valuable record of the early exploration of the area. Another treasure of the picture collection is a magnificent pen-and-ink sketch panorama by Walton entitled *The Chain of Mont Blanc* (1865), which may have influenced the Rev Bonney's illustrations in his *Outline Sketches in the High Alps of Dauphiné*, (1865). The collection also owns *Monte Viso* (1865),[38] a watercolour that was formerly owned by William Mathews and was presented to the Alpine Club by Mrs Mathews following his death in 1901.[39]

Although Walton was well established on the London art circuit throughout the 1870s and continued to exhibit until the last year of his life, it is clear that the art-loving public had seen his most innovative work by this date. They were being offered repetitions of a theme, as a review of new work exhibited at the Burlington Gallery indicated: 'The Nile, the Alps and the Isle of Wight still furnish themes for his pencil and we need scarcely remind our readers of his delicacy and brilliancy in rendering atmospheric effects.'[40] His critics referred to his repetitive mannerisms and it was these that led eventually to his artistic decline. A new integrity and a truthful representation of the mountains by other artists had developed. A comprehensive review in the *Alpine Journal* of Alpine pictures in the 1879 London exhibitions highly praised George Barnard's *Wengern Alp*, Mr Croft's *A View in the Rosegthal* and *The Matterhorn* and the work of Mons Loppé and Harry Goodwin. The review of Walton's work was scathing: 'Unfortunately there is little new to be said of it. Mr. Walton can paint a brilliant snow-peak or mountain mists better than anyone. But he is content to repeat year after year one or two effects ... and for their sake to neglect all that gives their individual character to the various Alpine regions.'[41]

This derogatory review from an establishment that had once praised his work must have been difficult for Walton to accept. However, Bonney's judgement of this repetitious 'devotion to peculiar effects of atmosphere and colour' is attributed to Walton's deliberate isolation from 'the society of fellow workers and from study of their works.'[42] The following February, in failing health, insolvency forced Walton to sell the entire contents of his home and on 25 August 1880 Walton died of cerebritis – inflammation of the brain – leaving slender provision for his three sons.[43] The obituaries were generous in their praise and *The Times* noted how Walton had combined 'in a quite exceptional manner the rigidly technical with the highly artistic.[44] And the Rev Bonney himself provided the most comprehensive account of Walton's life in his moving obituary in the *Alpine Journal*.[45]

Following his death Walton's work was frequently shown in AC exhibitions. While the reviews showed great admiration for Walton's work they also acknowledged his decline, with comments like 'he fell under the baleful influence of the chromolithographer.'[46] Another remarked: 'The studio dreams of later years are altogether inferior.'[47] An Alpine Club exhibition catalogue noted:

> He delighted in atmospheric effects ... drew mountain form with a skill and knowledge that has never been equalled. This merit did not meet the eyes of most critics, who found fault ... with his frequent carelessness in foregrounds and repetitions of a single effect. He was a true artist spoilt by a public, which called for chromolithography.[48]

It seems there were those in the Alpine Club who considered Walton's pragmatic commercialism to blame for the decline of his reputation. Paradoxically, it was the embrace of this medium that had initially enabled Walton to forge his career. Whilst the development of chromolithography had democratised the ownership of art, it appears that in retrospect it was credited with lowering the respectability of art reproductions and for presenting them as being of dubious taste, associated with the lower-middle classes who could not afford original works. The limitations of the chro-molithographic process negated texture and individual brush strokes and presented flat planes of colour that relied on the skill in colour judgement of the lithographer. The process was well utilised for the production of Walton's illustrated books, but the sale of individual plates became associ-ated with cheap commercialism and not representative of his skill as an artist.

Whilst Alpine Club literature has been the source of discredit, a review of the Club's Winter Exhibition of 1901 provides perhaps Walton's ultimate acclaim from this arena:

> The Club hall was again well filled in December with a collection of recent works by our Alpine artists. ... But we must admit that if so far we have produced many talents the genius is yet to come. No successor of Turner or even of Elijah Walton has yet appeared on our walls, no one with the power of grasping mountain scenery as a whole, of painting its atmosphere as well as its forms.[49]

There can be no doubt that the friendship and support of Mathews and Bonney allowed Walton to achieve wide contemporary recognition and to play a considerable role in the development of the genre of mountain painting. Surely it was the picture and art-loving public who bought Walton's pictures and illustrated books that were his true judges. His lasting legacy is illustrated in contemporary reviews: 'Elijah Walton, the artist whose drawings of Egypt and Switzerland are a joy to many;'[50] or: 'To picture these grand and mighty summits has been the work of a life. They take the art lover on easy terms into scenery the grandest in nature.'[51]

Today Walton's work holds the interest of many lovers of the mountains and collectors of mountaineering history. As the Rotary Club of Aosta has shown, Walton is also remembered in the places that he visited and repre-sented.[52] While his lesser watercolours appear on the market occasionally, those of the respected peaks of The Alps, and Walton's illustrated books, are infrequently seen. They form a valuable part of museum collections and the collections of many lovers of the high Alps, in Britain, Europe and further afield.

Walton's contribution to the representation of mountain scenery continues to be recognised at the Alpine Club where he retains a unique position for his association with William Mathews and the Rev Bonney. The Club's reproduction of *Monte Viso* as a Christmas card and postcard is testament to this and has kept Walton very much in mind.

REFERENCES

1   Sidney Lee, ed, T G Bonney, 'Walton, Elijah, 1832-1880' *The
    Dictionary of National Biography* (London, 1899), vol LIX, p272
    'Obituary', *The Times* (31 August, London, 1880), p8, col F
    T G Bonney, 'In Memoriam, Elijah Walton. FGS '*The Alpine Journal*
    (November, 1880), vol X, pp74-8
    The Proceedings of the Geological Society, 'Elijah Walton '*The Quarterly
    Journal of the Geological Society* (1881), vol 37, p48
    A L Mumm, ed, *The Alpine Club Register* (London, 1923), pp363-5
2   *Alpine Club Committee and General Meetings Minutes, 22-12-1857 –
    10-12-1867* Archive ref AC2S/1
3   A L Mumm, 'Elijah Walton', *The Alpine Club Register, 1857-1863*
    (London, 1923), p364
4   Dr J Lovatt, *Peaks Passes and Glaciers* (London, 2001), p3
5   President 1869-71
6   President 1881-83
7   A L Mumm, *The Alpine Club Register 1857 -1863* (London, 1923),
    pp209-216
8   *Ibid*
9   He owned a large number of Walton's paintings, several of which were
    presented to the Alpine Club by his widow following his death.
    George Yeld, ed, *The Alpine Journal* (London, 1903), vol XXI, p135
10 T G Bonney, 'In Memoriam, Elijah Walton, FGS' *The Alpine Journal*
    (November, 1880), p75
11 A L Mumm, 'Rev Thomas George Bonney', *The Alpine Club Register
    1857-1863* (London, 1923), pp41-50
12 Elijah Walton, *Clouds, their Forms and Combinations* (London, 1868),
    p29
13 T G Bonney, *Memories of a Long Life* (Cambridge, 1921), p84
14 Walton entered the Royal Academy Schools in 1855 Royal Academy
    Archives
15 'Birmingham Society of Artists', *The Art Journal* (London, 1868),
    vol VII, p121
16 1867, (69 x 107 inches) oil on canvas. It is held in store away from
    public view.
17 He was president from 1873-79. *The Bromsgrove, Droitwich and Redditch
    Weekly Messenger and General Advertiser,* (17 February, 1872).
18 *The Camel, Clouds; Their Forms and Combinations, Peaks in Pen and Pencil.*
    Ibid (20 December, 1878)
19 A J & D R Freke, eds, *Recollections of Victorian Frenchay by Charlotte
    Howard, (nee Tuckett) (1994),* p20
20 *Ibid*
21 The National Library of Art, Victoria and Albert Museum

22   Examples of Walton's Eastern drawings and oil paintings can be viewed at the Fitzwilliam Museum, Cambridge, Victoria and Albert Museum, the Birmingham Museums and Art Gallery, the Smith Gallery, Sterling and the Frenchay Museum, Bristol.

23   Victoria and Albert Museum, Pictures, Prints and Drawings Department. Museum no SD1172

24   Cat no 346

25   'The Royal Academy', *The Art Journal* (June 1, London, 1865), vol IV, p170

26   A watercolour of identical viewpoint, *Afterglow at the Tombs of the Mamlik Sultans, near Cairo*, 35cm x 50cm, that may have been the study for *The Tombs of the Sultans, near Cairo, Sunset*, is in the Frenchay Museum, Bristol, and was given by Walton to Francis Fox Tuckett.

27   'The Camel, its Anatomy, Proportions and Paces', *The Athenæum*, No 1955 (April 15, 1865), p518

28   Briony Llewellyn, *The Orient Observed, Images from the Middle East in the Searight Collection* (London, 1989), p142

29   Elijah Walton, *Peaks and Valleys of the Alps* (London, 1867), p8

30   John Ruskin, *Modern Painters* (London, 1868), vol IV

31   *Ibid* p1

32   Ruskin wrote of 'Turnerian Mystery' in *Modern Painters*, vol IV, part V, 'Of Mountain Beauty'

33   T G Bonney, 'The Lofoten Islands', *The Alpine Journal* (London, 1870), p429

34   H B George, ed, *The Alpine Journal*, 1865-1866 (London, 1866), vol II, p95

35   H B George ed, 'Notes and Queries. New Expeditions in 1865, Elijah Walton, 'Col de Planaval', *The Alpine Journal* (London, 1866), vol II, 1865-66, p267

36   John Ruskin, *Modern Painters* (London, 1868), vol IV, p355, 4

37   H B George ed, 'Elijah Walton, 'Gouffre du Busserailles' *The Alpine Journal* (London, 1866), vol II, 1865-66, pp271-2

38   This may have been a preparatory watercolour for a larger oil version of the same title that was exhibited at The British Institution in 1866 (no 544), priced at 200 guineas, and later at Walton's 1868 exhibition *Sinai, Egypt and the Alps*, priced at 180 guineas.

39   George Yeld, ed, 'Presentations to the Alpine Club', *The Alpine Journal* (London, 1903), vol XXI, p135

40   'Elijah Walton's Water Colour Drawings', *The Art Journal* (London, 1879), vol XVIII, p98

41   Douglas W Freshfield, ed, 'Alpine Pictures in 1879', *The Alpine Journal* (London, 1880), vol IX, pp302-305

42   T G Bonney, 'In Memorium' *op cit*

43   *Ibid*

44 *The Times,* 'Obituary of Elijah Walton', (London, 31 August, 1880), p8, cf

45 T G Bonney, 'In Memorium' *op cit*

46 A J Butler, ed 'Pictures at the Alpine Club Winter Exhibition', *The Alpine Journal* (London, 1893), vol XVI, pp74-78

47 A J Butler, ed 'The Alpine Club Exhibition of Pictures and Photographs, 1892', *The Alpine Journal* (London, 1893), vol XVI, pp342-347

48 Alpine Club Exhibition, *Catalogue of a Collection of Mountain Paintings and Photographs at the XIXth Century Art Gallery* (London, 1894), p31

49 'The Winter Exhibition', *The Alpine Journal* (London, 1901), vol XX, p327

50 A J & D R Freke, eds, *Recollections of Victorian Frenchay by Charlotte Howard, (nee Tuckett)* (1994), p20

51 'Chromolithographs after Mr Walton', *The Art Journal* (London, 1874), vol XIII, p352

52 The Rotary Club of Aosta produced a facsimile edition of *Vignettes Alpine and Eastern* (London, 1873) reprint (Turino, 1988).

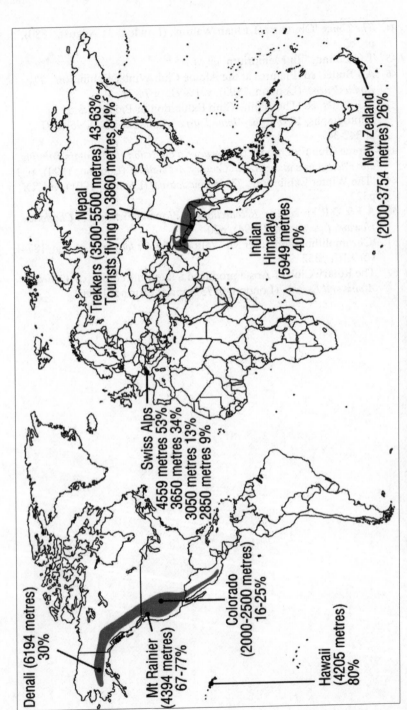

Reported incidence of acute mountain sickness at different locations

Denali (6194 metres)
30%

Mt Rainier
(4394 metres)
67-77%

Colorado
(2000-2500 metres)
16-25%

Hawaii
(4205 metres)
80%

Swiss Alps
4559 metres 53%
3650 metres 34%
3050 metres 13%
2850 metres 9%

Nepal
Trekkers (3500-5500 metres) 43-63%
Tourists flying to 3860 metres 84%

Indian
Himalaya
(5949 metres)
40%

New Zealand
(2000-3754 metres) 26%

P A BARRY & A J POLLARD

Altitude Illness - An Aide Memoire

Altitude illness is common in people ascending to more than 2500 metres, especially if the ascent is rapid. In most cases it will manifest as a mild, self-limiting illness but in a few cases it will progress to more severe, life-threatening forms. This article first appeared in the *British Medical Journal* and is published here to offer readers a synopsis of current thinking and an easy reference source.

As more people travel to high altitudes for economic or recreational purposes, altitude medicine has become increasingly important. Altitude illness should be anticipated in travellers to altitudes higher than 2500m, although for most it will be mild and self limiting, and will not require the intervention of a doctor. On rare occasions altitude illness may progress to more severe forms, which can be life threatening. The best method of preventing altitude illness is to ascend slowly, allowing time for acclimatisation. The mainstay of treatment is descent, and drugs and other treatments should be used mainly to aid this.

We gathered information for this review from several sources: our own experience and reading of the relevant literature, a search of the Cochrane database, a search of Medline using the terms 'altitude sickness' and 'altitude', and consulting a specialist database of altitude related articles.[1] We used two recently published texts, especially in regard to diagnosis, [2, 3] and information from a recent course on high altitude medicine and physiology organised by ourselves and held at the National Mountain Centre, Plas Y Brenin, Wales. The research evidence in altitude medicine is scanty and hampered by differences between studies in ascent rates, environmental conditions, and definitions of illness. We therefore used observational studies and clinical experience to formulate recommendations.

Three main syndromes of altitude illness may affect travellers: acute mountain sickness, high altitude cerebral oedema, and high altitude pulmonary oedema. The risk of dying from altitude-related illnesses is low, at least for tourists. For trekkers to Nepal the death rate from all causes was 0.014% and from altitude illness 0.0036%.[4] Soldiers posted to altitude had an altitude related death rate of 0.16%.[5] In British climbers attempting peaks over 7000 metres, altitude related illnesses contributed to death in 17%.[6]

Risk factors for developing altitude illness include the rate of ascent, the actual altitude reached, the altitude at which the traveller sleeps, and individual susceptibility.

Key points are:
- Physical fitness is not protective,[7] and exertion at altitude increases a traveller's risk of becoming unwell.
- Genetic make up may also influence performance at altitude.[8]
- Most pre-existing illnesses, such as chronic obstructive airways disease or diabetes, are not in themselves risk factors for developing altitude illness.

Acute mountain sickness

Acute mountain sickness consists of a constellation of symptoms in the context of a recent gain in altitude. (The map on the opposite page shows the reported incidence of acute mountain sickness at different locations.) These include headache, anorexia, nausea or vomiting, fatigue or weakness, dizziness or light-headedness and difficulty sleeping. These non-specific symptoms may be attributed to other conditions, especially by people who are anxious to stick to a preplanned schedule. Symptoms typically occur six to twelve hours after arrival at a new altitude – but may occur sooner – and resolve over one to three days, providing no further ascent is made. Acute mountain sickness is unusual at altitudes below 2500m. Peripheral oedema may be seen, but there are no physical signs that are diagnostic of acute mountain sickness, and the presence of neurological signs should imply the possibility of high altitude cerebral oedema or an alternative cause. Symptoms of acute mountain sickness can be quantified by using the Lake Louise scoring system,[9] but this epidemiological research tool should probably not be used to direct the management of an individual case.

Pathophysiology

The pathophysiological processes that cause acute mountain sickness are unknown. However, symptoms of acute mountain sickness may be the result of cerebral swelling, either through vasodilatation induced by hypoxia or through cerebral oedema.[3] Impaired cerebral autoregulation, the release of vasogenic mediators, and alteration of the blood-brain barrier by hypoxia may also be important.[10] Similar mechanisms are thought to cause cerebral oedema at high altitude, which may represent a more severe form of acute mountain sickness. Differences in individual susceptibility to acute mountain sickness are striking and inadequately explained. A reduced ventilatory drive in response to hypoxia may be important,[3] as may an individual's relative volume of cerebrospinal fluid to brain tissue. People with relatively more cerebrospinal fluid are able to displace it to compensate for cerebral oedema.[10]

Treatment

Resting at the same altitude often relieves the symptoms of acute mountain sickness, and most patients will improve without treatment at the same altitude in 24 to 48 hours.[2, 3] Simple analgesics and antiemetics may reduce headache and nausea in mild acute mountain sickness.

Box 1
Acclimatisation and rates of ascent

- Above 3000 metres increase your sleeping altitude by only 300m to 600m per day
- Above 3000m take a rest day for every 1000m of elevation gained
- Different people will acclimatise at different rates
- If possible, don't fly or drive directly to high altitude
- If you do go directly to high altitude by car or plane, do not overexert yourself or move higher for the first 24 hours
- Climb high and sleep low
- If symptoms are not improving, delay further ascent
- If symptoms deteriorate, descend as soon as possible

A carbonic anhydrase inhibitor, acetazolamide, is effective in reducing the symptoms of acute mountain sickness, although the optimum dosage is unknown; 250mg every eight hours is widely used and has been shown to be effective. Dexamethasone, 8mg initially, then 4mg every six hours, may also be used to relieve symptoms.

The main principles of treating acute mountain sickness are to stop further ascent, to descend if symptoms do not improve over 24 hours or deteriorate, and to descend urgently if signs of high altitude pulmonary oedema or high altitude cerebral oedema occur.

Prevention

A body exposed to hypobaric hypoxia makes a series of adjustments, known as acclimatisation, that serve to increase the delivery of oxygen.[11] Acclimatisation is best achieved by a slow ascent, allowing the body to adjust before going higher, and minimising the risks of succumbing to altitude related illness. This has led to recommendations for maximum rates of ascent – see Box 1. Slower ascent may be necessary for some individuals, but others may be able to ascend much faster without symptoms. A flexible itinerary is important, to allow days of rest without further ascent if needed.

A large part of acclimatisation takes place over the first one to three days at a given altitude, but the rate varies between different people. Full acclimatisation takes considerably longer. No reliable predictors for good acclimatisation exist, except that people tend to be consistent in how well they acclimatise on different trips.

Drug treatment may also be used for prophylaxis against acute mountain sickness.[12] Acetazolamide has been recommended for people who are susceptible to acute mountain sickness or when ascent rates are unavoidably greater than those recommended. Several randomised trials have shown a notable reduction in symptoms of acute mountain sickness with the prophylactic use of acetazolamide 250mg-500mg twice a day. A recent meta-analysis concluded that acetazolamide 750mg per day is efficacious in preventing acute mountain sickness but that lower doses are not.[12] However, this analysis has been criticised for its choice of outcome variable and for analysing trials with different ascent rates together. Lower doses of acetazolamide of 125mg twice a day have been recommended to reduce symptoms while minimising side effects, but the minimum effective dose remains unknown. If acetazolamide is used, treatment should be started at least one day before ascent and continued until adequate acclimatisation is judged to have occurred. Side effects, which include paraesthesia and mild diuresis, are common but usually well tolerated. Acetazolamide is a sulphonamide, and allergic reactions can occur.

Box 2

Treatment of altitude illness

Mild acute mountain sickness
- Rest days, relaxation; consider descent
- Aspirin, paracetemol, ibuprofen
- Antiemetics may be useful
- Acetazolamide may be considered

Severe acute mountain sickness and high-altitude cerebral oedema
- Descent, evacuation, oxygen
- Dexamethasone
- Pressure bag to facilitate descent

High-altitude pulmonary oedema
- Descent, evacuation, oxygen
- Nifedipine
- Pressure bag to facilitate descent

Altitude illness, type unknown
- Descent, evacuation, oxygen
- Dexamethasone
- Nifedipine
- Pressure bag to facilitate descent

Dexamethasone 4mg every six hours reduces the incidence and severity of acute mountain sickness at altitudes above 4000m.[12] Lower doses or the same dose given every twelve hours are less effective.[12] Prophylaxis may be started a few hours before ascent. Dexamethasone is not the first choice for the prophylaxis of acute mountain sickness because of its side effects. It may, however, be useful in people who have to ascend rapidly or who are predisposed to acute mountain sickness and are intolerant of or allergic to acetazolamide.

Many other substances have been considered for preventing acute mountain sickness, supported by anecdote or, in a few cases, small randomised trials.[12] Ginkgo biloba and aspirin are more effective than placebo in preventing symptoms of acute mountain sickness. Evidence for the use of spironolactone is conflicting, and there is no convincing evidence for using nifedipine, furosemide (frusemide), or codeine in preventing acute mountain sickness.[12]

High altitude cerebral oedema
Diagnosis

High-altitude cerebral oedema is usually preceded by acute mountain sickness and may lead to coma and death. Prodromal symptoms of early mental impairment or a change in behaviour may be ignored by patients and their companions. Headache, nausea and vomiting, hallucination, disorientation, and confusion are often seen; seizures are less common. Clinical signs include ataxia, a common early feature that may be disabling and is often the last sign to disappear during recovery; a progressive deterioration in conscious level, proceeding to coma and death; and papilloedema and retinal haemorrhages. Focal neurological signs may occur, but in the absence of other signs and symptoms of cerebral oedema these should prompt consideration of other diagnoses.

Severe illness due to high-altitude cerebral oedema may develop over a few hours, especially if the prodromal signs are ignored or misinterpreted, and may be accompanied by high-altitude pulmonary oedema. Like acute mountain sickness, the incidence of high altitude cerebral oedema depends on the speed of ascent and the altitude reached, and is less than 0.001% for people travelling to 2500m and approximately 1% for lowlanders travelling to 4000m to 5000m.

Treatment

Anyone with symptoms of high-altitude cerebral oedema should descend immediately. Delay may be fatal. Dexamethasone, 8mg initially, then 4mg every six hours orally or parenterally, will usually relieve some symptoms, making evacuation easier. Similarly oxygen, if available, should be used as an aid to evacuation. Hyperbaric chambers improve oxygenation and relieve symptoms, making unaided descent easier. Even with descent, recovery may be delayed, and good supportive care is essential.

Box 3

Pre-existing medical conditions and altitude illness

Cardiac disease
- The risk of ischaemic heart disease in previously well trekkers is not increased
- Angina of effort at sea level is likely to worsen at altitude, and ascent to moderate altitude may precipitate angina in patients with previously stable coronary artery disease
- Well controlled hypertension is not a contraindication to travel to altitude
- Tests such as an electrocardiogram have no benefit in predicting potential problems at altitude
- Echocardiography while the patient is breathing a hypoxic gas mixture will identify someone whose hypoxic pulmonary vascular response is brisk, but this test is not discriminatory for the development of altitude illness

Asthma
- Asthma is generally unaffected by travel to altitude
- There is no evidence that people with asthma are at greater risk of altitude illness than people without asthma
- Some peak flow meters may be inaccurate at altitude

Chronic obstructive airways disease
- Symptoms at sea level will be worse at altitude, and performance will deteriorate. Infectious exacerbations are a greater risk, so appropriate antibiotics should be carried and treatment started early
- Patients with interstitial lung disease, such as cystic fibrosis, are at high risk of deterioration on travelling to altitude

Diabetes mellitus
- Exposure to altitude in itself does not worsen diabetes
- Symptoms of hypoglycaemia may be confused with high altitude cerebral oedema
- Diabetic patients should have ready access to glucose supplements, and their companions should be aware of the symptoms and management of hypoglycaemia
- Some blood glucose monitors may be inaccurate at altitude

Epilepsy
- Altitude in itself does not increase the risks of seizures in patients with well controlled epilepsy
- The consequences of an epileptic seizure may be more severe in a remote mountain area

High-altitude pulmonary oedema
Diagnosis
Symptoms of high-altitude pulmonary oedema occur most commonly two to three days after arrival at altitude and consist of dyspnoea with exercise, progressing to dyspnoea at rest, a dry cough, weakness, and poor exercise tolerance. As the disease worsens, severe dyspnoea and frank pulmonary oedema are obvious, with coma and death following. Early clinical signs include tachycardia and tachypnoea, mild pyrexia, basal crepitations, and dependent oedema. Patients with high-altitude pulmonary oedema tend to have lower oxygen saturations than unaffected people at the same altitude, but the degree of desaturation by itself is not a reliable sign of high-altitude pulmonary oedema.

High altitude pulmonary oedema rarely occurs below 2500m. Its incidence is 0.0001% at 2700m, increasing to 2% at 4000m. Speed of ascent, exercise during or immediately after ascent, male sex, youth, and individual susceptibility are all risk factors.

Pathophysiology
The pathophysiological cause of high altitude pulmonary oedema is still unknown, although several mechanisms have been proposed.[3] Due to patchy pulmonary hypertension, stress failure occurs in capillaries of over perfused areas, leading to pulmonary oedema. It is not clear whether the inflammatory mediators detected in the oedema fluid reflect an underlying inflammatory cause or are a consequence of another process.

Recent work with people susceptible to high-altitude pulmonary oedema indicates that deficiencies in clearance of alveolar fluid may also contribute to high altitude pulmonary oedema.[13]

Treatment
Descent is the mainstay of treatment. Descent of even a few hundred metres may be beneficial.[2, 3] Supplemental oxygen should be given if available. Nifedipine is effective in preventing and treating high altitude pulmonary oedema in susceptible individuals (10 mg orally initially, then 20 mg slow release preparation over 12 hours). A portable hyperbaric chamber has been developed that simulates descent. This consists of an airtight bag, which is pressurised by means of a manual pump. Continuous pumping is needed. The chamber may be claustrophobic, and lying down in it may worsen orthopnoea. Despite these problems the chamber remains popular and is carried by many larger expeditions.

Predicting altitude illness
Can doctors predict who is likely to develop altitude illness? An individual's past experience is in general a good guide, although there have been well-documented exceptions. Otherwise, tests undertaken at sea level are disappointingly poor at predicting altitude illness. Level of fitness, simple

Box 4

Children, pregnant women, and elderly people at altitude

Children
- Altitude illness seems to have the same incidence in children as in adults, but the diagnosis may be delayed in children too young to describe their symptoms.
- Any child who becomes unwell at altitude should be assumed to be having altitude illness unless a clear alternative diagnosis is obvious.
- The principles of treatment are the same as in adults.
- Lowland infants taken to altitude are at risk of developing pulmonary hypertension and subacute mountain sickness, also called high altitude heart disease.
- It remains unclear whether ascent to altitude increases the risk of sudden infant death syndrome.

Pregnant women
- There are very few data on the risks of travelling to altitude when pregnant.
- Studies from altitude residents indicate few differences in fetal oxygenation at altitudes below 3000 metres.
- Data from small studies and the experience of the airline industry indicate that exposure to normal aircraft cabin pressure or altitudes above 2500 metres in later pregnancy up to 37 weeks is safe, provided that no other complications of pregnancy have occurred.
- There are very few data about pregnant lowlanders travelling to altitudes above 2500 metres.
- Conditions that reduce maternal oxygenation, such as altitude illness, carboxyhaemoglobin (exposure to cigarettes and fires), or other conditions impairing oxygen carriage, should be avoided or treated aggressively.

Elderly people
- The risk of altitude illness does not seem to increase with increasing age.
- Provided a traveller is fit, age in itself is not a barrier to travel.
- Exercise capacity and performance may be reduced and may also be affected by other medical conditions.
- Elderly patients should limit their activity during the first few days at altitude to allow acclimatisation to take place.

measures of lung function, and vascular or pulmonary responses to hypoxia are all inconsistent in predicting individual susceptibility to altitude illness,[2,3] and small innovative studies have not as yet been confirmed in larger trials.[14]

Additional educational resources

Societies

- Medical Expeditions (www.medex.org.uk/) is a research charity dedicated to investigating the mechanisms of altitude related illness. The organisation runs courses in high altitude medicine and physiology and from 2003 will be organising a diploma in mountain medicine
- The International Society for Mountain Medicine (www.ismmed.org/) aims to encourage research and the dissemination of practical information about mountain medicine around the world
- The International Mountaineering and Climbing Federation (UIAA; www.uiaa.ch/) is the umbrella society for climbing organisations
- The Wilderness Medical Society (www.wms.org/) aims to improve scientific knowledge in matters related to wilderness environments and human activities in these environments

Journals and journal articles

- *High Altitude Medicine and Biology* Wilderness and Environmental Medicine
- Bibliography of *High Altitude Medicine and Physiology* (http://annie.cv.nrao.edu/habibqbe.htm) lists 8600 references on high altitude medicine and physiology
- A J Pollard, D R Murdoch, *The High-altitude Medicine Handbook*. Abingdon: Radcliffe Medical Press, 1998
- M P Ward, J S Milledge, J B West, *High-altitude Medicine and Physiology*[2], the definitive UK text for altitude medicine.
- T F Hornbein, R B Schoene, *High-altitude exploration of human adaptation*[3] contains a collection of detailed essays on the pathophysiology of altitude related disease.
- J B West, *High Life - A history of high altitude physiology and medicine*. New York: Oxford University Press, 1998
- S Niermeyer, *The Pregnant Altitude Visitor*. Adv Exp Med Biol 1999; 474:65-77
- A J Peacock, *Oxygen at High Altitude*. BMJ 1998; 317:1063-6. (See also references 3, 11, and 16.)

Information for patients

- Emedicine on line: (www.emedicine.com/emerg/ENVIRONMENTAL.htm) is an online emergency medicine textbook with chapters on altitude illness.
- CIWEC Clinic Travel Medicine Center (http://ciwec-clinic.com/) provides information from Kathmandu on altitude illness and traveller's diarrhoea.
- The Himalayan Rescue Association (HRA; www.himalayanrescue.com) is a voluntary organisation that aims to reduce casualties in the Nepal Himalaya.
- *The High Altitude Medicine Guide* (www.high-altitude-medicine.com/) provides current medical information for doctors and non-doctors on the prevention, recognition, and treatment of altitude illness.

REFERENCES

1 R Roach, C Houston, P Hackett, J P Richalet, *Bibliography of high-altitude medicine and physiology*. April 2002 http://annie.cv.nrao.edu/habibqbe.htm

2 M P Ward, J S Milledge, J B West, *High altitude medicine and physiology*. 3rd ed. London: Arnold, 2000.

3 T F Hornbein, R B Schoene, *High-altitude Exploration of Human Adaptation*. New York: Marcel Dekker, 2001. (*Lung biology in health and disease*, Vol 161.)

4 D R Shlim, J Gallie, 'The causes of death among trekkers in Nepal' in *Int J Sports Med 1992*; 13 (suppl 1): S74-S76.

5 I Singh, P K Khanna, M C Srivastava, M Lal, S B Roy, 'Subramanyam CS. Acute mountain sickness' in *N Engl J Med 1969*, 280: 175-184.

6 A J Pollard, C Clarke, 'Deaths during mountaineering at extreme altitude' in *Lancet 1988*, i: 1277.

7 J S Milledge, J M Beeley, J Broome, N Luff, M Pelling, D Smith, 'Acute mountain sickness susceptibility, fitness and hypoxic ventilatory response' in *Eur Respir J 1991*, 4: 1000-1003.

8 D R Woods, H E Montgomery, 'Angiotensin converting enzyme and genetics at high altitude in *High Alt Med Biol 2001*, 2: 201-210.

9 R C Roach, P Bärtsch, P H Hackett, O Oelz, 'The Lake Louise acute mountain sickness scoring system' in J R Sutton, G Coates, C S Houston, eds. *Hypoxia and molecular medicine*, Burlington, VT: Queen City Printers, 1993: 272-274.

10 P H Hackett, 'High altitude cerebral oedema and acute mountain sickness: a pathophysiology update' in *Adv Exper Med Biol 1999*; 474: 23-45.

11   N P Mason NP, 'The physiology of high altitude: an introduction to the cardio-respiratory changes occurring on ascent to altitude' in *Curr Anaesthesia Crit Care 2000*, 11: 34-41.

12   L Dumont, C Mardirosoff, M R Tramer, 'Efficacy and harm of pharmacological prevention of acute mountain sickness: quantitative systemic review' in *BMJ 2000*, 321: 267-272.

13   C Sartori, Y Allerman, H Duplain, M Lepori, M Egli, E Lipp, et al. 'Salmeterol for the prevention of high altitude pulmonary oedema' in *N Engl J Med 2002*, 346: 1631-1636.

14   D Austin, J Sleigh, 'Prediction of acute mountain sickness' in *BMJ 1995*, 311: 989-990.

15   A J Pollard, S Niermeyer, P Barry, P Bärtsch, F Berghold, R A Bishop, et al, 'Children at altitude' in *High Alt Med Biol 2001*, 2: 389-403.
     A J Pollard, D R Murdoch, P Bärtsch, 'Children in the mountains' in *BMJ 1998*, 316: 874-875.

ACKNOWLEDGEMENTS

We thank Jim Milledge and David Murdoch for their helpful comments on the paper and Brownie Schoene and David Murdoch for permission to reproduce figures.

The third edition of the *High Altitude Medicine Handbook* by Andrew J Pollard and David R Murdoch was published in August 2003.

KEN ALDRED

Bill Tilman's Flower

When the Yorkshire Rambler's Club made their visit to the Rolwaling in 1997 a small group of less energetic members accompanied the main party as far as Kathmandu and then carried on to trek into the Khumbu region with the intention of meeting up later in Namche Bazar. The main purpose of this group was to walk to Everest Base Camp and to include a few peaks such as Kala Pattar on the way. A bonus, however, as far as some of the members were concerned, was the flora encountered, growing often in places and at heights not anticipated. Just below the summit of Gokyo Ri at 17,000ft and with the early morning sun offering some warmth, we saw beautiful examples of *Saussurea tridactyla*. With almost no snow about, this hairy plant provided its own microclimate in an area where temperatures would often be well below freezing point.

Later, when camping at the foot of the Cho La at 14,000ft and enduring a night-time temperature of minus 12°C, we saw *Delphinium glaciale* in flower. There were no traces of snow at the foot of the pass so that it appeared that our lack of success at home with these plants could no longer be explained by the excuse that in the wild they were protected by a deep cover of snow.

Between Namche Bazar and Phortse were numerous patches of *Gentiana depressa* but we saw one plant which no member of the party could identify. It had a small pale starry blue flower and lanceolate leaves. Shortly after returning home, I was watching a video of *Flowers of the Everest Region* (Alpine Garden Society) when I saw what appeared to be the same flower referred to as *Gentiana tilmanii*. *The Encyclopaedia of Alpine Flowers* made no reference to the plant and three specialist books on gentians also didn't list it. The Alpine Garden Society couldn't throw any light on the matter and the maker and presenter, George Smith, had died. The Royal Horticultural Society didn't have the plant listed on their internet site. The lack of information was puzzling. An appeal in the newsletter of the Alpine Garden Society for help brought a reply from a member, Peter Boardman, that he possessed some of the field notes and slides of the late George Smith. In them was a reference to *Gentiana tilmanii*, giving its location and a brief description but no indication of the origin of its name. The original naming of the plant became more intriguing.

Tilman's book *Nepal Himalaya* gave some useful clues. In 1949 he was in the Langtang valley with Oleg Polunin, the botanist who produced an excellent book on Himalayan plants, although it makes no reference to

Gentiana tilmanii. An interesting note which unfortunately didn't help the search was that when seeds were sent to the British Museum from this expedition they were labelled 'HWT'. A year later Tilman had Col D G Lowndes, another eminent botanist, in his party. Lowndes had a number of plants, such as *Rhododendron lowndesii* and *Gentianella lowndesii* named after him, but the flower *Gentiana tilmanii* does not appear in any of his papers.

A search through the British Museum publication of the plants of Nepal resulted in no information on this particular plant but did note that George Smith was in Nepal with Christopher Grey-Wilson in the early 1970s. Grey-Wilson wrote an article in the *Alpine Garden Society Journal* which included a comment that the gentian had been found in the lower Khung Khola.

Following searches in the library of the Royal Botanic Garden in Edinburgh it was their herbarium which supplied the first positive results. The herbarium possesses four samples of material listed as *G. tilmanii*, found at Lula Khola (1952), Muktinath (1954), above Seng Khola (1954) and Tegar, not of Mustang (1954). There is a further sample listed as *G. huxleyi* (syn *G. tilmanii*). All the samples are credited to Harry Smith. A helpful note from the herbarium states that '*G. tilmanii* is one of Harry Smith's many unpublished names. He sometimes put names on herbarium speciemens and never published them.' The report then goes on to state that 'we have them listed under *G. marginata* but this is a species which needs further work to determine whether it includes more than one thing or not. Harry Smith obviously thought that these were different.'

The Natural History Museum provided more information on Harry Smith's part in this work. It appears that he went through the museum's *Gentiana* holdings in 1958 and 'found what he considered to be a new species, which he called *G. tilmanii*. He identified five specimens as this species, four of them being Stainton, Sykes and Williams specimens and the fifth being from D G Lowndes, collected on 9 September 1950. It was this last one which Smith intended to cite as being the type – the original – specimen for his new species.' These last two sentences appear to supply the final piece to the puzzle. Tilman and Lowndes were together in 1950 and it was specimens collected by *them*, which became the intended type species.

Until further work is done with the existing herbarium material it is doubtful whether we shall hear anything further of *Gentiana tilmanii*. Searching for it has been an interesting exercise, and it would appear that our only hope of growing this plant at home is to search for *Gentiana marginata*, as an alternative in specialist seed catalogues. Oleg Polunin describes *G. marginata* as 'from Afghanistan to Uttar Pradesh 2700m-4300m. Open slopes. May-Aug. Like *carinata* but differing in its more crowded out-curved sickle-shaped leaves, its conspicuous out-curved calyx-lobes, and its corolla-tube without scales at the throat. Flowers bright to pale blue, to 12mm long. Plant usually densely branched and forming a nearly stemless domes cluster usually 2cm-5cm across, but sometimes more.'

176 THE ALPINE JOURNAL 2003

ACKNOWLEDGEMENTS

The brief report in the preceding article is the result of considerable help from a number of sources. Thanks to Marissa Main of the Herbarium at the Royal Botanic Garden in Edinburgh, Roy Vickery, Curator of Vascular Plants at the Natural History Museum and Dr A C Leslie, the Senior Registrar of the Royal Horticultural Society. Also, Jim Jermyn, Tony Schilling, Peter Boardman and David Hardman for their useful leads.

Looking Back

Looking Back

DENNIS GRAY

Down and Out in Kathmandu and Bombay

And the end of the fight is a tombstone white,
   with the name of the late deceased,
And the epitaph drear: 'A fool lies here
   who tried to hustle the East.'

Rudyard Kipling, *The Naulahka*

Early in December 1964, at the end of an expedition to Gauri Sankar, I was camping on my own in the grounds of the British Embassy in Kathmandu. Don Whillans and the other four members of our team, Ian Howell, Dez Hadlum, Ian Clough and Terry Burnell, determined to get home for Christmas, had departed just a few days earlier in our expedition Land Rover to begin the drive back to England. I had travelled out by the same means, while Don had accompanied the gear by ship, train and road to Nepal. It was now my job to escort our remaining stores back to the UK, travelling in reverse order.

In those days the Nepalese customs were merciless and you paid duty on the stores you used up: food, fuel, or ropes, and any items such as a tent abandoned damaged in a storm. Everything else had to be crated and taken back to where it had come from or you faced severe financial penalties. In the early 1960s there were no trekking agencies and very few expeditions, so there was little or no market for high-priced climbing equipment and personal effects. This, then, was the daunting task that faced me.

I had two shipping crates, each weighing several hundredweights, to get from Kathmandu to Bombay, but before their lids could be nailed down I had to clear every single item with HM Customs. This took many days of patient negotiation, but life did have its compensations. First and foremost was my situation in the Kathmandu Valley, with outstanding views while I moved around its environs on foot from a base camp in the grounds of the British Embassy. The ambassador, Mr Duff, had arranged for me to be served breakfast, the full English variety, in my tent on a tray, with the food set on silver platters with a royal crest engraved upon them and a beautiful china tea service alongside. All this was delivered each morning by a bearer in full dress uniform.

The weather in December was stunning, cold enough at night to wake up each morning to a ground frost, but pleasantly warm during the day. The atmosphere was crystal clear with little in the way of pollution from the wood fires used for cooking and heating in the city. The Kathmandu Valley was enchanting, with no tourists to speak of, for entry into the country was tightly controlled. A visitor's visa allowed travel just within the Valley itself and there was accommodation available only in a single hotel. This was the famous Royal which had the only bar in town, the Yak and Yeti, run by an archetypal, thickset and heavily-jowled White Russian named Boris. He had, I was told from several reliable sources, escaped the Russian revolution, riding a mule laden with gold and crossing the main Himalayan chain to reach this Shangri-La. One night, after a few beers, I challenged him with the truth of this story. He smiled enigmatically and assured me that he was 'only a poor man trying to make a living'. In an alcoholic mood of bonhomie I sympathised with him because my own funds were rapidly diminishing, and I had no idea whether I had enough money to get home again to Yorkshire.

Before I could set out to test my penny-pinching skills, relying on our scant remaining funds to blag my way to Bombay, I had to shrug the customs men off my back. They were probably giving me a hard time because Whillans, on arriving in Nepal with our gear by road, had been involved in a physical confrontation with some of their colleagues at Raxaul on the frontier with India. Perhaps not such a good idea when dealing with bureaucrats.

But there were further compensations for these delays. I used to toddle off down to the huge building where the government was housed in the old Rana palace, the Singha Durbar, and sit and drink tea and have a chat with the Foreign Minister, himself a Mr Rana. He was a tiny, jolly, friendly old chap whose family had ruled Nepal for a hundred years. He dressed traditionally and as we drank our tea he schooled me about the country and its history. Kathmandu had then about 100,000 inhabitants and the whole valley probably five times that number. This is a huge area and to travel out to one of the small towns on the perimeter could take hours. It was also a journey back in time to almost medieval conditions. The airport at Gauchar – 'Cow's Field' – was small and couldn't take jet planes. There was a single road out of the valley, the Rajpath completed in the late 1950s, leading south towards India.

Mr Rana could not understand why Western people were always in such a hurry, and he assured me that once all the formalities had been completed I would be allowed to leave with my precious boxes. Meanwhile, why not enjoy myself, explore the valley, find out more about his country's history and people and make new friends?

Boris was not the only escapee in Kathmandu at that time. It was like a frontier town, and camping down on the banks of the Bagmati River were many Tibetans. They were not then allowed into town in any numbers. In fact the Nepalese were quite frightened of them, but the man in charge of their welfare as the commissioner for refugees was Peter Aufschnaiter, the man who had led the German 1939 Nanga Parbat expedition, of which Heinrich Harrer had been a member. With Harrer, he had later escaped from a British internment camp in India to reach Tibet and Lhasa.

Reading Harrer's *Seven Years in Tibet* you do not find out much about this interesting man, and it was not clear to me what his exact role had been in that famous adventure. Now I feel privileged to have met him. I was introduced to him by Erwin Schneider and was subsequently invited to visit the Tibetan refugee camp, which was extensive with hundreds of men, women and children living in primitive conditions of extreme poverty. The thing that initially impressed me about the man, apart from his physical presence – he was a big fellow – was his command of languages. He seemed to be able to speak so many. Tibetan of course, but all the other local dialects, and we held a discourse in the Yak and Yeti speaking in a mixture of several European tongues. His knowledge of the Nepalese languages and Tibetan was so good that he was the advisor on place names to the government on what were to be the first complete maps of Nepal, an exercise then under way and led by Schneider and Kinzl.

It was fascinating to hear from Peter at first hand about his participation in the early attempts on Kangchenjunga (1929 and 1931), and about the 1939 Nanga Parbat expedition. His party had reconnoitred the Diamir flank, had found a possible route and had intended to return to attempt it in 1940. Most interesting of all were the stories about his escape from India and his years in Tibet. The thing that remained uppermost in his mind from this escapade was the journey from Dehra Dun to Lhasa when he and Harrer had crossed the Himalaya and journeyed for many months to reach their goal. He was neither a critical nor a bitter man. The mood he struck was one of serene gentleness, which perhaps his life in Tibet had developed. He was obviously totally committed to his work with the Tibetans who had fled the Chinese occupation of their homeland. However he did warn me not to accept the whole of the story as portrayed in Harrer's book. He pointed out that without him it was unlikely that the latter would have been successful in reaching Lhasa and getting accepted there, for Peter was the linguist and had been East several times before 1939, whereas Harrer had not. Furthermore, Harrer had over-dramatised their roles and positions in Tibet. But it was also obvious that Aufschnaiter was not seeking any kind of redress, and still thought well of his companion. He would not be drawn any further and changed the subject to ask me about our trip to Gauri Sankar during which we had actually been inside Tibet while high on the mountain.

Erwin Schneider was someone I kept running into, either in the Royal Hotel or about Kathmandu, and we became friends. He was then working on the mapping of the Rolwaling Himalaya and he was keen to get as much information a possible from me about the Gauri Sankar area. I may be wrong but I think in that era no one had the depth of knowledge of the mountains of the world, or had made so many important first ascents as he had. He seemed to have been everywhere, for he was one of the pioneers of the Cordilleras Blanca and Huayhuash in Peru, the Pamirs, and of course the Himalaya. Along with his colleague Hans Kinzl he was a cartographer of the highest ability – the Austrians were the official map-makers to HM government – and their maps of Mount Everest, the Cordillera Blanca, Mount Kenya and so on set a standard that others were to follow. Later I felt privileged to be invited to Innsbruck in 1965 to visit their map-making department, and to watch them working on a section of the Rolwaling map aided by some of my transparencies from the northern side of the range.

I imagine that as a young man, Erwin was a bit of a Whillans figure. The stories about him on the disastrous 1934 Nanga Parbat expedition, when he emerged along with Peter Aschenbrenner as the lead climber, are ones of a pushy, aggressive and very determined character. In old age he still looked like a bit of a bruiser, squat and physically powerful, but by the time I knew him he was avuncular and very kind to me. To hear from him first-hand about that 1934 expedition was gripping. He and Aschenbrenner reached over 25,000ft and were within striking distance of the summit, still feeling fit and strong. But due to poor organisation, and a lack of back-up in the supply chain, they were forced to descend. It was during this descent that a storm of the utmost ferocity hit the mountain, and six Sherpas plus Merkl, the expedition leader, Wieland and Welzenbach all died.

The story is well known and has become one of the most written about and analysed events in mountaineering history. Claims have been made that Aschenbrenner and Schneider abandoned the porters, and skied off down the mountain to save their own skins.* Knowing Erwin as I did after our time in Kathmandu, I find this hard to believe, for the storm they were in was one of those that comes along perhaps once in a generation. The only explanation I can think of for what happened is that the effects of altitude and Himalayan conditions were not as fully understood then as they were later. And the European climbers of that time had come to an exaggerated opinion of a Sherpa's ability to withstand cold and hardship, and to move around safely in a mountain environment.

In terms of technical climbing experience they were near novices, and once Europeans had acclimatised, Sherpas were not superior to them physically. But because of their hardiness, willingness and outstanding good nature, a myth had grown up that they were able to withstand any amount of bad weather conditions. I can imagine how Erwin would think that on such easy ground, down which he could ski, these hardy hill men would have no difficulty in following them. Whatever the truth as to their motivation, Aschenbrenner and Schneider did come to regret their decision and tried several times to get back up the mountain to execute a rescue. But each time they were beaten back by snowfall and avalanches.

* **Editor's note:** These allegations were largely accepted among older Sherpas in Darjeeling and were repeated to the Editor by Ang Tsering, who died in 2002 and was the last Sherpa to make it off the mountain in 1934, having also been on Everest with Mallory in 1924.

It was meeting Erwin that made me want to go to Peru. He sent me photographs of Alpamayo, pointing out that despite claims to the contrary by a Franco-Belgian team that had included Claude Kogan, its north ridge had still not been successfully climbed to the main summit. This party had actually only reached the north peak, but in bad weather had mistaken this for the top.

Erwin had been one of the mentors to Hermann Buhl, and when the latter and Kuno Rainer had been amongst the first Austrians to visit the Western Alps after the war, he had accompanied them. It was obvious that he had the highest regard for Buhl, but he was surprised when I told him my opinion that apart from our own stars, Brown and Whillans, this Austrian climber had had more of an impact on British mountaineers of my generation than any other.

'What was he really like?' I asked him one night in the Yak and Yeti after a few beers.

He thought for a while and replied: 'A good singer and guitar player, so he was good company!'

Someone I also kept running into was Kathmandu resident Jimmy Roberts. Jimmy had been military attaché at the Embassy and was a former Gurkha officer. Then recently retired, he had been with the Americans on their successful Everest expedition the previous year. For our attempt on Gauri Sankar he had been very helpful, hand-picking four of the best Sherpas to go with us.

He had an encyclopaedic knowledge of the Himalaya. After our near success on Gauri Sankar, when Whillans and Ian Clough had nearly succeeded in climbing the north face of the mountain, I had become interested in trying one of the higher mountains by such a route. After talking with Jimmy and Erwin about this possibility, I settled on the South Face of Annapurna of which the former produced a fine photograph. As soon as I saw it I decided that this was to be it, for running the height of the face was a spur similar to the Walker on the Grandes Jorasses. Before I left Kathmandu I went to see Mr Rana, and gained a promise of permission for this route, but it was not to be. An incident the following year stopped my plan dead in its tracks. A group of Tibetan Khampas attacked a Chinese baggage train. A Westerner, who was also a mountaineer of sorts, filmed the fighting and his film was smuggled out of Nepal inside a diplomatic bag. This led to a confrontation with China and the closing of Nepal to mountaineers almost until the end of the decade.

In retrospect Kathmandu in 1964 was poised on the edge of the biggest change in its history. India and China, with the USA putting up the largest number of dollars, were all vying for influence and offering to fund aid projects. And the British in their own quiet and quaint way were also, as the original and oldest foreign power in town, doing their best to keep up with these competing forces. One initiative taken by Britain under the Colombo Plan was to set up the first printing plant in Nepal. Because of my background in the industry I was invited along by Mr Duff to observe its progress. The sight that greeted me on arrival was incredible. The operation was set in a huge yard, which looked more like a brick works than a printing press. A Brit by the name of Mr Page was in charge and he was teaching the Nepalese involved how to set lead metal type. Arranged around the yard were heaps of letters, a huge pile of 'As', in another pile 'Bs', and in yet another 'Cs' and so on. The compositors had their sticks and were wandering from pile to pile trying to set up words. I was gob-smacked to learn later from Mr Page in the Yak and Yeti that he was charged with printing for the first time the laws of Nepal. He was expecting later that week to receive via India two Heidelberg cylinder printing machines and had been given about three years to finish the job. Through the diplomatic bag he was getting a regular supply of Johnny Walker, so he and I became friends as I commiserated with him over a dram or two about the difficulties he was facing.

Another British initiative I came across while hanging out in Kathmandu, was a plan to introduce the Nepalese to the works of William Shakespeare. A cast of locals directed by a thespian imported by the British Council were to perform Macbeth and I was invited along to this performance in an assembly hall not far from the Singha Durbar. Unfortunately for the actors, it had a tin roof, as well as a stage.

The night was unusually cold, even for December, and it looked stormy as I walked along to the venue from the Embassy where we had gathered for a pre-performance drink with the cream of the diplomatic corps. No sooner had the performance started than it began to hail and then thunder. Sitting at the back of the hall all I could hear was the crash of huge hailstones on the roof, which sounded like an enormous drum being beaten again and again. This continued on and off for most of the evening but putting on a brave face at the end of the performance, which few if any of the audience had heard, Mr Duff congratulated the cast and declared the evening a resounding success.

It was after this performance that I met my first-ever hippy in the Yak and Yeti. In 1968, when I was again climbing in the Himalaya and taking up a travelling fellowship around India, they were ten a penny, but in 1964 in Kathmandu she was a trailblazer. Sue had come from California to seek enlightenment. A wonderful blonde goddess of 21 from Los Angeles, she was looking for a guru, and I think she found him. The next time I saw her she was with someone who looked a little like the Maharishi of Beatles fame. She was following two paces behind him wearing a sari, bedecked in beads and bangles and walking barefoot through the bazaar. She carried a drum which she kept hitting at irregular intervals.

After an introduction by Jimmy Roberts I went to visit Willi Unsoeld, who was then head of the Peace Corps in Nepal. Willi was still learning to cope with the loss of most of his toes after his great climb the year before of the West Ridge of Mount Everest with Tom Hornbein. It was impossible to be indifferent to Willi. He was a muscular Christian, a professor of religion and philosophy no less, and he soon made me aware of this fact. Bearded, powerfully built, he seemed to me unorthodox. If it had not been for his higher religious calling, I could have imagined him embracing the hippy lifestyle. He had not been in post long, but already he was the subject of gossip amongst some I talked to in Kathmandu; how he simply sent his Peace Corps volunteers out into the villages of Nepal in a sink or swim approach. Most seemed to survive the experience and do well, which was probably Unsoeld's intention. I found him an open and enthusiastic talker and his story of the Everest adventure held me enthralled. But he seemed to me, like so many Americans to those of us who grew up as part of the working class in northern Britain, a mixture of obvious goodness and earnestness, but heavy on sentiment and with not a trace of irony. I couldn't imagine Joe Brown talking like that, but then Willi grew up in a different country and another culture.

At last I was given the all clear by HM Customs to nail down my boxes, and I set out with my cargo, riding in a Sikh's lorry to the Indian border. As we left the Embassy the whole staff turned out to see me off. I had a lump in my throat as I waved goodbye to them all. The Duffs had been more than kind and I owed them a debt of gratitude. But in all truth my main concern was how I was going to travel to Bombay to catch the boat back to Liverpool.

The first leg of the journey set the pattern for what was to follow. It took two days to get from Kathmandu to Raxaul, with the road best described as challenging. I already knew what to expect for I had travelled up and down to the Indian border in a lorry when Whillans arrived. Thanks to his difficulties with the Nepalese authorities, he arrived in Kathmandu minus our gear, which was impounded. I had to go down and retrieve it. It was an adventure just to travel this route, and the way was littered with wrecks and lorries in various states of disrepair. All movement had to finish before dark since it was judged too dangerous to drive at night. I slept with the driver and his mate in the lorry, and arrived hungry and tired at Raxaul late on the second day.

Moving the crates into the railway station waiting room, where I spent the night lying on them for security, was a major operation, and took the effort of twenty men. I was living off bowls of rice and mugs of sweet tea. Next day I got a shock trying to book through to Bombay on the train. It transpired that I could only book to Benares and there had to change stations onto another railway line, and then pay from there to Bombay.

Later that same morning the boxes were loaded into the luggage car of the Benares train, again by twenty hired men. Riding third class to conserve what few rupees I now had left, I became very worried as the train rumbled southwards. The boat journey would be alright because I had the return ticket that Don had come out on, and the shipping line was carrying our gear for free, but had I enough funds to get me to Bombay?

If you have never travelled third class in India you may have missed out on a life-changing experience. I still thank my good luck that this took place at the end of December and not in July. If it had been hot I might not have lasted the course.

Getting from one railway station in Benares to the other, across the city, with my two boxes carried by twenty porters, created a sensation. And when I paid them, the hired hands must have thought me the meanest sahib this side of the Ganges. I had to sleep on the boxes again, but lying in this elevated position set on the station platform, I felt like a potentate compared to the mass of Haridjans sleeping in their thousands around me. It was the only home they knew.

The last leg to Bombay was totally without comfort, taking the best part of two days, in the most cramped, uncomfortable conditions one could imagine. The smell of human sweat and excreta hit the olfactory senses like a Whillans right-hander.

Arriving in Bombay I spent the last of my rupees getting the two crates moved from the railway station into the shipping company's go-down. What a relief! But the boat home was not leaving for another five days, and what do you do for that length of time with no money, without a single anna? And as I became ever more hungry I decided I would have to try to steal some food. I was also worried where I might sleep in Bombay, somewhere that I would be physically safe.

I spent the first night sleeping on the pavement outside the Taj Mahal hotel. Believing this to be the finest hotel in India I assumed the area around it would be secure. I woke up in the early hours when a pair of hands tried to pull the rucksack I was using as a pillow from under my head. I jumped up and screamed, and a little boy of about eight or nine ran off terrified.

Next morning and now desperate with hunger, I walked back down to the harbour, and found, quite literally, salvation. I came across the Red Shield House, the Bombay headquarters of the Salvation Army. I staggered inside, weak from lack of food and drink, to be greeted by a major from Barnsley. Ever since, I have had a high regard for the Salvation Army, for they fed and watered me, and offered shelter until the boat sailed for Liverpool. I had to clean the toilets and join in with the hymn singing in return.

The boat trip, taking place during the festive season, chugged slowly back to Britain, calling at Karachi, Port Sudan, Aden, Suez, Naples, Cyprus and so on. I had little or no problem, being the object of charity from my mainly wealthy fellow passengers, eating and drinking like a trencherman. When I arrived in Liverpool five weeks later, Don Whillans and Terry Burnell were waiting on the quayside as our shipping crates were unloaded. They soon had them broken open and the gear stuffed into the expedition Land Rover, which they had driven back to the UK.

'Don't think I came here to meet thee,' Whillans informed me. 'I've only come to get me bloody gear!' I had left home eight months earlier, travelling out for six weeks by road, spending ten weeks in the mountains, and then the wait in Kathmandu followed by the long journey home alone. 'Yer can drive,' Don decided, handing me the keys. Expeditions these days just aren't what they used to be.

SHARON WOOD

Rising

> You experience God when you're extended a long way out beyond
> yourself and still trying to lift up from your fears. Get caught on a rock
> and of course you want to howl like a dog. Surmount that terror and
> you rise to a higher fear. That may be our simple purpose on earth. To
> rise to higher and higher levels of fear.
>
> Norman Mailer

In the summer of 1985 my partner, Carlos Buhler and I climbed a difficult,
untried route on Cerro Huascaran, the highest mountain in Peru. Early
on in the climb my shoulder was broken by a falling rock. We could have
turned around but we didn't. Instead we chose to climb another six days to
the top, the hard way.

This story begins in the pre-dawn light, on the third day of our climb.
Caught, on the side of a massive vertical ice and rock-strewn face, 18,000ft
feet above sea level, in the middle of nowhere, I want to howl like a dog.
We are so committed that I am jolted into being fully extended and alive,
where the only option is to start moving.

It often seems miraculous to me, that we can put ourselves into such
unnatural places as this, places we don't belong and shouldn't be. What is
natural, yet so deeply buried in millennia of domestication, is our instinct
to fight our way through danger and fear and in doing so, discover strengths
that astound us and leave us wanting for more.

My legs dangle over the edge of our small icy ledge chiseled out of the
mountainside. I peer down over my boot tops at the steep ground we have
climbed up and imagine the path of my fall, should I take one. I guess, in a
disconnected way, where I would hit, bounce and slide before I finally came
to a stop on the glacier three thousand feet below.

All climbers do this, I'm sure. There is a fragile denial of this possibility,
a tacit agreement to not challenge it. My mind, in its undisciplined moments
of respite, wanders toward the morbid. As though channel surfing on
television, I'm drawn to the images that most stir my senses.

It is comfortable to consider this now because I won't fall. I am trussed
and tethered firmly to the anchors we pounded in the night before. We
trust they will hold our body weight and a few thousand pounds more.
Save for an earthquake or an act of God, our stance is bombproof. Nothing
is going anywhere. But, in my waiting, I consider this possibility too. After
all, earthquakes frequent this area. In the early 1970s a large piece of this
mountain calved off and obliterated a town miles below. There is way too
much time to ponder and entertain the worst.

This climb is all business and a serious one at that. We eat for fuel, rest to recharge, and look only for information to aid our progress. The object in these kinds of climbs is to impose upon ourselves a challenge that is just a little beyond our reach. The goal is to test and extend that reach. On this climb we are moving too slowly. We never seem to be as far along as we want to be. At yesterday's end we were racing the dying light to find shelter for the night. Our headlamps cut through darkness as we chipped and dug out a ledge big enough to spend the night.

We have spent the last few dark hours sharing a ledge that is no bigger than a small narrow coffee table, sitting up, cocooned in our sleeping bags, fully dressed, our lower bodies crammed into our packs for extra warmth and support to give our feet something to push against. It's bitterly uncomfortable and the only way to relieve this is by shifting from butt cheek to butt cheek. The discomfort is constant and more intense in the night, when we have the time to entertain it.

All I care about is the grey light growing at the edges of the horizon. With the coming of the light the other senses can kick in and distract me, draw me out of the darkness. Fear grows best in the dark. At night's end it has had the longest stretch to run its course. I can't see what it is I fear; therefore it grows ever larger and more menacing. This is when the resolve to be here is at its weakest. What releases the tension is the day's new light. Moving on promises relief.

My right shoulder is stiff from our night's wait. Painkillers – and denial that anything more than bruising has resulted from the blow to my shoulder the day before – tempers the pain. I want to take more drugs but I have to wait. The drugs take a long time to kick in and a long time to leave. Too many drugs deaden my senses, too little causes the pain to distract me from my climbing. Thank God the light is coming.

In the darkness my thoughts race and veer down paths of worry, fear and chance. The severity and consequences of my injury amplify the doubts I have about the climb. Like most climbers, I start monitoring my body, looking for symptoms of something malevolent.

My head hurts, that hangover kind of headache where every movement increases the painful throbbing. The stress of my injury, so it seems, has reversed the acclimatization I have gained from living between 12,000ft and 20,000ft for the last couple of months. The headaches grow stronger, my resting heart rate has increased, and I am coughing more. The fear that I have high-altitude sickness nags away. Give me light, movement and something I can see to rise to. Let this new day begin.

The pain seems worse. I tell myself: 'Pain is just information, not an obstacle nor a reason to stop.' It has to be. It has to be, because my injury is the only hurdle that lies between success and failure. Failure is not an option. Rescue is not an option. No one even knows where we are. By deciding to continue up yesterday we passed the point of no return. The only way out now is up and over. Besides, we will probably top out tomorrow and then be off the mountain the following day.

I tell myself this climb is just a practice joust. Thinking this way diminishes the gravity of our present situation. Everest looms, and not just the ordinary route, but the West Ridge, complicated, technical and demanding. I have to be ready. Climbing a new route on Huascaran is essential to earning my place on the team. There was no one I needed to prove this to more than myself. Only Huascaran can resolve my doubts.

My monomaniacal climbing partner also fuels my resolve to go on. Carlos is a tortured man, plagued by the idea of failure and low self-worth. He defines himself as a climber, a good one when he succeeds and a bad one when he fails. He is as good or as bad as he climbs. He is also my partner in life, and I fear having to live with the same man I climb with through the aftermath of an unsuccessful climbing season, a season of approaches.

But the fear of failure serves me well. Negative reinforcement is my greatest motivator. I fear the aftermath of failure even more than the consequences of going on. Every experience, epic, setback and conquest is an investment in getting better. Better is always possible. Pain and suffering are necessary precursors to the realization of my potential. I thrive by this tenet. I eat it for breakfast, lunch and dinner. Maybe I am borderline monomaniacal myself. I am as good or as bad as I climb.

But the most important thing of all is this question: When I'm on Everest next year and I'm in trouble, in a place I shouldn't be, will I be able to rise and meet the challenge or will I shrink back and succumb to fear? This climb is the test. My performance is the answer. In the two months Carlos and I were climbing in the Cordillera Blanca we had yet to complete a climb together. Each climb we had approached was out of condition, due to dangerous conditions and weather. We could write a guidebook on how to get to climbs where the only thing missing would be the rest of the route to the top of the mountain.

Just last week we reached the crescendo of the season's failures. Our objective had been the steep and intimidating South-west Face of Chacaraju. Following a few days of preparation and heavy load-carrying up to the base of the climb we settled in, prepared to begin the face the next morning. Then it snowed that night and next morning a heavy blanket of new snow clung to the face putting another route out of condition.

I was privately relieved. Thousands of feet above us, rimming the summit ridge like gargoyles menacing the face, cornices the size of small houses teetered on the brink of collapse, waiting. One tap of an axe, a hint of a tremor, a little more weight could cut it all loose to crash down, sweeping anything off the face in its path. Anywhere else in the world, you would not dare climb beneath the fall line of these things. There was little history of climbers being killed by cornice fall but I reasoned there was little climbing history, period. And while luck is often a factor in the climbing recipe,

I didn't want to rely on it until I had to. Good judgement strikes me as more reliable.

Aside from the detail, things just didn't feel right, even though not feeling right can be easily misread for fear. I was dreading the argument, my grappling for the words to articulate and justify this intangible sixth sense. The steadily falling snow made the decision easy. Turning around cost us time and the effort to get up there but even worse was the disruption to our momentum, the erosion of our confidence, even depression. I am left believing I am the obstacle, the one at fault for my reluctance and fear. The 'fraidy cat. Nothing is done on Carlos' part to tell me any different. If I weren't comfortable then we wouldn't do it. It was never him that called it.

It was on our retreat from Chacaraju that I first noticed the East Face of Huascaran, the face we are now on. Sitting atop our packs on a hillside we mused over the possibilities of meddling with that nasty-looking face. The entire side of the mountain was unclimbed. It was an obvious challenge, easy to access but not to climb. Carlos had considered it in the past but deemed it too unsafe. Others had written it off as a 'death route'. The bottom of the face was pockmarked black with rock fall. The north-east exposure was most vulnerable to the heat of the sun, turning the whole face into an active missile range.

I, the 'fraidy cat, was becoming more compelled by the minute to climb it. The appeal of outwitting the danger with good strategy was the very essence of great climbing style, to make the impossible possible, to defy the perceived odds. Or, perhaps it was because this would be our last climb, our last chance to get up anything this season, that we tried so hard to make it seem possible. Or was it because I picked it, not Carlos. I saw it and it called to me.

We determined there was a long enough portion of the day when the face fell into shade to cause the temperature to drop below freezing and keep everything stuck together. We would climb this untried face of Huascaran in the cool of the day and during the hours of sunshine we would seek shelter and sit it out. It was the following week, our spirits buoyed with this strategy, that we alighted from the minivan just below the base of Huascaran Sur.

Early on the morning of 24 July, equipped with four days' food and supplies, we wove our way through the large séracs of the glacier below the face. We had anticipated it would take us a long day to get to the base but we were there in just a few hours. Elated with this boost to our schedule we began to climb.

Eager to begin with the face still in the shade, I burrowed my way through the bergschrund and hoisted Carlos up and through. Together we moved quickly, daggering over the next few hundred feet of 45° to 50° ice to reach a small hole marking the second bergschrund and a point of shelter. There in the cave, poking our heads in and out to look up at the face, we briefly discussed whether to spend the rest of the day and night here in safety or hopscotch a few hundred feet more to the next point of shelter. The air was still cold, the face in shadow, quiet, with no sign of rockfall. Carlos was passive and quiet, while I was eager. The momentum gained from better than anticipated progress pulled me out and set me climbing.

I felt strong, the ice took the tips of my crampon points and tools with a satisfying sound and the feel of a knife puncturing dense Styrofoam. Relief and uncontained excitement fuelled a fast pace despite the sixty-pound pack on my back.

Racing the impending arrival of the sun, Carlos paid out the rope as I climbed the steepening ice. Moving as fast as possible I climbed the full length of the 70-metre ropes, slowing as their weight grew at the end of the pitch. Labouring under the weight of my heavy pack, I hauled the ropes with one hand as I strained for each step. Finally I reached their end and began to set the station, threading a screw into the dense ice.

As its teeth slowly bore into the ice, a sense of foreboding grew turn by turn, eclipsing the previous moment's optimism and feeling of control. My focus narrowed to the small radius I was working over. I was rushing, not panicking, channeling all I had to get the screw in quickly. If anything should cause me to fall this screw would be the only barrier between me and a fall of almost 500 feet. Only when the screw was in just enough to hook my rope over it, to anchor myself temporarily, did I first let myself register my surroundings, the change in quality of light, the feel of the warmer air, and the high-pitched whining of rocks falling past.

An abrupt heavy blow slammed me hard against the face. I heard myself grunt as all the air exploded from my lungs. Not yet registering the full impact of the assault, I thought, 'This must be what it feels like to get shot.' Frozen, like a deer in headlights, with no reference point for what had just happened, I lay still. I could hear the escalating intensity of the barrage of falling rocks and the transition from whistle to whine as they shot by me.

'Sharon! Sharon! Are you okay?' My partner's calls, the coolness of the ice seeping into my chest flattened against the face, and the return of the air to my lungs drew me back up the tunnel to awareness. A force from deep within kicked in, delaying pain and fear, impelling me to action. I yelled down to Carlos, 'I'm getting out of here as fast as I can!'

I know this place, I know enough about getting hurt and the state of shock to know that there is a finite window of time where one has the gift of extraordinary strength and presence of mind to get out of danger's way before immobilization sets in. Much internal dialogue all at once, my inner coaches all worked in perfect unison to take advantage of this window. Another part of me engaged, racing to assess range of mobility, not injury – that would come later. My brain was intact. I could use my left arm and my legs worked.

With slow, mechanical, persistent deliberation I attached myself to the screw with one hand, threaded another screw in and re-rigged the ropes for descent. Calmly, after checking and double-checking, I began lowering, knowing Carlos must be frustrated, helpless to aid me, every passing minute feeling like an hour to him. I yelled down once more, 'Coming. Down. Now!' Making myself as small a target as possible, willing the rock missiles to part around me, I slid down the ropes to the small hole in the face that marked the ice cave where he waited safely.

Carlos popped out of the hole in the face and hauled me in. I slumped down on the snow and before relief could find its place a heavy cloak of dejection settled over us. 'Let's not talk or make any decision now.' Either one of us could have said this. Instead I silently berated myself. How could I have done something so stupid, so easily avoided? There would be no decision made until the next morning. And then, it would be all up to me. I was the injured one. I was the one that had made the bad call. At least we could lie down in the cave and be safe for the time being. Maybe with the night's passing the gravity of this near miss will have diminished and the day will dawn with nothing more than a bruise and renewed resolve.

A new day and a silent face assured us that if we were more vigilant in sticking to our original strategy we could pull this off yet. To start I went second, testing my shoulder. Throughout the day it loosened and my mobility improved. And it is at this place, the chiselled out ledge we reached on the second day, that I now sit, waiting anxiously. In the growing light I can look up the face and see ramps and passages where in the dark my imagination could only see impossible ground.

We leave our alcove of safety and climb over the next couple of days to within reach of the top of the face. By a stroke of good luck we have to wait just a few hours before a thick veil of mist shrouds the face, keeping it cool and safe for us to continue. I can do my share of leads alternating with Carlos, thank goodness. I would lead out to the full extent of the rope's length and fix an anchor point to bring Carlos up and then he would lead out the ropes to establish the next anchor, establishing the familiar cyclical rhythm of engagement and disengagement with our day.

One point on my shoulder is pierced by pain whenever I try to reach above the level of my chest. But it is just information. I can avoid reaching. The muscles in my upper back are in spasm under my heavy pack. I can feel a knife lodged between my shoulder blades. The pain fades when I'm climbing. Better to be distracted, engrossed in finding the next hold, to be simply straining, getting closer to a goal, than to have yet more time to entertain the discomfort. Time slows when my mind and body are still, as I pay out the rope inch by slow inch to my partner as he moves up. Here, my thoughts drift easily to the pain and the impatience of getting up, getting off the climb. I will myself not to anticipate progress or early escape.

The third and final night we bivouac at the base of a 300-foot rock band rimming the top of the face. Hope and optimism prevail, diminishing the fear and symptoms of the altitude sickness I once suspected. Once we reach the East Ridge it will be over. Just one day to a well-trodden route and it will be all downhill.

But it wasn't to be just one day. The next day, hours come and go traversing the base of the rock band looking for a way through to the top. Feeling more and more disheartened as we look for a weakness through the band, we finally settle on a line through the steepest part. It is my lead up through the rock. Eager to sink my teeth into this last problem I start up. But within a few feet I have to do a manoeuvre involving the full extension of my right arm above my head and hauling up on it. This move is impossible but it takes a few moments to convince myself of it. I finally admit defeat and climb back to hand the lead over to Carlos. As I anchor myself back in to prepare to belay him I castigate myself for my inability to pull my weight. Over the course of a couple of hours, Carlos worked slowly, doggedly, winning through to the top of the band. That's his trademark: slow but sure. At the top Carlos starts hauling me up after him.

Just as I dare to anticipate progress I pull up over the top to a sight that makes my heart sink. Carlos had hoisted me inside a cornice where he was belaying me, just like the one I refused to climb under on Chacaraju. Through the hole of the wind-sculpted snow curl I view an endless, serrated knife-edge ridge capped with massive cornices stretching into the mist. This ridge is our only way off. We have not topped out; our climb has just begun. Overtaken by the encroaching darkness, disappointment and trepidation, we make our home inside the cornice for the night. Every move, every turn has to be made carefully for fear of disturbing its fragile hold on the mountain ridge and sending us careening down the West Face. Now, through this night, is where luck comes in.

I am relieved to see next morning that the ridge is shorter than I feared. We thread our way through the gauntlet of giant hanging cornices, climbing on opposite sides of the knife-edge ridge. The rockfall and my injury we could manage, minimising risk and taking control. This traverse is altogether different. We are forced to go this way, there are no options. I pray quietly to keep us from falling the 8000 feet that looms below on either side.

As we arrive at the vast summit plateau, we are engulfed in a shroud of mist, the same mist that had aided us with longer climbing days now rendering us blind to continue. We are forced to spend another night out. The only respite is that we can stretch out to sleep for the first time in five days. At 3.30am with nothing left to drink or eat it takes no time to rise and get moving. We have to get down today.

But within a short time I am too cold to continue. There is no fuel in my tank, my belly empty from lack of food, my extremities stiff and clumsy. We stop once more and share one sleeping bag to wait for light and more warmth. Now I am drifting dangerously close to the edge of losing resolve and faith. But this is Peru, I say to myself, not the Himalaya.

Light brings warmth and we start out once more. I swear silent oaths to believe in God forever more if I reach the well-trodden trough that will guide us back down the other side with relative ease. At midday we intercept some Spanish friends of Carlos who had just climbed the regular route the day before and are camped before they descend. Coming upon the Spanish camp was like discovering an oasis in a long desert march. We get a warm welcome and plenty of food, delicious cheeses, breads and meats. I draw strength from their robust congratulatory handshakes and hugs. Discreetly we snatch bits as often as possible without looking as desperately hungry as we really are. We gorge ourselves to fuel the rest of the long slog down the mountain.

Two days later we got home. Just days before I had been immersed in the intensity of staying warm, alive and resolute. I only wished to feel safe and comfortable. One part of me wished that a climb like this could bring me satisfaction and lessen the need to rise again to the fears these extreme experiences imposed. Another part of me was already nurturing a restlessness, craved that altered state of feeling, of being purposeful, fully engaged and alive.

As though looking at scenery from a moving car, memories of Huascaran fell behind as fast as the forward view rushed in. It was business as usual. Carlos went back to training and raising money and enthusiasm for the next climb and me to guiding.

I still could not raise my arm without pain. That evening after work I went to the hospital for answers and an hour later a doctor confirmed the thin white line running through the illuminated x-ray of my shoulder was a fracture. I arrived home later that same evening to find Carlos sitting at our kitchen table absorbed in telling our story to a newspaper reporter. To the delight of both of them and – dare I admit it – even myself, news of my broken bones made the story larger and better. When he had his story, the reporter asked what was next. I felt that anticipation rising inside me again. Everest. Everest was next.

In 1986, Sharon Wood became the first North American woman to climb Everest, via the West Ridge.

JOHN JACKSON

Skye - Sixty Years Ago

In the late 1930s my brother Ron bought a motorbike and sidecar for £5. It was an old side-valve Ariel, which never went very fast but slogged away all day, without any trouble. We called it the 'Iron Lung' and it was really, because it transported us to the fresh clean air of the moorlands and hills. Ron quickly learned to drive and after a few sorties to Ilkley, Almscliffe and the Lake District, we planned to have two weeks in Scotland and the Isle of Skye.

I remember my feelings of excitement and anticipation as we sped northwards across the border for the first time, knowing we were on the road to the Isles. We threaded our way through Glasgow, took the twisting road by Loch Lomond, climbed over Rannoch Moor and then swept into Glen Coe. Evening clouds drifted slowly down the valley and swirled among the deep gullies of Aonach Eagach. Away to the left, the rocky bastion of Crowberry Ridge loomed through the mists that twisted and curled over the faces, ribs and clefts of Buachaille Etive Mór. It seemed appropriate for our first visit to the Glen of Weeping.

At Arisaig the next day we arrived at the western seaboard, looked across to the misty Hebrides and saw our first Scottish black-faced sheep. Further along the road we reached Mallaig where the herring fleet had returned the night before. All the boats were tied up at the jetty and the fishermen were mending their nets, tough, kindly and soft-spoken men. They took us over the sea, to Skye.

It took a long day riding past Beinn na Caillich and round the shores of Loch Ainort to Sligachan where we caught sight of the jagged dark line of peaks, the Cuillin. Out came the guidebook, revealing the magic of the Cuillin names, Sgurr nan Gillean, the peak of the young men, the axe-shaped tooth of Am Basteir, its name obscure but often supposed to mean 'the executioner'. Beyond we could see Bruach na Frithe, the brae of the deer forest, and the start of Bidein Druim nan Ramh, the peak of the ridge of oars.

From Sligachan we sped round by Carbost then bounced along the dusty, boulder-strewn track into Glen Brittle. There ahead was Sgurr an Fheadain, the peak of the water pipe, the serrations of the many peaks of the foxes, Sgurr a'Mhadaidh and the noble Sgurr a'Ghreadaidh, the peak of the mighty winds. These strong names made a permanent impression on my mind, perhaps even more because of the wet and windy days that followed. It also helped that later we made friends with two Gaelic speakers who carefully trained us in the meaning and pronunciation of the names.

At the end of the day we stayed at a little white-washed cottage then owned by Mr and Mrs Chisholm. It was the post office with the unforgettable number of Glen Brittle 1. The waters of Loch Brittle came right up to the little cottage garden which grew crops of peas, beans and potatoes and because of the seaweed being used for fertiliser smelled strongly of the sea. That evening was a fitting end to an exciting day as the sun sank down into the western sea and its ruddy glow lit the massive gabbro walls of Sron na Ciche and the rock ridge of Sgurr Dearg, the red peak against a soft blue sky. Unfortunately this was the last distant view we had of the ridge. For the next ten days the misty island lived up to its name. Despite the weather they were a memorable ten days as is often the way in mountains when difficult conditions extend achievements and experiences.

After the short fierce gritstone ascents at Widdop, Almscliff and Ilkley, and then the longer routes in Cumbria, Sron na Ciche seemed a good progression. We climbed the gully, face and direct of the Cioch, the rough rock smoothing our finger ends until they were almost too sore to grip, the crystalline gabbro biting deep into the soft iron of our climber nails. Heavy rain swelled the hemp rope, its weight a hindrance as the wind curled it away from us, across the water-washed rock face. Up into the clouds we went, towards the Crack of Doom and climbs on Cioch Upper Buttress.

It was on the Upper Buttress that Ron and I saw our first rope slings and a strange, artificial contraption a small team of Welsh climbers called a karabiner. We were surprised that such aids and safety devices should be used in a sport that we felt depended mainly on personal skill, judgement of difficulties and conditions, and assessment of one's own ability. Years later I trained people in the use of all this equipment but always felt unease carrying chocks, wires, slings and karabiners. Without them we climbed the hardest routes in Britain before the war and we had a great time doing them, sometimes in rubbers, often in nails, occasionally solo but generally the two of us together. With the two of us linked by a Beale's red three-stranded hemp rope there seemed to be no problems in the whole wide world other than getting up the next stretch of intriguing and alluring rock.

You can go through almost the whole gamut of mountaineering experience in Scotland, and on the Skye ridge they come together. We practised moving alpine style over Sgurr Alasdair, onto the Thearlaich Dubh Gap and then traversed Sgurr Mhic Choinnich via King's Chimney and onto An Stac. As we climbed the Inaccessible Pinnacle the mist swept about us, the sun shone weakly. Wind from the deep depths of Coruisk whipped between the rock teeth, making a cleaving sound, like that of a swooping falcon, and then when the sunlight strengthened a Brocken Spectre appeared. My own shadow seemed huge within the circular rainbow – the glory! White light from the sun split into the spectrum as it shone through the spherical droplets of mist and then projected onto the screen of the cloud beneath. Such moments are never forgotten.

As we neared the top of the Pinnacle the mist thinned out, the sunlight was strong enough to disperse the clouds and when it cleared the next group of peaks was revealed to us. The barren-looking ridge, fractured and shattered by fierce freeze-thaw action over a million years, is surprisingly dry, and it's worth seeking out the hidden springs. They also offer a welcome display of colour as alpines stretch towards the sun from these rare sources of moisture.

Of course, there is much more to Skye than the Black Cuillin. There is, for example, much fine walking on the softer, rounded granite hills of the Red Cuillin. And then there are the strange volcanic ash formations of The Storr and the Quirang, the softer rocks eroded into strange pillars and rock windows and steep gullies, looking across the Sound of Raasay to Rona where the seals breed each summer. And beyond Rona, the pre-Cambrian sandstone of the Torridon hills.

Once at the Quirang I saw a golden eagle circling above the vertical rock walls and sky-reaching pinnacles of 'The Prison'. This is a strange, hidden place where Skye crofters hid their sheep and cattle when rustlers arrived from over the sea. The livestock were driven up the narrow gullies to reach areas of flat grassy grazing land surrounded by crumbling walls of rock. Their defence was easy – the only way in or out was by the gullies. Once the raiders had gone, the crofters returned to the thatched roofs of their shielings and their runrigs, the strips of lands running down to the sea.

Always in the Western Isles you come back to that unique balance of sea and mountain. Once, camping with my wife Eileen and our two sons at Achiltibuie, north-west of Ullapool, I visited the mountaineer and explorer Tom Longstaff. Few have done as much to travel, explore and climb as he did in different parts of the world. Together, with a few drams of Glenlivet as a lubricant, and maps to stimulate the memory, we discussed countries and mountains far afield. Before dark I asked, 'Why did you retire to this spot?'

He took me to the window. There I looked out across the loch to the Summer Isles, then beyond to the rugged mountainous coastline stretching south and west as far as the serrated peaks of the Cuillin of Skye. The sea was on fire from the setting sun and the toothed gabbro of the ridge was etched against the golden clouds.

'I have travelled far and wide,' he said, 'climbed in most mountain areas of the world, but this is the finest panorama of the mountains and the sea I have ever seen. This is where I want to end my days.'

I've been back to Skye many times since those early days and often camped on the green stretch of *machair* by the shores of Loch Brittle. There the Atlantic Ocean rolls right up to the tent doorway and you look across to the islands of Rum, Eigg and Canna. Once, two of us camped behind Mary Campbell's cottage, which at the time was a favourite grazing ground for her long-horned Highland cattle. Early in the morning we were away up onto the Cuillin ridge via Choir' a' Ghrunnda.

Weather signs were not good and by noon we were in the middle of a classic Skye deluge. Rock walls and slabs, gullies and cirques became a vast watershed made up of hundreds of foaming, rushing streams and waterfalls. Thoroughly drenched and cold, we made our way back down to the camp thinking of warmth, shelter and steaming mugs of tea. To our horror we found that the long-horned cattle had ripped the tent apart, trampled over our food and eaten our only packet of tea. Worst indignity of all, they had left 'visiting cards' over the rest of our equipment.

Early starts became the norm for us. We would climb up to the ridge and be on top as the early morning sun slanted into the curving, glaciated basins. Sparkling lochans winked back from the sombre deep-lying hollows and the frost-shattered scree would begin to shift in the sunshine, sending a clattering of stones down that would echo from the shadowy rock walls.

The mountains offered us a silence that was yet not quite a silence, for these sounds filtered quietly into our consciousness. These, along with the satisfaction of knowing that we would share yet another exhilarating day on the ridges of Skye, ensured that we would 'live life to the full, blend dream with the deed, and drink deep of the draught'. For me, in the 1930s, the Brontë moors, Lakeland and then Skye, and our 'iron lung', were the motivation for a lifelong connection with the high hills.

History

MICHAEL WARD

The Pundits Beyond the Pamir
The Forsyth Missions of 1870 and 1873

(Plates 51–55)

B efore the middle of the 19th century the mountain ranges north of the Pamir in Chinese (East) Turkestan and the western Kun Lun were virtually unknown, as was the southern part of the Silk Road that ran from Kashgar to Kashmir, with the only available information coming from Mediæval and Chinese sources. In 1812 Mir Izzet Ullah had visited Yarkand, whilst in 1852 Adolph Schlagintweit approached Yarkand but was murdered a few days later outside Kashgar. One of Montgomerie's pundits had managed, in 1866, to locate and place Yarkand on the map, but unfortunately he also was murdered whilst returning to Dehra Dun. Even the position of these two major Central Asian cities remained uncertain.

Then, in 1868, Yakub Beg (Athalik Ghazi), a Moslem usurper, drove the Chinese out of East Turkestan; but eight years later he became yet another murder victim, and the Chinese repossessed the country, renaming it Sinkiang (Xinjiang or New Province). The political position now resumed the status quo, but during his few years in power, Yakub Beg had allowed two missions of British and Indian explorers, soldiers, surveyors and traders to go to East Turkestan to explore, measure, map and trade. The aim of the British had been to make Yakub Beg an ally and his state a buffer against the Russians who were expanding south towards India.

The ignorance of the British Government in India about this immensely important strategic area of East Turkestan, the pivot of Asia, was profound, and the overthrow of the Chinese provided it with a window of political opportunity. In addition, the markets of Central Asia appeared to be there for the taking, particularly if it were possible to avoid the usual route from India using the Karakoram Pass and Leh, where the Maharajah of Kashmir's customs officers imposed heavy tariffs. A more eastern route across the Aksai Chin, connecting with Kulu and Lahul in British India, might be easier and also cheaper.

After Yakub Beg had driven out the Chinese in 1868, three separate individuals visited East Turkestan. Robert Shaw, a tea planter, went in search of Central Asian markets, George Hayward aimed to explore the Pamir and the ranges beyond, whilst the Mirza, one of Montgomerie's pundits, went to survey and obtain political and cultural information. All three were more successful geographically than as traders, and the Mirza was the first to give an accurate account of crossing the Pamir. Tenuous relations were established with Yakub Beg whose potential alliance with Russia had failed to materialise, and all three travellers were allowed to leave unharmed.

In 1870, partly in response to a request from Yakub Beg, Lord Mayo, the Viceroy, despatched the first-ever British mission to Yarkand. Although ostensibly a friendly visit, its main purposes were to establish a political alliance, obtain information about the Russians and develop trading opportunities. Douglas Forsyth, the leader, was Commissioner for the Punjab and an expert on Central Asia. Some years previously he had been responsible for placing a British agent in Leh, a key town, where routes from West Tibet and East Turkestan joined. With Forsyth were Dr George Henderson and Robert Shaw. This mission never met Yakub Beg, who was away fighting insurgents, but their observations enabled them to lay the foundations for the Forsyth Mission of 1873, 'one of the best appointed missions to leave India'.

The 1873 mission was despatched by Lord Normanbrook, the new Viceroy, with Col T E Gordon as second in command. Other members were Dr H W Bellew, Captain Chapman, Captain Biddulph, Captain H Trotter of the Survey of India, and a scientist Dr F Stoliczka. Attached to the party at various times were the pundits Kishen Singh, Nain Singh, Kalian Singh and Abdul Salam, code-named 'the Munshi', who was not an 'official' pundit but a native surveyor who carried out important exploratory surveys during the mission. There was also an escort of 22 soldiers from the Guides, and the whole mission comprised 300 men and 400 pack animals.

This time Yakub Beg was in residence in Kashgar, and during a state visit in full regimental dress Forsyth personally delivered a letter from Queen Victoria. The effect of this impressive display on the court of Yakub Beg, his advisers and on the local population was profound.

Trotter wished to extend the survey to the Tien Shan range to the north, and south-west to the Pamir and the Oxus river. However, the most notable geographical prize was the unknown country to the east of Kashgar – to Aksu, a town on the northern edge of the Taklimakan desert and further east to the Lop Nor marshes and lake. The unknown Kun Lun range, too, extended for a thousand miles or more on the southern edge of the Taklimakan desert and delineated the northern edge of the Tibetan Plateau. Although the pundits were not able to visit and map the whole of this vast area, they gained much valuable geographical information.

On its way from Leh across the Karakoram Pass to Yarkand, the mission split into two parties; the eastern party went by the Chang Chenmo valley and the western party via the Karakoram Pass. For much of their journey both parties were at altitudes of over 15,000 feet and the temperature at night reached minus 26°F. The Munshi (Abdul Salam) was sent to fix the position of several Karakoram peaks already surveyed by the Great Trigonometric Survey (GTS). However, as the days were short, cloudy and cold, the survey yield was not as great as Trotter, a perfectionist, would have liked. On reaching Yarkand, the mission left all the pundits behind for political reasons, except for Kishen Singh, and arrived in Kashgar on 28 November 1873.

After a formal meeting with Yakub Beg, one group went north to the Russian frontier by a route surveyed by Trotter. Another group set off east to Aksu but did not reach the town because time was short. On 2 February 1874 a treaty of commerce was signed and the political part of the mission was complete, but winter snows blocked their return to India. As a result, Forsyth organised another excursion, to the north, passing through a region inhabited by nomadic Kyrghiz. Reaching the Below Pass they returned to Kashgar on 3 March having covered 340 miles. A fortnight later, on 17 March, the mission left Kashgar for Yarkand. On 21 March, at Yangi Hissar, Gordon, Trotter, Biddulph and Stoliczka, with Kishen Singh and Abdul Salam, were despatched to the south and west, passing between the Kongur massif and Mustagh Ata.

A vast, high, 25,000-foot icy rampart of peaks, visible from Kashgar, blocked the southern route to India. The main mass was the Kongur–Kongur Tiube, while adjoining them to the east were the Tigurman and Shiwatke mountains. Passing around the eastern end of this range and then along the southern border just north of the Mustagh Ata, the mission joined the route south to Tashkurgan from the Karakul Lakes, which were first visited by the European explorer Ney Elias in 1888.

Surprisingly, the position and heights of Kongur I (Kongur Tiube, 7595m), Kongur II (Kongur, 7719m, the highest peak in the Pamir) and Mustagh Ata (7456mm) were not established until the Anglo-Russian boundary commission determined them in 1895. All these peaks had to wait until the end of the 20th century for their first ascents, Mustagh Ata and Kongur Tiube by a Sino-Russian party in 1956, and Kongur by a British party in 1981.

Reaching Tashkurgan, Gordon's party traversed the Wakhan corridor but at Kula Punjam on the Oxus river they received information that they were not allowed to continue south to Kabul. So except for Abdul Salam they returned to Tashkurgan and reached Yarkand on 26 April. Abdul Salam was ordered to continue the Oxus survey which he did for a further 85 miles, gaining in addition much political intelligence. Finally, he returned secretly to India via Kabul. The last stretch of the Oxus was surveyed by the pundit M.S. (Mukhtar Shah). Several years later, at the end of the 19th century, George Curzon, later Viceroy of India, also travelled in the Pamir and investigated the source of the Oxus.

When Gordon returned to Yarkand, Forsyth had already left for Leh but by a more easterly route before joining the normal Karakoram Pass track. They arrived at Leh on 17 June 1874. Kishen Singh also undertook the other important exploration of the Mission, going east to Khotan. This oasis region lay on the south side of the Taklimakan between the desert and the Kun Lun range, and had first been visited by Johnson of the Survey

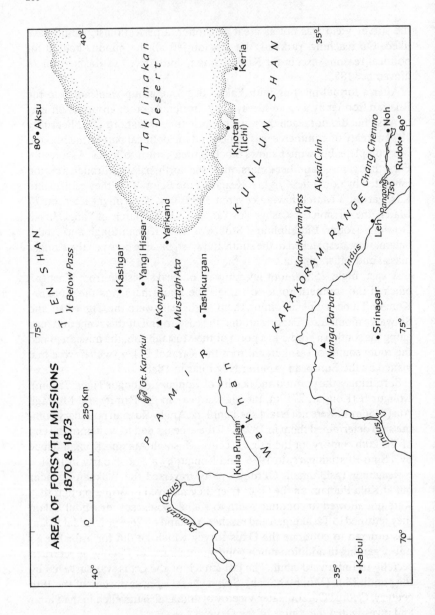

AREA OF FORSYTH MISSIONS
1870 & 1873

of India in 1865. Kishen Singh continued as far east as possible, passing through the main town of Ilchi (Khotan) and reaching Keria on 18 June. In a further three days he visited the Sorghak goldfields which were worked all the year round. Returning to Keria he turned south, crossing the Kun Lun by a route well to the east of the Karakoram Pass, and gained the Chang Tang (northern plateau of Tibet). This route had abundant grass and fuel despite their being no inhabited villages for 250 miles, and he passed no other travellers. Best of all, this route avoided the tariffs imposed by the Maharajah of Kashmir. Despite all these advantages, foreigners being rigorously excluded from Tibet, it was to be eleven years before Carey and Dalgleish and Ney Elias travelled this route, though from south to north, using Kishen Singh's directions which they found outstandingly accurate. Approaching the village of Noh on the north bank of the Pangong Lake, and knowing that he would be searched, Kishen Singh buried all his instruments and notes. Unfortunately he was not allowed to continue to Rudok in western Tibet, so retrieving these he turned west to Leh which he reached at the end of July 1874.

Because of the excellent and accurate work of the pundits, the Survey had great confidence in the newly established positions of Kashgar and Yarkand, the Oxus, the main ranges of the Chinese Pamir, parts of the Tien Shan, the western end of the Taklimakan desert, the Kun Lun range, the southern part of the Silk Route and the route from Keria to Leh. Kishen Singh, in particular, was marked down for further exploration in Tibet, and his later outstanding work confirmed his position as one of the leading explorers of Central Asia.

The Forsyth missions of 1870 and 1873-74 were outstandingly successful geographically and the British made their presence felt in this vital border area. However, although there was an initial boost to trade, this later tailed off. As an increasing number of military operations took place in the northwest frontier region, the pundits' main efforts were switched to Tibet, the north-east frontier and the independent Himalayan Kingdoms of Sikkim, Bhutan and Nepal which, at the time, were still virtually unknown.

BIBLIOGRAPHY

G N Curzon, *The Pamirs and the source of the Oxus*. Royal Geographical Society, 1896.

T D Forsyth, *Report of a mission to Yarkand in 1873 – with historical and geographical information regarding the possessions of the Ameer of Yarkand, Calcutta*. Printed at the Foreign Department Press, 1875.

T E Gordon, *The Roof of the World*. Edmonston and Douglas, 1876.
The narrative of a journey over the high plateau of Tibet to the Russian frontier and the Oxus sources on Pamir.

G W Hayward, 'Journey from Leh to Yarkand and Kashgar and exploration of the sources of the Yarkand River' in *Journal of the Royal Geographical Society 40*, 33-166, 1870.

W H Johnson, 'Journey to Ilchi, capital of Khotan in Chinese Tartary' in *Journal of the Royal Geographical Society, Vol 37*, 1-47, 1867.

T G Montgomerie, 'Report of the Mirza's exploration from Kabul to Kashgar' in *Journal of the Royal Geographical Society 41*, 132-192, 1871.

Gerald Morgan, *Ney Elias, explorer and envoy extraordinary in High Asia*. Allen & Unwin, 1971.

R B Shaw, *Visits to High Tartary, Yarkand and Kashgar and Return Journey over the Karakoram Pass*. John Murray, 1871.

R B Shaw, 'Journey to Yarkand: letters from R B Shaw, longitude of Yarkand' in *Proceedings of the Royal Geographical Society, Vol XV*, 175-180, 1871.

H Trotter, 'On the geographical results of the mission to Kashgar under Sir T Douglas Forsyth in 1873-4' in *Journal of the Royal Geographical Society 48*, 173-234, 1878.

Mir Izzet Ullah, 'Travels beyond the Himalaya' in *Calcutta Oriental Quarterly Magazine*, 1825.

Unattributed paper, 'Journey of Carey and Dalgleish in Chinese Turkestan and Northern Tibet and General Prejevalsky on the orography of Northern Tibet'. *Supplementary papers, Volume 3, Part 1*. Royal Geographical Society, 1890.

Derek Waller, *The Pundits:' British Exploration of Tibet and Central Asia*. The University Press of Kentucky, 1990.

Michael Ward, Peter Boardman, 'The history of the exploration of the Mustagh Ata – Kongur Massif'. Appendix in Chris Bonington, *Kongur: China's Elusive Summit*. Hodder and Stoughton, 1982.

Michael Ward, 'The Survey of India and the Pundits: The Secret Exploration of the Himalaya and Central Asia' in *Alpine Journal 103*, 59-79, 1998.

DENIS GREENALD

Johnnie Lees: A Memoir

(Plates 46, 47)

Since Johnnie's death I have been reading his early log books and re-living the adventures of a lifetime's friendship. We were first cousins, and the fact that our mothers were not just sisters but best friends too, ensured that from the earliest days there was close family contact. At first this was sporadic, on our grandfather's farm near Halifax in Yorkshire, with other cousins, and in Chingford, Essex, where the Lees then lived. In 1939 John's father was transferred to Hexham-on-Tyne. Travel to the West Riding, where all our relations lived, became much easier. They were also nearer to the Lake District, and John's log starts in 1940 significantly, with a postcard of Helvellyn. It was captioned 'My first real mountain' and he climbed it with his father, a keen fell walker. This year also marked the start of our cycling partnership. During the holidays we met at Piercebridge-on-Tees, staying overnight and returning together to Hexham or Bradford. Soon we were doing the trip in a day and all our holidays were spent touring in the Dales or Northumberland.

Each August there were longer expeditions, when we worked at a student forestry camp in the depths of Aberdeenshire, all part of the war effort. The work itself was dreary and monotonous, but we had enormous fun, especially in getting there by bike and staying at Youth Hostels. We loved the hut near Rhynie we used as our base. John wrote of his last trip there, just after VJ day, on his own after a delay for his RAF interview. "I was pleased to see the old 'Buck'," he wrote. "I had been able to see [it] for the last ten miles on my right, and to see that grand little mountain and friend of ours, Tap o'Noth, with Blackstripes down below and the forestry road winding down past it into the white mist in the valley bottom."

For the next two years we saw little of each other, except when our leave coincided, though at the end of that stint we managed a week's fell walking in the Lakes, taking in the Langdales, Gable and Scafell. "Pavey Ark by means of a grand little gully which even called for a bit of 'rocking'" Johnnie wrote, recalling also a retreat from Broad Stand. "After shedding rucsacs we followed nail scratches down to the left which led to a narrow cleft in the side of the face – presumably *Fat Man's Agony*. Half an hour or more of reconnoitring, during which we found ourselves on a tricky rock climb ... convinced us that it was too 'dicey' with Bergens and without ropes."

This was in September 1947. John, already a corporal PT instructor, decided to sign on in the RAF and was posted to Hendon. By a happy coincidence I had a place at the LSE and through the college's mountaineering club we started climbing at Harrison's in the summer of 1948. It was a turning point; we were hooked and the outcrop became our Mecca. This was the time when Nea Morin, the discoverer and undisputed authority on the rocks, held court. She and her two brothers, her children Denise and Ian, together with Hilary Longley-Cook – an Alpine Club member – were to be found there most weekends, demonstrating, encouraging, cajoling the would-be tigers. It was the friendliest of climbing schools. The routes were short, steep, slippery and hard, the competition fierce, but good-natured and relaxed. Friendships made there were to last a lifetime, especially amongst the group which called itself, somewhat tongue-in-cheek, 'The Bar Room Mountaineers'. And John – or JRL as we then called him – was undoubtedly our outstanding member by his energy, enthusiasm and sheer appetite for rock climbing. Technically, too, he was just that bit better than the rest of the local experts, with a phenomenal knowledge of the climbs and the minutiae of the holds. Undeterred by the 'NL' symbols in the guide book, he proceeded to lead these routes and create variations in a restless search for new lines. A year after starting, he circulated his typescript 'Some New Additions' to E C Pyatt's *Sandstone Climbs in SE England*.

With our new-found friends we climbed at a frenetic pace for the next two years, weekends at Harrison's interspaced with longer trips to North Wales, the Lakes and Scotland, repeating classic routes and getting used to mountaineering in all seasons. And then there was gritstone. The Lees family had finally come home to Yorkshire and were living at Otley. Almscliffe near Harrogate, and the Cow and Calf at Ilkley, were only a bike ride away. Caley Crags and Chevin Buttress were within walking distance of their house in Station Road. The latter crag in particular we made our own, top-roping and eventually leading its steep, serious lines.

This pattern continued in 1950, with skiing in Glencoe thrown in for good measure, and excursions to Oxted chalk quarry for Alpine training. The season was a vintage one for British climbers and just about everybody seemed to be in Chamonix. The BRMC were there *en masse*, about a dozen camping on the Blaitière *alpage*, whilst JRL, Geoff Millwood, Gwen Guntrip and myself annexed the Baraque Forestière, on the lower path from Montenvers. From these bases climbs were made in all directions, but we four concentrated on the cirque around the Nantillons glacier. The climax was a traverse of the Grépon, with ten in the party. Gwen remembers the descent particularly:

"After about twenty minutes my broken crampon packed in again, the boot lace having rotted through ... there was no time to fiddle again, so off with it, and onward by slithers and hops, now held firmly from behind by JRL, equipped with axe and crampons and an excellent good temper. We reached the rock of the rognon just as it was dark and slithered down, with two feeble torches between us. I doubt whether I should ever have seen a hand or foothold, had it not been for the untiring generosity with which Johnnie shared his torch glimmers."

That year he had joined both the Climbers' Club and the RAF Mountaineering Association, and on his return from the Alps was immediately involved in a RAF College Mountaineering Club meet in Glen Coe. The other instructors were Wing Commander Tony Smyth, Chairman of RAFMA, and Flight Lt Gordon Parrish. Also present was Prof T Graham Brown, a Vice-President of their Club, and at that time Hon Editor of the Alpine Journal, who was keenly interested in mountain rescue. Clearly he hit it off with JRL and, after the meet, invited him and Parrish to spend some time on his boat on Loch Etive, to explore the now well-known Trilleachan slabs on his 'mystery mountain'. They were joined by Dan Stewart, a leading member of the Edinburgh University Mountaineering Club, who later found himself strategically drafted to Kinloss when his time came for National Service.

For some time there had been concern in the RAFMA committee regarding the lack of mountaineering expertise in the rescue service, and ways of involving RAFMA in training programs were being considered. These concerns were given impetus in March 1951, when the crash of a Lancaster on Beinn Eighe cast serious doubts on the ability of the local team to work in severe winter conditions on high, inaccessible mountain crags. Top brass, in the shape of the President of RAFMA, Sir Ralph Cochrane, who was also Vice-Chief of the Air Staff, took action and his staff convened a conference of interested parties. Recommendations for the recruitment and training of NCOs and airmen volunteers were agreed, and, at the same time, Mike Holton, a founder member of RAFMA now working in the Civil Service, was seconded to the Air Ministry to write a training manual.

Thus, in October 1951, Sgt Lees instructed on the first RAF Mountain Rescue Course, and in the following January was posted to Valley, in Anglesey, as NCO in full-time charge of the MR team. This first year was a busy one, with training courses in Wales and Scotland, taking part in rescues and visits to London for RAFMA and Air Ministry meetings. Interspersed with all this was recreational climbing managed during periods of leave. Indeed, personal and professional life merged into a seamless whole, with amateur friends such as Bill Trench and Geoff Roberts often giving a hand on courses. His personal standard moved up a notch, membership of the CC giving access to the club's huts, the chance to climb with many of the best rock climbers of the time, and to lead Hard VS climbs in the Llanberis Pass and on Clogwyn d'ur Arddu.

It was also the year when he met Gwen Moffat, the most experienced of the post-war women climbers and an original member of the Alpine Climbing Group founded later that year. Their relationship got off to a happy start, Gwen finding her climbing feet again three years after the birth of her daughter, respecting Johnnie's technical ability and careful style. He was delighted at finding an attractive girl-friend capable of following and even leading through on hard routes. It seemed a perfect partnership, full of promise and potential. He wrote that 20 April was "definitely a day to remember, walking over the Pass, rather warm, with Gwen, and Sheena on my back. Crackstone Rib. Moffat soon in bare feet. ... absolutely bubbling over with delight at climbing again, and soon talked me into giving her the lead."

With their new relationship, and the constant demands of the team, there was no opportunity to fit in an Alpine season in 1952. The year finished with the traditional New Year's Eve ascent of Snowdon in blizzard conditions, a warm-up for the winter mountain rescue course in the Cairngorms in February 1953. David Dattner, the widely respected officer heading the Kinloss team, was in charge of the course. Lees was Chief Instructor. In March, Lees himself was posted to Kinloss and shortly after, Dan Stewart, now an Education Officer, replaced Dattner. This was the start of a formidable partnership which was to last for the next two years, Scotland becoming the preferred venue for training courses.

In the summer of 1953 Johnnie was back in Chamonix, climbing with Bill Trench and Dennis Kemp, partners in many of his Welsh rock climbs of the previous year. They started with the NNE arête of the Aiguille de l'M, and the Charmoz-Grépon traverse, then went up to the Leschaux refuge. From this base they climbed a short route on the Pointe Cupelin, before embarking on two longer climbs. The first of these was a traverse of Mt Mallet, the Aiguille de Rochefort and Dent du Géant to the Torino. Approaching the Dent, they had a good view of the south face and saw two climbers high up on the TD route, later meeting them on the summit. They were Arthur Dolphin and his Belgian partner, shortly before the former was tragically killed, soloing down the easy but exposed rocks below the foot of the Dent. It was late afternoon when they reached the Torino hut but instead of staying there, they now charged down the Géant glacier and back to the Leschaux by 9pm. Next day, they made a trip to Chamonix for reprovisioning and a slide show given by Kemp, an accomplished professional photographer. Then they returned to the hut, having acquired an experienced French climber to make up a four for the Old Brenva. The next day they were at the Col de la Fourche, in deteriorating conditions. They decided to go to Col Moore to have a look. They looked and went on, with some argument, and reached the ice wall beneath the summit plateau by midday. They forced this and continued to the top in poor visibility. There the team met "a party of Dutch and one odd Italian, whom we took care of," and by the time they reached the Vallot hut at 2pm blizzard conditions had set in. Next day, in foul weather, they nursed him down to the Grands Mulets and eventually on to Montenvers. Here they left him and slogged back to the Leschaux hut at dusk, in heavy rain.

4. Geoff Cohen climbing the steep snow and ice pitch on the first ascent of Switchback (2010m) in the Lemon mountains, Greenland. (*Dave Wilkinson*) (p57)

45. Dave Wilkinson on the summit ridge of The Spear in the North Lemons; the Courtauld glacier appears below. (*Geoff Cohen*) (p57)

46. Johnnie Lees with Vic Bray during a reunion at RAF Valley in 1993. (*Derek Walker*) (p209)

7. Johnnie Lees on Kaisergebirge Wall in the early 1950s. (*Ray Tanter*) (p209)

48. The most likely birthplace for Tenzing Norgay, the holy lake of Tshechu overlooking the Kama valley and opposite Makalu on the eastern side of Everest. (*Ed Douglas*) (Book Review, p338)

49. Elijah Walton's 'Bedouin Encampment in the Desert with the artist sitting in his tent looking at a sketch' dated 28 February, 1864. (*Courtesy of the Victoria and Albert Museum*) (p151)

50. Gabriel Loppé's 'Sunrise on the Grandes Jorasses seen from Mont Blanc', 1869. (Book Review, p350)

51. Lower Kumdan Glacier – Shyok. (T E Gordon, *The Roof of the World*, 1876) (p203)

52. Kila Panja on the Oxus – looking east. (T E Gordon, *The Roof of the World*, 1876) (p203)

53.   The Karakoram Peak – from the southern side of the pass – looking NW.
      (T E Gordon, *The Roof of the World*, 1876) (p203)

54.   Aktash Valley – looking NW. (T E Gordon, *The Roof of the World*, 1876) (p203)

55. Andrew Dalgleish and his Yarkand household including Abyssinian servant and Yarkandi wife. (John Keay, *When Men and Mountains Meet*, 1977) (p203)

JRL was now an accomplished alpinist – this was his third season – and a strong contender for a place on the RAFMA Himalayan Expedition planned for 1955. It was led by the veteran Wing Commander Tony Smyth, and besides Lees and Stewart included John Sims, Donald Bennet, Jack Emerson and Mike Holton, all of whom had climbed together previously, either in mountain rescue teams or the association. Despite initial difficulties due to exceptionally heavy snow, this was a successful venture with several first ascents of 6000m peaks in the Kulti Himal. Johnnie played an important part.

Returning to Britain he was posted to Valley again, where he was to remain for the next five years, creating the best-known mountain rescue team in England and Wales, and exerting great influence on the young men in his charge. The incident for which he will always be remembered, and which captured the imagination of the public at the time, was the dramatic rescue of Major Hugh Robertson from a ledge on Amphitheatre Buttress, on a dark winter's night in January 1958. The climber had come off while leading an ice-covered pitch, fracturing his skull in the process. Help was sent for and the Valley team reached the site in three hours to find the injured man delirious. Time was precious and urgent action needed if the man's life was to be saved. A stretcher rescue would be difficult and time consuming, but Johnnie knew of a continental device, the *tragsitz*, which enabled a casualty to be carried on the rescuer's back. He immediately improvised one from the ropes and slings available and, with the injured man thrashing about in delirium, was lowered some 200ft to the bottom of the cliff. Vic Bray, responsible at the anchor for controlling the descent, has vivid recollections of the nightmare scene, the difficulty in communicating and the constant anxiety that the knots joining the 120ft ropes might snag. The exhausted team still had an arduous two-mile stretcher carry across ill-defined boggy tracks to reach the ambulance at the road head in Cwm Eigiau; they remained with the casualty during the journey to Bangor and later kept vigil at the hospital. Robertson recovered from his injuries and later showed his gratitude by purchasing a commercial *tragsitz* in Austria and donating it to the Valley team. For his crucial role in the rescue, Johnnie was awarded the George Medal, the only time this decoration has been given to a British climber. It was richly deserved, demonstrating as it did his mastery of mountain craft and mountain terrain in severe conditions, his quick thinking and initiative, his courage in taking the most dangerous and arduous role, and his confidence in the ability of the men he had trained. He rarely spoke of it, except to correct a detail or misconception, but remained quietly modest, insisting that it was a team effort.

He and Gwen Moffat had married in 1956, and continued to climb at a high level both in Britain and in the Alps, though their partnership there was often dogged by adverse conditions. Their best routes were an epic ascent of the Breithorn Younggrat in 1957 and, in the Dauphiné in 1959, the Aiguille de Dibona – Direct with Stofer variation – and a traverse of the

Meije. The romance and the strains of their climbs and life together are described, with at times heartbreaking candour, in Gwen's three mountain books. The first of these, *Space Below my Feet*, published in 1961, rightly became a classic. Johnnie celebrated it, with dry humour, by a new route on Craig y Wrysgan, in the Moelwyns, *Space Below MY Feet* (HVS 5a). With him was Derek Walker, one of the many young men who had been inspired by Johnnie and introduced to climbing when a member of the Valley team. It was in an area he knew well, having used it for MR training exercises and when researching the first Moelwynion guidebook, which was published in 1962.

The same year, he left the RAF and worked for a short time with Ron James at Ogwen Cottage, at that time an independent Outdoor Centre, with its own rescue team which Johnnie had helped to train. Indeed, many rescues had been joint efforts, in the course of which they both became alarmed at the number of incidents involving badly led or inadequately equipped school parties. Together with others in the field, they began to press for some form of training in basic mountain craft and navigational skills for leaders of groups. These ideas were later developed by Sir Jack Longland and led to the formation in 1964 of the Mountain Training Board and the Mountain Leadership Certificate of the BMC, notable milestones in the history of accident prevention.

His next moves were to more conventional Outward Bound schools in the Lake District and Scotland, as a climbing instructor. But the transition to civilian life was not proving easy. Freelance guiding might have offered a career, since both he and Gwen had qualified as mountain guides in the mid-1950s, she being the first woman in Britain to have this distinction. Private clients, however, were difficult to find with the explosion of demand in this field yet to occur. Financial security came eventually in 1966 with his appointment as Warden Service Officer for the Peak Planning Board, and they moved to Derbyshire. Sadly, it did not resolve the tensions in their marriage, and they divorced in 1971. Four years later Johnnie married Dorothy Pleasance, a colleague at work, and settled down to a more peaceful but no less busy life. In this new career he continued to insist on the same high standards in training and safety as formerly, and in his spare time was much in demand on voluntary committees. From 1974 to 1977 he was Chairman of the BMC Safety Committee and served on that body's Peak Area Committee, becoming Secretary in 1992. He was also heavily involved with the Duke of Edinburgh Award Scheme, being Chief Assessor for the Peak area.

His contact with the active climbing scene continued, and he was hut custodian for the Climbers' Club, at both Helyg and Cwm Glas Mawr, in the 1970s. He loved to attend the annual reunions of the Valley teams of the 1950s and in 1993 became the first President of the RAF Mountain Rescue Association formed fifty years after the service was founded. His contribution to guiding was recognised by the British Association of Mountain Guides when he was made an Honoured Guide.

Even after retirement in 1985 he continued to climb at a high standard. Ron James remembers doing *Vector* with him about this time, and *Dream of White Horses* considerably later. My own last climb with him was more modest. A family wedding had brought us to Glasgow, and afterwards we had a nostalgic drive along Loch Lomond side to stay with our old friends Don and Val Aldridge in Perthshire. The next day we climbed on Craig y Barns, a small crag above Dunkeld, in the autumn sunshine. The route was about VDiff; we both failed on the crux, but found an alternative line, delicate, but with plenty of holds; a good, old-fashioned climb like the climbers themselves. This was in 1996, some two years after Dorothy's death. Their relationship had been warm and companionable, full of good-humoured banter, and he missed her terribly. They had no children, but Johnnie had always kept in touch with Sheena, Gwen's daughter, to whom he had been a loving and conscientious stepfather. Grown-up and living an independent life, she was a comfort to him now.

Despite his reputation as a hard man, Johnnie was a very caring person. He cared passionately for the mountain environment and for the safety of the people who ventured into it. His wrath and indignation was reserved for the incompetence, or ignorance, of those who should have known better. He came into rescue work largely by accident, but once involved his commitment was total. To risk one's life for others – surely there is no finer epitaph.

Johnnie Lees GM BEM, 1927-2002

I am indebted to the generous help given by Mike Holton and Derek Walker – both former General Secretaries of the BMC – in the preparation of this memoir.

C A RUSSELL

One Hundred Years Ago

(with extracts from the *Alpine Journal*)

(Plates 56–60)

T he weather during the early part of the winter had been unusually
bad – thoroughly unsettled, in fact – and numerous heavy snowfalls
had made it look as though any expedition would be out of the question.
However, about the middle of January a break came. The sky cleared,
the wind dropped, and the glass began to rise.

The improvement in the weather experienced in many Alpine regions during
the opening weeks of 1903 was recorded by C M Murray who completed a
winter ascent of the Jungfrau on 18 January, accompanied by Christian
Jossi junior and Peter Bernet.

The views were superb. The keen frosty air was clear right to the horizon,
and all the principal mountains in Switzerland seemed spread out close
before us. We could see the Bernina group, Monte Rosa, the Dom, and
Matterhorn, standing up clear in the distance.

On the following day Murray and his guides reached the summit of the
Mönch where the views 'were even better than those from the Jungfrau on
the previous morning'.

Two months later an outstanding expedition was completed by Gustav
Hasler and his guide Christian Jossi senior who on 15 March made the
first winter ascent of the Aiguille Verte. After reaching the summit by way
of the Whymper Couloir and descending by the same route Hasler and
Jossi enjoyed hot tea provided by their porter, Henri Devouassoud, before
continuing the descent to Chamonix in bitterly cold conditions.

An important event in the development of ski mountaineering was the
first attempt to complete the high-level route – the Haute Route – from
Chamonix to Zermatt. Leaving Chamonix on 16 January Dr Payot, Joseph
Couttet, Alfred Simond and Joseph Ravanel[1] crossed the Col du Chardonnet
and the Fenêtre de Saleina to the Val de Bagnes, reached the Chanrion hut
and ascended the Otemma glacier before bad weather forced a retreat to
the valley. Resuming the expedition further along the chain the party crossed
the Col d'Hérens before descending to Zermatt. In the following month a
notable expedition on ski in the Pennine Alps was undertaken by Robert
Helbling and Friedrich Reichert who reached Arolla from the Val de Bagnes

by way of the Col de Cheilon and other passes. On 13 February Helbling and his companion continued to Zermatt, crossing the Col d'Hérens and making the first ski ascent[2] of the Tête de Valpelline. Another successful tour, in the Bernese Alps, was completed by Henry Hoek and W Schiller who on 26 January, accompanied by Alexander Tännler and K Moor, made the first ski ascent of the Wetterhorn.

A period of high temperatures during May and June was followed by cold and unsettled weather which persisted for much of the climbing season. Although conditions were, in the main, unfavourable in the principal regions many expeditions were undertaken and a number of new routes was completed. During the season Victor de Cessole continued his exploration of the Maritime Alps where on 22 August, accompanied by Jean Plent and André Ghigo, he made the first ascent of the Corno Stella, the famous rock peak to the north of the Punta dell' Argentera.

In the Mont Blanc range Emile Fontaine completed several new routes with Joseph Ravanel and Léon Tournier, making the first ascent, on 16 July, of the Aiguille Mummery above the Col des Cristaux and on 8 September, from the Col des Droites, reaching the summit of the unclimbed Tour des Courtes by way of the SW face. On 9 August a classic route was followed by Karl Blodig and Max Horten who completed the first traverse,[3] in ascent, of the W ridge of the Aiguille de Rochefort – the western end of the Rochefort Ridge – and the first ascent of the SW ridge of the Dôme de Rochefort. Another fine route was established on 6 September when Etienne Giraud with Joseph Ravanel and Armand Comte made the first unaided traverse from the Petit to the Grand Dru.

In the Pennine Alps on 28 August E A Broome accompanied by the brothers Alois junior and Heinrich Pollinger made the first recorded ascent[4] of the N ridge of the Schalihorn. A week later, on 5 September, Miss Grace Filder with the guides G B Pellisier and Antonio Curta reached the E, higher summit of the Liskamm after following a new line on the SE face.

In the Bernese Alps on 14 July O K Williamson with Jean Maître and Raphael Lochmatter forced a route up the steep N face of the Tschingelhorn. On 31 August Fräulein Helene Kuntze and Gustav Hasler accompanied by Johann von Allmen made the first ascent of the long ENE ridge of the Morgenhorn in the Blümlisalp group. On 2 September a notable expedition was completed by C F Meade and the brothers Ulrich and Heinrich Fuhrer who made the first descent of the NE ridge of the Jungfrau – a ridge which at that time was still unclimbed.

To the east in the Bernina Alps on 8 September P J H Unna with Martin Schocher made the first complete ascent of the difficult SSE ridge of Piz Morteratsch. In the Dolomites on 10 August the Mosca Chimney route on the S face of the Cima Grande di Lavaredo – the Grosse Zinne – was opened by E Stübler with Giovanni Mosca.

On 27 and 28 June ceremonies were held at Samedan to mark the official opening of the Albula Railway, the extension of the Rhaetian Railway from

Thusis to the Engadine. This major engineering project required the construction of numerous viaducts and tunnels including the Albula tunnel, nearly 6km in length, between Preda and Spinas.

During the year many parties were active in other mountain regions. In Norway J N Collie returned to the Lofoten Islands, accompanied on this occasion by W C and W E Slingsby and D Northall-Laurie. Starting on the island of Moskenesøy the party climbed to the summit of Hermandalstind (1034m), the highest point on the island, on 29 July and completed the first ascent of two other peaks: Munken (805m) on 30 July and Ertenhelltind (942m) on 2 August. A week later, on 10 August, Collie and his companions became the first party to reach the W, lower summit (1035m) of Rulten, the famous peak on the island of Austvågøy. Addressing the Alpine Club later in the year Collie recalled that

> Although we had climbed our peak, and although a perfect sunset and a marvellous view was spread out in front of us, yet Rulten was still unvanquished, for the eastern peak, some third of a mile away, was evidently about 20ft. to 30ft. higher; also, to our disgust, the connecting ridge between the two was quite hopeless.

After further investigation the party with the addition of H S Mundahl succeeded, on 18 August, in making the first ascent of the E, higher peak (1062m), completing the climb by way of the E ridge and S face.

In the Caucasus, where the weather was exceptionally fine for much of the summer, a large party organised by W R Rickmers spent several weeks in the central region climbing numerous peaks and making a number of outstanding ascents. On 21 July an attempt to scale the unclimbed S, higher peak (4710m) of Ushba by Rickmers, Fräulein Zenzi von Ficker, her brother Heinz, Adolf Schulze and a hunter named Muratbi had to be abandoned when Schulze, the leader, fell and was injured. Five days later Schulze, Robert Helbling, Friedrich Reichert, Oscar Schuster and Albert Weber succeeded in making the first ascent of the S peak, a fine achievement for the period. Other notable expeditions by members of the party included the first ascent of two high peaks: Shkhelda (4320m) by Helbling, Reichert, Schulze and Weber on 1 August; and, on 7 August, the W, higher peak (5051m) of Jangitau, with the addition of a traverse to the E summit (5038m), by the same climbers accompanied by Mito Arkhulian, a local porter.

Another fine expedition was completed by Hans Pfann, Ludwig Distel and Georg Leuchs who made the first traverse of both summits of Ushba. Reaching the N, lower summit (4696m) on 10 August by way of the NE ridge Pfann and his companions were obliged to spend the next three nights without shelter before descending to the Gul valley on the southern side of the peak.

T G Longstaff and L W Rolleston who arrived in the region at the end of July also completed some notable expeditions, reaching the summit of the unclimbed Tikhtengen (4610m) on 5 August and, on 24 August, making the first ascent of the W, lower peak (5057m) of Shkhara.

Earlier in the year, in March, Samuel Turner travelled south from the Trans-Siberian Railway to carry out winter exploration in the Altai mountains. Accompanied by an interpreter and two local hunters, Turner overcame numerous difficulties to reach the Ak-Kem valley below Bielukha (4506m), the highest peak in the region. Although forced to abandon an attempt to scale Bielukha Turner climbed to a height of nearly 4000m during a solo ascent of another peak above the Ak-Kem valley which he named Willer's Peak.[5]

On 14 April, after passing the winter in Kashgar, Gottfried Merzbacher resumed his expedition[6] to the Tien Shan where he hoped to obtain a comprehensive plan of the higher regions and, in particular, to establish the correct location of Khan Tengri (6995m) which at that time was thought to be the highest peak in the range. Accompanied by the geologist Hans Keidel, the guides Franz Kostner and Sigmund Stockmayer and a number of Cossacks, Merzbacher continued his exploration but was still unable to determine the exact position of Khan Tengri. Finally, after Keidel had left the expedition on 7 August, Merzbacher and the guides obtained a complete view of the peak from a point on the snowfield of the southern branch of the Inylchek glacier.

> A fine snowy summit, glittering in the sun, appeared aloft, colossal white marble buttresses projecting from it; a few steps farther, and a huge pyramid stood out freely, its base also soon coming into view. The giant mountain, the monarch of the Tian-Shan, revealed himself to my enraptured gaze in all his naked majesty, from his feet, rooted in the glacier ice, up to his crown, wrapt in sunlit shifting mists.

From his observations Merzbacher was able to establish that Khan Tengri does not form part of the central chain as had been supposed but stands on a ridge to the south-west of the main range.

In the Karakoram Dr William Hunter Workman and his wife Fanny Bullock Workman undertook the fourth of their mountain journeys accompanied on this occasion by B H M Hewett as topographer, the guides Joseph Petigax and Cyprien Savoye and Laurent Petigax junior as porter. As in the previous year the Workmans spent several weeks exploring the Chogo Lungma and other glaciers, climbing on neighbouring peaks and taking a large number of photographs. On 12 August, starting from a high camp above the Chogo Lungma glacier, the party ascended a peak to which they ascribed a height of 6878m.

In the Punjab Himalaya H Sillem and his wife explored the approaches to the Nun Kun group. On 12 July Sillem and two local men climbed to a height of some 6400m, reaching and photographing the snow plateau between the main peaks.

Later in the year Henry Hoek arrived in Bolivia as a member of a geological expedition. Travelling with G Steinmann and Baron von Bistram, Hoek explored several of the southern ranges and climbed a number of peaks including Cerro Campanario (5050m), ascended on 10 October, and Cerro Liqui (5115m).

In the Canadian Rockies an outstanding climb was completed on 21 July by H C Parker who with Christian and Hans Kaufmann made the first ascent of Mount Hungabee (3493m). On 1 September Parker and his guides, accompanied by August Eggers, reached the summit of the unclimbed Deltaform Mountain (3424m), the highest of the Ten Peaks near Moraine Lake, and two days later the same party made the first ascent of Mount Biddle (3319m). Other notable expeditions included the first ascent, on 16 July, of the S Tower (3562m) of Mount Goodsir by Parker and C E Fay with Christian Häsler and Christian Kaufmann and, in the same month, the first ascent of the NE ridge[7] of Mount Assiniboine (3618m), by W Douglas with Häsler and Christian Kaufmann.

Another visitor to the Canadian Rockies was Edward Whymper who completed his second expedition on behalf of the Canadian Pacific Railway Company. Accompanied by a young man named Harry Tattrie, Whymper spent several months travelling on foot and undertaking further exploration in the region.

To the west in the Selkirk range a new route on Mount Sir Donald (3297m) was completed on 3 September by E Tewes who with Eduard Feuz senior and Christian Bohren made the first ascent of the NW ridge.

In Britain many strong parties were in the field and several climbs of note were completed. In Wales on 24 April J M Archer Thomson and Oscar Eckenstein made the first ascent of the *Central Route* or *Route 1* on the E buttress of Lliwedd. In the Lake District on 7 April E Rigby, D Leighton and J Sandison opened the *'A' Route* on Gimmer Crag. Two months later on 3 June F W Botterill, leading H Williamson and J E Grant, completed a famous climb: the first ascent of *Botterill's Slab* on Scafell Crag. On 21 September a climb on the Pinnacle Face of Scafell ended in tragedy when R W Broadrick, A E W Garrett, Henry Jupp and Stanley Ridsdale all died after falling from the face during an attempt to reach Hopkinson's Cairn from Lord's Rake. In Scotland Harold Raeburn returned to Ben Nevis where on 29 June, with Dr and Mrs William Inglis Clark, he made the first ascent of the *Original Route* on Number Three Gully Buttress.

A notable event during the year was the foundation of the Ski Club of Great Britain. The idea of forming a club was discussed by W R Rickmers, E C Richardson and other enthusiasts during a dinner held on 6 May at the Café Royal in London.

The meeting was a complete success, and was unanimous in advocating the formation of the club, the objects of which were then set forth as being: The development of the sport in the British Isles; the effecting of improvement in the style of ski-ing amongst members who already had experience; the assistance of novices; and the bringing together of persons interested in the sport.

Another event of note was the publication of *Round Kangchenjunga*,[8] the account by D W Freshfield of his celebrated Tour of Kangchenjunga four years earlier. This fine work, illustrated principally with photographs by Vittorio Sella, was reviewed in the *Alpine Journal* where it was described as 'a contribution to science, as well as a record of arduous travel, excellently illustrated and admirably written.'

This account is concluded with the following extracts from reports published during the year in connection with proposals for another engineering project in the Alps.

The much talked of railway to the top of Mont Blanc has got as far as the adoption of plans by municipal councils, and work is to be begun immediately. Whether it will ever be finished is another question which, in the absence of any exact precedent, it is difficult to answer. ...

Sentimentalists will hope that the famous mountain may be spared this desecration, and climbers will be equally opposed to the idea. Fancy arriving at the top after risking one's life a hundred times in the perilous ascent, only to find your friend Jones enjoying his lunch and tantalisingly flaunting his return ticket in your face!

REFERENCES

1   The famous guide Ravanel, *le Rouge*.
2   A ski ascent is defined by Sir Arnold Lunn as 'an expedition on which ski were used until the foot of the final rock or ice ridges.'
3   The ridge had been traversed in descent by Ettore Allegra with Laurent Croux, Pierre Dayné and Alexis Brocherel on 18 July 1900.
4   The ridge had been descended by W E Davidson with Christian Klucker and Josef Imesch, accompanied by the Hon Gerald FitzGerald with Ulrich Almer and Fritz Boss on 14 August 1900.
5   Now known as Ak-Ayuk.
6   For further details of this expedition see *AJ 101*, 131-139, 1996.
7   Known as the N ridge. The ridge had been descended by the Rev James Outram with Christian Häsler and Christian Bohren on 3 September 1901.
8   Douglas W Freshfield, *Round Kangchenjunga; a Narrative of Mountain Travel and Exploration*. London, Edward Arnold, 1903.

Area Notes 2002

EDITED BY JOSÉ LUIS BERMÚDEZ

Alps	*Lindsay Griffin*
Russia and Central Asia	*Paul Knott*
Greenland	*Derek Fordham*
Scottish Winter	*Simon Richardson*
Middle East & North Africa	*Tony Howard*
India	*Harish Kapadia*
Pakistan	*Lindsay Griffin*
North America	*Ade Miller*
Cordillera Blanca	*Antonio Gomez Bohorquez*

LINDSAY GRIFFIN

Alps 2002

This report on selected activity in the Alps during the winter 2001-02 and all seasons during the following year relied on the generous assistance of the following activists and correspondents: Lionel Daudet, Ivano Ghirardini, Andy Kirkpatrick, Villiam Jakubec, Stephen Koch, Mireille Lazaravitch, Vlado Linek, Ian Parnell, Michel Piola, Urs Odermatt, Tony Penning, Hilary Sharp, Thomas Tivadar and Ivan Zila. The report is arranged from west to east, beginning with the Mont Blanc Massif and ending with the Dolomites. All notable ascents on a particular mountain are grouped under one heading, with nearly all ascents dated for clarification of the climbing period.

The Alpine Journal particularly welcomes details of new routes and information on members' activities in the Alps, as well as changes to established routes. These should be sent to the Club.

MONT BLANC MASSIF

Mont Blanc On the *Grand Pilier d'Angle* (4243m) Swiss aspirant guides, Denis Burdet and Nicolas Zambetti, made the long-awaited first completely free ascent of *Divine Providence* (Gabarrou/Marsigny, 1984: 900m on the pillar followed by 600m up the Peuterey Ridge: 6b and A3 but now 7c). Burdet, an experienced big-wall climber, led all the hard pitches on sight. Technically, every pitch of the route had been climbed free previously, but not by the same party. In July 1990 Frenchmen, Alain Ghersen and Thierry Renault, virtually free climbed the entire route. A long overhanging A3 corner was led completely free at 7c;

higher, the pair were thwarted by a wet roof, which required three points of aid. In August 1991 British climbers, Andy Cave and Paul Jenkinson, climbed the route in two days, this pair also managing an almost free ascent. Unfortunately, Jenkinson was forced to use four rest points on the overhanging 7c corner, which was very sustained and a little damp. However, the 'wet roof' higher up the route was bone dry and went relatively easily at 7a.

Mont Maudit The well-known French guide, Ivano Ghirardini, accompanied by Rahel Maria Liu from Germany, made the first ascent of a well-defined rock pillar on the SW Face. Climbed in about five hours on 28 July, starting from a bivouac on the Col de La Brenva (4303m), the *Éperon Gousseault* is 300m high and III-IV with one pitch of V, ending at c.4315m on Mont Maudit's NW Ridge. It is dedicated to Serge Gousseault, the young French guide who died in 1971 during an epic attempt, with René Desmaison, on a hard new route up the left flank of the Walker Spur .

Aiguille Noire de Peuterey Over 28-29 July Dave Hope, Nic Mullin and Tony Penning climbed the excellent *Lost to Obsession* left of the 1976 *Nardella Diretissima* on the SE Face. The route has 12 pitches and gave 530m of climbing above the approach gully (Cretier Couloir), the key pitches occurring at the start of the second day. The continuation corner above the bivouac was blank, so after some probing both left and right, Penning eventually made a c.12m rappel right, followed by a c.12m traverse to a long corner, which went at British E4 6a (F6c+). The crux was a bold and difficult leftward layback into a wide crack out of sight of the belay. The whole section took around four hours to complete, leaving the climbers just half a rope-length above their bivouac site. The climbers rappelled from the top of the diamond-shaped buttress and did not continue up the easy ground above to the summit. This was Penning's fourth visit to the cirque to climb this route and his second serious attempt

At the end of August Slovakians, Dino Kuran and Ivan Zila, made a rare repeat of the 1994 Patrick Gabarrou/Manlio Motto route, *L'Équipée des Bras Cassés*, on the now seldom visited West Face. This 500m-high ED2 (6c+, 6b obl. 50 in-situ bolts) follows a direct line up the left side of the West Face of Pointe Brendel (3498m). The crux pitches are in the first part but the upper half of the route follows a very steep and sometimes overhanging crack and corner system on beautiful golden granite (which the first ascensionists compared to climbing on the Grand Capucin). This gave classic Alpine rock-climbing at steady 6b and almost constantly protectable with natural gear.

Pointe Gamba Prior to their ascent on the Noire, Hope, Mullin and Penning climbed a short new route on the lower SSE Face of this 3067m tower. The very difficult and sustained rock route takes the central groove in the wall overlooking the couloir leading to the North gap of the Col des Chasseurs and finishes at the obvious large shoulder on the South Ridge. Climbed on 24 July with a crux of E5 6a, the 180m *Third Time Lucky* was, as the name suggests, completed on Penning's third attempt. In common with the new route on the Noire, only natural protection was used throughout and this brought the total of Penning's new routes in the vicinity of the Chasseurs to three.

Trident (du Tacul) During early summer Oliver Besson and François Pallandre put up *Les Enfants Gateux,* a nine-pitch (c.250m) route at 7b, 6c obl. to the right of the celebrated *Les Intouchables* (7c+) on the South Face.

Cosmiques and Simond Huts An ominous development during the winter was the closure of the Refuge Simond. This appears to have been instigated by the guardian of the luxurious and highly expensive Cosmiques Hut little more than 200m away. Understandably, he wants to make as much money from the hut as possible and feels the Simond Bivouac should only be made available in situations of emergency, when problems arise with accommodation at the Cosmiques.

Grandes Jorasses In early January Lionel Daudet made the second overall and first winter ascent of the 1999 Valeri Babanov route, *Eldorado* (1000m ED4: A3/A4, 6b, 90°). The Frenchman found the difficulties reported by the first ascensionist to be a trifle over-rated and he was also somewhat critical of the number of drilled bathook placements and a certain overuse of bolts on several pitches. The maximum difficulties he encountered were A2/A3 and 6b, with an overall grade of ED3 deemed appropriate.

Daudet progressed slowly up the route in relatively settled but very cold weather, on one day climbing no more than one pitch. By the time he was rappelling from the summit of Pt Whymper, both the length of the route and the weather had taken its toll. The portaledge, which had already been damaged lower down the face, could not be properly closed and spindrift was making Daudet's clothes and equipment extremely damp. The result was some degree of frostnip to his extremities. He finally managed to descend to the Leschaux and onwards to Chamonix Hospital, arriving on the 28th, having spent a total of 14 days away from the valley on his successful adventure. However, as will be read elsewhere in this report, the frostnip sustained to his digits would cost him dearly a few weeks later.

Later in the month Stéphane Benoist and Jérôme Thinières made a rare ascent of *Rolling Stones* (Kutil/Prochaska/Slechta/Svejda, 1979: 1200m: ED3: VI, A3, 80°) on the left flank of the Walker Spur. The French pair found excellent conditions, climbing the ice runnels with crampons yet able to tackle the difficult pure rock sections, which were completely snow free, in boots and thin gloves. In more snowy conditions the two felt the route would involve considerably more difficult mixed climbing.

Benoist and Thinières, who climbed with all their 35kg of equipment packed into a single haul sac, found two full pitches of A2 on rather fragile rock, together with a double pendulum. They agreed with other recent ascensionists that this was a route established well-ahead of its time, the only fault with the line being the slanting rightward traverse at around three-quarters height to join the Cassin. If a more direct, four-pitch continuation up obvious mixed ground was followed to reach the upper section of the 1973 Gousseault Route, this would provide a much more elegant finish.

Col des Hirondelles The north-facing couloir leading directly to the col has been climbed throughout for the first time by Patrick Gabarrou and Italians, Massimo Farina and Ezio Marlier. The ascent took place on 1 April and the capping sérac was simply a plain ice wall c.120m high and around 80°+. After the initial c.300m ice slope at 65° max, the three climbed the sérac in two very long and impressively positioned pitches at V/4+. For these three talented climbers this must have proved easy and after reaching the col they made eight rappels down the couloir left of the sérac. An apt name of *Poisson d'Avril* was given to this new line.

Aiguille du Tacul The day following the ascent above, the 19-year-old Farina and the well-established 50- year-old Gabarrou headed for the Aiguille du Tacul (3444m), where they had spied a thin runnel in the back of a corner on the East Face. On closer inspection they found hard mixed climbing with a few sections of aid needed in the upper section of the corner. After five difficult pitches at IV/4 and A1, easier ground led up to an exit just left of the summit. *Ice for Good* was 400m and the pair descended their route by rappel. The next day, 3 April, the pair returned for a line they had noted just to the left. *Stupenda* gave four pitches of ice and mixed climbing on excellent granite but was often difficult to protect. After 300m at IV/4+ the route joins *Ice for Good*, which was rappelled from that point

Evêque - Pointe 3019m On 2 August Tony Penning, with Nic Mullin, added his third new route to the NE Face of this remotely situated peak above the Frébouze Glacier. *The Eve of our Return* is a good 500m climb to the left of the *1990 Cresswell Route*, reaching the obvious white triangle high on the face. Climbing up to the triangular was enjoyable British HVS/E1 but it was then necessary to make a desperate tension traverse across a blank wall to a hanging stance followed by a pitch of E3 (F6c).

The c.500m face lies above the lower eastern section of the Frébouze Glacier and has a complex approach from La Vachey up the left side of the valley, involving a slabby section with difficulties up to British 4c/5a to the left of glacial séracs. Route-finding is not obvious, so reaching the foot of the face from the valley on the first attempt will probably take around three-and-a-half hours. The descent necessarily takes a different route and involves two long rappels down a large wet chimney further west (bolt at the top).

Aiguille des Pèlerins/Aiguille du Peigne Jean Christophe Lafaille made the third overall but first solo ascent of *Pèlerinage* (VI/6), a highly serious, thin ice climb put up in November 1991 by Christophe Beaudoin and Andy Parkin. However, the line is really not so different from that first climbed back in March 1982 by Andy Bailey and Andy Nisbet. These two British climbers, who had attempted the route the previous year, used a fair bit of aid on the first two pitches, the first of which they fixed, before completing the route in a day. They refer to their line as a *Direct Start to the North East Couloir of the Col du Peigne*. Lafaille climbed the first serious pitch on 13 February, taking three hours to manage 50 metres in very delicate conditions. He returned on the 16th for an all-out attempt but was forced to retreat in bad weather. Finally, on the 18th he climbed the route in five hours. He used a backrope on all the hard pitches, though it appears he still climbed significant sections of the route unroped. The second ascent was made in late spring 2001 by Marco Gaïani and François Marsigny.

Further left in this austere amphitheatre, the famous 1992 Parkin/Twight route, *Beyond Good and Evil*, appears to have evolved into 'an easy day for a lady' (to use that overworked and sexist Mummery quotation), as scores of parties made ascents during the winter season. At the start of the season it was quite well-formed with certain French specialists reporting the technical difficulties to be no more than French 4/4+. As the season progressed, much of the ice fell off, leaving sections with little more than isolated blobs stuck to the granite and conditions probably similar to those experienced on the first ascent, when the ice was too thin to use screws and the grade was quoted as a very serious V/5+ F5+ and A1/A2. British parties at the end of the season report sections of hard Scottish 7. How many from all these parties completed the original finish is unclear but it was certainly climbed all free and with the original finish in a racy five hours by American, Stephen Koch, and Slovenian, Marko Prezelj. British climbers completing the route included Andy and Pete Benson, Jon Bracey, Nick Bullock, Jules Cartwright, Kenton Cool, Tim Emmett (reportedly making his first Alpine ascent), Stuart McCleese and Mike 'Twid' Turner.

Pointe Migot On 12 December 2001, and therefore a little before the start of the official winter season, François Marsigny and Thierry Renault, the latter making something of a comeback to alpinism, climbed a very hard new mixed route on the North Spur of this 3311m peak. The pair christened it *One Step Beyond*, no doubt as something of a snub to the neighbouring super-route, *Beyond Good and Evil*.

The route takes a parallel lower ramp system to the rarely repeated *1964 Bonington/Brown/Ford/Patey Route* (600m: TD–/TD: VI). To reach the start of this ramp the French pair followed a difficult dièdre to the right of the initial section of the *Carrington-Rouse*. Two points of aid were used low down, though these were eliminated by Bruno Sourzac and visiting Argentinean, Rolando Garibotti, during a subsequent but unsuccessful attempt. Once the crest of the North Spur was gained, the pair rappelled 20m left into the couloir leading to the Col Supérieur des Pèlerins and followed this for its upper 150m. No grade has been quoted.

Aiguille de Blaitière Michel Piola continues to spend part of his summer re-equipping his old classics. This year it was *Majorette Thatcher* (Piola/Steiner, 1984: 200m: five pitches: 6b) towards the right side of the Red Pillar and *Fidal Fiasco* (Piola/Steiner, 1984: 350m: 11 pitches: 7a, 6b obl) towards the left side of the West Face.

Petit Dru One of the more notable ascents in the Massif during the winter took place from 28 January to 13 February, when British climbers, Andy Kirkpatrick and Ian Parnell, climbed a partial new line on the West Face based on the 2001 *Lafaille Route*.

The pair were unable to locate the original start and in the end climbed a weakness just left of *C'est Arrivé Demain* (Berhault/Remy/Remy, 1979: 6a and A1), reaching the left edge of the large snow terrace after six largely independent pitches at Scottish VI, A2 and British HVS. The haul bags now had to be dragged almost horizontally across the terrace and this proved disastrous. As Kirkpatrick was manhandling the bags on to a ledge, the straps broke and one bag and the portaledge took a c.300m flight to the glacier below.

Leaving the remaining haul bag, the pair descended via the North Face and continued on down to Chamonix to find a replacement portaledge. Two days later, on 4 February, they were back at their high point in surprisingly milder, rainy conditions. Several hard mixed and aid pitches led to the high point gained by Lafaille on his first attempt. Abandoned here were considerable amounts of static rope together with a full rucksack (which the British pair cleaned from the mountain). Above, they inadvertently managed to avoid the A5 pitch, one of many route-finding problems on the route due to the placement of Lafaille's original bolts. The Frenchman had used standard screw-thread bolts and removed the hangers, so the remaining small studs were often impossible to see under the frosting on the rock, even at close quarters.

Kirkpatrick and Parnell continued through deteriorating weather, climbing several pitches of A4, making a couple of pendulums and overcoming some Scottish 7 mixed, before finishing on the North Face at the big ledge harbouring bolts used by the TV crew who filmed Profit's solo ascent of the *American Direct* in the 1980s. Here, the cumulative effects of constant cold, fatigue and extremities now beginning to succumb to frost nip, forced them to forego the summit and make a rappel descent of the *American Direct*.

The pair report snowfall on most days but on seven of these it was quite heavy. Temperatures reached as low as −15/−20° C but fortunately it never got really windy. Both climbers were full of praise for Lafaille's effort, noting that the route took a logical line and contained little drilled equipment. They felt that the 26-pitch route as a whole was of a similar standard to Yosemite's *Aurora*.

Since the big rockfall in 1997 the *Bonatti Pillar* has, understandably, not been attempted on a regular basis. In fact, most of the route is undamaged but the rockfall most certainly altered a c.50m section in the lower part of the pillar; the old fourth and fifth pitches, formally graded V, are now 6b and A1. However, during the summer of 2002 the route began to gain popularity once more and around one dozen ascents were made. There are few pegs in place on the first half of the route.

Aiguille Sans Nom American, Stephen Koch, and Slovenian, Marko Prezelj, made the third overall and second winter ascent of *There goes the Neighborhood,* a c.900m mixed route on the North Face climbed over two days in October 1993 by Americans, Scott Backes and Mark Twight. This much misquoted line, which takes its name from a song title by the rap artist Ice-T, was originally graded at 5.9 A3 90°+ with an overall rating of at least ED3. On the second ascent, in excellent conditions, Thierry Braguier and François Marsigny were able to climb a thin ice variation to the A3 pitch, making a completely free ascent, and this was also achieved by the American-Slovenian pair. Despite several attempts during the winter, these climbers were the only two to successfully repeat the route.

Pointe 3064m On 4 July François Pallandre continued his explorations of the Charpoua side of the Moine satellites with an ascent, with Jean-Pierre Juillard, of the SW Ridge of Pt. 3064m, a rock tower on the long SW Ridge of the Aiguille du Moine. The 280m new route has a total of nine pitches up to 6a+ (6a obl) and was christened *Nos Vices*. From the summit of Pt. 3064m the pair rappelled directly down the NW Face via the anchors of *La Voix du Druide*, a reportedly excellent eight-pitch route at sustained 6c, 6b obl, climbed by Pallandre himself (with Didier Gumy and Karen Pallandre) in 2001.

Les Courtes On 15 June two Swiss, Thomas Schonz and Gabriel Voide, climbed a new c.800m line up the NNW Spur, the rocky buttress lying right of the classic *1938 Swiss Route*. The pair climbed more or less up the middle, following a line of thin goulottes falling directly from the apex of the buttress. Eight hours were taken, the route named *Mama Mia* and graded ED1 or V/5+ and F5+.

Aiguille du Chardonnet On 16 December 2001, just outside the official winter season, Stéphane Debruyne and Didier Manu climbed a new route on the NW Face, right of the prominent Aureille-Feutren North Couloir. The fine new 500m mixed route starts up a ramp below a red pillar, lying between the *1977 NW Buttress Direct* (Gabarrou/Gabarrou: TD-: III/4) and the *1979 NW Face* (Gabarrou/Michod: D+/TD-: III/4 and F4+). Higher, it cuts through the *Escarra Route* (D+ or III/4) and continues up mixed ground to the summit. The overall grade was III/4+ M with rock at 5/5+.

AIGUILLES ROUGES

Although for good reason climbing in the Aiguilles Rouges during the summer has been gaining in popularity due to the increasing trend towards easy accessibility, moderate altitude, a magnificent panorama and first class quality rock (which in the case of the Aiguilles Rouges is generally well-protected with bolts and bathed by considerable amounts of warm sunshine), this venue has seen heightened activity in the last couple of years since the publication of the definitive topo guide, *Aiguilles Rouges - Escalade au Soleil*, by Thomas Dulac and the late Godefroy Perroux.

Aiguille de la Floria Michel Piola has added another two routes, solo, to the fine South Face of the 2888m Aiguille de la Floria directly above the Index Téléphérique Station. The routes are as yet unnamed and lie to the left of Asia. One is seven pitches and 5c, while the other is five pitches and 6a.

Tour de Crochues On this tower of the 2837m Aiguille Crochues, which lies on the main ridge a little north of the Floria, Michel Piola has added two new lines to the right of the *Galbert Route*. With Christian Hug he climbed a five-pitch 6a+ and then soloed a six-pitch 6a.

Aiguille de la Belvédère On the South Face of the well-known 2965m peak above the Lac Blanc, Piola, with Christian Hug and Pascal Strappazzon, has added a new route up the centre of the face between *Luchini Arsène* (Abderrahame/Lisko/Passy/Ravanel/Schwarz, 1995: 300m: 6c+) and *Baisers Orageux* (Piola/Strappazzon, 1996: 300m: eight pitches: 6c+). This so far unnamed route is eight pitches long and 7a.

Aiguille Pourrie Eric Belin, Mathieu Leclet, Daniel and Emmanuel Meot have established a new route on the lower section of the Aiguille Pourrie, conveniently approached from the Grand Balcon Sud used on the Tour du Mont Blanc. *Linéa Bianca* (270m: 5c max and obl) climbs a small pinnacle from a hollow frequented by skiers and known as Combe Lachenal, approximately 20 minutes from the ski station. The climbing is sustained at 5a to 5c, well-equipped with stainless steel bolts, and the line is seven pitches in length.

MONT BUET REGION

Corne Est de Loriaz (2699m) In the Vallée de Bérard, a relatively wild and remote valley behind the Aiguille Rouges and accessed from Le Buet, Jean-Marc della Volpe and Pierre Marizy have added *Loriaz Express* (600m: 19 pitches: 6a+, 6a obl). The rock is compact gneiss and, not surprisingly for the altitude, is sometimes a little lichenous. The route is equipped with bolts and pegs, though these are often well-spaced on the easier sections and the foot of the face can be reached in around 45 minutes from the Refuge Loriaz (2020m).

Pointe Vouilloz Two new routes were recorded to this 2672m summit immediately south of the Grand Perron, overlooking Vallorcine. *Justine p'tite Goutte* by Jean-Marc Della Volpe, Hubert Dupessay and Yves Lagesse lies close to the right edge of the SE Face. The 180m route has six pitches followed by an airy summit arête and difficulties up to 5+. The climbing involves cracks and compact slabs and is well-equipped except when natural protection is possible. The best approach (2 hours) is from the Emosson Dam, following the path over the Col du Passet, then a cairned track on the west flank of the Chardonnet arête to a stony couloir and small col at the foot of the route. This pleasant climb is equipped for a rappel descent. The second route, *La Grevôle Directe* by Mathieu Bourrat, Christophe Fadda and Sylvain Ravanel, is an 11-pitch, totally-equipped climb, sustained at 6a and 6b.

VALAIS

Valais Traverse

Two young Swiss guides, Claude-Alain Gailland and Sébastien Gay, completed a mammoth traverse across the Valais Alps. They originally planned to follow the ridge that forms the border of the Canton Valais, which would have involved around 640km without descending from the crest, 330 summits, 18 of the 4000m peaks in the Alps and a total elevation gain of more than 70,000m. Beginning their project on 1 June at the shores of Lake Geneva, they followed the crest in an anticlockwise direction, crossing major peaks such as the Matterhorn and Monte Rosa. They had completed approximately two-thirds, climbing 250 summits, when during the descent of the Rhonenstock, north of the Furka Pass, Gailland was hit by a rock, which broke his hand. Sadly, the two had to abandon their ambitious odyssey before they were able to start the westward traverse across the Oberland peaks back towards Lake Geneva.

Matterhorn Towards the end of January Stéphane Benoist, Olivier Larios and Jérôme Thinières made a rare but notable winter attempt on the *Original Route* (Cerruti/Gogna, 1969: 1,000m: ED2/3) on the Zmutt Nose. This relatively rarely climbed line, probably Alessandro Gogna's most significant and impressive addition to the Alps, has seen little winter traffic since the first winter ascent over eight days in January 1974 by Thomas Gross and Eric Oberson.

The three French found the climb an altogether harder proposition than *Rolling Stones* on the Grandes Jorasses, climbing no more than 150m a day and discovering much steep and delicate rock-climbing with technical difficulties up to 6a and A3. They climbed through a rock scar and were four pitches from the top of the Nose, when they decided to retreat.

In February it was the turn of Lionel Daudet. After a period of rest following his ascent of *Eldorado* on the Grandes Jorasses reported elsewhere, the 34-year-old Frenchman made an attempt at the first complete ascent of *Aux Amis Disparu*. This route, which climbs the overhanging crest forming the right side of the Zmutt Nose, was climbed by Daudet and Patrick Gabarrou in 1992. However, Gabarrou had already climbed the lower section twice before with other partners, so on this occasion he opted to approach via the Zmutt Ridge to a point where he could traverse across to the base of the prow. From there the pair climbed it direct in an audacious position at A2/A3. It remained unrepeated.

Daudet set off up the initial slopes with only his portaledge for company. Barely above the initial gullies, he was trapped for two days by a storm that produced high winds, for which this section of the North Face is famous, and temperatures down to −30° C. Believing he could sit it out, he waited patiently, although frostbite may already have been insidiously developing. When conditions improved, he continued upwards, though somewhat hesitantly due to the uncertainty in the weather. On the 19th, positioned directly below the start of the prow on his eighth day on the face, Daudet was hit by a more violent storm. Two days later, with the portaledge becoming increasingly damaged, he began his retreat. Spurred on by the belief that his hands and feet were already frostbitten, he reached the Hörnli Hut after a very competent descent of just 12 hours. On the 22nd he was evacuated by helicopter. His fingers survived but after two weeks in a Grenoble hospital, eight of his toes had to be amputated, reducing, as he said in a press release, his size 43 feet to a mere 39.

During the summer the ubiquitous Patrick Gabarrou created a fine route on the Italian Flanks when, with Cesare Ravaschietto, he completed *Padrepio, prega per Tutti,* a direct line up the SSE Face of Picco Muzio. This new climb appears to run very close to (and possibly just right of) the *1970 Route* and is graded ED3 7a, 6c obl. It is reported to lie on good rock and appears to reach the crest of the Furggen just left of the summit of the Muzio, from where the overhangs of the *Direct Finish* (Carrel/Chiara/Perino, 1941: TD: sustained for 150m at V and V+), must be climbed to reach the top of the Matterhorn. The total height of this combination is 1200m.

Weissmies Over 10-11 December 2001 Italians, Stefania Merlo, Leonardo Ricalcati and Mauro Rossi, climbed *Via del Seracco Rosa* on the remote and rarely visited NE Face. For the first 400m they followed a fairly narrow goulotte with short sections of 85° until it terminated in a sérac barrier, which dominates the central part of the face and guards access to the upper slopes. After passing the sérac, they found these upper slopes, although less steep (c.60°), very demanding due to lack of decent snow cover. Approximately 500m of hard front-pointing on classic, winter, alpine concrete led to the top and the serious c.920m route was given a grade of TD V/3+.

BERNESE OBERLAND

The new AC Guide to this region, edited by Les Swindin, is completely updated from the previous volume, and sports improved features, notably topos included in the text alongside the route, rather than grouped at the end.

Eiger There were at least two ascents of interest on the North Face. Over 17-18 August Swiss climbers, Stephan Siegrist and Michal Pitelka, made a two-day ascent of the *1938 Route* using mostly original equipment from the 1930s. They were accompanied by Thomas Ulrich, who, equipped with modern gear, photographed the climb and also filmed it for a TV documentary. Much 1930s equipment was gathered for the event. Nailed boots and ice axes came from Swiss Army stocks, pegs and clothing from various sources, crampons were replicated by Grivel and, as the only comprise in this highly traditional venture, hemp ropes were constructed with a nylon core. Anderl Heckmair helped considerably in the preparations.

Later in the season, from 12-16 September, Swiss guides, Peter Keller and Urs Odermatt, put up a hard new route following, in its first half, an independent line right of the *Direct North East Pillar* (put up in 1970 by the Scots, Ian McEacheran, Bugs McKeith and Kenny Spence). Where the Scottish route climbs the First Buttress of the Pillar on its left flank, the Swiss route takes the quasi-overhanging prow direct. Keller and Odermatt first attempted the line in June, hoping to climb it alpine style, but soon realised that, for them, this was not feasible. A second attempt, this time fixing ropes, was made in August, the climbers taking two days to reach the ice field at the top of the First Buttress. Here, they encountered climbing up to 7b and one 50m section that overhung around 10m.

The third and final attempt began on Thursday, 12 September. They completed only 60m that day, fixing one rope before returning to their bivouac in the tunnel. On the second day they climbed just 90m in 14 hours of sustained effort. The buttress was continuously overhanging and although the weather was fine, it was very cold with a brisk north-easterly wind. On the third day they overcame a steep wall right of the crest of the Second Buttress, where the last two pitches to reach easy ground were 7c. Here they left the haul bag and much of their equipment (the pair carried 150 bolts to equip all the compact rock sections, always drilling on lead from skyhooks).

On the morning of the 15th they reascended their ropes and continued up mixed ground on the right flank of the Third Buttress, where difficulties of M5 and WI3 were encountered. Now, after 30 new pitches and halfway up the face, it was only five rope lengths of easier snow/mixed ground to the lower edge of the Lauper Icefield. The pair climbed this into the night for a further six pitches to reach the Mittellegi Ridge, where they spent an uncomfortable bivouac. By 10.00am on the fifth day they were at the 3970m summit. The route, which has 41 pitches and nearly 2000m of climbing on variable rock from loose to perfect, was christened *Griff ins Licht* ('Reach for the Light').

BREGAGLIA-MASINO

Monte Qualido In May probably the hardest and most sustained free route on the huge East Face was put up by talented local activists, Simone Pedeferri and Adrian Selva. *Yellow Butterfly* (named after a large yellow flake high on the route) is situated towards the left side of the c.600m vertical granite wall and shares some ground with existing lines (eight out of the 21 pitches are common to other routes). As it follows a series of hard cracks, the climbing can be almost entirely protected with natural gear. At the time of writing it is not clear whether the crux pitch (the 18th , estimated at 8a/8a+) has been climbed without rest points.

Around on the front face, referred to as the **Precipizio degli Asteroidi**, the naturalized Germans, Gabor Berecz and Thomas Tivadar, frequent visitors to this formation, completed two more big-wall routes. In mid-July they spent two days working on the lower part of their line, then set off with a double portaledge. After three nights on the face they completed their 13-pitch project, which lies towards the right side of the SE Face near the established 1988 Fazzini/Fazzini/Gianola/Pomoni route, *Pejonasa Wall* (V 5.10 A2). The result was *Abyss*, a moderate new-wave aid route at 5.11 and A3, which according to the authors is one of best routes of its type in the valley. Six days in total were spent on the face.

The pair had reckoned this to be the last worthwhile big wall line on the face but during their ascent spotted a nearby thin crack system. They returned almost immediately and climbed the route, making one bivouac at the end of pitch five on the large wooded terrace at half-height. The third pitch, led by Berecz on Beaks, heads and hooks, felt definitely A5 terrain but was awarded a slightly lower grade due to one good Lost Arrow placement. The route joins *Pejonasa Wall* for a section and then again at the exit, where the pair had to climb through a heavy electrical storm. *Discoteca con Franca* (named after a local girl) has one of the hardest technical aid pitches in the valley and was given a grade of VI 5.10 A4c. Twelve Bat holes were drilled, and 15 Beaks, 15 Copperheads and the full assortment of hooks will be required for a repeat ascent.

Piz Badile On 28 July two Slovakians, Villiam Jakubec and Jan Mierka, created the first new route in over a decade on the famous NE Face. *La Storia Lunga* starts up the First Dièdre (aka Rébuffat Dièdre) of the classic *Cassin Route* and at the top, where the Cassin traverses left, climbs straight up the slabs between *Linea Blanca* ('The White Line' – Koller/Silhan, 1978: c700m: VI) and *Another Day in Paradise* (Muller/Muller/Zgraggen, 1991: c600m: VII). Nine pitches above the Dièdre (IV and V with three pitches of VI+), the pair came to an overlap. Unable to continue directly, they were forced to make a relatively easy traverse right for around 30m to join the last four pitches of *Another Day in Paradise*. The route was completed in 12 hours. The unclimbed direct finish remains an obvious challenge for a strong party.

BERNINA

Piz Gluschaint On 30 January local activists, Luca Maspes and G Ondaro, made the first ascent of *Delicatezze* on the South Face. The pair had gone up to the peak to attempt a rock route but finding favourable conditions turned instead to an unclimbed gully which they climbed at IV/5 M5.

Cime di Musella Maspes returned to the region on 2 February with Marco Colombo and guidebook author and local guru, Giuseppe Miotti. They first looked at one of the 2800m subsidiary summits of the Musella and on its SW Face climbed a new 300m high, six-pitch rock route with difficulties of V+/VI.

The following day they made the second overall and first winter ascent of *Spigolo Asimmetico* on the South Spur of the West Ridge of **Cima Occidentale** (3094m). This is a very fine 250m high, eight-pitch route characterised by wonderful red gneiss, and put up in September 1991 by Celio Gatti and Mario Vannuccini at a maximum grade of V+.

Piz Palu Swiss guides, Walter Hölzer and Toni Steurer, linked all three classic arêtes on the N Face within 24 hours during the summer. They also managed this without using any mechanized transport from the Bernina Pass. The pair began a little after 8.00pm from the 2300m Pass and walked up to the Diavolezza Cable Car. After crossing the Pers Glacier they started the N Spur of West Peak a little before 2.00am and were on the summit in just two hours. After continuing up the ridge to the main summit, they began a difficult descent of the Bumiller-grat, down-climbing the sérac formation that generally forms the crux of the upper section, and the lower rock, which has difficulties up to V–. They then moved across to the Kuffner and made a rapid ascent of this to the 3882m E Summit before high-tailing it down c.1600m to regain their car at the Bernina Pass just 23 hours and 40 minutes after leaving. The total ascent and descent was reported to be around 7850m. While it is believed the three spurs have been linked before, they have not been crossed at this speed, car to car.

DOLOMITES

Brenta Group
Cima Brenta In early summer the talented Italian, Rolando Larcher, pulled off an impressive feat by making an all-free ascent of the *1964 Baschera/dal Bosco/ Navasa Route* on the East Face of Cima Brenta (3150m). The 650m *Via Verona* was originally climbed over 40 hours at V+ and A3, and normally parties re-peating the line still count on making a bivouac. Larcher, accompanied by fellow Italian, Franco Cavallero, climbed the whole route, onsight, in 11 hours. Larch-er led every pitch using the in-situ gear and placing his own natural protection. The crux was 7c.

Brenta Alta In early August Larcher, this time with Maurizio Oviglia, put up a new route on the South Face. *Dialoporco!* is a 350m climb on a yellow pillar with difficulties up to 6b+. The most sustained section is found in the lower part of the route, where the rock is continuously overhanging. Although rather devoid of natural protection, this section is well furnished with holds and features. The pair employed a combination of natural protection and eight-millimetre bolts. The latter were used quite sparsely, with only a maximum of two bolts placed, from skyhooks, on any pitch. This has resulted in a number of run-out sections, notably up to 15m of climbing at 6a+ without protection.

The Pala Group
Fourth Pala di San Lucano Ivo Ferrari, one of the most prolific activists and pioneers in the Dolomites during recent years, made the first solo ascent of the *Casarotto-Radin Route* on the East Face. Put up by the legendary Italian, Renato Casarotto with Piero Radin in 1974, the 1000m high route is not sustained but has a crux pitch of VI+ and A1, the only one on which Ferrari used a backrope.

Leaving the Valle di San Lucano at 5.00am on a warm summer's morning, Ferrari was on the top by 2.00pm.

Torre Sprit In mid-September Rolando Larcher completed yet another very demanding all-free multi-pitch route, when he made a redpoint ascent of the 465m-high *Grande Onda* on the SW Face of this 2392m summit south-west of Monte Agner. The new route lies to the left of the South Pillar taken by the fine and sustained *Spigolo della Melodia* (de Pellegrini/Zanolla, 1978: 450m: VI/VI+) and has ten pitches, eight of which are 6c and above. There are two pitches graded 7a and 7a+, one graded 7b, pitches two and three are 7c and the crux fifth pitch is rated 8a. The route has been equipped in typical Larcher style, bolted from the ground up but with the protection points very well-spaced, leading to quite run-out climbing and obligatory difficulties of 7b. Fifty-six bolts were placed and natural gear is not really needed except on the last easy pitch.

Civetta Group
Torre Venezia During the early part of the summer Christoph Hainz added a fine and very sustained all-free route to the South Face. The 450m line, on which the first ascensionist used only traditional protection, climbs through the big series of overhangs in the centre of the face, left of the *Tissi Route*, and has maximum difficulties of 7b.

Marmolada Group
Marmolada di Penia Not reported in last year's AJ but too significant an ascent (for more than one reason) to miss, was the first redpoint of the incredible route, *La Larcher/Vigiani*, on the SW Face of the 3343m Marmolada di Penia. This line, which was first climbed in the summer of 2000 by Italians, Rolando Larcher and Roberto Vigiani, lies immediately left of the classic *Solda Route*, taking the right edge of the *Cristina Pillar* before continuing to tackle the centre of the compact and overhanging *Lindo Pillar* directly above. The 10 pitches have the following grades: 6c, 6b+, 7c+, 7b, 7c+, 7c, 8a, 7b+, 7c+, 7b, and the redpoint was made by Larcher himself. The route is extremely sustained and Larcher reports the ninth pitch to be the best he has ever climbed. Bolts are sportingly placed, so the route also features rather run-out and obligatory high-standard climbing. But despite the fact that this is certainly not the first route on the Marmolada to be created with bolt protection, the great South Face is still considered hallowed ground amongst many Italians, and Larcher's use of the drill has been criticised.

Tre Cime di Lavaredo Group
Cima Grande The well-known German, Alex Huber, made the first ropeless solo of the highly exposed *Brandler-Hasse Route* (VIII) on the North Face. Huber first climbed the route on-sight the previous month, then practised the climb for five days until he had all the difficult sections well-rehearsed and knew which holds he could trust. He then opted for total commitment, starting his ascent at 7.00am on 1 August with no other equipment than climbing shoes, chalk bag and helmet. Four hours and 18 pitches later he was on the summit.

Cima Ovest Equal to, if not more impressive than Alexander Huber's achievement was Michael Mayr's completely free solo ascent of the 1935 *Cassin-Ratti Route* on the North Face (6c/6c+). In common with the *Brandler-Hasse* the rock is far from perfect, which makes this completely on-sight ascent by the 27-year-old climber from the Tyrol all the more impressive. The Austrian climbed with a small rucksack containing a 12m length of rope for emergency purposes but it was not used.

Alex Huber's own route on the face, *Bellavista*, received a second ascent on 16 September, albeit in two stages, by Mauro 'Bubu' Bole. Bole worked on the route for a couple of months and on the 16th 'warmed up' by top-roping the two hard pitches below the great roof (30m, 7a and 18m, 7a+). Feeling in very good shape he decided to immediately set out on the crux pitch. Everything went well and he was able to link the entire 55m 8c pitch and continue to the top of the route. He then rappelled and quickly climbed from the ground up to the crux, so freeing all pitches on the route.

PAUL KNOTT

Russia and Central Asia 2002

The author would like to acknowledge the help of correspondents including Viktor Vasyanin, Peter Solomatin, Vladimir Komissarov and Lindsay Griffin, and information resources mountain.ru, risk.ru and Babelfish.

As in 2001, the exploratory activities of international climbers were again concentrated almost entirely in the Tien Shan. Meanwhile, there was significant development by climbers from Russia and Central Asia, partly due to the introduction of a 'first ascent' class in competitions. There were also many purely independent endeavours and a plurality of styles from group ascents of hard routes over many days (a style that is awarded its own grade), to a lightweight 'alpine' approach.

The Caucasus
Exploration in this range included winter climbs on the major peaks, continued attempts at hard routes on serious faces, and lower altitude rock routes in outlying areas.

In the Western Caucasus in August Yuri Koshelenko, with Mikhail Astakhov, continued his Open Caucasus project with a trip exploring the potential of the area around **Great Tkhach (2368m)**. They found cliffs with a vertical drop of 250-350m and suggested that although the area has promise, the **Fisht/ Pshekhasu** area seems to have greater potential. At around the same time a group of Krasnodar climbers including Nikolai Rudenko and Natalya Grishenko visited the area. They made first ascents of several 3-6 pitch routes of an easy grade, reporting a total length of cliff over 10km.

In the Elbrus Region, several teams sought to climb new routes on the W/ NW Face of **Kiukiurtliu (4610m)**. This has been argued to be the hardest rock wall in Russia, and presently has only three routes: the 1974 *Giutashvili Route* on the W Face at 6A, the 1981 *Lukashvili Route* in the centre of the NW Face at 6B and the 2000 *Andreev Route* on the R part of the W Face, also at 6B. Typical difficulties include sustained steepness of 100° combined with unreliable rock, problematic access and poor weather. In 2000, an attempt at repeating the *Andreev Route* ended when Igor Nefedov was killed by rockfall low on the route.

In June Alexander Abramov returned to the mountain for a second attempt on the new 6B route on the NW Face that he first attempted with Sergey Shchepachkov in December 1999. On that occasion, they climbed a quarter of the route before Shchepachkov suffered pulmonary oedema, forcing a retreat. The 2002 attempt, with four other climbers, ended when ominous rockfall was encountered in the same place as in the 2000 Nefedov accident. A Dagestan team climbing early in 2003 was more successful, climbing a new route on the Central W Face between the *Lukashvili* and *Andreev Routes*. The team including

A Grigorev and Konstantin Dorro climbed from 7-26 February, reporting practically all pitches as having difficulties of 5B-6A.

On **Elbrus (5642m)** in late July an international clean-up expedition took place, with over 130 people taking part from cities in Russia and elsewhere. On one day alone an estimated four tonnes of metal cans and broken glass were carried down, in addition to which a large amount of rubbish was burned. From the nearby Adyl-Su Valley, early in 2003, the team of V. Volodin, Andrey Kazakov and G Kochetkov climbed a new route at 6A on the N Face of **Bashkara (4241m)**. They climbed in alpine style, in poor weather conditions, reaching the summit on 26 February.

In the Bezingi area, A. Rakhmanin's team from St Petersburg climbed a new route on the E Face of **Misses-Tau (4427m)** from 14-18 August. On **Koshtan (5151m)**, in December, the team of Ruslan Kochetkov, Ivan Artemov and Sergey Shchepachkov climbed a new 5B route which they named *Samara*. Taking an ice couloir on the N Face slightly to the right of the 1989 *Kolchin Route*, they summited on 15 December after spending three nights on the mountain. This was the second climb of a project to make ascents of Caucasus 5000m peaks in winter.

In February 2003 two teams made ascents of the rock face of **Ak-Kaya**. Kiril Korabelnikov's team climbed a new route left of the *Vasiliev Route*, finding climbing up to 6A. The *Vasiliev Route* itself received an alpine-style ascent by the St. Petersburg team of Valery Shamalo and Alexey Gorbatenkov.

The 1000m NW Face of **Erydag (3925m)/Erydag NNW (3887m)** in Dagestan was the venue for the rock class of the 2002 Russian open championships. The face has straightforward access and a dry climate with minimal build-up of snow and ice in winter. Routes climbed during the championship included the *Goloshchapov, Efimov, Shchedrin, Rodoshkevich, Babitskiy, Mikhailov* and *Nekrasov*. The 2001 *Voronin Route* received its second ascent by a Ekaterinburg team including Anatoliy Yarunov.

Konstantin Dorro with a team from Makhachkala climbed a new route on the face. The 1100m route took the 'nose' on the R part of the NW Face and was 6th class climbing with VI and A3. It was climbed from 17 July to 3 August using two camps on the wall. During that time there was at least one storm sending waterfalls and rockfall down much of the face. The ascensionists compared the route to the *Voronin Route*, considering it possibly to be harder overall.

Russia and Ukraine

In this mostly non-mountainous area, exploration highlighted surprising climbing potential in lower altitude arctic ranges. In the **Prepolar Urals** two separate teams made first ascents on the E Face of **Sablya (1497m)**. The St Petersburg team, led by Kiril Korabelnikov, climbed the Central NE Face in 20 pitches at 6A from 10-19 April. The team from Perm led by Vyacheslav Puchnin climbed the right side of the NE Face, finding the same grade and length of climb, which they completed in two pushes from 8-11 and 14-19 April. In the **Khibins Mountains** on the arctic Kola Peninsula there are reportedly potential routes up to 5B, and 400m unclimbed N faces on **Petrelliusa**, **Fersmana** and

Takhtarvumchorr amongst other peaks. On the NE Face of **Great Vudyavrchorr (1068m)** near Kirovsk, a St Petersburg team including A Andreev, S Sidorenko and M Pankov climbed a new 11-pitch 5B mixed route, completing it on 23 August after two days of preparation. Previous routes on the E Faces of this peak and its neighbour **Vudyavrchorr Lesser (1068m)** took various ribs at 3A-B. On 1 February 2003 a Moscow team including Ivan Ermakov climbed a new route taking the E Couloir of **Vudyavrchorr Lesser (1068m)** at 2A. In March a ski mountaineering competition was held in the range.

A number of new routes was reported on the cliffs and mountains of the **Crimea**. At the end of January 2003 Alexander Lavrinenko, Vladimir Mogila and Aleksey Zhilin completed the 310m new route *Centre*, 6A VI A3, on the well-known cliff **Foros Kant**. The route takes a central line, between *Semerkiy* 5A and *Left Rhombus* 5B. This followed the tradition in the last few years for Odessa climbers to climb significant new routes over the New Year period. In early 2001 A. Zhilin and team climbed the 400m *Renaissance*, 6A VI A3, on **Treugolnik**, and V.Yarechevskiy and V. Maruchin climbed the 300m Giperboreya, 6A 5.11d (F7a) A3+, on **Shaan-Kaya (871m)**.

In early 2002 Odessa climbers put up *Machombo*, on **Morcheka (980m)** (see AJ107). This route received a solo ascent over three days in February by Minsk climber Alexander Maksimen, who also completed a solo ascent of *Centre* (over two days, by Ershov's *Zamanikh* variant). In mid-May **Machombo** was again climbed by Latvians Kristaps Liepins and Janis Kigurs, who completed the route in 24 hours of active climbing time, grading it 6A VI A3, 335m.

On **Chelebi (657m)** in late February Kharkov climbers L. Volkov and A. Larionov climbed a new route on the right side of the S Face, estimating its grade at 5B and giving it the name *Extreme*.

The Pamir (including Chinese Pamir)

There remained little climbing activity in the Pamir other than on its three highest peaks, probably because of security concerns, which remain in some areas of Tadzhikistan. In contrast, there was much activity on **Pik Lenin (7134m)**. In February-March 2002 a team including Dmitry Shparo from Russia and Alexander Gubaev and Alexander Agafonov from Kyrgyzstan made a winter ascent. In the summer season 74 participants from 13 countries took part in a mountain festival. Of these, 41 from 9 countries reached the summit. A further festival is being held in 2003, which is an important anniversary of the first ascents of the Pamir 7000m peaks: the 75th, 70th and 50th for peaks **Lenin, Communism (Ismaila Samanievo)** and **Korzhenevsakaya** respectively.

In an area sometimes referred to as the Chinese Pamir (and otherwise as part of the Kun-Lun), in August-September a team of five led by Andrey Ledebev made a 195km traverse over the **Ulug-Arttag, Kongur-Tag** and **Muztag-Ata Ranges**. The Ulug-Arttag has seen little attention since Eric Shipton's attempt on its highest peak Chakragil (Karabentertag, 6760m). In the Kongur-Tag the team made the first ascent of the westernmost summit Pik Aklangm (6995m), approaching from Bulunkol to join the upper SE Ridge. The 30-day trip was concluded with a N-S traverse of the 'crater' of Muztag-Ata (7546m), over the Kuksay Glacier.

The Pamir Alai

As in 2001, climbers were deterred from visiting much of this area by the unstable security situation. Concerns remain despite the reduced capability of the IMU following the military action in Afghanistan. Conflicting views about the situation have been expressed by local sources.

One of the few reported climbs from 2002 was that of the Central N Face of **Ak-Su (5217m)**, by the Kirov team of Ilyas Tukhvatulin and Pavel Shabalin. A new variant on the left of the 'nose' in the centre of wall was climbed over 16 days, starting at the unusually late date of 20 September. The pair descended via the *Cold Corner*. This was Pavel Shabalin's tenth ascent of the face, with all ten ascents having been by different routes.

In the nearby **Fann Mountains** an alpine rock-climbing championship was held in July-August. Ascents included the 1987 *Arkhilov Route* taking a pillar on the N Face of **Parandas (4250m)** at 5B, the 1966 *Usenov Route* on the N Rib of **Chapdara (5049m)** at 5A, and the W Face of **Zamok (5070m)** at 5A. Also in the Fann Mountains an international expedition took place, during which the first ascent was made of a 5800m summit in the Darvazskiy Range. The team led by Alexander Kirikov from Tomsk summited on 15 August by a route graded at 5A. The peak was named **Druzhby Narodov** ('friendship of peoples').

The Tien Shan

The interest of non-Russian climbers continues to be concentrated in this range, and this is being paralleled by continued development of access and facilities. In May the Irkeshtam Pass was opened between Kyrgyzstan and China, making combined trips easier between Pik Lenin and Muztag Ata. Climbers will also be interested to note that Globalstar satellite phones are now available for rent in Bishkek. On a less encouraging note, the impression of more unsettled weather is reinforced by recent measurements showing rising levels in the Issyk-Kul Lake, reversing the earlier trend towards shrinkage.

During the summer season there were ten ascents of **Pik Pobeda (7439m)** by climbers from Russia and beyond. There was one fatality from cerebral oedema. The mountain received its first ski descent in August by Nikolai Pimkin from St Petersburg, who had climbed the mountain in the company of two friends from Novgorod. Both ascent and descent were by the standard route via **Pik Vazha Pshaveli (6918m)**. In 1997, Americans Tyson Bradley and Dave Braun skied from 6700m on Pobeda's *Abalakov Route*. The team of Nikolay Chervonenko, Dmitry Muravjov, Sergey Samoilov, Alexander Krynin and Ali Nasuh Mahruki (Turkey) attempted the second winter ascent of this route in February 2003, the first having been in 1990 by a very strong team. After an initial push was made to 5650m heavy snowfall prevented further climbing.

In the **Kyrgyz Range**, in February 2003 Kyrgyz climbers Vitaliy Akimov and Nikolai Gutnik climbed a new 5B route on Svobodnaya Korea (4740m).

A number of teams visited the area around **Kyzyl Asker (5842m)** in the **W Kokshaal-Too**, attracted by its potential for fine technical lines on mostly good granite. The Scottish team of Esmond Tressider and Guy Robertson made two attempts on the SE face of **Kyzyl Asker** by its central ice couloir. Both attempts were thwarted by rapidly thawing ice as the sun hit the face. The highest point reached was a little under halfway up the 1300m face, just past the first section of very steep ice. The climbing was up to 95°, with more of the same above, plus difficult mixed climbing high on the face.

Blair Fyffe and Neal Crampton from the same group repeated the N Face of **Pik Babuchka (5225m)** ('butterfly peak') at the head of the Central Komorova glacier, reporting quality climbing with a crux of Scottish V. The route was first climbed in 1998 by a N American team (*see AJ104*). Following this they made the first ascent of the N Ridge of **Pik 4850m** from the Kyzyl Glacier. This was the second ascent of the peak, which they provisionally named **Pik Sabor** (Cathedral peak). The 1200m route took two days at TD with Scottish V,6, tricky route finding, and a novel bivvy behind a huge flake.

In September a team including Cecilia Buil and Iñaki Cabo climbed a multi-day big wall route *Ak-Shaitan* ('white devil') on the Ochre Walls. The route involves a 500m rock tower at around A3+ 6A 80° followed by an alpine arête. Fixed ropes and some bolts were used on the wall, but nights were spent at its base because of the unsettled weather. The attempt was interrupted for four days during which a metre of snow fell at base camp. After this, a cold clear spell allowed an ascent to the summit.

In October a group from Bishkek and other cities coordinated by Vladimir Biryukov visited the same area, with new route objectives including the SW Face of **Pik 4716m** (often called Petit Dru). An attempt on the face was started on 15 October, but this was curtailed by heavy snowfall that soon confined the team to base camp. Their retreat to Bishkek was something of an epic, in which even Ural trucks became stuck on a number of occasions.

There were also several teams exploring smaller ranges in the same general area. In September a trip guided by Pat Littlejohn, Adrian Nelhams and Vladimir Komissarov first visited the **At-Bashy Range** of limestone peaks immediately north of the Kyzyl Asker group. There are no records of previous climbs in this range. From a base camp at 3800m in the Aksu-lu-tor Valley ascents were made of **Ak-Kalpak (4673m)** at PD and the W Ridge of **Pik Troika** at AD, and a traverse was made of **Berkut (4717m)** at AD+ and **Kenesh (4630m)**. After this they moved to the previously unvisited Ak-bai-tal Glacier, the third to the W of Kyzyl Asker, via a 25km drive up a river bed. From a camp at 4200m they climbed routes including both summits of **Ak-bai-tal Peak (4981m)**, the technical W Ridge of the same peak, and a traverse of the distinctive 'White Fan' (**Belyi Veer, 4757m**). Finally, at the end of the trip, a number of 3-pitch HS-E2 limestone rock routes were climbed in an area christened Nomad Domes.

Approaching from the same direction, a UK team including Mike Rosser, Wayne Gladwin and Sharon Abbott made the first visit to the SW end of the **Khrebet Borkoldoy**, where they climbed **Peaks 4655m** at PD (which they named **Peak Alexander**), **4850m** (named **Ata Peak**) and **4655m** (named **Peak Ibex**).

The similarly unexplored **Khrebet Kyokkiar**, situated by the Chinese border and reached by skirting the At-Bashy Range, was visited by David Gerrard's UK team in August. As acclimatisation, David with Karl Baker climbed several new peaks in the Gory Sarybeles including **4300m**. In the Kyokkiar they made the first ascent of the highest **Peak 4760m** at AD, and of two nearby peaks, both at **c.4600m**. Meanwhile John Cuthbert and Graham Sutton had explored a separate cwm and attempted an ice line on one of the faces. The greatest potential of the area would appear to be the 500m-1000m limestone walls, which are highly featured and have snow-free descents.

Siberia and the Russian Far East

Here the exciting development highlighted in AJ107 continued both in the previously reported areas such as the Ergaki Massif, and in even less known regions.

The more established **Altai Range** also saw some activity. In the **Katun Range**, early in 2002 **Altai Crown (20th October Peak, 4160m)** received a winter ascent of its NE Face by a team including A. Afanasev. The route was climbed over 15 days at 6A. In the same area on 21 August a speed competition was held on **Belukha East (4506m)** from the 1900m base camp to its S. The winner was Sergey Brodsky with a time of 6 hours 45 minutes. In July members of the Sakharov alpinist movement of Russia including E Maltsev and E Onishchenko made the first ascent of a peak from the Shavlo area of the **Northern Chuisky**, which they named **PL Kapitsy (3500m)**. The ascent was from the NW at 2B.

Several new routes were climbed in the **Western Sayan**. A Krasnoyarsk team including V. Balezin, D. Tsyganov and E. Dmitrienko climbed a new route on the N Face of **Sphinx North (1915m)**, climbing from 23-26 August at 5B/6A. In the Ergaki Massif from 3-6 August, D Morozov and team from Chalabinsk climbed a new route taking the left part of the N Face of **Parus (2137m)**.

In the **Eastern Sayan**, Andrey Afanasev and Bair Khandzhapov from Irkutsk gained first place in the climbing championship in the new class of first ascents, with their route on the N Face of the E shoulder of **Kupol (2921m)**. They climbed the route from 18-24 September at 6A. In the same range from 5-8 August a Krasnoyarsk team including S Cherezov made the first ascent of the E Face of **Golova (1970m)** at 5B.

In the **Barguzin Range**, immediately E of Lake Baikal, a new route was climbed on **Argada (2340m)** by P Kolesov, P Tugarin and I Sherstnev from the Buryat Mountaineering Federation. The route took the Central E Face at 5B.

In February 2003 there were two major winter ascents in the **Kodar Range**, one day's train journey NE of Lake Baikal. The Angarsk team of Sergey Kosoturov, Andrey Kustov, Oleg Pedenko, and Denis Veretenin climbed the 600m S Face of **Obrez (2980m)** (aka. **Pioneer**) at 6A-6B. This peak immediately N of **Pik BAM (3075m)** was previously unclimbed in spite of several prior attempts. The team started climbing on the 9th in calm sunny weather at − 25C, and after losing many days' climbing to bad weather, finally summited on the 21st. They used one portaledge camp on the face, which is mainly rock. They approached the mountain via 50km of off-road driving by Ural truck followed by five days of load-hauling over the remaining 17km.

In spite of the low temperatures encountered on their winter 2001 expedition, Krasnoyarsk climbers including Valeriy Balezin, Vladimir Arkhipov and Zhenya Dmitrienko returned to **Pik Tsarskiy Tron (2820m)**, also in February, 2003. They climbed a 1000m new route on the SW Face of the main summit, making two camps on the face and mostly using aid to overcome the 6B climbing because of poor rock. They avoided a lengthy approach by using helicopter access.

DEREK FORDHAM

Greenland 2002

These notes are based on the 24 reports received in response to over 40 requests for information.

Ice Cap crossings

As in previous years, expedition activity in Greenland during 2002 was dominated by ice cap crossings. From a total of 60 applications the Danish Polar Centre received for 'sport' expeditions, 33 were from groups intending to make a crossing, most planning to use the 'trade route' between the airfields at Kulusuk (east coast) and Kangerdlugssuaq (west coast). Several factors emerged in 2002. Firstly, more parties chose to make the crossing from west to east than in previous years. Secondly, the start dates were spread more evenly over the period April to August than in other years. Thirdly, at last the time taken for the fairly straightforward 'trade route' crossing of about 600km was substantially reduced by a number of parties, the current record set in 2002 being eight days, closely followed by one of nine days and another of ten days. This particular form of speed skiing is so far the sole prerogative of the Norwegians.

One of the first of the crossing expeditions was the 'Swedish Arctic Girl Adventure', composed of Maria Hedman and Kristin Lundgren (Sweden) who started on 10 April from **Kangerdlugssuaq** and reached **Isortoq** on the east coast 33 days later.

They were followed a day later by Anders Voll and Yngve Torjussen (Norway) of the Ajungilak 02 Expedition who, finding no snow on the last few kilometres to the ice cap, had to take a lift to **Pt.660** along the controversial road to the VW test circuit on the ice cap. From there, using pulks but eschewing sails or kites, they reached Isortoq in 23 days.

On 16 April Aslak Prestbakmo and Lars Helgaker (Norway) set off from Isortoq and with the aid of kites reached a speed of 15km/hr on their crossing to Kangerdlugssuaq which took 18 days despite losing 1½ days due to bad weather.

Kites were also used by Denis Bonnefous and his three companions (France) in their attempt to make an east-west crossing in less than 15 days starting on 17 April. They made slow progress to a point 100km in on the ice cap where they encountered high winds followed by a four-day storm which dumped large quantities of new snow in low temperatures. Realising that they were moving too slowly and as a result were low on food, fuel and time, they used a satellite telephone to arrange to be picked up by helicopter.

Kites also featured large in the plans of Freddy Markham, Roger Mear and Bill O'Connor (UK) who on 26 April were landed by helicopter on the eastern edge of the ice cap. However, the inexperience of one team member with the operating technique required for the large powerful kites taken meant that the expedition had to be abandoned shortly after starting.

Reverting to more traditional means of ice cap travel Sjur Mørdre (Norway) led a group of eight with dog sledges on a 21-day traverse from **Kangerdlugssuaq** to **Isortoq**, starting a 19 day return to Kangerdlugssuaq on 7 August.

On 11 May the Greenland veteran Ramon Larramendi, together with Roberto Lema and Carlos Mengibar (Spain), started from **Narsaq** in the south of Greenland and using an innovative 'Kitesled' of their own design, reached Qaanaaq in the north on 13 June, having covered 2408km in 33 days. The 'Kitesled' was made of three sledges lashed together to make a platform of 6x3 metres riding on four runners. A tent was permanently pitched on the platform and Ramon claims it was possible for one person to sleep and cook while the kite pulled the sledge at speeds up to 383km/day!

This impressive journey followed a similar south-north traverse made in 2001 and technical improvements in the 'Kitesled', resulting from experience gained on the two traverses, are being made in preparation for a planned traverse of the East Antarctic ice sheet.

The Greenland Bicycle (yes, BICYCLE!) Expedition was equally innovative in another form. Ralph Tuijn and Pierre Deroi (Netherlands and France) left the east coast on 12 May and made the crossing to Kangerdlugssuaq in 26 days, having lost two days to storms. On the ascent to the ice cap the bicycle needed to be carried on the pulk. Storms and later soft snow hindered its use until the central plateau where at times the bicycle, fitted with very wide tyres, was used to tow the pulk with the other member either riding on top or using snow shoes. Problems with crevasses were encountered near the west coast just before the cyclists encountered the road to the VW test track.

The hard surface from **Pt.660** to **Kangerdlugssuaq** gave a last day of cycling with a top speed of 20km/hr. On the whole crossing the bicycle was used for 180km and the expedition plans to use the same technique on an Antarctic expedition planned for 2003/4.

The members of the Piteraq 2002 expedition, Egil Nilsen, Knut Holmann and Richard Larsson (Norway), which left Kangerdlugssuaq on 16 May, planned to make the crossing in less than 10 days and to this end took food and fuel for only 13 days. Their total load amounted to 110kg carried in backpacks and two pulks. They skied for 12-14 hours per day until, on day five, one of the party was diagnosed as having blood poisoning in his heel and had to be evacuated by aircraft summoned by satellite telephone. The remaining two members then made a big effort to make up the lost time and despite bad weather they skied long hours and made it off the ice in 9 days, 4½ hours, each 9kg lighter than when they started.

On 13 June Alice Henderson and Kirsten Dunne were landed by helicopter from Ammassalik at their starting point on the east coast and proceeded for 27 days, many with poor visibility, to a point only 6-10km from Pt.660. Here it was necessary to use their PLB to summon a helicopter, since Kirsten Dunne was suffering from the effects of falling into several crevasses. Prior to their pick-up the party had used some of the emergency huts provided along the ice road from Pt.660 to VW's 'Aurora' test track. Their encounter with much rubbish and worse around these huts gives further strength to the question, why on earth did the Greenland authorities allow VW to desecrate such a wonderful unspoilt natural feature with a test track for motor cars?

In the south of Greenland Jakob Fink and four companions (Norway), starting on 23 July, made a journey of approximately 120km along the edge of the ice cap between **Nanortalik** and **Narssarssuak**. Delays with freight and terrain difficulties associated with being near the edge of the ice delayed the party and they were pushed to make their rendezvous by the appointed time ten days after leaving Nanortalik.

On 23 July one of the few expeditions to break away from the 'trade route' left **Isortoq** heading for **Port Victor**, some 80km north of Ilulissat on the west coast, following in reverse the route of A de Quervain's 1912 expedition. Led by Weiland Adler the four-man team (Germany) took 40 days to complete the 705km traverse using pulks with loads of 110kg each at the start, and sails where possible.

A seasonally late start took its toll on Thomas Klovland, Andres Storeng and Fredrik Rommen (Norway) who left Kangerdlugssuaq on 27 July. On the first day they only made 4.2km and during the first six days only 60km owing to lack of snow and much melt water in the form of rivers and lakes. However, once the snow was reached they made good progress and completed the crossing in 20 days.

Armin Wirth and Jarle Heimdal (Germany) started from Isortoq on 1 August also following in reverse the route of A de Quervain's 1912 expedition. Using kites and with a mid-ice cap visit from a TV crew they completed the crossing to Ilulissat in 25 days, despite encountering the bad weather and heavy snow typical of this time of year. They were lifted by helicopter the last few kilometres across a crevasse field and on to Ilulissat.

A delayed departure was made by Gard Telje and a companion (Norway) who started on 9 August from Isortoq. They encountered bad weather and difficult terrain conditions on the ascent to the ice cap but made it to the west coast in 22 days.

One of the last and certainly one of the fastest crossings was made by Yvind Sandbakk, Eirik Haugsnes and Ottar Haldorsen (Norway) who left Nativiit on the east coast on 20 August and reached Kangerdlugssuaq in 10 days, 21 hours and 32 minutes! They started fast, in the first eight days travelling 14 hours a day until slowed by whiteout and new snow followed by a dramatic drop in temperature. On the last few days the weather and travelling conditions improved and they arrived on the west coast with five days' food and fuel in hand.

The crossing record set by the Piteraq 2002 expedition in May stood for only three months, since Bjerg Odd Harald Hauge, Trond Hilde and Ivar Tollefsen (Norway) left the east coast on 23 August and even that late in the season reached Kangerdlugssuaq in an amazing 8 days and 9 hours!

East Coast
During July Steve Fisher (UK) led a six-strong expedition to the **Knud Rasmussen Glacier** area of the **Caledonian Alps** north of Semiligak. The snowline was at 600m and about 15km from the coast, much higher than in previous years, making the hauling of pulks harder work than anticipated. A base was established at the junction of the KR Glacier with an un-named side glacier from the east at about 66°11'N. From this camp three possible first ascents were made. Return to the coast was by the upper **Idrac Glacier** and this route

is recommended when the KR Glacier is dry. The expedition's lasting impression was that there are some big alpine objectives in the area which they were not equipped or experienced enough to undertake.

In July and August Roy Ruddle (UK) led a team of eight members of the Alpine Club and Alpine Climbing Group to the **Lemon Mountains** (*see article 'Citrus Delights', page 57*). Poor conditions on the glaciers forced their aircraft to land some 14km from the previously selected site. This revised base site, close to the **Lindbergh Mountains**, enabled the party in three groups to explore the glaciers to the north of the **Courtauld Glacier** and also the Lœbœltet Glacier. The North Lemon mountains were penetrated and two members made a first ascent of **The Spear, c.2500m**, via the NE face. Other team members made first ascents of six peaks in the North and East Lemons in addition to other climbs in the area and three first ascents in the Lindbergh range adjacent to the landing site. These included the most southerly of the Trillingerne group and the two mountians directly to the north. Second ascents were made of the **Trillingerne Central and Main peaks**. Unsuccessful attempts were made on Mitivagkat East, Cathedral East and Narren.

In June Bjerg Odd Harald Hauge (one of the three Norwegians who later set the record for crossing the Inland Ice in August) took a six-person group (Norway) further north to the **Watkins Bjerg** where they climbed **Gunnbjørnsfjeld**. They then moved to the mountain group to the north, **Knud Rasmussens Land**, which they mistakenly believed had not been visited before (Jim Lowther and his party were there in 1988), and made the ascent of a 3015m peak which they named **Hannbjørnsfjeld**, 'as it is definitely more aggressive and impressive than its sister (Gunnbjørnsfjeld) to the south'.

Also in the Watkins Mountains in May was a five-person group led by Paul Rose (UK). The team made two abortive attempts on **Gunnbjørnsfjeld** before achieving an ascent of the north ridge. They climbed several other peaks in the area and abandoned attempts on others, being progressively hampered by bad weather before flying out on 17 June.

June also saw John Hulse and Al Read (UK) in the Watkins. They had planned to traverse Knud Rasmussens Land but bad weather forced their aircraft to divert to a site near Gunnbjørnsfjeld. In this area they made four ascents, commenting that the climbing was relatively easy and that their 'joy was enhanced by the sense of pure exploration in this challenging and remote part of the world'.

Further north, Hans Laptun, who had spent his childhood at Nyhavn adjacent to **Mestersvig**, led a Franco-Norwegian group of three to revisit the area and the old coastal trappers' huts his father had used long ago. They travelled by Zodiac through the fjords to **Strindberg Fjord** before returning to Mestersvig.

The old trappers' huts were the focus of a group led by Anders Bjerregaard (DK) who spent three weeks restoring a hut at Kap Herschell last used in the 1940s. These small isolated huts, often in the most beautiful locations, are reminders of the period of intense Danish and Norwegian fur trapping activity during and after the war. They are not often a feature of climbing expeditions but many climbers who have had occasion to travel to or along the coastal areas of NE Greenland will know how welcoming they can be.

John Thorogood and his four-person group (UK) also used Zodiacs to travel from **Mestersvig** to the head of **Dicksons Fjord**. They then travelled up the **Langenthaler Glacier** onto the ice cap before skiing with pulks to the foot of **Shackletons Bjerg**, (first climbed by Swiss geologists Haller, Diehl and von Gunten in 1953) which was easily climbed by its SW ridge. Several other peaks to the south and east of Shackletons Bjerg were climbed before the party retraced its tracks to the Zodiacs and Mestersvig.

In early July, about a month prior to John Thorogood's expedition, the five-member Cambridge Glaciology Expedition, led by Chris Lockyer, flew by Twin Otter into **Louise Boyd Land**. They carried out a field research programme into the glaciology and geology of the area and made some first ascents of 2000m summits before commencing a 200km ski journey southwards to a pick-up in Dicksons Fjord. The journey took 21 days, passing close to **Petermanns Bjerg** and Shackletons Bjerg, and provided interest in the form of numerous melt river crossings, damage to pulks and a blizzard.

Owing to the non-production of the Greenland notes in the last issue of the *Alpine Journal* it was not possible to mention the latest expedition of the intrepid Dennis Schmitt (US). In July 2001 he led a NGS-sponsored expedition to the **Warming Land peninsula** in the far north of Greenland, where he found a valley reminiscent of Yosemite with a castle-like peak at its head, an ascent of which was later made. The party crossed and re-crossed the peninsula from **St George's Fjord** to **Hartz Sund** and found the limestone terrain provided useful natural bridges over the large rivers encountered.

Later in the year Dennis completed a multi-year Arctic project; the first longitudinal crossing of the **North American Brooks Range** from **Point Hope** to the **Mackenzie River**. Dennis had lived at **Anaktuvuk Pass**, about halfway along the traverse, in his youth and conceived and executed much of the traverse of the western section while hunting caribou and dog-sledging in the area. In the '80s and '90s he climbed in the Franklin and Romanzof icefield areas and completed much of the eastern half of the route; and in September 2001 the final leg of the eastern section was completed by crossing the Barn Range to Bonnet Lake. This was a journey of about 1500km through some of the most remote mountains in the Arctic.

SIMON RICHARDSON

Scottish Winter 2001-2002

The 2002 winter season had a very slow start. There were no snowfalls during October and the first real blast of winter did not occur until the second week of November. A pattern of short cold snaps followed by thaws continued through the month until high pressure centred over Scotland in early December. The weather was calm and the glens were below freezing, but a temperature inversion meant the tops were sunny and warm. Winter weather finally arrived in earnest just before Christmas when a series of northerly winds brought copious amounts of snow to Northern and Western Highlands.

Despite the variable conditions there was a high level of enthusiastic activity, especially over the New Year period. A noticeable trend was the number of second ascents and early repeats of high-standard routes by a large number of teams. Fewer new routes were climbed than in previous years, a recognition perhaps of the huge resource of existing quality climbs throughout the Highlands.

Two of the finest new routes of the early winter took place in the West. Andy Nisbet and Jonathan Preston visited **Ben Nevis** straight after the first November snows and made the first winter ascent of *The Slab Climb* (VI,7) on South Trident Buttress. This gave a superb and well protected mixed climb through some impressive ground. Across on **Aonach Mor**, Mike Pescod added a fierce route to *Homo Buttress* with the first ascent of *Piranha* (VII,8) with Jonny Baird and Tim Riley. This takes the right facing corner right of *Homo Robusticus* and was described as 'quite nippy' with a long technical crux section climbed on adze torques.

The weather steadily got colder over the Christmas period and strong northerly winds brought copious amounts of snow to the Northern Highlands. Climbing in the Torridon area was almost impossible without drowning in powder, but further north the lower peaks in **Coigach** provided some good climbing. Chris Cartwright and Simon Richardson visited Cul Beag and added the first winter climb to the cliffs on the West Face with *Cul of the Wild*, a six pitch V,6 mixed route based on the icy grooves right of *Lurgainn Edge*. The neighbouring **Cul Mor** also saw some activity with a bold solo ascent of *The Cul* (V,5) with a new variation finish by Iain Small.

The Applecross hills did not catch as much snow as their bigger neighbours. This allowed Blair Fyffe and Es Tresidder to visit the awesome Giant's Wall in Coire nan Fhamhair on **Beinn Bhan** and make the second ascent of *Divine Retribution* (VII,6). This major route starts right of *Die Riesenwand*, and then joins it for the exposed traverse right, before moving up and left to gain a groove system that leads directly up the cliff. Fyffe and Tresidder thought they were on new ground, but the route had previously been climbed by Robin Clothier and Chris Cartwright in 1991 and was never recorded. This only added to their adventure, and Tresidder later commented that the uncertainty of not knowing what lay above them and whether the route would go, meant it was one of the best days he had ever had in the mountains.

Central Highlands

One of the most significant events of the winter was the development of Coire an Laoigh in the **Grey Corries** by Andy Nisbet and Dave McGimpsey. This quartzite cliff which is clearly visible from Spean Bridge had been probed by several parties over the years, but Andy and Dave started developing it in earnest during 2001. Pride of place went to *Centrepoint* (VI,7) that tackles the imposing tower block shaped buttress in the centre of the crag. During the 2002 season, they added a new *Direct Start* (V,5) before adding four more routes. Pride of place went to the three star *Taliballan* (V,6), an improbable chimney blocked by a huge roof and the very imposing line of *Serve Chilled* (VII,6) that takes the icy vertical groove to the left. Always keen for some exploration, Erik Brunskill and Dafydd Morris also visited the crag and added *The Chaf* (IV,5), a mixed route on the left wall of *Central Gully*. Nisbet and McGimpsey continued their development of the cliff with four more routes in February. The highlight was *Blue Rinse* (VI,7) a sensational line up the big roofed corner on the right side of Centrepoint Buttress. Eric Brunskill and Daffyd Morris got in on the action with *Popped at the Piste* (V,6), a direct line up the steep slabby wall on the left side of Centrepoint Buttress, and Blair Fyffe and Andy Lole made the second ascent of the superb *Taliballan* (V,7).

The good ice extended to the North Face of **Aonach Beag**, where the modern classic *Royal Pardon* (VI,5) saw many ascents, and Stewart Anderson and Stuart MacFarlane climbed the very steep icefall to its right resulting in *Monarch's Crown* (VI,6).

Cairngorms

Conditions in the **Northern Corries** were not as reliable as usual. The finest individual performances came from Scott Muir. Taking advantage of a welcome Saturday night snowfall he made the first ascent of *Wedgewood* (VII,7) with Gordon Lennox. This is a winter version of the summer E2 *Edgewood* on Aladdin's Buttress in Sneachda, taking a more direct line than the line climbed by John Wiggins and Kathy Grindrod the previous season. Muir commented afterwards that the route is made for winter climbing with good torquing cracks. A week later Muir visited the neighbouring Coire an Lochain with Kevin Kelly and made the second ascent of *The Millennium Line* (VII,7). It was a wild day with rime galore and the ropes blowing horizontally in the wind.

In the Northern Cairngorms, Mark Garthwaite and Graeme Ettle made two significant ascents on the Upper Tier of **Carn Etchachan**. First they repeated *Snake Charmer* (VI,6) before returning the following weekend to make the first winter ascent of the summer line of *Poison Dwarf*. This technical VII,8 mixed climb was climbed on an atrocious day of high wind and spindrift and ranks as one of the finest performances of the winter.

The steep faces on **Lochnagar** came into good icy condition in February. Capitalising on a rare ascent of *Tough Guy* earlier in the season, Guy Robertson and Jason Currie returned to make the second ascent of *Rolling Thunder* on the

Tough-Brown Face. This summer E1 was first climbed in winter by Alan Mullin. Climbing solo in powder snow conditions in December 1999, he took several falls onto a back rope before succeeding on the route with a variation he called *Death by Misadventure* (VIII,8). Robertson and Currie made a more measured ascent, taking advantage of the icy nature of the right side of the face, describing the route afterwards as 'Lochnagar mixed climbing at its best'.

Further left, Blair Fyffe and Es Tresidder made the third ascent of *Trail of Tears* (VII,8). This was their third visit to climb this outstanding line that has become the most sought-after route on the Tough-Brown Face. Fyffe and Tresidder made it a fine three days in the corrie, by climbing *Shadow Buttress B* and then making an early repeat of *Pinnacle Grooves* (VII,7) on The Pinnacle. This latter route requires particularly icy conditions and Robertson and Tim Rankin teamed up to take advantage of the welcome ice when they made an early repeat of the nearby *Epitome* (VII,7). At the crux, they swung left round the arête, then went immediately back up right to join the original route.

Deeper in the Cairngorms, Chris Cartwright and Simon Richardson visited Dividing Buttress on **Beinn a'Bhuird**. This steep buttress separates Coire an Dubh Lochain from Coire nan Clach, but it is more exposed to sun and thaw than the deep corries on the mountain so it rarely holds snow for long. Conditions in mid-February were perfect for the rib and over-hanging flared slot to the right of *Sentinel Gully* on the right edge of the buttress. As expected, the slot of *Big Bertha* (VII,7) proved the crux, with a bold exit on thinly-iced slabs leading to easier but still intricate ground above.

Northern Highlands
In February, Martin Moran and Paul Tattersall climbed a major new line on the huge Giant's Wall of Coire nan Fhamhair on **Beinn Bhan**. Their ascent of *The Godfather* (VIII,8), which takes the face between *Gully of the Gods* and *Great Overhanging Gully*, caused great excitement amongst NW regulars and was immediately recognised as the most significant new route climbed last season.

Another fine ascent in the Northern Highlands was the first ascent of *The Big Chill* (VII,7) on **Beinn Dearg** by Guy and Pete Robinson. The route takes the first obvious line right of *Ice Bomb* on the Upper Cliff of Coire Ghranda and involves some hard mixed climbing to gain a striking ice plume flowing from a groove at the top of the crag. This route was a long time coming and was only climbed after three previous visits to the crag. Guy Robertson had another great day on the imposing Mainreachan Buttress of Fuar Tholl when he made the first ascent of *Supersleuth* (VII,8) with Pete Benson and Jason Currie. This begins with the first two pitches of *Sleuth Start*, and then takes a direct and unlikely line through two barrier walls to give a steep and very direct version of *Sleuth*. Robertson also scored a notable coup with the second ascent of the famed *West Central Gully* on Beinn Eighe with Es Tresidder.

Andy Nisbet was delighted to finally make the first winter ascent of *Rampart Wall* (VII,8) in Coire Mhic Fhearchair on **Beinn Eighe** in early March with Brian Davison and Dave McGimpsey. It took five visits to the cliff before the route was climbed, but it was clearly worthwhile as it was described as a superb three star mixed climb.

Southern Highlands

The Southern Highlands witnessed some important repeats. An on-form Tim Rankin made the third ascent of *The Screaming* (VIII,8) in the North-East Coire of **Beinn an Dothaidh** with Gordon Lennox. Rankin described the overhanging crux pitch as being as pumpy as an E5 rock climb. On the **Cobbler**, James Baillie and Ben Wilkinson made the third ascent of *Punster's Crack* (VII,8), and high upon **Beinn Ime**, Andy Clarke and Frank Yeoman scooped up the second ascent of *Headfault* (VII,7) with a variation on the crux headwall. The same pair also made a major addition to **The Brack** by climbing the well-named *Hogwart's Express* (VI,7), a very steep line up the right edge of the *Resolution* wall finishing via the top fault of the summer route *Mainline*.

It is a measure of the difficulty of the conditions that the first new Grade VIII of the winter was not climbed until the end of February. Cold northerly winds brought The **Cobbler** briefly into condition at the end of February and there were ascents of *Chimney Route*, *Maclay's Crack*, *Ramshead Gully*, *Ramshead Ridge*, *Recess Route* and *Deadman's Groove*. The outstanding performance came from Dave MacLeod and Gareth Hughes who made the first winter ascent of *McLean's Folly* (VIII,8), the spectacular hanging arête left of *North Wall Groove* on The South Peak.

The finest new route of the New Year period fell to Scott Muir and Graham Little with their ascent of *Planet Fear* (VII,7) on Arrow Buttress on **Meall nan Tarmachan**. This very serious route takes the fragile free-hanging icicle well right of the diagonal gully of *The Dambusters* and can be clearly seen from the dam at the head of the **Ben Lawers** road. In many respects the route is more Continental than Scottish in nature and involved a skilful combination of delicacy and pure strength to pull through the impending headwall above. It was an outstanding lead by Muir, and Little was just as delighted. He had been watching this route for the past twelve winters, and the long wait was finally over.

Ben Nevis

For many winter climbers, the 2002 season will be remembered for the extraordinary ice climbing on Ben Nevis in March and early April. Extraordinary is no exaggeration, because the consistently poor weather earlier in the winter laid the foundation for the finest thin face climbing on the mountain in living memory.

Thin face routes rely on a build-up of snow-ice on steep slabs and are normally climbed when the covering is only two or three inches thick. Rarely does the pattern of freeze-thaws allow the snow-ice to form thicker than this, and once committed to the route the climbing is a delicate game of mind control whilst balancing on tip-toe up thinly iced slabs far above protection. The transitory nature of the climbs adds to their attraction, for it only takes one quick thaw to strip the routes entirely.

But 2002 was different. The combination of wind direction, snowfall, and short thaws during February built up a layer of thick water ice on the high north-west facing crags that had never been seen before. *Galactic Hitchhiker* (VI,5), the Mick Geddes and Con Higgins masterpiece up the thinly-iced slabs and grooves right of *Hadrian's Wall*, saw probably more ascents this season than it had during its entire 24-year history. The *Great Slab* to its right, long lusted after by Nevis winter aficionados, was climbed by Mick Nunwick and Stephen Reid thinking it was the original route and the most obvious way to go. And so did Nick Bullock who soloed past them and Alastair Robertson and Luke Arnott who followed on behind later that day. It was only days afterwards they all discovered that they had just climbed a last great problem.

This is only one example. There was so much ice on Observatory Buttress, that routes like *Match Point* (VI,5) dropped two full grades, and big much-feared routes such as *Pointless* (VII,6) had almost too many ascents to count. Indicator Wall, high up below the very summit of the mountain, has probably the highest concentration of thin face routes in Scotland. These routes have big reputations, or at least they did have until March 2002. *Albatross* (VI,5), *Riders in the Storm* (VI,5), and *Psychedelic Wall* (VI,5) had so many ascents that they dropped out of the aspirational category to classics that should be on every winter climber's tick list.

As word got around that the Ben was the place to be, Observatory Gully was packed with teams queuing for the test-pieces of old. It was a delight to see so many climbers enjoying themselves on these great routes, but there was just a hint of sadness that the Ben had let its defences down so totally. Not only was the ice thick enough to take screws almost on demand, grooves and corners were so well delineated with ice that it was immediately clear from the foot of a climb whether it was in condition or not. Typical Ben Nevis horror scenarios, such as discovering the good-looking icy groove you started climbing has deteriorated into centimetre-thick sugar 20 metres above your last runner, were few and far between. The predictable conditions were a soloist's dream. Several climbers had marathon days soloing multiple Grade V's and VI's demonstrating impressive levels of fitness by climbing well over a thousand metres of steep ice in just a few hours.

Although many climbers rushed to fill their bag with long sought-after climbs, there were some good new additions. Conditions were particularly good on Number Three Gully Buttress, which saw four new routes. Andy Nisbet teamed up with Dave McGimpsey and Mark Edwards to fill a prominent gap with the first ascent of *Vulture* (V,5), which climbs the huge icy slab between *Diana* and *Quickstep*. They followed this ascent with the outstanding *Boston Two Step* (VI,5), a snaking line of ice left of *Two Step Corner*, but they were beaten to *Artemis* (V,5), the parallel line of icy grooves to the right of *Diana*, by Ed Horne and Graeme Gordon who had climbed the route two weeks before.

Over on the Little Brenva Face, Dave McGimpsey and Hannah Burrows-Smith solved a long-standing problem with the first ascent of *Super G* (VI,6), the long admired icefall hanging down the headwall above *Slalom*. Although this route forms consistently each season around mid March, its existence is often short-lived as it faces the sun and can become rotten and detached. Careful timing was the key to success with Burrows-Smith making a fine lead of the steep undercut crux pitch. On the West Face of Observatory Ridge, Simon Richardson and Chris Cartwright took advantage of the exceptional ice build-up in March to climb *Maelstrom* (VI,6), the prominent groove to the left of *Antonine Wall*, and Robin Clothier and Paul Thorburn climbed the left rib of *Point Five Gully* to give *Bombing the Pilgrims* (VI,5).

The finest ascent of the season however was Blair Fyffe's *Rhyme of the Ancient Mariner* (VII,7) on Indicator Wall. His first attempt with James Edwards climbed the rib right of *Albatross* to escape up the rising traverse of *Flight of the Condor*, but two weeks later he re-climbed the route with Es Tresidder and forced a way through the imposing headwall above to create a compelling and futuristic looking line. Along with 1986, the 2002 season will be long remembered as one of the great winters on the Ben. But it was also the end of an era when the reputations of the big 1970s routes were finally put to bed. No doubt other climbers will soon be following Fyffe's vision to create the next series of test-pieces for future generations.

TONY HOWARD

Middle East & North Africa 2002-2003

Despite the infamous 9/11 and the subsequent collapse of tourism in much of the Islamic world, climbers, albeit in reduced numbers, have continued to visit North Africa and the Middle East during 2002 and have been greeted with the usual welcoming friendliness.

MOROCCO

This is one of the least affected North African countries. The following notes have been mostly compiled from info supplied by Les Brown. The peak **Jebel el Khest** (2374m) is the highest point of a 40km long quartzite ridge at the western end of the Anti-Atlas above the pleasant market town of Tafraoute. It presents on all its flanks an array of rock buttresses, pinnacles, ridges and gorges offering immense scope for traditional adventure climbing on good rock. Tony Howard and friends climbed on the area's massive granite boulders reminiscent of Joshua Tree or Hampi in 1962/3 winter. They were rediscovered by Dennis Gray, followed by Ron Fawcett. Then, in 1990, Les Brown and friends made their first visit and have been every year since, Les and Trevor Jones doing the first new routes in the mountains that dominate the area. There are now about150 climbs, varying in length from 100m up to the 750m 4+ *Great Ridge* of **The Lion's Head**. Other climbs range from severe to E2.

The team bases itself in Tafraoute, on the south side of the massif. In 2002 a team consisting of Les Brown, Claude Davies, Joe Brown, Pete Turnbull, Derek Walker and Chris Bonington continued the explorations, adding about 30 routes. Locations included climbs above the villages of Inergui, Assgaour and Tafghalt on the south side and Sidi Mzal, Assandrar on the north side.

Other climbers have undoubtedly visited the area and no doubt the French have made ascents, as elsewhere in the Moroccan mountains. Some bolted routes of unknown origin have been found amongst the boulders. The main climbs are described in a log book kept in the Hotel Les Amandiers in Tafraoute. The season 2002 saw the first forced bivouac and the first leader fall since climbing began here. Considerable scope for new routes still exists, particularly on the north side where the rock topography has prominent lines and where it is cooler in hot weather.

A guidebook is being prepared by Claude Davies.

TURKEY

I am informed that there is now a company which organises rock-climbing holidays of various standards. Trans Nature are based in Antalya and have an agency in Marmaris: info@transnature.com.tr. They also have a website at www.transnature.com.tr

ALGERIA.

This country is deeply troubled by internal unrest but the south, including the mountains of the **Hoggar**, seems little affected. Climbers are still visiting in limited numbers, flying into Tamanrasset and thereby avoiding the north.

EGYPT

Little seems to be happening in the mountains of Egypt whose Red Sea coastal mountains seem to have been deserted following our brief spell in Cairo's military jail in Dec 2001 for being (unknowingly) in a closed military zone! There's lots to be done there once the area opens up again. Sinai, once popular with Israeli climbers, is open but quiet.

SUDAN

French climbers David Jonglez and Matthieu Noury visited the exfoliating granite **Kassala Domes** on the Ethiopian border in winter 2002/3. They repeated R.A. Hodgkin and L. A. Brown's 1939 route to the main summit **Jebel Taka**, probably making the fourth ascent, the second being by a Czech team in 1981 and the third by the author and friends in 1983. Apparently the first ascent pitons are still in place, in 'a splendid 5+ dihedral'. They also repeated the Czech climb on nearby **Jebel Totil** up 'athletic fissures, ED, 6c' before adding three routes of their own, all at around Fr 6b with lengths between 120 and 300m, the longest being 'a beautiful route finishing near the top of Jebel Taka'. They correctly point out that 'the compactness of the rock offers only rare lines of natural protection'. I would also add that most of the possible climbable features are already home to enormous Ruppel's Vultures! It is nevertheless a fascinating and remote place and well worth a visit for lovers of exotic rock and African culture. See the web report by David Jongles at www.camptocamp.com.

ETHIOPIA

This country had a visit by Andre Hedger and friends who, with a hint from our trip some years ago, climbed some towers and faces in N Tigray Province, to the NE of the Simiens and 800km N of Addis Ababa. (High Dec 02). These gave routes of between 100m and 300m at grades up to E2 5c. The Simien Mountains, where North Africa's highest mountain **Ras Dashan** (4620m) is located, have numerous big walls, but they are mostly grass and baboon covered! However, in N Tigray where Andre Hedger's team climbed, the spectacular towers have better rock and more good climbing should be found. For advice and assistance with travel, contact Tony Hickey at Village Ethiopia: village.ethiopia@telecom.net, and website: www.village-ethiopia.com.

JORDAN

There was quite a lot of new route activity in Wadi Rum in 2002 (*High 239*) though some involved the creation of pure bolt-protected sport routes. Not, in my opinion appropriate in a 'wilderness' area and disapproved of by the new Rum Park Authority. More traditionally, the key to a long lost Bedouin Route, the S to N Traverse of **Jebel Rum** was finally found by Rum regular Gilles Rappeneau with aspirant Bedouin Guide Talal Awad. The route was later completed in full in one day by resident French guide Wilf Colonna and friends.

Also in 2002, the Rum 'Protected Area' was finally set up by Jordan's Royal Society for the Conservation of Nature and handed over to the Aqaba Authority early in 2003. After considerable debate, including input from regular Rum climbers and the BMC, the park regulations, aimed at protecting the environment and wildlife, seem quite amenable towards the climbing and trekking community. Previous concerns about the park's impact on the local community also seem to have been overcome. At the request of the RSCN, the author and Di Taylor, again with input from the BMC, have prepared a leaflet on 'Safety and Environmental Awareness in the Rum Protected Area'. The question of Guides and Rescue is also being considered again and the park authority are proposing to further train the local Bedouin guides and equip and train a rescue team. (*See High & Summit, March 03*)

In week one of the Iraqi war, March 2003, the Rum Bedouin told us all was well. There were no visitors but they were fine, many having returned to life with their animals.

OMAN

Geoff Hornby sent the following report on recent developments in the Western Hajar mountains:

In early 2001 Oswald Oelz and Robi Boesch climbed a fine line through the middle of the SE face of Jebel Misht. This route appears to follow much of the existing route *Eastern Promise*, first climbed by Paul Ramsden and Tom Nonis.

I returned in early 2001 with Aussie Dave Wallis to explore the further potential of the huge faces of Misht. Our first offering was a new 750m line on the S face. Kicking off to the right of my previous route *Madam Butterfly*, it provided some excellent and bold face climbing in the lower third before finishing with a definitive sting in the tail. From the summit the stinging wasn't over as Dave was bitten by a snake on the descent. The route *Snakes and Ladders* weighs in at TD 5.10 –.

After this warm-up we set about our main objective, the unclimbed groove line on Misht's SE face. The first eleven pitches passed with sustained 5.8/5.9 climbing leading up to an obvious bowl in the face. From there, easier ground for half-a-dozen rope lengths led to a rising line of corners and bulges which led to the summit ridge with one pitch up an overhanging groove (5.10). *Intifada*, TD, 23 pitches and 1000m is an excellent route and worthy of further ascents.

Our route was small beer, though, compared with what was to follow. Pat Littlejohn and Steve Sustad blew through town, with the rapidly warming temperatures of March, and climbed the superb hanging line up the left edge of the SE face. After 15 pitches they crossed the French pillar and then forged a route just left of the upper arête to the summit. Pat reports that the temperature on the face was so hot that he took his rock shoes off on every stance and hid them in the shade to get them to cool down a little. They completed *Icarus* in 27 pitches to ED3 (5.11+) in two days.

In November 2002 possibly the best line in the range was climbed on Misht by resident Austrian guide Jacob Oberhause and Brian Davison. They stormed the direct line up the crest of the South Pillar in a day at ED3 (5.11+) and 1200m in length, and named their line *The English Arête*.

An interesting and possibly frightening development during the winter of 2001/02 was the arrival of the highly prolific Austrian team of Albert Precht and Sigi Brachmayer. This pair have dominated new route developments in Jordan's Wadi Rum over recent years and have now turned their attention to the cream of Arabian limestone, all at the invitation of Oswald Oelz. Oswald and Albert were part of a team attempting Makalu 25 years ago. Since then Albert has given up high-altitude mountaineering in favour of exploratory alpine and sub-alpine rock-climbing. Oswald went on to climb many Himalayan peaks, sometimes with Reinhold Messner. So this invitation was designed to be a reunion.

The Eastern Wall of Jebel Misht, known as the Al Jil Wall, had received an ascent by Geoff Hornby and David Barlow in 2000, but our route avoided the obvious difficulties of the central pillar. After an exploratory ascent of a line called *Half Moon Corner* with Gerhard Hafner, the Precht, Brachmayer and Oelz team climbed the central pillar and named it in Oswald's honour as the *Doc.Bulle pillar*, TD and 500m.

The Precht/Brachmayer team then took to the SW face of Misht to climb the left edge of the wall. *Watergate*, TD and 500m, takes the obvious corner system with the difficulties predominantly in the lower half. The Austrians then swung around the back and climbed a 200m new route on the N face of the First Tower at TD, just to fill in the rest of the afternoon!

In March 2003 Geoff Hornby with Mark Turnbull and Susie Sammut climbed the face right of *Watergate* to finish up the front face on the upper pillar. *Sorely Misht* is D.Sup and 600m.

The Austrians added another independent line up the central section of the S face of Misht at TD with 800m of climbing. Yet again, they were up and down with a fair amount of the day remaining and Oswald, who watched them through binoculars, described them as mutant dwarfs. *Way of the Dwarfs* or *Wichtimannchen* looks like a good outing.

The British team of Peter Bishop, Aqil Chaudhry and David Barlow attempted the right-hand pillar on the SE face. *Riddle in the Sands*, 850m, TD inf, traverses into *Intifada* for three pitches at half height and so loses some of its attractiveness, but was an excellent voyage up an obvious feature.

From Misht, the view southwards is dominated by the mass of Jebel Kawr. This so-called 'mountain of waterfalls' is surrounded on all sides by walls of between 400m and 900m in height. On the NE side a system of towers becomes visible with the changing light of the late afternoon. The Austrians invited me to join them in exploring the potential of these towers.

Our first venture was the striking N ridge of Jebel Asait. This beautiful towered ridge rises for 600m above the small village and provided us with steady climbing, a few pitches of 5.9 and a steep 5.10c. *Internationale* is one of the finest routes I have ever done and deserves repeat ascents.

The north pillar of Jebel Asala gave 500m of TD rock and a further 500m of scrambling, which is a good day in its own right, but not enough for Precht, so he soloed a 500m line on Asait's N rib, as he passed it on the way down! *Solo climb*, D Sup, now has a pair of parallel lines, courtesy of myself and Susie Sammut, named *Two's Company* and *Three's a Crowd*, both 500m and D.Sup. Brian Davison soloed the wall left of *Three's a Crowd* to give *Alone in Space*, TD, 500m, and two shorter and easier lines further to the south end of the face.

An attractive tower to the west of Asala's summit has become known as the Asala Tower. The full Austrian contingent climbed the Luadabuam pillar at TD and 250m. While the others wound their way down the back, Albert soloed down another line before soloing back up a third line. These two lines are *Down Hill* and *Straight Up* and both contain climbing to 5.9!

Meanwhile, Peter Bishop and I were beavering away on Asait's W face. This 600m wall is brilliant. Our route, *Snake Charmer*, climbed the pillar separating the NW and SW aspects and went straight to the summit. Face climbing, cracks and grooves, never harder than 5.10a, it is truly superb. Our ascent was made during the Islamic festival of Ramadan. After descending from the hill and into the village at sunset, we were invited by the shepherds, who had been watching us all day, to break the fast with them. Sitting around the camp fire with the whole village, sharing dates and drinking cardoman coffee, whilst the children did imitations of bouldering moves, was very, very special.

Aqil Chaudhry and David Barlow worked away at a steeper line to the left of *Snake Charmer*. After six pitches, including E2 offwidths, the boys hit a patch of soft rock and were forced to rap down. Left as a climb in its own right, they named it *Muscat Rap* and graded it TD Sup.

The next day, Albert and Sigi left their last mark on the range for the year with a second line up the N face of Asala. *Rock Fascination* weighs in at TD and has 600m of climbing and 500m of scrambling.

The British posse then took off to investigate the potential of Jebel Misfah at the head of Wadi Ghul. The only existing rock climb on Misfah was the excellent looking Sisi pillar up the S buttress. We took to the SE face and added a pair of fairly moderate 400m climbs called *Sunburst* and *Shadowlands*.

Our last route of the trip was a second line on the beautiful Mistal Tower. This gorgeous looking feature did not provide us with the quality climbing we were expecting and *The Way of the Goat* is an apt name, TD– and 450m.

Oswald Oelz was not finished. Back he came in January 2002 with Robi Boesch to add a third line to the W face of Asait. Close to the top of this sustained TD route (5.9), the pair found a bizarre man-made bridge between two towers of rock. Unable to guess how and why this feature had appeared, they named their route *Mystery*. I presume that the shepherds had found a spot that their goats occasionally escape to.

The Austrian-Swiss team returned in November to continue their explorations. First, accompanied by Italian Dolomite guide Hans Peter Eisendle, they climbed two lines on the Karn Sheik S face in Musandam, *Windjammerer*, 450m and 6+, and *Meerresleuchten*, 400m and 6+. Subsequently they moved to Central Oman and climbed another pair of lines on the mystery wall of Asait, *Annas Tango*, 400m and 6+, and *Mish Mushkila*, 400m and 8– (with Jakob Oberhauser from the North Tyrol). On the W face of Asala they added *Jebelistas*, 400m and

6+, whilst on the N face of the same peak they added *Ramadan for Bolts*, 450m and 6+, and *Omaniak*, 300m and 6+.

As this team left the mountains so Brian Davison, Susie Sammut and myself arrived from the UK. Davison completed an extensive programme of soloed first ascents on Jebels Asait, Asala and Khormilla, whilst the three of us added two important first ascents on previously untouched mountain features. Jebel Manzoob is a subsidiary peak of Jebel Kawr and provides a handsome looking 600m N face. Our line climbs a 400m arête on the left side of the face, *Gully Arête*, weighing in at ED2 (5.11).

On the other side of the range, Jebel Ghul has an extensive ridge line with north-facing buttresses on it. From the highest point drops a pair of 650m-high pillars and we climbed the eastern one via a series of walls, ramps and covers to give *Original route* (5.11).

Brian Davison's other solo routes were on Jebel Asala's N face with three easy routes and on Jebel Khormilla with four routes.

Note: Info on all the above areas will also be found on Tony Howard's website: www.nomadstravel.co.uk

HARISH KAPADIA

India 2002

In the year 2002 there were 108 expeditions to the Indian Himalaya. Out of these 73 were Indian expeditions. This report covers the 53 expeditions to notable peaks. There was a drop in the number of foreign teams climbing in the Indian Himalaya and only 35 expeditions climbed here in 2002.

Many popular areas, like Nun-Kun in Zanskar, Kishtwar and the entire Kashmir valley, remained closed for mountaineers due to security concerns.

Climbs

Amongst notable climbs were two first ascents: **Padmanabh** (7030m) by an Indian-Japanese team, and **Suj Tilla West** (6373m) by a two-member British team, followed by an Indian Navy team. **Arwa Tower** (6352m) and **Arwa Spire** (6193m) in Garhwal were climbed in good style, while smaller peaks like **Little Kailash** (6321m) and **Brahmasar** (5850m) were climbed.

Explorations

There were two major explorations and discoveries in the East Karakoram. The vast and unique Teram Shehr Plateau was explored for the first time by an Indian-Japanese team. They traversed the valleys along the Shyok River and stood on the historic Karakoram Pass. Later they crossed the high Col Italia, the first team to do so for 72 years. Two members of the team then trekked up the Teram Shehr Plateau which lies at an average height of 6000m. It is unique to find so high and vast a plateau surrounded by peaks and packed with snow and ice. It was first seen by mountaineers climbing the nearby Rimo I in 1985.

The Indian Army, stationed on the vast Siachen Glacier, also did some exploration. They discovered the remains of the old Balti settlement and the camp of an Italian team led by Prof G Danielli in 1930. The army found a large stone with inscriptions possibly in the Balti language, old human bones and a large inscription by the Italian team. This was certainly an important landmark in the rediscovery of the history of the Siachen glacier.

SIKKIM

Nepal Peak (7153m)

Expedition: DAV Summit Club, Germany
Leader: Herbett Streibel (12 members)

This was a rare attempt on Nepal peak. They followed the route from Gangtok to Lachen and then via Yakthang and Yabuk Rest Camp. Base camp was established on the Nepal Gap Glacier at 3900m and Camp 3 on the SE Ridge of Nepal Peak at 6620m. On 21 October three members climbed the S Ridge to the summit. The summit was reached by the leader with Ms Carl Claudia and Johann Paul Hinterimmer.

UTTARANCHAL

KUMAON

Changabang (6866m) and Purbi Dunagiri (6523m)

Expedition: German
Leader: Jan Mersch

This 11-member German team had an ambitious plan to attempt Changabang by the northern route and Purbi Dunagiri by two different routes. Base camp was established on 17 September with 65 porters, and the final camp was established on 26 September. Changabang was attempted and they reached 5700m. As there was too much snow they gave up the climb. Purbi Dunagiri was initially attempted by the W and S ridge, reaching 6100m. The expedition subsequently reached 6200m on the ESE ridge. On both routes the climbers were stopped by very loose rock and dangerous conditions.

Little Kailash (6321m)

Expedition: Indian-British Joint Expedition
Leader: Martin Moran (11 members)

Martin Moran, a regular visitor to the Indian Himalaya, organized this expedition to an unknown and remote peak. Proceeding from Dharchula on the pilgrim route, they turned towards Shin la and the Jolingkong lake to attempt the summit. Base camp was established on 26 September and the higher camps were in place by 6 October. On 3 October a peak which they called **Rajula** (c. 6000m), adjoining **Baba Kailash** to the north of Shin la was climbed. The summitters were Martin Moran, T Rankin, M Singh, S Ward, A Williams and R Ausden.

The height of Little Kailash according to them is 6191m. They attempted it from the N side from the Jolingkong lake with the intention of climbing to just 10 metres short of the summit, because of the holy status of the peak. However they were stopped by very loose snow and rotten rock at about 6000m. They climbed through a prominent rock band under very heavy snowfall in early September; but later, although the weather was good, conditions did not improve.

Suj Tilla West (6373m) (earlier known as Suitilla)

Expedition: Indo-British team, **First Ascent**
Leaders: Paramjit Singh and Graham Little

A small team attempted this virgin peak in the Ralam Valley in the eastern Kumaon. Paramjit Singh and Alka Sabarwal had to return early because of an infection and ailment, while Graham Little and Jim Lowther continued the attempt. They approached via the Shyangalpa Glacier and established base camp on 17 September and subsequent camps by 27 September. They climbed a superb line, free and without any fixed rope. Abandoning their initial attempt on the NW Face they climbed the SW Face on 27 and 28 September. They called the route *Moonlight Route*. Jim Lowther described the climb:

'Graham and I climbed the peak in pure Alpine style in a 22-hour continuous push. By the time we got to the western summit at 6373m (which we thought was going to be the highest point on the ridge but turned out not to be) we were totally spent and didn't have any reserves left to traverse the ridge to the other, higher, eastern point which we now believe to be 21 metres higher. We had to get down fast because we had no bivvy gear. This we did, and when we met up with the Navy a day later we told their leader about the height differences of the two summits. The western summit that we climbed is the one which you'd naturally assume to be the highest point, as it is the dominant snow peak visible from Ralam; the eastern summit is set back along the ridge.'

Suj Tilla West (6373m)
Expedition: Indian Navy, **Second Ascent**
Leader: Lt Cdr Satyabrata Dam
Suj Tilla West (6373m) was climbed by the SW Face, as a second ascent, by Divyesh Muni, Lt Amit Pande, Sherpa Nima Dorje on 6 Oct and by Lt K S Balaji, Lt Amit Rajora, Chera Rajkumar, A Chaudhury, Sherpa Tsange Puri and Nima Thondup on 11 Oct. A small peak, **Ralam We** (5350m) was also climbed by the team.

GARHWAL

GANGOTRI AREA

Shivling (6543m)
Expedition: Austrian
Leader: Herbet Volf (4 members)
Shivling was climbed by the W Ridge on 26 September by four members including their leader. The other summitters were Mattle Rolande, Moritz Ijoachim and Bitscanu Leander.

Expedition: Swiss
Leader: Walter Hungerbuhler (6 members)
All seven members of this Swiss team climbed Shivling by the W Face on 30 September. They had excellent weather after establishing base camp on 20 September on the south side of the Gangotri glacier. The names of other summitters, with the leader, were Rita Schoppmann, Florian Stroub, Bammert Oliver, Hnopeter Hug, Franh Mavcel, Melanie Blatter.

Expedition: Israel
Leader: Ran Kagan (3 members)
A four-member team from Israel climbed the W Ridge of Shivling, reaching the summit on 29 September. The leader and the other three members all reached the top. They were Morah Levy, Alan Hod and Goy Hasson. Some members

suffered from frostbite and had to be evacuated on donkeys to Gangotri on the way to Delhi.

Shivling (6543m) (Continued)

Expedition: Hungarian
Leader: Bela Mester (2 members)

Shivling was climbed by the normal W Ridge by two members, Casadaba Toth and Gabor Babscan. They established their final camp at 5520m and reached the summit on 2 October.

Expedition: Spanish
Leader: Jorge Corominas Garcia

A team of 15 members attempted the W Ridge of Shivling and the Gangotri glacier. On 5 October the leader, with Eva Zarzuvuelo and Jam Buenaza, reached the summit, followed next day by Msax Msesek and J Rimon Agras. They established base camp on 24 September and returned on 23 October.

Swachand (6721m) and Meru (6350m)

Expedition: Canadian
Leader: Guy M Edwards (4 members)

This team followed the Gangotri glacier, established base camp by 10 September and was climbing in the area for a month. Owing to recent snow, the climbing on Meru Shark's Fin became very dangerous and they gave up the attempt. However, the W Face of Swachand peak was climbed between 3 and 7 October. The summit was reached on 6 October by Guy Edwards and John Miller.

Meru Shark's Fin (6350m)

Expedition: British
Leader: Jules Cartwright with Jon Bracey and Matt Dickinson.

They approached this attractive rock face from the Gangotri glacier and established base camp by 16 September. High camps and summits were tried between 23 and 27 September by the E Face. The weather was good, but they were carrying too much equipment and were unable to reach the summit.

Bhrigupanth (6772m)

Expedition: Korean
Leader: Woo Suk

A Korean team with 8 members attempted the SE Face, establishing base camp at 5200m and further camps up to 6300m. On 28 August Evn Soo Koo and Kwnchul reached the summit, despite some inclement weather.

Chaukhamba II (6974m)

Expedition: French
Leader: Wagnon Patrick and Peter Trommsdorff, with Sauget
               Gregoria and Ziania Yannick, mountain guides from France.

They climbed Chaukhamba II by the W Face in perfect style and in a quick push. Braving some early bad weather, they finally ascended the peak in alpine style with three bivouacs, quickly returning to Delhi.

Sudarshan Parvat (6507m) and Saife (6166m)

Expedition: Indian, from Pune
Leader: Shripad G Sankpal (11 members)

This young team attempted Sudarshan Parvat by the SW Ridge which is not very often climbed. After passing Gaumukh they entered the Thelu bamak. Bypassing peak Thelu to the west, they climbed the SW Ridge to reach the summit of Sudarshan Parvat. Camp 3 was established on 4 July by Shripad Sankpal, Santosh Bomkar and Chandra Bahadur Sahai and H.A.P. On 7 July, starting early, they made a summit attempt along the sharp snow ridge and going across two rock humps and a hard ice wall on their way to the top. The weather was clear and they had excellent views. On 8 July, Avinash Khandekar and Sachin Naidu reached the summit at 1.30 pm following the same route.

Kedarnath (6968m)

Expedition: Italian
Leader: Moretti Martino (5 members)

A 5-member Italian team of doctors and an Alpine Guide attempted this high peak in the Gangotri valley. They established their camp ahead of Tapovan on the Kirti Glacier on 26 September. A high camp was made at 6100m by 2 October. They intended to follow the N Ridge of **Kedar Dome** to Kedarnath Peak. However, too much soft snow above 6100m stopped them.

Thalay Sagar (6904m)

Expedition: Japanese
Leader: Hiroshi Kawasaki with Kanji Saito

This two-member team set up base camp at 4700m on 31 May at the foot of Thalay Sagar intending to attempt its N Face. However, they could only reach a height of 6200m and because of tiredness gave up a further attempt. The last camp was established on 16 June at 6100m.

Chaukhamba I (7138m) and Chaukhamba II (6974m)

Expedition: Korean
Leader: Man Jae Lim (8 members)

An eight-member Korean team attempted the twin peaks of Chaukhamba from the Mana village going to Vasudhara Col and establishing camp at Satopanth tal. They established base camp at 4300m on 25 July and subsequent camps up to 6200m by 19 August. They attempted the E Face of Chaukhamba I and II, but the terrain was full of crevasses and there were several hanging séracs on the route. The leader of the team was hit by a broken sérac, but luckily survived. They reached a height of 6500m on peak I.

Januhut (6807m)

Expedition: Austrian
Leaders: Jochler Josef and Zenz Christian

This was a two-man expedition, both being professional climbing guides from Austria. They established a base camp following the long Gangotri-Tapovan route on 19 May to the head of the long Gangotri Glacier in early June. However, they had plenty of porter problems on their approach march, with too much snow on the glacier and later bad weather which affected the fingers of one of the members. No serious attempt was made on the peak.

Chaturangi IV (6304m)

Expedition: Indian, from Calcutta
Leader: Dipankar Ghosh (12 members)

Chaturangi IV is situated on the Gangotri glacier. The team established three camps in early summer and 7 members reached the summit.

Gangotri III (6577m)

Expedition: Indian, from West Bengal
Leader: Suman Guha Neogi

Gangotri III lies to south of Gangotri temple at the head of Rudugaira glacier. This team established three camps, the last one being at 5900m. Finally, after braving some bad weather, on 2 June they reached the summit from the SSE Ridge. The summitters were Dipankar Ghosh, Debnath Das, Subashish Banerjee, Jaisingh Sahji, Jaisingh Thakur and Laxmansingh Thakur.

CENTRAL GARHWAL

Devban (6852m)

Expedition: Indo-Tibet Border Police
Leader: Y S Sandhu

This is a high and difficult peak near Kamet in Garhwal. A strong ITBP team reached the summit on 19 September. The summitters were Vijender Singh, Jyot Singh, Mohammed Ali and Tashi Motop. They followed the S Ridge, approached from eastern sector.

Rataban (6166m)

Expedition: Indian, from Chandarnagor, W Bengal
Leader: Gautam Banik (16 members)

They approached this peak, meaning 'Red Arrow', from Malari and crossed the Bhuidhar Khal to establish a camp at its foot. The summit was reached via the W and NW Ridge on 27 August by 12 members.

Kamet (7756m) and Abi Gamin (7355m)

Expedition: Indian
Leader: R C Bharadwaj (10 members)

The expedition, from the Uttaranchal Tourism Board, attempted two high peaks on the border with Tibet in Northern Garhwal. On Abi Gamin the summitters were Rakesh Joshi, Ashish Singh, William Akbarchandra, Chanda Bist with Sherpa Mig Tamba and the summit was climbed on 3 October. After suffering some delays on 5 October, Kamet was climbed by team member Satish Chandra Bhat with 3 Sherpas, namely, Pasang Dorje, Dawa and Purba Gyalzen. The team was climbing along with and at the same time as an Indian army team, which was also attempting the summit. Owing to the late season, several members suffered frostbite and other cold injuries.

Peak 6075m (On Kakodagad near Harsil)

Expedition: Indian, Indian Mountaineering Foundation, New Delhi
Leader: Ms. Chandraprabha Aitwal (9 members)

The team approached the unclimbed peak via Harsil on the Gangotri motorable road in early September. They acclimatised at Kana tal and a low base camp was made at 3100m. They made two camps en route to the summit which was climbed on 19 September after a long day. Climbing in two groups, seven members reached the summit. They were Sushma Thakur, Kavita Burathoki, Reena Kaushal, Sundri Devi, Babita Gosawi, Ekta with 3 HAPS and Narendra S Kutyal.

Brahmasar (5850m)

Expedition: British
Leader: Martin Moran (8 members)

A small British team led by energetic Martin Moran made ascents of six smaller peaks in Garhwal. These peaks are situated around Khatling glacier at the head of the Pirangla Valley. They established a base camp on 1 May and higher camps between 4 and 13 May. The following summits were climbed:

> **Rabbit's Ear**, 5530m, by E Ridge
> **The Cathedral**, 5360m, by W Couloir
> **The Fortress**, 5541m, by N Couloir
> **Point Walkers**, 5260m, by E Ridge
> **Point 5709m** by NW Bank
> **Brahmasar II**, 5800m, by SE Couloir

An attempt on Brahmasar I by Martin Moran and two other members failed 60m below the summit on 11 May. They climbed 15 pitches at grades 4, 5, and 6 and reached a maximum height of 5790m. Descent was done by 11 abseils. They had excellent weather throughout.

Jaonli (6632m)

Expedition: British
Leader: Oliver Clayton and Ed Cropley

This two-member team climbed Jaonli by the NW Ridge on 6 June 2002. They had approached from Lod Gad Valley to Jaonli Glacier to reach the foot of the NW Ridge. Base camp was established by 31 May and Camp 2 at 5800m by 5 June. Both the young summitters reached the summit in Alpine style.

Arwa Towers (6352m) and Arwa Spire (6193m)

Expedition: French
Leader: Antoine De Choudens (11 members)

This strong French team climbed Arwa Tower by two different routes. First they established base camp on 4 May and climbed the S Face in a three-day push by Emanuel Pellissier and François Savarx, reaching the summit on 11 May. Then another team climbed the NW Face, with the leader and three other members. Arwa Spire was climbed on 16 May in a three-day push by the leader

with François Savarx, Philip Renard and Thomas Pauchevre. The expedition
enjoyed excellent weather, withdrawing on 21 May.

Arwa Spire (6193m)

Expedition: Swiss
Leader: Bruno Hasler with Stephen Harvey and Roger Schaeli

This team of three mountain guides established base camp at 4660m and abc
at 5400m. On 24 May Hasler, Harvey and Schaeli reached the summit by the
Central Pillar in a three-day Alpine-style push. On 5 June, all the three members
climbed the W Pillar of Arwa Spire in a seven-day Alpine-style push. These
were some of the finest ascents in the Indian Himalaya this year.

Arwa Tower (6352m)

Expedition: Swiss
Leader: Frederic Roux

This was a four-member team consisting of three guides and one manager.
They climbed the N Face and the E Ridge of Arwa Tower in 17 hours of Alpine-
style climbing on 7 October 2002.

HIMACHAL PRADESH

LAHAUL

Ramjak (6318m) First Ascent

Expedition: Indian Mountaineering Foundation
Leader: Sangay Dorjee Sherpa

Two earlier attempts by IMF Expeditions in 2000 and 2001 were unsuccessful.
The expedition left Delhi on 22 July and established Base Camp at 4620m on
27 July after fording several icy streams on the way. They established Camp 1
on 3 August after negotiating difficult terrain, crevasses and exposed slopes.
Finally, on 4 August, the Leader reached the summit along with HAP Dawa
Wanchuk, Nima Dorjay, and Mul Dorjay.

Unnamed Peak (6265m) and Tung Ring Ho (5865m)

Expedition: Indian, from Calcutta
Leader: Prasanta Roy (8 members)

This unnamed peak is located N of Kharcha Parbat in Kharcha nala. The
attempt on the peak failed because of steep snow conditions. However, after
establishing two camps, the team reached the summit of Peak 5865m which is
known locally as Tung Ring Ho.

Lion (6164m)

Expedition: Indian, from Aarohi, West Bengal
Leader: Satyajit Kar (10 members)

Lion is a peak situated in the Barashigri glacier which was approached from
Baltal. On 23 August the summit was reached by Dilip Sadhu, Pasang Bodh
and Prakash Thakur.

Unnamed Peak (6107m), Koa Rong group
Expedition: Polish
Leader: Andrzej Zbinshki (Aged 67) (9 members)
The Koa Rong group lies SE of Darcha and there are several peaks in these groups of Koa Rong and Tela. The N Face of unnamed peak 6107m was attempted on 18 August by Kryuztof Gardyna and Krzysztof Bigta. They reached 5500m on its steep face.

Shiva (6142m)
Expedition: Indian, Mountaineers Association of Krishnanagar, Calcutta
Leader: Basant Singha Roy
The summit was reached on 30 August by the leader with Debasis Biswas, Sange Sherpa and Dukka Sherpa.

SPITI

Kangla Tarbo I (6315m) and Kangla Tarbo II (6120m)
Expedition: Indian, from Calcutta
Leader: Chanchal Bhagduri (9 members)
This is a peak in the Khamengar Valley in Western Spiti. The team approached it by going from Mikkim and trekking 9 days to reach base camp. Kangla Tarbo I was climbed on 11 September by Gopal Das and Padma Anchule in excellent weather.

KINNAUR

Phawrarang (6349m)
Expedition: Indian, from Calcutta
Leader: Mohammed Mahjoob Khan (7 members)
This lovely peak is situated in the Tirung Valley in Eastern Kinnaur. The expedition approached it from Thangi and established base camp in early September. They reached the summit on 17 September via the SE Ridge. The summitters were Pasang, Jayanta and Pangba followed by Ramesh and Subrata.

Leo Pargial II (6792m)
Expedition: Indian, Ordinance Factory Trekkers, West Bengal
Leader: Sajal Kumar Kundu (13 members)
This is the high peak situated north of Leo Pargial I in NE Kinnaur. They attempted it from Yangthang and Nako and made a base camp at the foot of the Leo Pargial Glacier. Summitters were: Baryui, Ratikanta Hembram, Subendru, Subhajit Roy, Subrata Mondal.

KULLU

Deo Tibba (6001m)

Expedition: Tokyo Alpine Club
Leader: Hiroaki Aarikava (with Tadashi Hirano, Kagu Shibata,
              Tatsuya Ajaiki)

The expedition established their camp from Chandra Tal valley in late September and the final camp was made at 5300m. From here the leader and the three other members climbed the S Face to the summit on 2 October.

EAST KARAKORAM

Saser Kangri IV (7416m)

Expedition: Indian, from Chandigarh.
Leader: Satyander Singh Rana (14 members)

This team attempted the peak from the western approaches moving on from Leh to Nubra valley and Phukpoche glacier. They set up base camp on the glacier and made steady progress, establishing Camp 4 at 6500m. Their intention had been to attempt Saser Kangri I, but the difficulties of the route combined with illness to members of the team made them give up that attempt. However, on 14 July the summit of Saser Kangi IV was successfully climbed, in two ropes, by Shivjit Singh, Ajmer Singh and Sange Sherpa. Three members accompanying them stopped after a few hours as two of them fell in a crevasse; happily, they were rescued. The second team, consisting of the leader, Rakesh Kumar, Ganesh Jaina, Pemba Sherpa and Thandup Sherpa reached the summit on the same day.

The Indian-Japanese East Karakoram Expedition 2002

Five Indians and five Japanese mountaineers undertook a long traverse of the East Karakoram valleys for two months. The team covered almost 550km (including some repeated load-carries), took with them almost 2500kg of food, equipment and personal gear, first carried on 55 mules, and later by 11 members and 15 Sherpas and porters. They lived continuously on snow for almost 35 days, braving rather cold temperatures. There were no injuries, accident or sickness (except to one porter).

   The team traversed an historic route in the Shyok valley and returned via the Nubra valley (the Siachen glacier). Five passes were reached or crossed, two large glaciers were traversed and a vast unknown ice plateau was explored. The first ascent of the virgin and difficult peak, **Padmanabh, 7030m**, was achieved.

1   The team traversed the Shyok river valley from the Shyok village (Tankse-Darbuk) to the Karakoram Pass, along the ancient winter Trade route – the first expedition to achieve this in five decades.

2   The historic Karakoram Pass, on the border between India and China, was reached. It was the first time in the history of independent India that a team involving foreign mountaineers was permitted to visit the Pass. (One sole British photographer had reached the pass in 1997). Japanese mountaineers were the first from their country to stand on the Pass for 93 years.

3   The team traversed the central Rimo glacier and the Teram Shehr glacier by crossing Col Italia, the high pass between the two glaciers. It was for the first time, since its first crossing in 1929, that this pass had been crossed. (An Indian team consisting of almost the same members had reached the pass in 2000 but had not crossed it).

4   The high and vast Teram Shehr Plateau was explored and various cols surrounding the plateau were investigated. The plateau is a unique feature in the Karakoram, with ice and snow at a height of about 6200m, surrounded by high peaks on all sides. This was the first time that anyone had reached the plateau (Harish Kapadia and Ryuji Hayashibara) seen so often in photos taken from peaks like Rimo.

5   The first ascent of peak **Padmanabh** (7030m) was made on 25 June by Hiroshi Sakai and Yasushi Tanahashi. After setting up a second base camp (5650m) at its foot, another high camp was made at 6250m near a col at the foot of the S Ridge. In the next four days, 16 pitches of ropes were fixed up to about 6750m. Two teams of Japanese and Indian mountaineers worked together to push the route. Finally a team of two Japanese and one Indian (Lt Cdr S Dam) started for the summit. However, Lt Cdr Dam had to drop out of the final attempt. Two Japanese, in a long push of almost 11 hours of continuous climbing, reached the summit. Both had previously climbed Nanga Parbat but rated this peak more difficult in some respects than that famous 'killer mountain'. A team of Indians and Japanese (Motup Chewang, Rushad Nanavatty and Dr Oe, each of them having worked hard and reached high in preparing the final route) was poised to attempt the summit again in the next two days, but due to the onset of bad weather, this plan had to be abandoned. This was the highest peak on the Teram Shehr plateau and a major first ascent in the Siachen glacier group after many years.

6.   The team returned via the Siachen glacier to the Nubra valley. This was the first international team to climb on this war-torn glacier since 1986. These were the first Japanese mountaineers to visit the glacier from the Indian side since the conflict on the Siachen glacier began in 1984 (many Japanese teams had climbed on the Siachen glacier between 1972-1983, approaching it from the west).

Despite gathering war clouds between India and Pakistan while the expedition was on the mountains, the Indian army fully backed the team and at no point were we asked to stop or change our route.

FIRST ASCENTS OF SUMMITS OVER 6400M

A study by Prof Josef Hala of Prague involved mountain expeditions from 40 countries and included 923 virgin peaks in the Himalaya and Karakoram. The first three entries are as follows:

Country	No. of expeditions to virgin peaks organized by that country *	No. of virgin peaks above 6400m climbed by summitters of that country ‡
Japan	290.5	219
UK	136	169
India	106	170

* For joint expeditions a half credit is given to each country.
‡ No second or further ascents of the same expedition are included.

The full list is available in the *Himalayan Journal* 59 and the *Himalayan Club Newsletter* 56.

CLIMB FOR PEACE IN THE SIACHEN GLACIER

A group of four mountaineers from India and Pakistan (Harish Kapadia and Mandip Singh Soin from India and Nazir Sabir and Col Sher Khan from Pakistan) climbed peaks in Switzerland in response to a joint initiative of the World Conservation Union (IUCN) and the International Mountaineering and Climbing Federation (UIAA) for a 'real' summit in the Jungfrau-Aletsch-Bietschhorn region which has recently been designated the first UNESCO World Natural Heritage Site in the Alps. Their aim was to promote mountain protection, co-operation and peace during the UN's 'International Year of Mountains 2002'. The flags of India and Pakistan, were hoisted together on three Swiss summits. It was the special hope of the climbers to give a call for peace on this long war-torn glacier where the armies of India and Pakistan have been fighting a high-altitude war since 1984. This war has caused many deaths and injuries, brought major destruction to the environment, and trapped some most beautiful mountain areas in the conflict zone.
    As the climbers stated:

On the entire climb our minds remained occupied with thinking of how often the people of India and Pakistan had been kept away from so much happening between them. It is such a tragedy that such a commonly enjoyed sport is not allowed between our two countries. Yet thankfully, through such events, there is hope of bringing our two nations closer. Even the staunch enemies of the Cold War have overcome old barriers and come closer together. The Berlin Wall was dismantled, so let us hope the psychological wall that exists between our people can also be dismantled and we can live like natural neighbours and friends.

As mountaineers they have shown the way that it is hoped that others will follow to promote peace through sport and promote 'peace zones' as a means to overcome border disputes, protect mountain regions and the freedom to enjoy the mountains, particularly a peace zone for the Siachen Glacier

ELIZABETH HAWLEY IS HONOURED

The Kathmandu International Mountain Film Festival 2002 paid tribute to one of the most important figures in the climbing world. In 1960 Nepal got its first full-time mountaineering correspondent in the form of a young American woman, Elizabeth Hawley. 42 years later, Hawley is still in Nepal and is the repository of every detail of every expedition mounted in the Himalaya over the last four decades.

Hawley first came to Nepal as a political correspondent but at the same time she was meeting returning expeditions and gathering information while it was still fresh in climbers' minds. Things have changed over the past decade or so; it is now considered mandatory for climbers to pay their respects to the 77-year-old Hawley. The developments in satellite technology and live coverage of climbing exploits have only strengthened Hawley's work; she continues to be the person to assess the significance of a climb and put it in perspective.

Sometime in the next year, with the help of fellow-American, computer expert and climber Richard Salisbury, Hawley will publish the results of a lifetime of meticulous interviewing, reporting, and collecting of information in a comprehensive volume. Her lifetime's work has met a major need for information about the Himalaya.

ANG TSERING SHERPA

The climbing world lost a legendary figure when Ang Tsering passed away at Darjeeling on 22 May 2002 at the age of 97. He was perhaps the last person still alive from the 1924 Everest expedition and the last to have climbed with Mallory and Irvine. In 1924 he was 20 years of age.

Ang Tsering also took part in the fateful Nanga Parbat expedition of 1934. He was the sole survivor of a party of four German climbers and five Darjeeling Sherpas who were stranded at a high camp in a blizzard. One by one his companions died, and he descended the face alone. When he reached Camp IV, barely alive, he told a simple and straightforward tale of the tragic events that had taken place above. 'What suffering this loyal man must have endured and what a superhuman achievement!' remarked one of the other members.

In 1935 Ang Tsering was awarded the German Red Cross Medal. He was also a holder of the 'Tiger Badge' awarded by the Himalayan Club. Ang Tsering had witnessed and participated in Himalayan climbing from its infancy until all the highest peaks had been climbed.

LINDSAY GRIFFIN

Pakistan 2002

Thanks are due to Asem Mustafa Awan, David Hamilton, Tamotsu Nakamura, Aris Theodoropoulos, Thomas Tivadar, and UIAA Expeditions Commission for their help in providing information.

In 2001 around 70 expeditions came to the Karakoram. However, with the change in political climate following the events of the 11th September and reprisals in neighbouring Afghanistan, plus the subsequent threat of an all-out Indo-Pakistan nuclear war, a little less than 40 were due to turn up at the start of the 2002 season. Then, a dozen or so cancelled at short notice, leaving no more than 28 permits being taken up by visiting expeditions. As several expeditions operating on the high Baltoro mountains had more than one peak booked, the actual number of climbing teams on the ground was somewhat less than 28.

Many of the last minute cancellations came from commercially organised enterprises which, because of the prevailing political situation, either did not get enough clients or felt it unwise to visit Pakistan at the time. However, as many suspected, those who did decide to continue with their plans generally experienced no real problem travelling through the country and found almost everyone they met extremely pleasant. From the point of view of the local economy a far greater effect was felt by the drop in number of trekking parties, which was, proportionally, considerably greater than the drop in mountaineering expeditions.

The next two years witness the Golden Jubilees of both Nanga Parbat and K2, and although celebrations are planned, these are not expected to be anything like as well-supported as those for Everest in 2003. However, there are many who believe it is not only the threat of violence in the country that is deterring climbers. There has been no real motivation to improve mountaineering bureaucracy in recent years and Mountain Wilderness, which began a training program for Liaison Officers, has recently stopped its work, as the Pakistan Government has sadly neither used these officers on expeditions nor employed them to train others. With Nepal's recent introduction of new peaks, greater freedom of access and a much reduced need for Liaison Officers, Pakistan should also be looking towards revising its regulations in order to provide a greater incentive for prospective expeditions. As noted below, further inducements may already be under discussion.

Peak fees

In an attempt to encourage more expeditions to the Karakoram in 2002, the Government of Pakistan reduced all peak fees by 50%. Although unofficially announced earlier in 2002, it was not until very late last year that the Government confirmed that the peak fees for 2003 (and it would appear 2004) will remain the same as in 2002. The UIAA have continually campaigned for an improvement in the regulations, but highly instrumental in this recent decision have been local agents such as the well-known Pakistan mountaineer, Nazir Sabir, who pushed strongly for a continuation of the reduced fees. Sabir also reports that other incentives, for example the simplification of climbing and trekking procedures and an easier visa availability, were discussed.

Royalties for 2003 and 2004 in US dollars:		
Peaks	Royalty for up to seven members	Additional members
K2	6000	1000
Other peaks above 8000m	4500	750
7500-8000m	2000	250
7000-7500m	1250	200
6000-7000m	700	100

The Weather in 2002
Very poor summer weather, with frequent snowfall and high winds above 6000m for much of the time, and unreliable satellite-transmitted forecasts, combined to produce almost zero success for expeditions attempting the big peaks. Only five expeditions operating on permitted peaks above 6000m reached the summit of their intended goal and significantly four of those were on the same route.

K2
Eight independent teams attempted various routes on 8611m K2 last summer, though the majority were on either the Abruzzi Ridge or SSE Spur (*Basque Route*). Several of these brought Nepalese Sherpas to help on the mountain. There was a six-member Spanish-Mexican team led by the female climber Araceli Segarra, who was attempting to become the only living woman summitter of this mountain. There was also a five-member team led by the Spanish climber, Jordi Tosas, a third Spanish expedition led by Oscar Cadiach, with strong climbers like Eduárd Sanchez and Eloi Callado (new route on the SW Face of Xixabangma in 2000), a fourth Spanish team led by Carlos Suarez that included 63-year-old Carlos Soria, a fifth led by Luis Fraga – a Spanish politician, Henry Todd's multi-national expedition on the Abruzzi Ridge, Sam Druk's very strong Tibetan team attempting to climb all the 8000m peaks, and a six-man Japanese expedition led by 60-year-old Kondo Kazayoshi, who already has six 8000m peaks to his credit and is trying to notch them all by 2008. The Japanese also had a permit for Gasherbrum II.

Kazayoshi was the first to arrive at Base Camp and start work on the SE (Abruzzi) Ridge, the venue for his 2000 attempt when he reached 7300m. In common with the other teams, the Japanese were hoping for reasonable weather during June with a summit attempt possible by mid-July, as has been normal in past years. However, the weather remained very poor, and throughout July there were probably only two days when the skies were completely clear. Together with the Tibetans it was the Japanese who opened the lower section of the ridge but they only once reached the site of Camp 4 at 7900m on The Shoulder and this became their altitude high-point for the entire expedition.

With generally dangerous conditions prevailing, some consider it lucky there were only two fatalities. On 22 July Captain Muhammud Iqbal was descending from Camp 3 on the Abruzzi Ridge. While he was rappelling the fixed ropes, it appears that one of them (possibly an old rope he had clipped into by mistake) broke. He fell nearly 1500m to his death, narrowly missing members of Henry Todd's expedition ascending from Advanced Base. Iqbal was the Pakistan liaison officer to the joint Chinese-Tibet/Pakistan Expedition attempting the Abruzzi Ridge and was a popular figure at Base Camp. This Tibetan team, which included three members who have climbed 11 of the 8000m summits, reached a higher point on the mountain than any other last season. Their best attempt took them to c.8400m, ie above the Bottleneck, where they were forced back by a sudden storm. Caught in a ferocious blizzard not far short of the 7900m camp on The Shoulder, they were unable to locate their tents. Worried about straying off the ridge, they spent a reported seven hours waiting for the wind to drop and the visibility to improve. When it did, they found the tents to be less than 30 metres from where they were standing.

Prior to this, on or around 13 July, a huge avalanche swept down the gully alongside the SSE Spur and caught six Sherpas and a number of Pakistan high-altitude porters ferrying loads near the base. One of the porters, Sher Ajman, was struck by large chunks of ice and died instantly. Several others were hit and most were lucky to escape alive.

Jordi Tosas was attempting the *Basque Route* and hoped to snowboard from the summit. He only reached about 6300m on the spur, but was able to snowboard down to c.5000m from that point. His team included the Georgian double Everest summitter, Gia Tortaladze, who has recently launched the International Mountaineering Association. The IMA comprises a group of well-known climbers such as Carsolio and Wielicki, who will be organizing major climbing projects that will also involve clean-up expeditions.

63-year-old Carlos Soria, who has four 8000m peaks to his credit including Everest in 2001, also attempted the *Basque Route* but his expedition reached no higher than 6600m. Oscar Cadiach's team made an unsuccessful attempt on the SW Ridge or Magic Line but never got above 6000m.

Most of the expeditions gave up towards the end of July and headed for home, but Segarra's team, which included the Mexican, Hector Ponce de Léon, and American cameraman, Jeff Rhoades, remained and were, to their surprise, rewarded in August with more than a week of fine weather. Unfortunately, this brought different problems. The temperatures soared, avalanches poured from the mountain and subsequently the Abruzzi was subjected to severe stonefall, cutting some of the fixed ropes and making climbing extremely dangerous.

The Spanish also had to admit defeat at 7100m and return home empty-handed. However, one day during the expedition Rhoades and fellow film maker Jennifer Jordan were exploring the Godwin-Austen Glacier when they discovered the remains of human bones, alongside which were the remnants of an old canvas tent, clearly marked with the tag 'Made in India'. Later, some tattered clothing, labelled 'Cambridge (Massachusetts)' came to light, pointing towards the owner being a member of the ill-fated 1939 American-German expedition led by Fritz Wiessner. Then finally a glove was uncovered with the name Wolfe clearly written on it. It is presumed that the bones formed the remains of Dudley Wolfe, a very rich American climbing novice, who had been invited on the expedition largely to help finance it. He and three Sherpas were the first four fatalities on the mountain, whereas Ajman and Iqbal were the 51st and 52nd respectively

Nobody attempted K2 from the north or Chinese side.

Broad Peak

There were five separate expeditions on 8047m Broad Peak: the well-known guide, André Georges, and eight fellow members from Switzerland who also had permission for Gasherbrum I; a 15-member commercially organised German expedition led by Robert Rackl; a seven-member Korean expedition led by Han Wang-Yong, who only had Broad Peak and Gasherbrum II to climb in order to become the 11th person with all 14 8000m peaks (starting with Cho Oyu in 1994); a two-man German team hoping to complete a new route up the SW Face; a multi-national expedition led by Henry Todd. The two Germans quickly decided their proposed route was impractical and joined the others on the *Normal Route*. No one reached the summit.

On or around 19 July a big push by many of the teams working together saw a high point reached a little below the col on the ridge before the foresummit. The Koreans were trying to fix ropes across this section and with the American Chris Warner, from Henry Todd's expedition, in the lead, reached a point 50-60 metres below the col. Here, at c.7800m, the 45-60° slope of deep unconsolidated snow was deemed far too unstable and all descended.

Gasherbrum I

Only three expeditions attempted 8068m Gasherbrum I and while two failed (Swiss, led by André Georges, who were not able to get beyond 6300m and Spanish, led by Oscar Cadiach, who never made a serious attempt), Iwazaki Hiroshi's strong four-member team from the Himalayan Association of Japan recorded the only success on the Pakistan 8000m peaks during the season. Using the *Standard Route* up the Japanese Couloir the team reached the summit at 2.00pm on 5 August. It appears that on the descent the climbers were forced to spend an unplanned night on the mountain at 7000m and on 5 August Fumiako Goto became ill and fell into a coma. His team-mates lowered the unconscious victim down the route and were fortunately assisted by members of Kazuyoshi's K2 expedition. The latter climbers also had a permit for Gasherbrum II and, after abandoning their attempt on K2, were preparing to make a swift alpine-style attempt on the lower of the two Gasherbrum peaks when they received word of the accident. They quickly reacted with man-power, oxygen bottles and climbing gear, assisting with the lower and the subsequent evacuation from Base Camp. Goto regained consciousness before he reached Islamabad and doctors in Japan appear optimistic for a full recovery.

Point 7062m - Borges Peak
Having failed on K2 and then found conditions on Gasherbrum I too dangerous to make a serious attempt, the four-man Spanish team of Oscar Cadiach, Eloi Callado, Lluis Rafois and Eduárd Sanchez turned their attention to an unclimbed summit of 7062m, which they refer to as Gasherbrum 0. They reached the top on 19 July after what appears to be a technically difficult ascent and have proposed the new name of Borges Peak. The exact location of this peak is unclear though it is thought to be part of the Gasherbrum I complex.

Gasherbrum II
Gasherbrum II (8035m) is Pakistan's most popular peak. In 2001 a total of 17 expeditions attempted its *Normal Route*. Last year only two expeditions had a permit and only one, a six member Korean team, actually set foot on its flanks (the Japanese, who also had a permit for K2, were tied up with the rescue on Gasherbrum I as mentioned above). Their high point was 6300m.

Nanga Parbat
Only two teams attempted Nanga Parbat in 2002. A six-member Basque expedition reached c.7000m on the standard *Kinshofer Route* up the Diamir Face but found too much snow on the face above, while one Japanese and one Pakistani attempted the Rupal side of the mountain. The Japanese, Ichiro Hosada, was making his fifth attempt on the 8125m peak, which included a solo winter attempt in 1995. Although it is not entirely certain what route he was attempting last August, he failed fairly low on the mountain.

Gasherbrum IV
One of the more unusual expeditions to Pakistan last summer was the attempt by a six-man Swiss-Italian team to repeat the *Original 1958 Route* up the NE Ridge of 7925m Gasherbrum IV. Mario Casella was the leader and the members included the prominent Swiss-based activist, Roberto Bassi, the well-known mountaineer and film-maker, Fulvio Mariani, and the Lecco climber, Dario Spreafico. From Base Camp at 5100m on the South Gasherbrum Glacier the team established the route via the long glacier approach and the 500m-high dangerous icefall, dubbed the *Serracata delgi Italiani*, to the upper combe and col marking the lowest point between Gasherbrums III and IV. Camp 2 was established at around 6100m, after which chest-deep snow made it impractical to continue. Above, there are sections of hard mixed and rock climbing on the ridge, which the first ascensionists, Walter Bonatti and Carlo Mauri, graded V.

Batura II
A six-man team from the Saxon Alpine Club of Germany made a spirited attempt on the unclimbed Batura II (7762m), one of the highest unclimbed points remaining in the Karakoram. Tilo Dittrich, Günter Jung, Jan Lettke,

Tom Niederlein, Christian and Markus Walter set up Base Camp on the Baltar Glacier in June and followed the route of the first ascensionists of 7786m Batura I.

The 2002 Saxon expedition crossed the rubble-covered Baltar Glacier to an Advanced Base at 4250m and established Camp 1 towards the end of June at 5240m. To reach the site of Camp 2 they had to climb through a narrow and dangerous couloir, dubbed the Gunbarrel by the 1976 German team, which squeezed through a small gap between a rock wall and large sérac barrier. Camp 2 was placed at c.5800m on 2 June and, shortly after, Camp 3 above the Batokshi Pass. The team took around 250m of fixed rope and placed most of it on this section. On 15 July several team members were situated at Camp 4 (6560m) on the South Face of Batura II, somewhat left of the German line, preparing for a summit assault the following day.

Generally the weather had been very mixed with frequent snowfall but on the 16th the day dawned gloriously and Jung with the two Walter brothers set off at 3.30am. The snow conditions seemed reasonably acceptable to about 7000m but the névé field they were climbing was loosely bonded over ice and they realised that it would undoubtedly slide when hit by the rays of the sun. The three progressed to 7100m before deciding it was too dangerous. The route was subsequently abandoned but not before four members had climbed Batokshi Peak.

Back at Base Camp the group split, half going for an exploratory walk up the Toltar Glacier, while the rest climbed a 150m rock tower above camp. This gave three bold pitches (IV, VI and VII or 5.10c) on excellent granite and was christened Phalwan Chish (c.4200m).

Spantik

It seems that four expeditions attempted 7028m Spantik by its increasingly popular *Normal Route* up the SE Ridge and significantly, in a season where almost every team failed to reach its goal, all were successful.

Spantik remained more or less unknown until 1987 when Mick Fowler and Victor Saunders climbed the Golden Pillar, completing what was probably the most technical mixed route climbed to that date and at that altitude in the Karakoram. Interest then developed and since the mid-1990s, the SE Ridge has rapidly gained popularity. Despite the length of the route, technical difficulties are relatively low, there is only one real section where avalanche conditions can prove threatening. Significantly, much of the ridge is still negotiable in poor weather, making Spantik very much the peak of choice for those wishing to climb a non-technical, low 7000m peak in Pakistan.

The first group to succeed in 2002 was a primarily Pakistan expedition on which eight members from Shimshal, two from Passu, two from Skardu and two from Lahore (including a tour operator) reached the summit between 17 and 20 July. Accompanying this expedition was a Spanish climber, Victor Suanzez, who also reached the summit. Shimshal is the home of one of Pakistan's top high-altitude climbers, Rajab Shah, the only Pakistan mountaineer to have climbed all five of his country's 8000m peaks. With nearly two decades of mountaineering experience, Shah currently operates a climbing centre in Shimshal and is working with the youth of his area to bring them to the forefront of Pakistan mountaineering.

Next to summit on the 25th was a French Expedition, on which seven Europeans and three more high-altitude porters from Shimshal made the top. The group was led by the French guide, Christian Trommsdorf, and all but one foreign member made it to the summit. The team established three camps, the highest at 6050m, and was fortunate enough to be established at this camp at the start of a two-day period of fine weather. The summit day was 18 hours long.

The third team on the mountain was Japanese and comprised seven members led by the experienced Himalayan veteran, Omiya Motomu. Four members of this team together with three Pakistan high-altitude porters/guides reached the summit on 21 August.

The fourth and last expedition was formed by two mature Japanese, 57-year-old Hatsuyoshi Nori and 59-year-old Kenji Saito. Together with a Pakistan high-altitude climber, Akbar, the three reached the summit from Camp 3 (6200m) at 1.00pm on 1 September. The weather was good on the descent but Saito became exhausted and rather than continue further down the mountain, the three elected to spend a second night at Camp 3. During the night it began to snow hard and the three were pinned down for the next four nights. Saito deteriorated and eventually died from AMS.

The two survivors ran out of food on the third day and by the morning of the 5th an estimated three metres of snow had fallen. The pair set out in better weather and began to struggle down towards Camp 2 at 5500m but it took them all that day and the following night before they reached it. When they arrived at the site early on the morning of the 6th there was no sign of the tent, which was buried under tons of snow. The two had no option but to continue. Halfway to Camp 1 Akbar asked if he could stay for a rest. Nori left him with his sleeping bag and continued down to Camp 1 at 5200m, which he reached at 5.00am on the 7th. He was just able to make out the top of the tent and on digging it out managed to consume some food and drink. He then continued down to Base Camp (4580m), pleased to see that Akbar was now following. At 2.00pm the Japanese reached Base Camp. His fingers and toes were frostbitten but otherwise he was in relatively good shape. Akbar arrived later that day and was subsequently hospitalised before making a recovery.

Attila Ozsváth

The noted Hungarian rock climber and mountaineer, Attila Ozsváth, disappeared in the Charakusa region of Hushe on 24 July. He had gone to the area with a partner, Peter Tibor, although they do not appear to have been climbing together at the time. According to a spokesperson from North Pakistan Treks and Tours, who believe Ozsváth was swept away by an avalanche, a search was conducted but no trace was found.

The Flame

The only known significant rock climbs achieved in the Karakoram last year took place from the recently frequented Hainabrakk Glacier when Americans Bruce McMahon and Josh Wharton achieved the first ascent of *The Flame* at the head of the Hainabrakk Glacier via a route they named *Under Fire*.

McMahon and Wharton spent around seven weeks on the glacier, most of it suffering the bad weather prevalent in the range at the time. The pair made three trips up the glacier to the foot of the c.6310m spire, where they established a camp at c.5600m. Each journey was doomed to failure by the weather and as this approach involved considerable height gain and two dangerous icefalls, it took some motivation to return for the fourth time when the weather cleared at the beginning of August.

Their perseverance paid off. On 3 August, in an 18 hours' round trip from their tent, the two made the first ascent of this spectacular monolith via a 700m route they named *Under Fire*. The climb involved some wet and icy cracks, a difficult aid section using Birdbeaks and hooks, and an extremely bold lead by Wharton up the final 50 metres to the summit. This last pitch was a very steep and compact slab, and with the hand drill now broken, there was no possibility of protection. Wharton reached the top of this 5.10 pitch as the sun went down and the two rappelled through the night to the glacier. The route was graded 5.10+X, A3 and M5.

Shipton Spire

Returning to Base Camp after climbing *The Flame*, McMahon and Wharton took only one day's rest before setting out for a new route on 5852m Shipton Spire. Over the next two-and-a-half days the pair climbed the less-than-vertical but previously untouched South Buttress. This is the left edge of the SE Face as seen in the classic view of Shipton Spire and gave the two young Americans an almost entirely free climb. Only 30 metres was climbed on aid (C1) and in a dry year the pair reported that this section would go free at easy 5.12. The remainder of the climb went at 5.11 with some difficult snow-climbing needed to gain the summit. The 1300m, 30-pitch new route was christened *The Khanadan Buttress* (an Urdu name meaning family) and was the sixth line to be completed on this now famous formation (although not all of these have finished on the summit).

Other Peaks

Tadashi Kamei and partner from the Himalayan Green Club of Japan made an attempt on the NW Ridge of Khoser Gang, a prominent 6400m peak situated east of the Shigar to Dassu road and north of the Skoro La. After placing a camp at 5000m, the Japanese reached 5500m before giving up their attempt.

Three Koreans are reported to have more or less climbed the NW Face of a 5300m peak christened *Adil*. Unfortunately, at the time of writing there are no further details of either the ascent or the exact location of the peak.

Surprisingly, given its proximity to Chitral and the Afghan border, the Buni Zom region of the Hindu Raj was visited by a two-man Greek party. This mountain group is located a little east of the road connecting Chitral with Mastuj and was probably not explored until 1957, when Berry and Tyndale-Biscoe from New Zealand reached the summit of the highest peak, 6551m Buni Zom. Last summer Nikos Kroupis and George Zaralidis made an attempt on 6240m Gordoghan Zom, the fifth highest peak in the region and first climbed in 1965 by Alfred Koch and Ernst Lainer from Munich. Unfortunately, threatening weather turned them back at around 6050m.

ADE MILLER

North America 2002

The Area Notes for North America would not have been possible without the help of Kelly Cordes, the American Alpine Journal (AAJ), and Don Serl, who provided the original background material upon which these notes are based. For a complete report of all activity in North America, the reader is referred to the current editions of the AAJ and the Canadian Alpine Journal.

ALASKA

Conditions in Denali Park did not match those of the exceptional previous season, but that didn't prevent some significant activity, new routes, and repeats of major existing lines. As usual, the vast majority of climbers attempted the W Buttress route on **Denali**, leaving other areas to the more enterprising. Two paraplegic Russian climbers, Grigoriy Tsarkov and Igor Ushakov, did however climb the W Buttress. The pair climbed the mountain using mechanical ascenders on specially adapted sleds.

Kenton Cool and Ian Parnell (UK) made the second ascent of the *Denali Diamond* on the S Face of **Denali** over a period of five days, rating it Scottish VIII, 8. Cool and Parnell bypassed the Diamond's infamous 25-foot A3 roof by dry tooling an overhanging cracked wall to the left (at M7) avoiding the roof entirely. The route featured further sections of sustained mixed-climbing and vertical ice.

Stephen Farrand and John Kelley repeated the Twight-Backes line, *Deprivation*, on the N Buttress of **Mt Hunter**. This was the second complete ascent of the route (Hollenbaugh and Miller joined the *Moonflower* at the third ice band). The party bivvied twice on the ascent and again while descending the Moonflower Buttress.

After climbing **Mt Huntingdon,** Russ Mitrovich and Jimmy Haden climbed *Wall of Shadows* (VI, 5.9, A2, WI 6) on **Mt Hunter**. On their second attempt, they freed all of the remaining aid sections up to the last pitches of the *Moonflower Buttress* above the third ice band before being forced to retreat because of bad weather. **Mt Huntingdon** saw further activity when Chris Turiano soloed the W Face Couloir in 17 hours, finding exceptional conditions on the route.

In the Ruth Gorge region **Mt Dickey** saw several new routes and attempts this season. On the S Pillar of **Mt Dickey** climbers from the Fédération Française de la Montagne et de l'Escalade; Guillaume Avrisani, Yann Bonneville, Cédric Cruaud, Paul Robach, and Romain Wagner, put up *Crime of the Century* (1550m, 27 pitches, VI 6c, A4). The route consisted of a 1050m wall and 500m of mixed ground and was climbed capsule style over a period of eight days. Other members of the same group, Victor Charon, Alban Faure, Christophe Moulin, and Jérémie Ponson, established *Welcome to Alaska* (1400m, 31 pitches, snow/rock/mixed, VI 6b A3+ M6–) on the NE Spur of **Mt Bradley**.

Although it received scant attention in the US climbing press, one of the most significant new routes put up in the region during the '02 season was *Blood from the Stone* (5.9, A1, M7+, AI6+ X, 1600m) on the E Face of **Mt Dickey**. Sean Easton and Ueli Steck (Switzerland) climbed this mixed line in March over a period of four days. The route follows an ephemeral line of snow and ice with short linking sections of mixed ground.

Also on **Mt Dickey,** Mark Synott and Kevin Thaw attempted a new route between the *Roberts/Rowell/Ward Route* (1974) and the *Italian Route* (Bagattoli/Borgonovo/Defrancesco/De Dona/Leoni/Manica/Zampiccoli, 1991). The pair climbed 25 pitches free, with difficulties up to 5.11– before being turned around by bad weather, estimating that they were four to five pitches from the shale band.

Two parties also completed the second and third ascents of the Donini/Tackle route, *Cobra Pillar* (VI 5.10+ A3), on **Mt Barrill**. A Canadian team of Jean-Pierre Ouellet and Stefane Perron made the second ascent in a 37-hour round-trip, whilst Poles Maciej Ciesielski and Jakub Radziejowski, with Zack Martin (USA), completed the third ascent, freeing much of the route at UIAA VII/VII+ with two pitches of aid, to C2. The Poles also repeated several other routes, including *Game Boy* on **Stump Pillar**.

Elsewhere, Pete Lowney and Brian Teale climbed a new line on the E Face of **Mt Wake** (WI5, M4) in three days.

Mike 'Twid' Turner and Stu McAleese (UK) visited the remote **Kichatna Mountains**. Having been forced off the E Face of Kichatna Spire by a band of very loose rock, they redirected their efforts to the E Face of **The Citadel**. The pair put up a direct start to the East Buttress Route (Embick/Graber/Long, 1976) naming it *Off the Wall Madness* (VI, 5.11a, A2, 900m) after their state of mind at the end of a two-week wait for the flight out.

A four-man Polish team of Jacek Fluder, Janusz Golab, Stanislaw Piecuch, and Grzegorz Skorek established *You Can't Fly* on the left pillar of the **Bear's Tooth**'s E Face, starting on the pillar 250m left of *The Useless Emotion* (Bridwell/Christensen/Dunmire/Jonas/McCray). The route was climbed mainly free and given a UIAA rating of VII A0-A1, with one A2 and one A3 section. The Poles spent ten days on the wall after fixing the lower pitches from the ground; two of these days were spent waiting out bad weather. This is probably the first complete ascent of the peak from this side, as cornicing near the summit turned previous parties back.

In May 2002 Guy Edwards and John Millar (Canada) visited the remote **Stikine Icecap** in SE Alaska and NW British Columbia. Their primary objective, **The Devil's Thumb**, proved to be out of condition. Instead, the pair ascended the *Jack Hicks Memorial Route* (800m, V, 5.10+ A1) on the unclimbed S Face of the **West Witch's Tit** and established *Least Snowed-up Route* (900m, IV 5.10+) on **Cat's Ears Spire**. Tragically, Edwards and Millar were reported missing, presumed dead, on a subsequent attempt on *The Devil's Thumb* in early 2003.

CANADA

The **Kluane Park** saw somewhat reduced activity this year as fewer parties visited the park; the majority of expeditions attempted **Mt Logan**, mainly by the *King Trench*. One notable exception was the pair Jeremy Frimer and Jay Burbee, who made the first ascent of *The Orion Spur* on the NE side of Mt Logan between the *Centenary Ridge* (1967) and *Independence Ridge* (1964). The route itself was climbed alpine style in five days, but the summit plateau took several more days to cross because of bad weather.

Jesse Thompson, Rich Searle, and Joe Josephson climbed *Huge in Europe*, taking a line up the last unclimbed buttress on the S Face of **McArthur Peak** between the Statham/Kay *AstroFloyd* (1992) and the *Friesen/Scott/Wallator Route* (1988). *Huge in Europe* was climbed in 35 hours, ending on the summit ridge at 13,470ft. Due to a rapidly approaching storm, the team retreated rather than completing the line to the E Summit (14,134ft and five hours away). Thompson and Josephson then flew to the N side of the peak and climbed a new variation on the North Ridge route, *Night Shift*, to the lower E Summit in 24 hours round-trip. The team also attempted the unclimbed south-south-east buttress of **Mt Logan** from Water Pass, reaching a sub-summit on the ridge at 9,600ft.

Geoff Hornby (UK) was once again active in the park, this time with Glenn Wilks, Alastair Duff, and Susie Sammut. The team flew in to the SW fork of Goat Glacier in the Granite Range and climbed numerous peaks in the area. Kari Medig, Merrie-Beth Board, Jacqui Hudson, and Lena Rowat traversed the **Fairweather and St Elias Mountains**, starting at Haines and finishing at Miles Lake. The party took 55 days to traverse 675km, climbing the E Summit of **Mt Logan** on the way.

The Coast Ranges saw a good deal of activity during 2002 with many local parties getting out and climbing new lines. Craig McGee and Brad White climbed a new line on **Mt Waddington**'s SW Face. They climbed the initial couloir on the Wiessner-House then continued directly up the S Buttress following a chimney for many pitches at 5.9/10a then steep ice and rock until they rejoined the Wiessner-House at the traverse section a few pitches below the summit.

On **Mt Tiedemann**, Jia Condon and Guy Edwards ascended *SW Bartizans Rib* (V, 5.10, M4, 1400m), starting left of the initial couloir on the *SW Face* and eventually joining the *Cullum/Gerson*. The remote **Mt. Gilbert** (10,225ft) was visited by Simon Richardson (UK) and Chris Cartwright who climbed the impressive West Pillar (700m, V 5.10a), finding excellent granite.

Closer to Vancouver, Guy Edwards and John Millar added a new mixed line, *Smell the Roses* (TD-, M7-, some aid, 500m), on the NE Face of **Mt. Joffre**, while Jamie Chong and Conny Amelunxen added *Cheech and Chong* (V, 5.10d, 700m) on the W Face of **Mt. Dione** in the Tantalus Range. The **Squamish Chief**'s *Black Dyke* has long been a test piece for aid climbers. Matt Maddaloni finally freed the remaining pitches, helped by numerous Squamish locals with cleaning and partnering. The Dyke now goes free at 5.13b.

The **Bugaboos** also saw new route activity with Lizzy Scully and Heidi Wirtz climbing *Bad Hair Day* (V, 5.12-, 1,800') on the **South Howser Minaret** in two days, making the first free-ascent of the pinnacle. On **Bugaboo Spire**, Alex MacAfee (USA) put up *Symposium* (VI, 5.8, A2+) solo during a period of exceptional weather in August. The route follows a crack system R of the *Cooper/Gran*, which it eventually joins before ending at the N summit.

Sean Isaac (Canada), Brian Webster, and Scott Semple also visited the **South Howser Tower** in the fall to climb the mixed line *Perma Grin* (1000', TD- M5 WI4). Isaac and Semple also put up *Spinstone Gully* (1200' TD+ M7R). Although the Bugaboos isn't known for its ice/mixed climbing, these routes are two of a handful of such climbs in the range.

The **Canadian Rockies** saw several major new routes although the winter's unstable snowpack did not lend itself to ascents during the calendar winter; several major new lines were added during the fall.

Will Gadd (Canada), Kevin Mahoney (USA), and Scott Semple climbed *Howse of Cards* (3,500', VI M7– WI6 X) on the North face of **Howse Peak** on their second attempt, climbing in a two day round-trip. *Howse of Cards* is a new line, sharing only three pitches with the Blanchard/House/Backes route *M-16*.

Barry Blanchard (Canada), Eric Dumerac, and Philippe Pellet climbed *Infinite Patience* (VI, WI5, M5, 5.9) on **Mt Robson**'s Emperor Face. This was Blanchard's third attempt on the route, having previously reached the summit ridge (*The Emperor Ridge*, Perla/Spencer, 1961), but had not consider the route complete without the summit. Blanchard described the route as 'an absolute classic'.

Eric Dumerac and Philippe Pellet also established *Rights of Passage* (5.7, M5, WI8, 800m) on the far R-hand side of the N Face of **Mt Kitchener**. The route follows a gully system to a continually overhanging section of glacial ice for several pitches, hence their proposed grade of WI8. This line has possibly been climbed previously, but the glacial movement may have significantly changed the route during the intervening years.

Further N in **Baffin Island**, a team of Russian climbers, Alexander Odintsov, Valery Rozov, Alexander Klenov, Michael Devi, and Alexander Ruchkin, supported by Michael Bakin, Ivan Samoilenko, Lev Dorfman, Dmitry Lifanov, Sergei Porodnov, and Vladimir Morozov, travelled to **Great Sail Peak**. Their route, *Rubikon* (1154m, ED2, VI, 5.11a, A4, Russian 6B), took 16 climbing days to ascend, and additional days because of weather. Before the team committed to the wall, they fixed the first eight pitches from the ground. Rozov jumped from the summit, taking only a minute to descend the wall.

2002 also saw the first Polish climbing expedition to Baffin Island. Chris Belczynski, Marcin Tomaszewski, and Michal Bulik visited **Mt Thor** and climbed a new line on the N flank of the W Face. It took the climbers 18 days – the first 9 days they had poor weather – to establish *Absolute End* (1370m, VI, 5.11, A4) capsule style using three camps. The route follows a system of seams, cracks, and dihedrals broken occasionally by short blank sections or roofs.

Brad Barlage and Andrew McLean also spent a month ski mountaineering around the eastern fjords of Baffin Island, ascending and skiing numerous couloirs.

CONTINENTAL UNITED STATES

In **Yosemite,** the current trend of one-day and speed ascents continued this year, with the 9-year-old record of 4 hours 22 minutes for *The Nose* on **El Capitan** being broken on several occasions. This culminated in a new record of 2 hours 48 minutes for Hans Florine and Yuji Hirayama. Tommy Caldwell and Beth Rodden also freed the *Salathe Wall* (5.13b) in one day. Yuji Hirayama subsequently brought that time down to 13 hours by combining some of the crux pitches. Hirayama also onsighted Rob Miller's new line, *Quantum Mechanic* (see below), rounding off an impressive season for him. Dean Potter freed *Regular Route* (VI, 5.12, 24 pitches) on **Half Dome** and *Free Rider* (VI, 5.12d, 35 pitches) on El Capitan in one push, having previously worked the crux pitches.

On **The Sentinel**, Cedar Wright and José Pereyra freed *The Medicine Wall* (The Uncertainty Principle) 5.13a. Wright and Jake Whittaker also freed the Sentinel's *Psychedelic Wall* at 5.12. Both were freed from the ground up over a period of weeks and then redpointed in a single day.

On **Washington Column**, Rob Miller and Jay Selvidge (USA) put up *Quantum Mechanic* (V 5.13a, 15 pitches), right of *Mideast Crisis* (Bosque/Corbett, 1963). After numerous attempts, Miller managed to successfully redpoint the entire route.

Several new aid lines were also added in the valley. On **El Capitan**, Jacek Czyz (Poland) completed *Quo Vadis* (VI 5.9 A4/A4+) over a period of 25 days climbing solo. *Quo Vadis* is close to the *Muir Wall* and shares a couple of pitches with the *Dorn Direct*. Four of the route's 22 pitches are A4/A4+ with a further 13 or 14 pitches being A3.

Jim Bayer (USA) spent 24 days putting up *Martyr's Brigade* (5.11, A5c R), which takes a line between *Reticent Wall* and *Space*. The route takes 'Reticent-style' hooking to the next level with numerous reaching hooking moves, including one of 17ft and a 22ft dry-tool hook utilizing an ice axe. Bayer describes the route as 'probably the hardest and most dangerous big-wall route on El Capitan'.

Unusually, the **Grand Canyon**, more commonly known for its poor rock, was the scene of some climbing this year. Anne Arrans (UK), Roger Payne (UK), Nikolay Petkov (Bulgaria), and John Harlin III (USA) climbed *Comanche Ridge* (V, 5.10) on the canyon's south rim. The ridge rises 4400ft in 1.5 miles, although the first 2000ft do not require technical climbing.

On Utah's **Fisher Towers**, Stevie Haston (UK) and Laurence Gouault (France) free climbed *Sundevil Chimney* (5.9, A3). The route had been previously clean aided by Andy Dodson, but after further extensive cleaning, the Sundevil went free with five pitches of 5.12 and a crux pitch rated at 5.13–. The route was climbed in the same style as Haston's other free ascents in the Fisher Towers: clean without pins or hammer.

In the **Black Canyon** of the Gunnison National Park, Topher Donahue and Jared Ogden freed the aid line *Bull Girl* (5.11 A4) on the S Chasm Wall. Ogden had previously attempted to free the route with Mike Shepherd earlier in the year. The resulting route was named *Burlgirl* (V, 5.12– RX).

MEXICO

El Gigante saw the establishment of two major lines this year, utilizing different styles. Alard Hufner and Brent Edelen climbed *Faded Glory* (VII, 5.9, A3), a 14-pitch wall route up El Gigante's nose (between the NW and SW faces). This was climbed over 14 days ground up with minimal fixing and bolts. Luke Laeser, Peter Baumeister, and Bert van Lint created *Logical Progression* (VI, 5.12c, A0, 800m) on El Gigante's NW Face. The 28-pitch route was rappel-bolted and then climbed free. This was the first rap-bolted line to be established on El Gigante and the subject of some controversy.

ANTONIO GOMEZ BOHORQUEZ

Cordillera Blanca 2001-2002

Translated from the Spanish by José Luis Bermúdez

Cordillera Blanca 2001

Huandoy Sur (6160m) On 4 July Pavle Kozjek took five hours to climb the right side of the NE Face by a 900m new route, *No fiesta hoy día* (ED+). The Slovenian alpinist began on rock and continued on snow and ice. After reaching the summit at 12.50 at night he spent a further five hours and some abseils descending to the left side of the same face. The first 200m were climbed with Urban Golob who subsequently had to descend with altitude sickness.

Cerro Parón (5325m) The E Face of this granite peak, better known as **The Sphinx**, was climbed by Zack Martin and Joe Vallone. Over a period of 14 days in June and July the American pair connected up sections of new route with existing routes up the centre of the face, reaching the summit on 7 July. They called their route *Gringos* and graded it VI, 5.12–, A3+. The 700m climb had several sections of A2 through vegetated cracks that they cleaned. Subsequently Martin and the Peruvian guide Michel Israel climbed the 1985 *Bohórquez-García Route* in a single day, grading it V 5.11a.

From 11 to 29 July Andrej Grmovsek, Tanja Rojs and Aleksandra Voglar climbed a new route of nearly 800m on the same face. They graded *Mecho Taq Inti?* (*'Where are you, Sun?'*) VI 7a A2+ (approx VIII A2+ in UIAA grades). The Slovenian trio spent five chilly days fixing 360m of rope, descending each night to base camp to rest. They subsequently climbed in a single push from the end of the ropes leaving 25 bolts and some pegs in the route, which takes a line on the left side of the face between the 1987 Spanish route *Volverás a mí* (Olivera/ De la Cal/Madrid/Polanco) on the E Spur and the Italo-Slovenian route *Cruz del Sur* climbed by Bole and Karo in 2000. A week later (probably on 12 August) Rojs and Grmovsek freed the 15 pitches of their route, regrading it VI 7b (7a obl.). They then repeated the *Bohórquez-García Route* and made the first repeat of the 2000 Italo-Slovenian route, which they considered overgraded.

Quitaraju (ca. 6040m) On 21 and 22 July Nick Bullock and Al Powell put up a new route about 800m long on the S face. The route had sections of ice at 75°, 80° and 90° and some mixed ground near the rimaye. It took them seven hours to negotiate the sérac barrier at the base of the face, and they climbed to the right of the line taken by the Slovenians Svetici and Trusnovec in July 1986.

P. 4800m (ca.) in the Cerro Pumahuacanca Sur (or Pumahuagangan ca. 5050m) Roberto Iannilli and Luciano Mastraci climbed a new route on the NW Face of this rocky tower better known as **Punta Numa**. During a five-day period of bad weather they fixed 12 pitches on the right side of the face, climbing the remaining 11 pitches on 2 August. They called their route *Hasta luego zorro,* and graded it 7a A3+ (VII+ A3+ in UIAA grades). The route is probably 1200m long and its last two pitches are shared with the *Catalan Route* climbed by Eloi Callado and César Pedrocchi in August 1997.

Churup (5493m) Ricardo ('Richard') Hidalgo climbed on 4 October 2001 a 300m route, either a new route or an important variation, on the right-hand section of the central portion of the SW Face, starting up the first section of the 1982 *Lorenzo-Palacios Spanish Route* (*Princesa Malinche Route*) and then taking a direct line to the SE Arête and then for 50m to the summit. The Peruvian guide climbed sections of 70°, 80° and 85° on excellent ice and named his route *496 Spasmos.*

Taulliraju S or Taulliraju SE, c. 5400m   *Middle Earth*, the route climbed by Topher and Patience Donahue in 2001 and reported in the 2002 *American Alpine Journal,* is not on Nevado Tuctabamba, the peak climbed in 1960 by the Italians Andrea Farina and Nino Poloni. The peak climbed by the American couple, and which may not previously have been climbed, is somewhat closer to, and immediately to the SE of, the main summit of Taulliraju and should be known as **Taulliraju S or Taulliraju SE**. The peak is marked on sheet *0/3a* of the 2002 edition of the Austrian Alpine Club map, where it is shown with an altitude of 5400m (see also sheet *18-h* of the Instituto Geográfico Militar del Perú map). The peak was attempted by two Slovenians in 1995, who found evidence of a previous attempt (which may have been successful). The two Slovenians climbed the left side of the NW Face to the SE Ridge, which they then descended without reaching the summit. The American route is to the left of the line taken by the Slovenians.

Cordillera Blanca 2002

Alpamayo SW Face to the N Ridge. On 8 August the Catalans Josep Escruela and Tino Tain climbed the gully on the right of the *Ferrari Route.* From the Alpamayo-Quitaraju pass they reached the start of the *Spanish-Chilean Route,* subsequently climbing to the left along the base of the rimaye before crossing it at the start of the *French Gully.* They climbed 120m leftwards across *pendientes* of 45°-50° to reach the left-hand gully. Precarious curtains of ice at 90°-95° with poor belays led to a narrow gully between the *Ferrari Route* and the *French Gully* that was climbed on ice and snow at 60°-75° to the N Ridge. They descended the *Ferrari Route* without continuing to the summit. The team estimated that the route was 400m with a UIAA grade of ED, 45° 60° 95°. They called it *Sensations of History.*

Huandoy Sur (6160 m), S Face The French climbers Yann Bonneville, Benoit Chanal, Françoise Dupety and Pierrick Keller, assisted by T Dabois, climbed the S Face of Huandoy Sur in capsule style between 31 July and 21 August, fixing 600m of rope. They climbed the overhanging granite wall to the left of the 1972 *Desmaison Route.* Above the granite wall they followed the 1976 *Casarotto-Da Polenza Route* on vertical mixed ground with poor quality rock to the SW ridge 100m vertical below the summit, which they reached in cloud. The French team cleaned the route, which they called *Crisis de fe* (1000m, ED+, VI, A4, 6a, M5).

Cerro Parón (The Sphinx) 5325 m, E Face On 26 July 2002 the Colombian Agni Morales, the Catalan Isaac Cortés and the Basque Kepa Escribano made the fifth ascent of the *Bole-Karo Route*, reporting that the correct technical grade is 7a+ (7a obl.). Mauro Bole and Silvo Karo had climbed the route, which they called *Cruz del Sur*, in July 2000 with the photographer Boris Strmsek. They graded it VI, 7c+ UIAA. The route was repeated in July 2001 by Tanja Rojs and Andrej Grmovsek who downgraded it to 7b (7a obl.).

P 5375 m (P 5350 m), E Face According to the Spanish magazine *Desnivel* Alberto Urtasun climbed 'the E Face of an unnamed peak of 5375m or 5400m (depending on the map) close to the giant Ulta' in the Ulta valley. The climb took three hours. The 'instability of the summit mushroom' prevented the alpinist climbing the final 10m to the summit and he descended to the north glacier. Urtasun called his 500m route *Turmanyay* (*'Rainbow'*) and gave it a UIAA grade of TD, 80°/85°, III. In my opinion this peak is the mountain called **Allco (5454m)** in the *Revista Peruana de Andinismo*. This was recorded in Ricker's guide *Yuraq Janka* in 1977 and referred to as **Nevado Perro** (although Ricker did not point out that Allco – or Alco – means 'dog' in quechua). It is possible that the S Ridge of this mountain was climbed by Erhard Erdmann and Christian Schield on 7 July 1961. The peak is given an altitude of 5375m in the 1932 German and Austrian Alpine Club map, while sheet *19-h* in the map published in 1972 by the Peruvian National Geographical Institute records it as 5350m.

Nevado Ulta 5875m The W Face received its second ascent and first solo on a possible new line by Nick Bullock on 8 June. Two days later the NW Face was climbed by Al Powell and Owen Samuels.

Note: Contrary to the suggestion on p.302 of AJ 2002 that Santa Cruz Chico is unclimbed, it was ascended for the first time on 2 July 1958 by David 'Georgia' Michael, Irene Ortenburger and Leigh N Ortenburger by the NE Face and the N Face.

Mount Everest Foundation
Expedition Reports 2002

SUMMARISED BY BILL RUTHVEN

The Mount Everest Foundation was formed as a Registered Charity after the first successful ascent of Everest in 1953, and was initially financed from the surplus funds and subsequent royalties of that expedition: its declared aim is to encourage 'exploration of the mountains of the earth'.

Although some people assumed that it would be wound up after a few years, others thought differently, and it was agreed that only the interest from its investments should be given away as grants. Since then, some 1,400 expeditions have good reason to be grateful that the Foundation still upholds those original ideals, having received a share of the £750,000 dispensed in grants.

Each year potential leaders scour the world in search of unexplored mountain areas, and then submit applications for support from the MEF. Surprisingly more than half of the peaks over 6000 metres listed in the AC Himalayan Index still remain unclimbed – some because they are little more than minor bumps on a ridge, and others for political reasons – but there are still many worthwhile peaks awaiting the attention of adventurous young climbers. All that the MEF asks in return for its support is a comprehensive report. Once received, copies are lodged in the Alpine Club Library, the Royal Geographical Society, the British Mountaineering Council and the Alan Rouse Memorial Collection in Sheffield Central Library, where they are available for consultation by future expeditioners.

This year the Foundation has used the occasion of the Fiftieth Anniversary of the First Ascent of Everest to launch a major appeal for funds in order to improve the levels of grants offered. The principal function was a Royal Gala – 'Endeavour on Everest' – in the Leicester Square Odeon followed by a Reception in Spencer House, at which we were honoured with the presence of HM The Queen, and our Patron HRH The Duke of Edinburgh, together with several other Members of the Royal Family. Most of the surviving members of the original 1953 team were present at this and at a later Dinner given in honour of Sir Edmund Hillary to raise funds for the Himalayan Trust.

The following notes are a synopsis of reports from the expeditions and projects which were supported in 2002, and are divided into geographical areas.

AMERICA – NORTH AND CENTRAL

02/07 'The Longest Day' Ian Parnell (with Kenton Cool). May-June 2002
This two-man team had two objectives in mind for their return visit to Alaska, one being a new route on the SE Face of Mt Foraker, 5305m. However, they discovered that this route was threatened by at least 15 séracs, making it far too dangerous to attempt. As a consolation, they attempted the *Infinite Spur* on the same peak, but were forced to abandon due to appalling snow conditions. They therefore turned their attention to the other objective, the first free ascent of *Denali Diamond* on the SW Face of Denali, 6194m. Despite – or possibly because of – almost continuous snow, they climbed this in 5 days, compared with 17 days for the first ascent, using only two points of aid. (*See article 'Hell to Pay: On Denali's Diamond', page 23.*)

02/12 North Wales Alaska 2002 Stuart McAleese (with Rob Collister, John Cousins and Mike 'Twid' Turner). May-June 2002
Although nominally a single expedition, the climbers operated as two separate pairs on different peaks. Collister and Cousins made two attempts on the unclimbed S Ridge of Mt Hess, 3639m, but high temperatures caused instability and substantial avalanches made climbing too dangerous. However, a ski circuit of the Hess/Deborah massif was completed. McAleese and Turner made for the Kichatna Range, hoping to climb a new line on the massive 1300m East Face of Middle Triple Peak, described as the 'Cerro Torre of Alaska'. However, the approach to Middle Triple was considered too dangerous to attempt. Attention was therefore turned to the Citadel, 2597m (to its north-east) on which, over a 9-day period, an 18-pitch eliminate of one of Andrew Embick's routes was climbed on the East Buttress. Climbing was 'free' as far as possible, but most of the lower pitches required aid, and the route, named *Off the Wall Madness,* was graded A2, E3.

02/20 West Buttress of Mount Hunter Malcolm Bass (with Paul Figg) May-June 2002
Whilst descending the West Ridge of Mount Hunter in 2001, after making the first ascent of *The Prey* on its Eastern Buttress [*MEF Ref 01/ 04*], these Alaskan devotees decided that their next venture would be an attempt on the West Buttress of the South Peak, 4250m. However, their arrival in Alaska followed a period of incredibly warm weather, so before committing themselves, they examined the approach from the air, and decided that the broken ground and danger from massive séracs made it unjustifiable. They therefore flew to the Tokositna Glacier and attempted a repeat of the *Harvard Route* on Kahiltna Queen, 3773m (the highest peak on the French ridge of Mount Huntington). Although they reached pitch 27 (just above the first

ascensionists' camp 2) in under six hours' climbing, they were unable to progress further, as the next section – usually an icy chimney – contained neither ice nor snow, just creaking loose blocks. Other routes in the area appeared equally unsafe due to the generalised melt-out, so they decided to cut their losses and return home early, donating their remaining food to optimistic teams which decided to sit it out.

02/31 British Donjek Glacier 2002 Geoff Hornby (with Alastair Duff, Susan Sammut and Glenn Wilks). May-June 2002
The Donjek Glacier lies in the Canadian Yukon, and is surrounded by unclimbed peaks: this team planned to fly in from Alaska in a single-engined Otter to climb some of them. Due to poor visibility the pilot decided to drop the first pair, Hornby and Wilks, on the Eclipse Glacier (between the Hubbard and Donjek systems) but as a result, he was banned from further entry to Canadian airspace. Making the best of the situation, the pair made the first ascents of Pt 3390 via its SE Ridge and Pt 3320 via its E Face and also climbed a new route on the NW Ridge of Pt 3330. Meanwhile, Duff and Sammut were forced to drive to Kluane and then, after collecting the others, to Chitina, from where they were flown to Goat Glacier in the Granite Range of St Elias National Park. Three more first ascents were achieved in this area, Mt Lola by its SW Ridge, and Mounts Jennifer and Zaylie, both by their West Faces. New routes were also climbed on the West Face of Pt 2450 and the SW Ridge of Pt 2570 by its West Face. What would they have achieved if they had been in their intended area?

AMERICA – SOUTH AND ANTARCTICA

02/03 Maestri-Egger 2002 Alpine Style Alan Mullin (with Leo Houlding and Kevin Thaw). January-March 2002
Although Cesare Maestri said that he had climbed (with Toni Egger, who was killed during the descent) a route to the summit of Cerro Torre, 3128m, as long ago as 1959, there has always been doubt in some minds as to the authenticity of his claim, and the route has never been repeated. Viewing the peak in 2001, Mullin thought that much of the ice and summit mushroom had disappeared, thus reducing the objective danger at the crux, so he determined to attempt the route himself. Using a 'caterpillar style', with one man leading a block of pitches whilst a second cleans and the third Jumars on a free line, all went well for the first 360m, but then a small foothold snapped, and Houlding fell, causing serious injury to an ankle. After evacuating him to hospital, an American climber, Johnny Copp, was recruited for a return to the fray, but the window of 'good' weather was over, and no further progress was made – in fact retrieval of the abandoned gear became an epic in itself. (*See article 'Commitment and Bolts in Patagonia', page 139.*)

02/08 Towers of Paine 2002 Andy Cave (with Dave Hesleden, Leo Houlding and Simon Nadin plus Neil Harvey & Ross Purdy in support). January 2002
Despite the name of this expedition, no climbing was actually done on any of the 'Towers' themselves. However, from a base in the Bader (previously Pingo) Valley a number of successes were achieved. Cave & Houlding made the first free ascent of the 800m Spanish route *Illusiones* on Cerro Mascara (The Mask) in 1½ days at E4, 5C (the original team took 10 days and graded it A3+): Hesleden & Nadin made the first ascent of the West Couloir on Paine Chico, 2670m, and repeated the Spanish route on Los Cuernos.

02/09 Antarctic Convergence Zone Dr Alun Hubbard (with Fraser Birnie, David Fasel, Penny Goddart, David Hildes, John Millar, Andy Mitchell, Grant Redvers, Elliot Robertson, Lena Rowat and Peter Taylor). October 2001-March 2002.
In a voyage from New Zealand via Cape Horn totalling 15,000km, this team (which included representatives from Canada, NZ, Switzerland and the US, in addition to the UK) sailed to the Antarctic Peninsula on the leader's 15-metre ketch 'Gambo' to undertake a programme of mountaineering exploration and scientific research. Despite a particularly bad pack-ice year and exceptionally unstable weather, they achieved six first and a number of notable other ascents down the Peninsula and off-shore islands, including Mt Britannia, Stolze Peak, Laussedat Heights, Mt Luigi and two of the Seven Sisters of Fief on Wiencke Island. They also completed a two-week ski traverse onto the ice cap via The Downfall, but were forced to retreat from a first ascent of Mt Walker, 2200m, due to sustained poor weather and over-commitment. The expedition made 20 dives down to 30 metres at numerous sites, including the wreck of a whaling supply-ship at Enterprise Island. They also carried out a comprehensive environmental science programme on King Georgia Island, acquiring numerous radar profiles of the ice cap, along with snow and sub-glacial water sampling, to assess the region's long-term response to climate change before heading back to Cape Horn as winter set in.

02/23 Jirishanca Alun Powell (with Nick Bullock and Owen Samuels). May-June 2002
After acclimatising in the Cordillera Blanca by climbing the popular SW Ridge of Pisco, 5752m, (PD), Powell and Bullock moved to the Cordillera Huayhuash and made two attempts at the primary objective of this expedition, the first ascent of the Central Couloir on the SE Face of Jirishanca, 6126m. Each was thwarted by poor weather, prompting concern that another El Niño was starting. The second attempt ended after both climbers were avalanched down 60-metre gullies which they had just climbed at Scottish Grade IV, with Bullock sustaining a number of soft-tissue injuries.

At this stage, Samuels was recruited to the team, which moved back to the Cordillera Blanca. Powell and Samuels then made the first ascent of the 900m N Face of Ulta, 5875m, at ED2, Scottish VII, A1. Meanwhile, dosed up with painkillers, Bullock soloed a direct finish to the *Dawson/Cheesemond Route* on the NW Face of Ulta at ED1, Scottish 6.

02/29 Apolobamba 2002 Gareth Gretton (with Daniel Carrivick and Jonathan Ellis from UK and Catalina Llado from Spain). June-August 2002
Despite heights and names differing from 'official' maps, the sketch map produced by Paul Hudson in 1993 has proved very useful to subsequent climbers visiting the Cordillera Apolobamba, but it is most unlikely that all the peaks marked as 'unclimbed' remain so. However, this team used it as a basis for their exploration of the Cololo Massif, where they climbed three mountains from a Base Camp at the far eastern end of the Lago Pauoche. The first was Nevado Jacha Huaracha (*aka* Pelechuco, Pt 5527 and Pt 5488) by its N Face and W Ridge at AD–, although they stopped short of the summit because of a threatening cornice; next came Nevado Nubi, 5710m, on which they placed an intermediate camp before climbing its W Ridge at AD; and finally an unnamed peak – probably Pt. 5490 on the Hudson map – which they climbed via its E Ridge at F.

GREENLAND AND ARCTIC AREAS

02/17 Lemon Mountains 2002 Dr Roy Ruddle (with Derek Buckle, Geoff Cohen, Robert Durran, Andy Gallagher, Rachel Gallagher, Martin Scott and Dave Wilkinson). July-August 2002
This mainly Alpine Club team operated as four pairs to explore and make first ascents, particularly in the North Lemon Mountains, which cover an area of 300 sq km. The most significant achievement was by Cohen and Wilkinson who, in a 34-hour push, climbed one of the highest peaks in the area, The Spear, c.2500m, via its 1300m NE Face at Alpine TD mixed. Meanwhile, Buckle, Scott and the Gallaghers concentrated on exploration, between them climbing 13 peaks, most of them first ascents. Durran and Ruddle were less successful, failing on three major new lines due variously to technical difficulty, avalanche risk and illness. (*See article 'Citrus Delights',* page 57.)

02/19 Cambridge Greenland Glaciology 2002 Chris Lockyear (with Natalie Clegg, Sam Harrison, Madeleine Humphreys and Derek Marshall). July-August 2002
Louise Boyd Land is in NE Greenland and, being rarely visited, offered an ideal venue for a programme of field research into glaciology and geology, the first step towards making a computer model of the ice cap for comparison with data on Switzerland. Although it will take some time to complete the

analysis of readings obtained, initial results showed that glacier movement ranged from 10-75cm during the three-week period covered. Two different types of granite were identified, containing large rafts of metasediment, details that will be added to existing geological maps of the area. As well as the scientific aspects of the trip, the team climbed six new routes up to Grade IV on 2000-2400m peaks close to their base camp, and then carried out a 200km ski trek from Louise Boyd Land to their pick-up point on Dickson Fjord.

02/22 University of Wales Svalbard Glacier Survey Andy Pope (with Dr Adrian Luckman, and working in conjunction with a party from the University of Leeds). April-May 2002
With a 10-15cm rise in sea level during the last 100 years, the Arctic has been identified as an area particularly sensitive to future climatic change. This team therefore planned to quantify the volume change of a number of glaciers in the Svalbard archipelago using digital photogrammetry, and compare results with those obtained from traditional methods. Work was carried out from two field sites: Ny Ålesund (between Austre Brøggerbreen and Midre Lovéenbreen) in the north, and at Svea (near Slakbreen) in the south, where a network of high-accuracy GPS points was established to use as ground control. From these, Digital Elevation Models were generated, which will be compared with archived aerial photographs held by the Norsk Polar Institute. Mixed weather with temperatures ranging from above zero to minus 30°C caused inevitable problems with computers and batteries; nevertheless, analysis of the data obtained will occupy the team for several months.

HIMALAYA – INDIA

02/10 2002 Garhwal Virgin Summit Dr Roger McMorrow (with Connor Kane, Alan Manning, Mickey McCann and Angus Mitchell from UK, Sara Spencer from Ireland and Gustau Catalan from Spain). May-June 2002
The original objective of this team was to make the first ascent of Pk 6044 (NW of Badrinath) by two separate routes. However, on arrival in the area, it was discovered that the maps were unreliable, and that this was but an insipid peak in a long ridge forming the northern boundary wall of the Bhagirath Kharak Glacier. To gain the ridge it was necessary to scale Pk 6175, which they did by its SE Ridge at an overall grade of D/TD. Their arrival at the summit heralded a serious break in the weather, making safe descent a greater priority than a traverse of the ridge, and after 26 hours they eventually returned to their camp. When the weather improved, they carried out a comprehensive photographic survey of the area, which should prove invaluable to future visitors. Utilising a mix of Irish and local words, they have proposed that Pk 6175 should be named 'Draiocht Paravat', or 'Magical Mountain'.

02/14 West Gyundi 2002 Ms Mary Twomey (with Ms Penny Clay). August 2002
The Gyundi Glacier is situated in the Spiti region of the Himachal Pradesh (NW of the Bara Shigri Glacier system – one of the longest in the Himalaya) but has had few visitors despite a highway providing motorable access during summer months. This experienced duo first tried to reach the glacier from Hal in the NE, but were rebuffed by unstable terrain and swollen rivers. A jeep was therefore hired to take them NW to Losar, from where they were more successful. The Nala was explored and a photographic record obtained of unclimbed 6000m peaks on the ridge separating the Gyundi and Dongrimo valleys, and an unnamed 5000m rock peak was climbed.
This expedition was awarded the Alison Chadwick Memorial Grant for 2002.

02/13 British-Indian Suitilla Graham Little (with Jim Lowther from UK plus Ms Alka Sabharwal and Paramjit Singh from India). September-October 2002
Suitilla ('Peak of Needles') has been described as 'one of the finest unclimbed peaks in the Kumaon, if not the whole of the Indian Himalaya'. It is located in a fairly remote restricted area, 15km from the Tibetan border, not far from Pan Chuli. The walk-in was hampered by late monsoon conditions (and the unexpected arrival of a black bear), arrival at Base Camp coinciding with heavy snowfall which prevented a serious attempt at climbing the NW Face, the intended route. Singh then contracted a severe viral infection, and he and his wife, Sabharwal, left the expedition. Undeterred, Little and Lowther relocated to the south side, and succeeded in making an alpine-style ascent of the 1100m S Face, climbing continuously for 22 hours (15 up and 7 down), topping out on the horrendous cornice of the 6373m West summit. However, restricted military maps indicate that the East summit (marked as Suj Tilla), linked to the West by a serious corniced knife-edge ridge, is slightly higher at 6394m. (*See also 'India 2002', pages 259-260.*)

02/43 Shark's Fin Jules Cartwright (with Jon Bracey and Matt Dickinson). September-October 2002
Although the East face of Meru Central, 6350m, has now received its first ascent, the solo climber (Babanov from Omsk) avoided the central line on the Shark's Fin by sticking mainly to snow and mixed ground to its right (N). This team hoped to climb the true nose of the Fin – 850m of snow, ice and rock, followed by 450m of steep granite and mixed ramps, which the leader had attempted on an expedition in 1997 [*MEF Ref: 97/46*]. However, a late monsoon resulted in heavy snow with hoar frost plastering the fin, and that, combined with one member dropping out, meant that Cartwright and Bracey were unable to carry sufficient gear to get higher than 5500m.

HIMALAYA – CHINA AND TIBET

02/11 British 'Great Walls of China' 2002 Mike (Twid) Turner (with Paul Donnithorne, Alun Richardson and Louise Thomas). September-October 2002
Although the Qionglai Range of mountains in Sichuan Province lies in an easily accessible National Park much visited by local tourists, it has received little previous interest from mountaineers. This team planned to explore the area, and attempt rock routes on two of the many unclimbed peaks. Donnithorne and Richardson climbed an 8-pitch pinnacle with pitches up to E3 on one of these, but retreated without going to the summit due to storms and snow. Meanwhile, Turner and Thomas reached a col at c.5000m and began climbing a ridge above but were also forced to retreat, leaving equipment in place for a return visit.

02/32 British Siguniang Mick Fowler (with Roger Gibbs, Mike Morrison and Paul Ramsden). April 2002
In an attempt to attract visitors, the Siguniang area of Sichuan Province was declared a Reserve ('AAAA' rated!) by the Chinese a few years ago, but although popular with local tourists, it had not received any British visitors until now. Mt Siguniang, 6250m, the highest peak, had been climbed three times from the south, but the only attempt on the 1000m 'ice streaked granite' North Face (by Jack Tackle in 1981) had been unsuccessful. Over a period of eight days and nights that included his most uncomfortable bivouacs yet (during which he nevertheless endeavoured to keep abreast with the latest activities of Harry Potter) and nourished with little more than noodles, Fowler made its first ascent (ED sup) with Ramsden. After descending by the unclimbed North Ridge, he declared it 'one of the best climbs I've ever done': praise indeed! Meanwhile, Gibbs and Morrison explored the area, climbing Ptarmigan Peak, 4730m, via a mainly rock route, and then, Morrison being unwell, Gibbs made a solo ascent of the S Face of Snowy Peak – *aka* Pt 5484m – at the head of Changping Valley.
(*See article 'The North Face of Siguniang' page 29, and 02/11 to the same area.*)

02/45 British Nyewo Chu John Town (with Nicola Hart, plus Tibetan driver, horsemen etc). 20 March-7 April 2002
The aim of this enterprising pair was to reach and photograph peaks in the extremely remote North and Western flanks of the Upper Kongpo Range (East Nyanchentangla). A road goes from Nakchu via Atsa and the Sung Chu Gorge as far as Nye, crossing two 5000m passes, but is impassable for much of the year, and consequently sees less than 100 vehicles per year. (The only known British person to visit Nye was the plant-hunter Frank Kingdon Ward in 1936). After a three-day trek from Nye they reached the village of Ekar, and although they failed to gain a view of the highest point, Peak 6842/6920m, they climbed to Chung Tso to gain a view of the

spectacular NW Face of Nyenang (Kangla Karpo), 6870m/6730m, the N Face of Jomo Taktse plus many other unnamed (and unclimbed) peaks. (*See article 'Nyenang and the the Nye Chu', page 95.*)

02/48 Hong Meigui Yunnan 2002 Ms Hilary Greaves (with Richard Gerrish, Gavin Lowe and Paul Swire). August-October 2002
Until 2001, there had been little interest in the caves of North Yunnan, but that year a reconnaissance expedition indicated an overall depth potential exceeding 4000m – hence this return trip. At heights up to 4935m, there were several areas of particular interest – the south of Nu Tiang Valley (near Liuku), the limestone peaks 20km W of Zhongdian and the hills between Lugu Hu and the Yangtse. The final phase concentrated on the Zhongdian area where the height difference between a resurgence cave and a high-altitude draughting cave was c.2200m. The team returned home with plenty of scope for future exploration in the Province.

CENTRAL ASIA AND THE FAR EAST

02/26 British Mongolian Mountaineering 2002 Paul Hudson (with Ken Findlay, Stuart Gallagher, John Given, Les Holbert and Karl Zientek). July-August 2002
Information about mountaineering in Mongolia is fairly limited, and this leader described the area of his interest – Ikh Turgen Uul, a National Park situated N of Tsagaannuur Village, (itself N of Ölgiy) as 'Fuzziness on the Map'. Plans to fly to Ölgiy were thwarted by an outbreak of Foot and Mouth Disease, so the team was forced to make a horrendous multi-day overland journey from Ulaanbaatar instead. Glaciation in the area was far less than expected, making it possible to walk or simply scramble up most peaks. However, Findlay and Zientek found an unclimbed 'Alpine' Ridge (which they named '*Noodle Ridge*') on which they reached 4050m in a five-day exercise during the worst weather of the trip.

02/30 Khrebet Kyokkiar 2002 David Gerrard (with Karl Baker, John Cuthbert and Graham Sutton). August-September 2002
An expedition to Kyrgyzstan in 2001 (*MEF Ref 01/37*) only scratched the surface as far as this leader was concerned, so he returned in 2002 to explore further, hoping to make a number of first ascents in the process. Initially, they were unable to gain access to the Kyokkiar Range, due to high river levels making crossings too dangerous, so they returned to the Gory Sarybeles Range, the venue for the previous trip, and made first ascents of three peaks between 4200m and 4350m. Entry to the Kyokkiar was then made on horseback, and successful ascents made of another five previously unclimbed peaks between 4600m and 4760m.

02/35 British Heart of Asia 2002 Ms Nina Saunders (with Janet Fotheringham, Alan Halewood, Michael McLaughlan, Sebastian Nault, and Robert Watts). July-August 2002
Although a team of Polish visitors to the Mongolian Altai climbed many of the peaks and produced a sketch map of the area in 1967, subsequent visits have been few and far between, other than to the highest point in the area – Huiten, 4374m. This team hoped to explore further and use modern GPS equipment to augment the Polish map. Unfortunately, access to the Bayan Olgi Region was prevented due to an outbreak of Foot and Mouth Disease (Plague and Rabies are also endemic in the area!) but they managed to visit two other areas – firstly Otgon Tenga Uul where they climbed Otgon Tenga Uul, 3905m, itself, plus two unnamed peaks c.3100m, and then Altai Tavan Bogd (*aka* Taban Bogd) where they traversed all five summits of Huiten and also climbed Snow Church, 4100m, and Kowalewski, 3800m. Some of the peaks were receiving their first British ascents and the PD+ route up the North Ridge of Kowalewski was probably a new one.

02/41 Scottish West Face of Kyzyl Asker Es Tresidder (with Neal Crampton, Blair Fyffe and Guy Robertson). July-August 2002
There is only one recorded ascent of Kyzyl Asker, 5842m, in the Western Kokshaal-Too: siege style in 1985, as part of a Russian competition. This team hoped to climb a new route on the 1500m West Face using more modern techniques, but the vehicle taking them in could not get to their intended base camp due to boggy conditions. They did, however, reach the 1200m SE Face, which was attempted by Robertson and Tresidder who climbed a number of pitches (up to Grade VII), reaching approximately mid-height before aborting owing to rapidly thawing ice. Meanwhile, Crampton and Fyffe made the second ascent of the N Face of Pik Babuchka, c.5300m, and also the first ascent of the N Ridge of Pt. 4850, a peak previously climbed via its W Ridge by a Russian team. Both these routes were c.700m TD Scottish V and, being N facing, were not affected by the thaw.
(*This expedition received the Nick Estcourt Memorial Award for 2002. See article 'Kyzyl Asker', page 43.*)

02/44 Borkoldoy 2002 Stephen Saddler (with Sharon Abbott, Jill Barrow, Wayne Gladwin and Mike Rosser). August 2002
Borkoldoy Khrebet in the central southern area of Kyrgyzstan runs parallel with the Kokshaal-Too for 20km, but apart from a visit in 1994 by six Brits with some Russians, previous visits by western climbers were unknown. After a flight to Bishkek and then two days in a 4WD ex-military troop-carrier, this team reached their base camp. From here, with consistently fine weather and daily temperatures varying between –10° and +28°C, they explored the major peaks of Borkoldoy to its north, and the plateau south towards the Kokshaal-Too, achieving first ascents of three straightforward peaks, the highest being Ata Peak, 4850m.

02/47 British Tyva 2002 Mel Penn (with Linda Martin, Peter Martin, Allan Richardson, and Bill Thompson from UK plus many Russian cavers and supporters). August 2002
There were three parts to this expedition making a return visit to the Akdovurak region of Tyva (aka Tuva), a country the size of England and Wales in the Russian Federation between Siberia and Mongolia. Part 1 was an exploration of Shagonar Pothole *('Hole so deep man not been to bottom of')*, an exercise that, despite a surface temperature of 30°C, required crampons to descend an ice flow; however, other than an ice plug at a depth of 54 metres, nothing of great interest was found. It had been intended to use a helicopter for Part 2, but this was abandoned due to unreliability and a 6-wheel-drive 'mountain climbing truck' used instead to traverse Naryn and B'loo Valleys in the Sengilen Mountains, exploring and surveying more caves in a vast area of limestone. For the final part, the team climbed over 1400m up the western ridge to explore and survey more caves.

MISCELLANEOUS

02/38 High Altitude Medicine & Physiology Website Dr Mike Grocott (with Dan Martin). On-going from Autumn 2002
Although actual *'research into the effect of altitude upon the human organism'* (one of the topics eligible for support listed in the MEF's Memorandum of Association) must obviously be carried out 'in the field', there has long been a need to collate the results obtained by all the expeditions that have undertaken such work. Working in University College London, this is being done in the form of a database that can eventually be consulted by future climbers planning to explore the high mountains of the world. The structure of the website is now in place, but work will continue into 2003 to complete the information areas. Once this has been done, the MEF will advise how the database can be accessed.

In Memoriam

COMPILED BY GEOFFREY TEMPLEMAN

The Alpine Club Obituary		Year of Election
André Roch	HON 1979	1945
Comtesse Gisèle Pighetti de Rivasso		1976
Christopher Brasher	ACG 1953	1968
John Anderson		1972
Cdr Cortland James Woore Simpson		1947
Robin Cooper		2002
Elliott Viney		1945
John M S Lecky	Asp.	1996
Gino Buscaini		1980
Oliver Turnbull		1963
Jean François Saltet		1974
Samuel Stuart Ferguson		1978
Peter Henry Hicks		1945
Ursula Corning	LAC	1933
Sir Peter Averell Daniell		1932
Clifford Austin Fenner		1945
Joseph Fred Snalam		1978
Michael Hunter Johnston		1990
John Pitt Hull		1983
Brig Donald Ross		1951
Prof Maud B E Godward	LAC	1953
Harry Francis West Taylor		1980
Patrick Edmund Percy, The Rt Hon The Earl of Limerick		1964
Suzanne Irene Gibson	LAC	1938
Peter Lloyd		1934

The list this year is a particularly long one. Not only has there been a large number of deaths, but the list extends to April 2003 to allow for the fact that the Journal appears later in the year. It has not proved possible to include obituaries for a number of those listed above, but, as always, I will be very pleased to include any in next year's edition. Obituaries appear for Sir Alan Pullinger and Arthur Peters who were both in last year's In Memoriam list.

Geoffrey Templeman

André Roch 1906-2002

There cannot be many mountaineers, past or present, who could claim to have derived a spell of active enjoyment from their passion for over fifty years. André Roch, who died in Geneva on 19 November 2002, aged 96, was one of the few who did so. He attributed his good fortune to the enthusiasm provided by his father Professor Maurice Roch, a doctor of medicine, Rector of Geneva University, and President of the Geneva section of the Swiss Alpine Club, who, during his boyhood, used to take him out scrambling on the rocks of the Salève near his home. At 14 his ascents included the Fletschhorn, Weissmies, and Rimpfischhorn; three years later he traversed the Zinal Rothorn, and climbed the Zmutt ridge of the Matterhorn; the following year he arrived on the summit of the Grépon late in the evening in a storm. In the winter of 1926, accompanied by Armand Charlet of Chamonix, he climbed the Dent du Requin and the Aiguille du Plan. Beginnings filled with high promise, and followed by a career replete with a series of remarkable accomplishments.

But André Roch was not an alpinist pure and simple. He combined his passion for mountaineering with his interests in painting, photography, as a writer, a lecturer, and as a pioneer in scientific research relating to snow and avalanches. His life spanned practically an entire century, during which mountaineering methods as practised by the pioneers underwent changes to a degree that could hardly have been imagined. During civil engineering studies at Zürich University André Roch began to excel as a skier, winning competitions at Cortina in downhill racing, slalom, and jumping. In 1928 he was chosen to train an Italian University team at Val Gardena for slalom and downhill racing. During the winter of 1930-31 he undertook a course of study at the Oregon State College, USA, when he climbed Mount Hood. On returning to Switzerland, he worked as an engineer on a barrage south of Grenoble but, having qualified as an alpine guide, he quit the job to work as a guide and ski instructor, occupations much more to his liking. In 1934 he was invited to join Professor G O Dyhrenfurth's expedition to the Baltoro glacier in the Karakoram. A route was explored on the SE ridge of Gasherbrum I by which, with some variation, an American party climbed the mountain 24 years later. The SE summit of Baltoro Kangri, 7275m, was climbed on ski up to 7000m; also the central summit of Sia Kangri, 7300m.

André Roch joined the Swiss Federal Institute for the Study of Snow and Avalanches at its inauguration in 1940 on the Weissfluhjoch above Davos, where he worked for over thirty years on the study and structure of snow and the causes and prevention of avalanches. During the Second World War he conducted training courses for Army officers in snow conditions, weather, and precautionary techniques. Once, skiing off piste with his son above Davos, they were caught in a slab avalanche, and it was only after an hour of desperate digging that he was able to rescue his son.

In 1938 André Roch led a Zürich Academic Alpine Club expedition to East Greenland when six first ascents were made, including that of the second highest peak, Mt Forel, 3360m. He went there again in 1957 and 1959 with glaciological and topographical expeditions. He visited the USA in the winter of 1936-37, climbing and exploring some of the mountains above the old mining town of Aspen, Colorado. In the summer of 1937 at Aspen he surveyed and cut the resort's first ski run and designed the chair lift system. His subsequent visits to the USA included both skiing and mountaineering, and in 1950, he made the second ascent of Mount Logan. At Aspen, in 1967, by then well known and popular, he conducted an avalanche course, and attended a downhill ski race for the Roch Cup on the slope which he had designed and which bears his name. He returned to Aspen in 1987 where the 50th anniversary of his first visit was celebrated. As leader of two Swiss expeditions organized by the Swiss Foundation for Alpine Research, Zürich, André Roch visited Garhwal twice. In 1939, accompanied by two climbers F Steuri, D Zogg, and L Huber who carried out a photogrammetric survey, several climbs were made. Dunagiri, 7066m, first attempted by W W Graham with Emil Boss and Ulrich Kaufmann in 1883, and later by Peter Oliver and by Eric Shipton, was approached from the Rhamani glacier and climbed by its West Ridge on 5 July. Moving over to the Kosa glacier cirque, seven peaks were climbed including Rataban, 6150m, and Gauri Parbat, 6714m. An attempt on the SE face of Chaukhamba, 7138m, ended after an avalanche swept the party's camp 500 metres down a snow slope, killing two Sherpas. In 1947 André Roch led the first post-war foreign expedition to the Himalaya, the party including R Dittert, a leading Geneva climber, and the Zermatt guide Alexander Graven. I was privileged to be invited as a guest member. With a base below a moraine ridge on the left bank of the Gangotri glacier, Kedarnath peak, 6940m, was climbed, and a possible route was explored on the western approaches to Chaukhamba. We had a team of nine Sherpas with old Wangdi Norbu as sirdar, but following his removal to hospital after an accident, Roch appointed Tenzing in his place, which marked the start of his brilliant future career, and his special friendship with Swiss mountaineers. From a new base at Nandanban above the meeting point of the Chaturangi glacier with the Gangotri facing Shivling, Satopanth, 7075m was climbed. Two other mountains were ascended, Kalindi peak, 6100m, and Balbala, 6416m. On 10 September Roch, accompanied by Dittert and Angtensing, climbed Nanda Ghunti, 6310m, after a final climb of over eight hours, which Roch described as the hardest of the whole expedition.

André Roch was an obvious choice for the 1952 Swiss Everest team, which was the first to overcome the treacherous Khumbu icefall, openng the way into the Western Cwm. He had a lasting regret that the leader, Dr Wyss-Dunant, insisted on the return of all climbers from the South Col immediately after Lambert and Tenzing's attempt. Roch felt strongly that he and one or two of the other four climbers still on the col were in a strong position to make a bid for the summit. In 1953 Roch joined a team of seven from the Academic Alpine Club of Zürich for an attempt on Dhaulagiri by its forbidding North Face. After reaching about 7700m, the route was abandoned owing to serious objective danger. It was finally climbed 29 years later by a Japanese party after the failure of four further attempts and the loss of three lives.

André Roch first visited Britain in 1948 when he was taken rock-climbing in North Wales. On a visit to the Lake District in 1954 he climbed Kern Knott's Crack on Great Gable. During a short spell at Glenmore Lodge in 1978, ski resorts then under development in Scotland were able to benefit from his advice and experience. Broadminded, international in outlook, he was at home in any company; his humour, sometimes waggish, was always alive. He shrugged off any deprecatory comments about current styles in alpinism, implying that differences also existed between the methods followed in his day and those practised by the early Alpine pioneers – whom he admired. Commenting a few years ago about the proliferation of Alpine Clubs that spread across Europe and elsewhere following the founding of the Alpine Club in 1857, he wrote 'the die was cast, and alpinism was born in the congenial form introduced by the English.'

When I went to live in Switzerland in 1975, we resumed close contact, visiting each other regularly. At his house in Geneva, looking out on the Salève, surrounded by his library and his Alpine and Himalayan paintings, he loved to reminisce, to discuss mountains and mountaineers, and he would watch with rapt attention videos of mountain films, his eyes lighting up with the old sparkling smile. At a birthday party held in his garden he introduced me to some of his old climbing friends including Raymond Lambert, Ernest Hofstetter, Alfred Tissières, Georges de Rham, amongst others. André Roch was elected to honorary membership of seven clubs and societies, including the Alpine Club, and he followed his father's example by serving a term as President of the Geneva Section of the Swiss Alpine Club. He authored innumerable articles and thirteen books, including *Climbs of my Youth* (1942), *On Rock and Ice* (1946), *Mon Carnet de Course* (1948). His last book, superbly illustrated, *Exploits au Mont Blanc*, published in 1987, contains a history of ascents made on the great mountain.

There could be no better proof of his devotion to mountains than his acceptance, at the age of 84, of an invitation to visit the Baltoro glacier 56 years after his first visit, walking much of the way from Skardu to Concordia and returning with new sketches of the magnificent peaks which dominate the region. He was one of those few fortunate people able to combine a passion for mountains with a profession devoted to the study of their phenomena.

He was twice married; his second wife, Emilie Dollfus, pre-deceased him. He is survived by his son, daughter, grandchildren, and great grandchildren.

Trevor Braham

Gisèle Pighetti de Rivasso 1905-2002

The Comtesse Pighetti de Rivasso died in Chamonix on 16 December 2002. Few people remember that, under her maiden name of de Lonchamp, she made some exceptional climbs in the 1920s, including the first ascent of the Sans Nom Ridge of the Verte.

Born near Lyon on 8 October 1905, she was naturally attracted to the mountains by family holidays and in 1925 she started climbing properly. It was the period when the Groupe de Haute Montagne (GHM) was starting up, and she was drawn into a circle of friends whose passion was mountaineering. She quickly gained technical ability which, coupled with her powers of endurance, began to place her in their ranks.

Her climbing diary has survived and tells how she felt. For example, of the East Face of the Index, she writes: 'Horrid conditions, but few real difficulties despite snow and rain. Summit at 11.30 in storm: 6cm fresh snow. Nasty descent. Bitterly cold. In good shape.' When on 15 July 1926 she began the season by climbing the Requin with Armand Charlet, she obviously suffered: 'Poor form ... jittery.' She quickly recovered, to judge by the numerous attempts she made in bad weather with friends: 'Icy ... Cold ... Snow ... Storm', but 'Good training ... Excellent form.' At the start of August she traversed the Charmoz-Grépon and also surmounted the Bossons glacier: 'Great fun ... Extraordinary ambience lost in a world of séracs. Ever changing colours. Quite fantastic. Descent by lantern. An excellent piece of training.' She was ready for something serious and on the 19th she made the first ascent of the Verte by the Jardin Ridge with Armand Charlet and André Jacquemart. There follow a dozen or so pages left blank, certainly because she did not have time to write up her routes. Then comes 21 September and the first ascent of the Sans Nom Ridge with Armand Charlet and Marcel Bozon. After a series of technical details, she concludes: 'Joie intense. Pas de commentaires possibles. C'est tout intérieur. Mais à l'Aiguille Verte restent attachées mes joies les plus intenses et plus pures.' ('Intense joy. No way of describing it. Deep inside. But my fullest and purest happiness remains attached to the Aiguille Verte.')

She was only twenty years old.

The following summer was another good season, including a new variant of the Grépon-Mer de Glace with Charlet. But her main view had been 'the soles of Armand's boots', not quite the same thing as the 'serious long ridges, far from civilization, away from Chamonix' which she adored; but she loved mountaineering of all kinds. Elected to the GHM in 1926, she could not resist poking fun at the competitiveness of her fellow members when she took some friends to the Aiguille de l'M: 'Nice playing the guide ... Splendid view from the Col de la Bûche. The pleasures of the lower mountains. Not the place to make a name in the GHM!'

Her marriage in 1928, followed by the birth of three children, kept her away from serious climbing. Then came the war and her courage and sang-froid were exhibited when, during the exodus, she found herself with a group of women and children at Trinity-sur-Mer and stood up to some drunken German soldiers who entered the house and threatened them. She was not someone to recount such exploits, but we know she used her German to get her husband liberated from the Gestapo.

Later she managed to stay in Chamonix with her children and there she helped people trying to escape to Switzerland. Douglas Busk, in his book on Armand Charlet, speaks of her having got the celebrated alpinist, Dr Azéma, out of prison, and organizing passage for two dozen escapers. Busk met her, and it may be she did confide in him, but the stories have gone with her.

Nevertheless, we do know of one incident. To get a certain 'E' over the Swiss frontier Gisèle obtained an *Ausweis* from the Gestapo granting her permission to go crystal hunting with Charlet. Disguised as a peasant and carrying a milk pail, the young man 'E' made his own way to Lognan, where the two others met him before going up to the Argentière hut. The next day the three of them made their way to the Col Supérieur du Tour Noir in a thick fog. Here Charlet went on with the fugitive, leaving Gisèle alone for over seven hours ... It was a close-run thing because shortly after Charlet had left home a German arrived wanting to join the crystal hunt. Charlet's wife replied that she did not know where they had gone. The entry for 9-10 October 1943 in Gisèle's diary cautiously notes: 'Fresh snow, very tiring; dense fog; no crystals.' The only hint of what really happened is an enigmatic 'E' placed after Charlet's name and subsequently completed.

August 1944 marked the real return to mountaineering. The Pighettis constructed a chalet near Chamonix and family expeditions started, but the pleasure was terribly marred when the younger son, Christian, was killed climbing in 1957. In the winter of 1958 Armand Charlet encouraged Gisèle to find the peace of the hills once more, far from lifts and tourists, and she noted: 'Samivel scenery; quite beautiful; total silence. Just one track in the untrodden snow, ours. Christian with us.'

Age advanced, although she still went walking until the 1970s. Friends with Henri de Ségogne, Etien Bruhl, Robert Tézenas du Montcel whom she encouraged to write a superb book *Ce monde que n'est pas le nôtre*, Frison-Roche, Samivel, Gaston Rébuffat, James Couttet, Lionel Terray (who made her godmother of his second son), the Snell family and, of course, Armand Charlet and his wife Andréa. Gisèle was deeply involved with the climbing world for eighty years and always retained her love of the mountains.

It was a great privilege to have known her. Open, yet inwardly reserved, she was understanding and welcoming, always ready to assist. The kind of person who will help you see a problem in a different light. The kind of woman who, despite age, alway retains a youthful freshness of outlook.

Anne Sauvy Wilkinson

Sir (Francis) Alan Pullinger CBE, DL 1913-2002

Alan Pullinger was born on 28 May 1913 at Trowbridge, where his father was Wiltshire's first Director of Education. As a boy Alan developed a lifelong interest in the world of nature, beginning with childhood walks along the Kennet and Avon canal. He was educated at Marlborough and Balliol, where he read Engineering, much to the surprise of his Admissions Tutor, who pronounced dismissively 'Oh dear! You will find that very stunting.'

Nothing could have been wider of the mark. After Oxford he joined the Trowbridge based firm of heating and ventilating engineers, G N Haden & Sons – the Hadens and the Pullingers were family friends – and he spent the whole of his working life with that company. During the Second World War he was involved in the building of airfields and the development of air-conditioning for tanks.

He became Managing Director in 1958, and Chairman in 1961. During his long stint at the helm he managed to maintain the strong family ethos of the firm, whilst at the same time taking it to a position of undisputed prominence in the industry, building on its reputation for technical excellence and expanding operations by acquisition – the firm was renamed Haden Carrier in 1971. He undertook a number of important projects overseas, such as the Sydney Opera House and Jeddah Airport.

He became President of the Heating and Ventilating Contractors' Association, and later of the Institution of Heating and Ventilating Engineers which, under his leadership, received the grant of a much-coveted Royal Charter in 1976. Alan frequently described himself as 'just a plumber'.

He had many interests outside the firm. He became a governor of Benenden School in 1976 – his first wife, Felicity, had been head girl – and became vice-chairman of the Council in 1981. He was personally involved in a number of important building projects there. He was appointed a Deputy Lieutenant for Hertfordshire in 1982 and for 15 years was Chairman of the Hertfordshire Scouts. In 1970 he was appointed CBE and knighted in 1977.

Alan's passion for the mountains took off when he was at Oxford. He helped to revive the OUMC, and joined the Climbers' Club in 1934, taking over the editorship of the Journal from Elliott Viney in 1940, and held that post until 1946. He was elected to the Alpine Club in 1943, served on the committee in 1961 and as Vice-President in 1988. In 1991, he was made an Honorary Member, partly in recognition of his efforts in trying to secure alternative premises for the Club, following the move from South Audley Street.

In 1934 he was with a group of Oxford friends on an expedition to the Lofoten Islands, where he distinguished himself by leaping between the two precipitous rock towers on the summit of Svolvaer. With many of the same friends he made an adventurous crossing to St Kilda, notwithstanding an almost complete lack of sailing experience.

He climbed and walked extensively in Skye, the Cairngorms, North Wales, the Lakes, Connemara and Cornwall throughout the 1930s. He managed one Alpine season before the war, in the Dolomites where he climbed the Langköfel, the Fünffingerspitze, two of the Sella Towers and other climbs. After the war he returned to the Alps, and also travelled widely, making several visits to Nepal and Bhutan.

I can add one personal note. In 1963 I climbed in the Bernina with Alan, Charles Warren and Tony Dummett. Our aggregate age was a little over 200. On our ascent of the Biancograt we were rather held up by a party of four young Italians – estimated aggregate age about 80. As a result it was late when we reached the summit, and a blizzard had developed. We abandoned our intention of descending on the Swiss side, and made our way to the Marco e Rosa hut, where we found an Italian couple intent on being married on the summit on the following day. We put a blanket screen round them, but never knew whether a gun was jumped. The following morning we descended on the Italian side, and met the best man coming up. At a farmstead on a high Alpine pasture we received an offer of ham and eggs. The farmer's wife produced two chilled bottles to accompany this repast. I still remember Alan's ringing cry 'Orvieto Secco, a very good breakfast wine!'

The Alpine Club and the Climbers' Club will miss Alan Pullinger – a great character, mountaineer, beagler, sailor, ornithologist, naturalist and loyal friend. He was a marvellous companion on the hills, very fit, and a great goer. He kept up his activities into old age, making his first parachute jump on his 80th birthday, and travelling to the Galapagos and to Ethiopia, where he climbed Ras Deshan, 15,180ft, when well past 80.

He was a fierce driver, as many stone walls on the roads to North Wales and the Lake District can testify. On one occasion he drove through a bridge parapet on an old Roman road, having told his friends that there was no need to worry – Roman roads were always straight – he had failed to remember that there was one kink, where the road crossed a railway line.

Alan's life was not easy. He lost an elder brother, who died tragically during a routine appendix operation. He lost two wives, both of whom died of cancer, and his first-born son. He is survived by a daughter, Clare, and a second son, Anthony, to whom I am indebted for much of the detail in this obituary, delivered by him in a moving address which he gave at his father's thanksgiving service.

J H Emlyn Jones

56. Tschingelhorn (centre) from the Gamchilücke. (*C M Sleeman*) (p216)

57. Rulten, Austvågøy, Lofoten Islands. (*J N Collie, 1903*) (p216)

58. S (left) and N peaks of Ushba from the south-east. (*W Weckert, 1933*) (p216)

59. Members of Dr and Mrs Workman's party leaving Srinagar, 26 May 1903.
     (*Dr and Mrs W H Workman, 1903*) (p216)

60. View from Mount Huber, Canadian Rockies. From left: Deltaform Mountain,
     Mount Hungabee and Mount Biddle. (*B Harmon*) (p216)

61. André Roch, 1906-2002, with Peter Lloyd. (*F B Goodfellow*) (p302)

62. Chris Brasher, 1928-2003. (*John Cleare*) (p309)

64. *Left*
Gisèle Pighetti de Rivasso, 1905-2002. (*Marcel Bozon*) (p305)

Below
65. Jean François Saltet, 1920-2003, on the West Face of the Aiguille de la Tsa, 1957. (*Robbert Leopold*) (p327)

66. Gino Buscaini, 1931-2002. (*foto Altamura*) (p324)

Left
67. Oliver Turnbull, 1933-2002. (p325)

Below
68. John 'Andy' Anderson, 1944-2002.
(*Henry Day*) (p313)

69.   Peter Lloyd CBE, 1907-2003. (*John Cleare*) (p329)

Chris Brasher 1928-2003

'Ah, but a man's reach should exceed his grasp, or what's a heaven for?'
Robert Browning, and a favourite Brasher maxim

He was larger than life, a man of many parts. He was an enthusiast –
dynamic, inspirational, innovative, frequently infuriating. He was a can-
do man with time for neither red tape nor stuffed shirts and he never took
no for an answer. He brought a breath of fresh air and a ready chuckle into
any company and he was generous to an extreme. Chris Brasher, CBE, died
on February 28th at the age of 74.

Order a pint with Chris and the landlord would ask, *'Aren't you Chris
Brasher?'* Indeed, to anyone over 40, Brasher's distinctive, bespectacled visage
was familiar. Pacer for the first Four Minute Mile, Steeplechase Gold Medal
at the 1956 Melbourne Olympics, Observer Sports Editor, twice Sports-
writer of the Year, Head of General Features at BBC TV, a controversy-
stirring documentary presenter and with his long-time chum John Disley,
instigator of orienteering in Britain and founder of the London Marathon.
And then a final career as a highly successful businessman.

But Chris was much more than a mere celebrity. He was a mountain man
who escaped to the hills at every opportunity throughout his life, holding
that all mountain activities, from hiking the Downs to fighting a desperate
climb, were all part of the one great game.

I first met Chris in 1953 when he burst into the PyG where we were taking
tea en route from Lliwedd to the Ogwen valley. We were mere exhausted
schooboys but our mentor, Bertie Robertson, was an international runner
nearly twice Brasher's age who just happened to be planning a bid for the
Fourteen Peaks record. Chris had been out training hard for his own, high
key and highly organised bid and immediately laid into Robertson as being
too old and too casual to stand a chance. But we were introduced and as he
mellowed in later years, I never forgot that brash, mouthy and – I thought –
rather objectionable young athlete.

Introduced to the hills as a schoolboy Outward Bounder, Chris had led
student expeditions to Spitsbergen and Baffinland. He became President of
the CUMC and a member of both the CC and the AC. He held the Welsh
Fourteen Peaks record for a single day in 1954, and right into middle-age he
was a regular competitor in the Karrimor Mountain Marathon, the Vaux
Mountain Trial and other testing fell races. Membership of the first post-
war Western expedition to the Caucasus in 1958 resulted in his first book
Red Snows, written with John Hunt who led the party. Together they made a
fine second ascent of the Bezingi Wall but the descent in a storm proved
epic and marked the end of his hard climbing. Subsequently, Chris rocked
an Alpine Club AGM by declaring that the only privilege of membership
was access to the most expensive lavatory in London. He resigned and walked
out, although re-elected many years later.

Although his degree was in geology, after his Olympic success he drifted into sports journalism. As Sports Editor he angled the *Observer* at many mountain and outdoor stories, most notably a brilliant profile of Joe Brown which placed the 'human spider' in the all-time top rank of world-class sportsmen. Not surprisingly Chris gravitated to the BBC where he was instrumental in the creation of the so-called Climbing Circus. Here our paths crossed again when I was invited to join the team with my cameras. The spectacular Kilnsey Roof, televised live in 1964 with Chris as Associate Producer and Presenter, was the first really successful climbing broadcast. Pure theatre, the final pitch under the great roof was televised in late evening with floodlights illuminating the white limestone and dangling climbers. Next year, only a bad attack of piles prevented him from presenting the Matterhorn Centenary broadcast, McNaught-Davis taking his place on the climb at the last minute. That night, when our small team of British climbers who had actually carried the cameras and directed and shot the live coverage all the way to the summit, found ourselves destitute in Zermatt, every table booked and every bed taken, it was Chris Brasher who located us, gatecrashed a top restaurant and insisted we were properly wined, dined and entertained. He would always give credit where credit was due. He would alway say thank you. That was his style.

The Castell Helen broadcast followed, the Red Wall itself discovered by Chris, Rusty Baillie and myself. It was Tom Patey who suggested the Old Man of Hoy for 1967 but it was Brasher who enthused, who made it happen and who presented the programme. Teased unmercifully by the harder climbers for his climbing-groupie outfit and – for a climber – his clichéd commentary, he took it all in good part. There was also a Brasher-inspired reconnaissance to St Kilda – where we eventually pronounced the greatest sea cliff in the British Isles un-televisable live – and then the 1970 Spider's Web broadcast from Gogarth, a spectacular location and the first in colour, before the Circus disbanded.

At BBC General Features Chris brought the Outdoors in from the cold. His more notable projects included *Climb up to Hell*, a winter documentary actually shot on the Eiger; *Last Blue Mountain*, a reconstruction in the winter Alps of the Haramosh tragedy; *Lost River of Gaping Ghyll*, shot deep underground; and then sponsorship of Norman Dyhrenfurth's 1971 international attempt on Everest's South West Face. Unusually, Chris freelanced the BBC job, his dynamism and contempt for bureaucracy much resented by the BBC jobs-worths. Apparently, when in 1972 he resigned, his successor triumphantly proclaimed 'the end of Jock-Strap Television'.

Meanwhile, Chris was also freelancing for the *Observer* where his weekly *'Breath of Fresh Air'* column was highly regarded by outdoor folk. A brilliant journalist, he would jot a few key words on an old envelope and then dictate his story verbatim into the first available telephone. As a photographer on assignment with him, one could ask for no better, more understanding or appreciative journalist partner and we did many stories together including an entire issue of the *Observer Magazine* on the Highlands and Islands. Memorable were pieces on Mountain Rescue, on MacInnes and his Ice Axes, on the inter-island air service in the Orkneys – and, of course, on whisky. Always a bon viveur, he suggested in '*Brasher's Highland Choice*' the best places in which to wine and dine, shortlisting only establishments where the breakfast kippers were fresh rather than frozen. Our favourite was the Achnacellagh, a remote fishing inn above Inchnadamph highly recommended by our friend Tom Patey.

In the late '60s, with variously John Disley, Eric Langmuir and myself, his three epic January attempts to make the first ski crossing of Scotland from Fort William to Stonehaven were foiled around halfway by the weather. Adventures they were too, each preceded by a last-minute overnight sleeper journey up from Euston, during which optimism flowed in direct proportion to the British Rail wine. Chris did eventually ski from sea to sea several years later, though on a shorter line through Ross and Sutherland.

When the BMC's new *Mountain Life* magazine foundered in 1973, Chris took it over personally. Involving me as his co-editor, he published the magazine bi-monthly for nearly three years, providing both the working capital, the editorial direction and bright ideas galore. With coverage ranging from ice-climbing techniques to haunted bothies and a lively, irreverent, reader-friendly attitude, ML galvanized the then staid field of outdoor journalism, awarded prizes of gallons of ale for simple competitions and is still fondly remembered by many over-40s. But it was very much a spare-time task, and eventually we were bought out by the publishers of *Climber and Rambler*, but not before we had been sued for libel by opportunist bureaucrats working for the Snowdonia National Park.

Not content with his media interests and always interested in innovative gear, Chris entered the business world. Silva Compasses, the SweatShop and Fleetfoot, the running and training shoe distributor, were opened in partnership with John Disley in the early 1970s. By 1974 he was experimenting with a novel mountain boot based on the traditional curved last favoured by his Lakeland shepherd friend, the fell-race champion Jos Naylor. Early prototypes, hand made by a Snowdonia cobbler, were tested by his friends and in due course the boot evolved into the incredibly popular Brasher Boot of today. Under the motto '*Travel Light – Travel Far*' he launched a range of lightweight mountain clothing and popularized walking poles in Britain. In 1990 Fleetfoot was purchased by Reebok, Chris becoming chairman for a while and subsequently chairman of Berghaus after that firm was rescued by Pentland Industries.

By the early '90s Chris had become disillusioned with modern athletics, particularly by the Olympic scene, soured as he saw it by drugs and commerce, and he ploughed all his energies into the outdoors and his string of very successful racehorses. His wife Shirley, née Bloomer, the well-known fifties tennis player, had introduced him to racing late in life and it became something of a passion.

Inspired by Tilman and Shipton who had been Chris's heroes since boyhood, he now conceived OBOE – 'On the Back Of an Envelope' – which was how Chris also liked to plan his expeditions. OBOE was a loose-knit gang of invited chums, of all ages and all walks of life, whose like-minded company Chris enjoyed. Oboists would be circulated with brief details of forthcoming adventures and whoever could turn up at the rendezvous on the day was guaranteed good exercise, good fun, great company and excellent succour for the inner man – or woman. Such outings included three-day treks down the Thames or across the downs of Cranborne Chase staying in gourmet pubs overnight, a voyage to St Kilda by schooner or perhaps a ski crossing of the Chablis. Right to the end he continued to walk hard, ski hard or to ride, preferring a purposeful mountain journey of several days to a mere hike. Only his final illness prevented him setting out last autumn, with several OBOE chums, to hike the Yukon's Chilkoot Trail.

Last Christmas we biked out to Imber, the lost village in the heart of the Salisbury Plain battle area, closed except for few days each year. Chris was incensed to learn that the ancient church, previously upkept by the military, was now to be abandoned by Salisbury Diocese. 'I'll ring the Bishop,' he cried, 'it must be preserved. I'll get something going!' A short time later, scrambling over a wrecked tank a few yards off the track, we were arrested by an irate Range Warden.

'You're breaking the law!' he stormed, 'you were forbidden to leave the track! There are unexploded shells ... '

'Hang on,' Chris was vociferous as we were escorted off the site, 'there aren't any! And do I look daft enough to pick one up if there were?' That was Chris all over.

John Cleare

Roger Chorley writes:
I would like to add to John Cleare's admirable obituary by saying something about the work Chris did for wilderness and open space conservation.

I suspect Esmé Kirby got him into the outdoor conservation world with her battles over threats to Snowdonia. She too was a fighter, warm, passionate, relentless. A person right after Chris's heart. The mountains of Snowdonia were certainly Chris's first love and a lasting love. He climbed and explored from his Cambridge days in the Alps, the Arctic and further afield in the Caucasus, but abroad was not really his scene. Wales and later on the Highlands were what mattered, and few if any knew the Highlands better than he did, and at all seasons of the year.

Chris's first project was to get rid of the petrol pump opposite Pen y Gwryd. He managed to buy it and then set about getting rid of it. But decommissioning a petrol pump turned out to be rather complicated – red tape and regulations – so he turned to an old Cambridge mountaineering friend who just happened to be Chairman of Shell. We can all imagine how the conversation would have run: Chris (straight to the point), '*Peter, I've just bought a petrol pump and I need to blow it up. Can Shell do it?*'

I mention the petrol pump for two reasons. Firstly, it illustrates his unerring eye. One pump was not a big deal, but that pump was iconic and that was why it was important. Secondly, it was the first project of the Chris Brasher Trust. When Chris sold his share in the shoe distributorship business, he put a substantial sum into a Trust to support conservation. To this he added the royalties from the Brasher Boot. The total resources available were substantial. Over the years the Trust must have spent over a million pounds funding a wide range of projects. There was help to the National Trust for Scotland for two major acquisitions – West Glen Affric and islands in the Outer Hebrides, there was the help for the John Muir Trust, of which Chris was a founder. He was also instrumental in helping to secure the future of the crofting community on the Knoydart peninsula. This was a long drawn out and complicated affair that really needs the pen of a Compton McKenzie. It illustrates one of Chris's outstanding characteristics: once he had got his teeth into a cause, he never gave up. 'It was the nearest I ever got to divorce,' Shirley once said.

I will mention two more big projects, but they came in all shapes and sizes and there were of course many small, interesting projects where his funding made all the difference. He really enjoyed spending his money on worthy causes. When the Snowdon sale was announced in 1998, Chris went straight to the National Trust and said he would donate £200,000 if the Trust would launch a general appeal. This they did, and with BBC television at the foot of Snowdon, Chris, an excellent speaker, spoke movingly of the importance of Snowdon and of what it meant to him. Dafydd Elis Thomas also spoke. I didn't understand a word he said, but he was magical!

Finally, Petersham Meadows, the kernel of one of the great historic views and open spaces in London. Again a long drawn out saga illustrating Chris's relentless persistence and skill and also his generous funding.

John 'Andy' Anderson 1944-2002

Andy started climbing as a Sapper and we met up on being posted to the same troop in BAOR in Germany in 1965. We climbed on the outcrops near Osnabruck and Hamelin and got into bad habits with the un-English use of pegs. A trip to the Dolomites saw us on a great bolted wall called Via Olympia on the Catinaccio. A telephoto shot shows us changing leads in a novel fashion; I was mantleshelfing off Andy's helmet in order to bypass a missing hanger, our combined weight supported on a single bolt. The hole where the missing bolt had failed was only drilled a quarter of an inch deep and we wondered if they had all been like that.

Another scrape was in the Hindu Kush in 1969. The AMA had not been to the big peaks since Dick Jones and Jimmy Mills had been killed on Khinyang Chish. The President, Field Marshal Templar had recently galvanised the committee by marching out of an AGM when no plan for an expedition was on the agenda, so now we were off to Tirich Mir to try and repeat the original route from the South Barum Glacier. As a training climb Andy and Richard Summerton and I chose Little Tirich as yet unclimbed and 6361metres high. In an article by J R G Finch (*AJ73* 110) we had read that the Owir valley would be a better approach so we crossed the watershed lower down and descended until a snowed up gully seemed to run out simply onto the Barum Glacier. Andy decided that a sitting glissade was in order and soon after accelerating away was lost from view. It was such bad luck, he had nearly cleared the bergschrund but we found him jack-knifed over the lower lip, quite winded. In fact, we learnt later he had broken four ribs and deflated a lung. As the 'way down' was up, we carried on, made the first ascent of Little Tirich, followed by a hairy descent to rejoin the others in the Upper Barum four days later. (A fuller but sanitised version of this escapade appeared in *AJ75* 80)

Six months later we were lined up in the Alpine Club for our President to see us off to Annapurna. As the Field Marshal prodded Andy in the ribs to see if they were better, he asked if he was a Sergeant yet? No sir, said Andy. By the time we got to Nepal he was. There he carried a load to the summit camp and returned the following day to see us safely down.

After Annapurna he was recruited by Ian Leigh to become an instructor at the newly formed Joint Service Mountain Training Centre and later at Glenmore Lodge after he left the Army.

We met in the hills from time to time after that, the last time being in May 2000 to celebrate the 30th anniversary of our ascent of Annapurna. Andy was a strong climber and a fine man of whom many of us have fond memories.

Henry Day

At 'Andy' Anderson's funeral, Tim Walker, ex-instructor and current Principal of Glenmore Lodge, said:

> 'Just as important as mountaineering, of course, is that part of the mountain culture which requires one to tell stories, to sing, play musical instruments badly and to enjoy an occasional drink. Andy excelled in all these areas. In 1974 he joined the staff of Glenmore Lodge (the Scottish National Mountain Training Centre) as an instructor. Staff then were pretty much the 'who's who' in modern mountaineering and instructional development. My understanding is that Andy was the hard man; someone who seemed oblivious to the Scottish winter, wearing only T-shirts when lesser beings were wrapped in Helly Hansen and ventile jackets. During this time at the Lodge, Andy and Cattie were responsible for introducing a new member to the Glenmore Lodge family and that of course is Karen. Andy was appointed Deputy Director of Inverclyde (another of the

three Scottish Sports Council's sports centres, west of Glasgow) in 1979 after his active mountaineering and instructional career was hampered following a serious skiing accident. Not his fault, I hasten to add (he was 'taken out' by a military skier, skiing for the glory of his regiment). He regularly came back to the Cairngorms and I gained the impression that he rather considered himself to be in exile away from the Highlands. The opportunity for his return came when he was appointed Principal of Glenmore Lodge in 1986. He had by then developed a political acumen, I suspect with the help of friends here today, which was to see him survive in an environment which could be every bit as hostile as the Cairngorm plateau, and that is, of course, in the political wilderness of sport, where the avalanche dangers are not from snow and ice but from paper. As on the hill, Andy could remain calm and assured in the most frustrating bureaucratic crisis. The late 1980s was a critical time for Glenmore Lodge – the building was falling apart and badly needed investment and Andy can rightly be credited with masterminding the refurbishment of Glenmore Lodge, completed in 1996. In addition to being involved in a host of Sports Council working parties, reviews and initiatives he was appointed Technical Advisor to the Cairngorm Working Party, became the Training Officer for the Mountain Rescue Committee of Scotland and drafted the guidelines for the United Kingdom Mountain Training Board – work which remains very significant to this day.

'In 1996 he was appointed Director of the National Centres, Scotland, which resulted in even more time on the A9 and being away from home and I believe he was happy to eventually move on from the Scottish Sports Council after 23 years service in 1997 and settle in his house in Insh. He became the Project Officer for the Kinlochleven Land Development Trust working for the regeneration of the village. During these past few years he was pivotal in assisting the development of several new businesses including the Atlas Brewery and the Ice Factory Indoor Climbing Centre – two areas of real interest for Andy! Andy was a giant of a man who was generally considered by many to be indestructible. Since I first met him in the early 1970s he has been responsible for getting me into, and just occasionally out of, many challenging situations both on and off the hill and that continues to this day! He was always entertaining to be with and will be sorely missed by so many people. Life is a gift and Andy made the most of that gift, achieving so much in his lifetime.'

Arthur King Peters 1920-2001

Art Peters joined the Club in 1988, having been a member of the AAC since 1964. He was a climber, a scholar and a man of business, running his own importing agency in New York City, but finding time in the lunch hour to teach French at Hunter College or to play squash. He climbed mostly in the Tetons, having a summer home in Wyoming, and rock-climbed in the Shawangunks, as well as doing a number of routes in the Alps with guides. He served during the war in army counter-intelligence and, after the war, obtained a PhD in French literature from Colombia University. He had a special friendship with Gaston Rébuffat, climbing with him and translating some of his works. He published five books himself, including *Jean Cocteau and his World* and *Seven Trails West*, which begins with the story of the Lewis and Clark expedition and ends with the completion in 1869 of the first transcontinental rail link.

Art Peters had great charm and was a pleasure to climb with. His talent for friendship, shared by his wife Sally, made visiting their home a delight.

Michael Westmacott

Cdr Cortland James Woore Simpson CBE, DSC, RN 1911-2001

Enthusiasm and energy were Jim's outstanding qualities, coupled with great warmth for his friends, and a mischievous smile. To the end of his life he always had to have a 'project', which he tackled with determination and skill. His greatest project was the notably successful two-year Joint Services Expedition to North Greenland in 1952-1954, recognised by the CBE, the Polar Medal and the Founder's Medal of the Royal Geographical Society.

The son and grandson of admirals, he was destined for the Royal Navy from birth. He went to Dartmouth when he was 13. As a midshipman, he showed the zest for life and the enquiring mind that were characteristic – the logbooks he was then required to keep are full of beautifully drawn sketches and observations on the peace-time operations of his ship. He served as a junior officer until 1932, when he was transferred to the reserve list, the navy at that time being under pressure to reduce the number of active service officers. He then read for a degree in electrical engineering at London University. He was recalled in 1939, serving in the Mediterranean in an anti-submarine flotilla, and subsequently in destroyers in the North Sea and the Atlantic. In the Mediterranean his ship was sunk by a U-boat, and Jim distinghished himself in helping fellow-sailors into life-rafts. Continuing to serve in anti-submarine operations, he made use of his technical knowledge in the development of hydrophone and sonar operation and after the war was appointed first lieutenant of the Royal School of Communications and Weapons Engineering. He retired from the navy for the second time in 1961.

Jim first climbed in 1938, but the war precluded anything outside the UK, apart from a brief visit to the Lebanon where he learned to ski, as well as doing some rock-climbing. After the war there was no holding him. During the winter of 1945/46 he climbed in Scotland almost every weekend. The following summer he was on a Climbers' Club meet in Norway, climbing mainly with Bill Tilman. Their rope seems to have been faster and more persistent than others on the meet, and achieved ascents of eight peaks or major ridges, as well as traverses of eleven glaciers and cols. The next winter he was again in Scotland, doing a first ascent with Bill Murray and Doug Scott, and again climbing with Bill Tilman on Ben Nevis, where they were lucky to escape a fall on the descent without serious injury. The great man was so impressed that he warmly supported Jim's application to join the Alpine Club, though observing characteristically that Jim's qualifications were 'not up to pre-war standards'. Three Alpine seasons followed, mainly with Charles Evans, Richard Hull and Anthony Trower, during which they did a number of major traverses in very good time, notably the Dom/Täschhorn and the Old Brenva. Jim also had a spell with André Roch's research party on the Jungfraujoch.

In December 1947 Jim set up the RN and RM Mountaineering Club, initially as a section of the RN Ski Club, and was its moving spirit and first secretary. In addition to meets which he ran in Scotland and North Wales, there were a number on the Cornish coast, and Jim's name will always be associated with the first ascents he made there, notably *South Face Direct* on Chair Ladder, *Zig-Zag* and *Doorway* at Bosigran. But climbing was not an activity that found particular favour with the naval hierarchy, who presumably preferred to leave that sort of thing to the Royal Marines. Polar exploration might be another matter, and Jim developed an enthusiasm for a small naval expedition to explore Scoresby Sound in East Greenland. The idea was turned down by the Admiralty, but not without encouraging noises in some quarters.

Nothing daunted, he got permission in 1950 to join the summer relief party of a Danish expedition to Pearyland. During a flight, the mountains of Queen Louise Land were pointed out to him – entirely surrounded by ice, fleetingly visited but never explored. In a five-day solo journey, he reconnoitred the approaches through the coastal mountains to the 20-mile-wide glacier beyond, where lay his 'promised land'. He had seen from the air that this glacier was a formidable barrier of ice hummocks, melt water streams and gorges. The following year, with four companions, he crossed the glacier in three days, carried out a further reconnaissance and confirmed that a large lake to the north was deep enough to take flying boats. Plans which had been developing over the past year now crystallised into an ambitious programme – the exploration of Queen Louise Land, coupled with seismic and gravimetric work on the ice cap using tracked vehicles. It was typical of Jim that, having had a comparatively modest plan turned down, he should now propose a bigger and more complicated expedition.

He needed all his enthusiasm, tanacity of purpose and persuasive powers to overcome the numerous difficulties in his way. With the valuable moral support of Admiral of the Fleet Sir Algernon Willis, he obtained the blessing of the Scott Polar Research Institute, the Royal Society and the Royal Geographical Society and finance from Shell. He persuaded the Navy and the Army to help, with men, equipment and supplies, and the RAF to carry out an extended 'training exercise' which had better not be costed! Treasury approval was given only two months before the expedition sailed.

It was landed in Greenland at 75° N by the Tottan, a converted sealer. From there, the bulk of the expedition requirements was flown 150 miles north by RAF Sunderlands to the large lake in QLL, where the base was established. The only items that could not be flown in were the eight tracked vehicles and trailers. These were taken north by the Tottan, in the expectation that they would cross the great glacier after the winter snowfalls. Immediately the fly-in had been completed, Jim, with five companions, set off on a 250-mile dog-sledge journey to the centre of the ice cap to receive a large air-drop from RAF Hastings flying out of the American base at Thule. One plane crashed in a whiteout – luckily no one was killed and the crew were flown out, with great difficulty. Jim's party erected a prefabricated hut, where three of them were to spend the next eight months carrying out meteorological and glaciological research. Jim and the others sledged back to base, arriving just after the sun disappeared for the winter.

Meanwhile, the tracked vehicles had been landed 100 miles south of their intended destination, owing to bad sea-ice conditions. When the sea-ice froze, and with the help of the Danes, they were driven north to spend the winter at Danmarkshavn. In the spring, under Jim's personal leadership, they were driven across the sea-ice and the glacier with great difficulty in two separate parties, a trail blazer and a more heavily laden main party, the latter taking nine days to cross the glacier. After that, things ran reasonably smoothly and all the hard work paid off in terms of exploration and scientific results. With hindsight, some of the problems could have been foreseen, but if they had been taken too seriously, the expedition might never have started. It needed someone with Jim's optimism, drive and apparent refusal even to acknowledge the existence of obstacles, to get the venture off the ground and established in the field.

After this great success, it was back to naval service for another seven years, with retirement at the age of 50 to live in the family home in East Anglia; but not, of course, to an idle retirement. Jim taught mathematics for a number of years. He kept sheep. He was a churchwarden and a bell-ringer. He had hoped to establish a vineyard, but planning permission for an accompanying house was refused. Above all, he kept in touch with his friends and with the country he loved. Fishing was a passion. Every year, he would be in his van in Scotland for the climbing and fishing, and in Cornwall at the Climbers' Club hut, the scene of some of his rock-climbing triumphs. He continued to rock-climb until he was 80, with the determination he had shown all his life – and to the apprehension, sometimes, of onlookers.

In 1985 Jim finally left East Anglia for the West Country, with his beloved wife Ann, first of all converting a barn at Luxborough into a comfortable and elegant home, with a precipitous garden carved out of the hillside, and some years later moving to Iddesleigh. Even when compelled to move again in order to live more practically in a village with some facilities, Jim insisted on moving heavy rocks to landscape their garden.

Jim was recognisably and proudly an ex-naval officer, with what would now be called old-fashioned views on life, but to the end of his days he was young in heart – more an eager schoolboy than a distinguished explorer. He will be greatly missed by his many friends.

Michael Westmacott

Dr Robin Cooper 1945-2002

Robin Cooper was killed with Hunter Johnston on the north-east face of Les Courtes on 7 July 2002. I had intended to join them but got engaged instead. Robin was born on 8 April 1945 in Edinburgh and attended Morrison's academy before reading psychology at Edinburgh University. After graduating in 1968 he moved to London and became involved in the Philadelphia Association, a mental health charity. He obtained a PhD in Philosophy and married Hilary who is also a psychotherapist. His climbing career began in Scotland in his teens and continued throughout his life, though it was interrupted by the birth of his three sons, Lewis, Thomas and Joshua.

I first met Robin by chance in Courmayeur where he was staying in the same hotel and had just come back from climbing the Grandes Jorasses. Hearing English voices at another table talking about Alpine climbing meant that our respective parties soon introduced each other. At that time Robin was only an aspirant member of the Club but he joined our party on subsequent trips and qualified for full membership in 2002. Peaks we climbed together included the Barre des Ecrins, Zinal Rothorn, Durrenhorn, Hohberghorn, Nadelhorn, Point de Zinal, and the traverse of the Trifthorn. He also climbed the Piz Bernina with another party and had an awkward descent in stormy weather.

Apart from climbing, his other passions were his psychotherapy practice, his family and music. He also played a crucial role in the development of the Philadelphia Association and was influential in modernising the association to bring it into the 21st Century. He was a critic of the increasing bureaucracy and regulation of psychotherapy and tried to keep the Philadelphia Association true to its founding spirits.

Robin was a friendly, reliable character who will be sadly missed by his
climbing companions. He is mourned by his family for whom life will never
be the same again.

Hugh P Nettleton

Elliott Merriam Viney DSO, MBE, TD, DL 1913-2002

Elliott Viney was born in Aylesbury on 21 August 1913 and died there in
August 2002, a few days short of his 89th birthday. Throughout his life he
was closely associated with Aylesbury and the County of Buckinghamshire.
His family firm, Hazell, Watson and Viney, Printers and Binders, played a
prominent part in the life of the town, and Elliott became its Chairman in
1967.

He became involved in a large number of local organisations – including
the Aylesbury Chamber of Commerce (Chairman), the Aylesbury Orchestral
Society (President), Aylesbury Association for the Protection of Property –
he was bi-centenary President in 1985 – a county magistrate, and Chairman
of the Aylesbury bench from 1972 to 1983. He was High Sheriff of the County
in 1964-65 and a Deputy Lieutenant from 1951. He made a valuable
contribution to the life of the Church of England in the county, serving as
churchwarden, trustee of the Bucks Clergy Charity, the Diocesan Advisory
Committee and, most notably, as a founder trustee and subsequent chairman
of the Bucks Historic Churches Trust.

He will also be particularly remembered in the county for his work for the
Bucks Archaeological Society, where he served as Joint Editor over 30 years
– Secretary for 25 years and President from 1979 to 1997. On the national
stage he was a governor of the Museum of London, 1972-1988, President of
the City of London Archaeological Trust, 1985-1989, President of the British
Federation of Master Printers, and Master of the Worshipful Company of
Grocers. This long list of his outstanding service is by no means exhaustive.

Elliott Viney had a most distinguished war record. He had joined the TA
in 1932, went over to France with the Bucks Battalion of the Oxford and
Bucks Light Infantry, and took part in the gallant defence of Hazebrouck in
May 1940, where he was acting second in command and briefly the senior
surviving officer in the Battalion. This rearguard action contributed to the
escape of large parts of the British Expeditionary Force at Dunkirk, and
was commended by the Germans, who in a radio broadcast announced
that 'the defenders of Hazebrouck not only delayed the advance, but resisted
in a manner truly worthy of the highest traditions of the British Army'.

Elliott was captured and spent his next five years as a prisoner of war. In
1945 he was awarded the DSO for his gallantry at Hazebrouck, and also
became MBE in recognition of his service in the POW camps, where he ran
the camp library, edited a camp journal, and organised courses in professional
and academic subjects for his fellow officers. After the war he kept up his

connection with the regiment, and remained in the TA until 1988. He was President of the Bucks Battalion Old Comrades Association from 1960, and was awarded the Territorial Decoration.

Elliott's love of the mountains dates from his early days, with family holidays in Buttermere and walks in the Alps.

He was elected to the Climbers' Club in 1935, served on the committee from 1936 to 1939 and was Journal Editor from 1937 to 1940. He was elected to the Alpine Club in 1945, proposed by Leslie Shadbolt and seconded by S B Donkin. He served on the Committee from 1951 and on the Library Committee from 1972 to 1991. He was President of the Oxford University Mountaineering Club in 1934-35. He was a member of an Oxford party which climbed in the Lofoten Islands in 1934, and put in a good season in the Dolomites in 1938.

After the war two tragic events entered his life. In 1947 he climbed Mont Blanc with David Cox, Robin Hodgkin and Nully Kretschmer. They were joined by John Jenkins and two friends. From the summit Elliott and those two friends decided to go down on the French side by the Mer de Glace. The other four descended the Brenva face, by way of the Old Brenva route. Jenkins and Kretschmer fell and were killed. Cox and Hodgkin had the daunting task of climbing down after them, although their bodies were not found for several days.

Then again, in 1956, Elliott's younger brother Dick, who was Secretary of the Climbers' Club at the time, was killed climbing with Tom Bourdillon on the Jägihorn. These events didn't in any way diminish his love of mountains, but it did mean that he lowered his sights. He continued to walk in the hills of Snowdonia, the Lakes and the Cuillins. He also continued to run – he was field master of the Old Berkeley Beagles from 1952 to 1975. In fact, he first subscribed when still at school in 1929.

In 1950 he married Rosamund Pelly. They had two daughters. The Club extends its sympathy to his family on the loss of an outstanding character.

J H Emlyn Jones

John MacMillan Stirling Lecky CFA, MA, LL B
1940-2003

The 'Calgary Acquisitor', airline magnate, Olympic rower and philanthropist John Lecky died very suddenly, aged 62, on 25 February 2003 at home. He was a man of vision, passion and action and was an aspirant member of the Alpine Club.

Born in Vancouver on 29 August 1940, John attended Athlone school, Shawnigan Lake school and Neuchatel Junior college. He attained a BA in economics from the University of British Columbia and an MA and LL B from Cambridge University. He also read law at Middle Temple, Inn of Court, London from 1961 to 1964. John was on the Olympic eight rowing team that won the Silver Medal in Rome in 1960 and between 1962 and 1964 he was a member of winning crews in Oxford and Cambridge Boat races. In 1963 he toured the UK with the Canadian Rugby team and in 1964 was awarded the MacKenzie King scholarship in International Law. He was appointed the 'Chef de Mission' of the Canadian summer games team to the Los Angeles 1984 summer Olympics. For the Calgary 1988 winter Olympics, John was a member of the Executive, and the Nomination, Sponsorship and Licensing Committees. In his role as chairman of the finance and budget committee, he took the lead in staging the first ever financially successful winter Olympic games.

Meanwhile, his business career began in 1965 in the investment industry. In 1972 he founded the Resource Services Group Ltd whose diverse operations included drilling oil, acquiring companies and a helicopter business, Okanogan Helicopters. This brought John in a big way into the airlines business and he founded Canada 3000 Airlines which went on to be the biggest carrier in Canada after Air Canada. In the end he was running some 35 wide-bodied jets, buying from Airbus rather than Boeing which suited his operation. Besides internal Canadian flights he flew anywhere in the world where there was a niche market. He kept well away from the ultra competitive trans-Atlantic routes, and at the time of his death was pioneering a trans-polar route from Toronto to Delhi.

In 2000, the airline went public and was doing very well. Legal cases were pending against Air Canada on the basis of unfair competition, in so far as he thought it unjust that Air Canada should be getting public money, and Canada 3000 not. His solution was that neither company should get public funds but this of course was unacceptable to Air Canada who would go bust without that support. It was thought he was about to win the case. Then the 11th September attack on the Twin Towers came along and spelt the death knell to the company. Airlines run on cash flow and with money out due to recent expansion, the timing could not have been worse.

Although this shook John greatly he had many other ventures to keep going and they were nearly all successful even during recent stock market drops. That says a great deal for his ability to see through the fog of finance.

He loved shooting, buying one of the greatest grouse moors in north Yorkshire in the last four years, and came to love mountaineering which he took to in his late 40s and which, I believe, he regretted not getting into earlier in life. I had the honour to accompany John on various mountain-eering trips to Central Asia and I suppose I got to know him through these few climbing trips more closely than anyone, except of course his immediate family. When I met him some 15 years ago in Wales he had already climbed the Italian ridge on the Matterhorn and would later climb Aconcagua, as well as Kilimanjaro. Soon after I met John I received a rare permission through the Bhutanese royal family to attempt a 7000m peak called Masagang lying on the Tibetan border. John took no persuading in agreeing to come on a trip which would give him his first close-hand encounter with the main Himalaya, and a particularly remote section of it at that. As in his business life, John had that ability to immediately grasp those aspects of climbing which were the most relevant, these being attempts on unclimbed peaks or new routes. He understood the fundamentally non-competitive nature of climbing and took to that aspect despite Olympic days. He could never understand how Everest had been taken away from mountaineers and made into a rich man's playground. We were lucky to have like minded companions on Masagang, with Ed Webster, Steve Sustad and Sean Smith accompanying us.

John wrote fine accounts of his journeys and one very amusing Bhutan episode I must relate in his own words. So that the reader is in no way confused I would say before relating this that there are as many stories in Tibet about 'Tibetans and Yaks' as there are about 'Welshman and Sheep'. John wrote: 'While tents were being raised several of our members were well entertained by a twelve-year-old girl who led a Yak to them, raised its tail with one hand and made gestures with the other towards its nether regions. There followed a stunned silence as our party struggled to follow the intent of her proposal and then a somewhat embarrassed protest. This was interpreted by the girl, not that the assembled party were disinterested in Yaks in general, but were disinterested in this one in particular. She then proceeded to capture a blond and younger beast which in turn was presented to our party leader as more likely to find his favour. No doubt this hospitable game would have attained its natural conclusion had not our brave mountain men retreated in disorder from these all too obvious blandishments and the composure of the twelve-year-old native.'

The last expedition he accompanied me on was to a very remote and interesting region of the far eastern Himalaya between Bhutan and Burma on the Arunachal Pradesh border. I had finally received a permit from the Chinese army to make the first reconnaissance of the 23,000ft peak Nyegi Kangsang from the north. John loved that last trip to Tibet. We finally found the mountain with some difficulty after a seven-day walk-in through country marked blank on the Tactical Pilotage Chart map and invitingly captioned 'inadequately surveyed'. We made the ascent of a 6000m peak.

But what does a busy and successful businessman get out of roughing it in country where there is no hope of recovery in emergency and, possibly more importantly for John, no communications. Again his own words answer it... 'Two months on foot and in a tent does produce revealing encounters with oneself, and certainly any emotional baggage has to be dealt with. There is no option to this. However, the tranquillity and inner peace associated with eastern travel has more to do with the simplicity of daily existence and a struggle for thin air. The Bhuddist philosophy creates an atmosphere of live and let live, but the success of the individual to be happy in himself is more a function of timelessness, the uncomplication of material surroundings, and the absence of self-created stress. This is not a disappointing discovery, as two months of exertion, plain food, and a vacant mind does offer a marvellous feeling of renewal.'

John's friend, the Canadian Premier Ralph Klein, said of him, 'He was a huge, strapping individual and the epitome of health. He understood sport and that was his significance to the successful Olympic games.'

John and his wife Effy recently moved into Ven House in Somerset. He saw England as his natural home. He leaves five children by two previous marriages. The funeral was in Calgary and a memorial service was held at Chelsea Old Church on 24 April.

He will be much missed and was a great admirer of the Alpine Club.

Julian Freeman-Attwood.

Gino Buscaini 1931-2002

Gino Buscaini started to climb at 17; in a few years he had already climbed over 100 routes in the Alps, especially in the Monte Rosa and Mont Blanc ranges. These included first ascents and a solo ascent of the Bonatti route on Grand Capucin in 1959. In that year he met Silvia Metzeltin on the North Ridge of Pizzo Badile; in 1961 they married and since then they always climbed together, accomplishing around 1130 ascents, 110 of which were grade VI and 320 grade IV-V, all over the Alps and other European mountains. These included the North Face of the Aiguille de Triolet, the Gervasutti route on Pic Gugliermina, the South Ridge of the Aiguille Noire de Peuterey, the Cassin route on Pizzo Badile, the North Face of Piz Roseg, the Vinatzer route on the Marmolada, the Cassin route on Cima Ovest di Lavaredo, the Carlesso route on Torre Trieste, the Livanos route on Cima Su Alto, the Solleder route on the Civetta and many other classic routes. Some 40 of their routes were first ascents.

Gino and Silvia climbed mountains all over the world, often the two of them alone, in small self-supporting expeditions. Countries they visited included Turkey, Iran, Pakistan, India (Zanskar Himalaya), Algeria (Hoggar, Tefedest), Niger (Air), USA (Alaska, Mount Whitney, El Capitan, Half Dome), Korea, Japan, Argentina and Chile, establishing 125 ascents, 63 of which were to the summits of unclimbed mountains, and 21 new routes, especially in Patagonia, of which they became world-recognized connoisseurs.

During a few years in his youth, while serving in the Air Force as a pilot, Gino had learnt to draft topograpic maps, a craft which he employed as an author and editor of mountain guidebooks. For 33 years, until his death, he was editor in charge of the collection of guidebooks 'Guide Monti CAI-TCI' (published jointly by the Italian Alpine Club and the Italian Touring Club) which covers the whole range of the Alps and the other mountains of Italy, and he was the author of eight titles in that series. He was also the author, with Lucien Devies, of the Vallot guidebook of Mont Blanc. Gino Buscaini was extremely meticulous; he climbed personally many of the routes he described and cross-checked the information on which he based the descriptions of the routes he did not climb.

With Silvia, he wrote three illustrated books on selected routes in the Dolomites: *Dolomiti Occidentali*, *Dolomiti Orientali* and *Dolomiti, il grande libro delle vie normali*; and *Patagonia*, which is more than a guidebook, as it includes the mountaineering history of that area and some short stories. He was also the author, with Silvia, of eight booklets in Spanish on the history of exploration in Patagonia.

Gino and Silvia were the only Italians to be members of the most exclusive mountaineering clubs in Europe: the Italian Club Alpino Accademico, the British Alpine Club, the French Group de Haute Montagne, and the Austrian Oesterreichisch Alpenklub.

Mirella Tenderini

Oliver Turnbull 1933-2002

Oliver Turnbull's passion for mountaineering began during the Second World War, when his uncle, Professor Herbert Turnbull, a past president of the Scottish Mountaineering Club, took him walking in North Wales and later when they attended the SMC's Easter meet in 1949. His uncle, who was Professor of Mathematics at St Andrews, also introduced Oliver to golf and he soon had a handicap in single figures.

Oliver was born at Bowden, near Altrincham, Cheshire on 8 August 1933, the youngest child of the Reverend Peveril and The Lady Jane Turnbull (née Grey). He was educated at Marlborough, where he shared a study with John Emery, and there developed his three great interests in life: literature, mountains and music. It was these wider interests that made his holidays almost a cultural experience. Poor weather in the Dolomites and he would point towards Verona and an opera in the Roman Arena. After a hard climb on Mont Blanc he would relax in Aosta in an ornate rural church listening to an organ recital.

He served his National Service as a Second Lieutenant in the Royal Artillery, continuing his hill walking and taking up rock climbing. He went on to instruct, for a short time, at the Ullswater Outward Bound School, admitting that he had to learn quickly to keep one step ahead of the students. Later in life he became Chairman of the school and took a great interest in the young.

In 1957 Oliver joined the Wayfarers' Club and climbed in the Alps for the first time, with Richard Hobhouse, Eric Lodge and Alan Stuart. This was the first of over twenty seasons in the Alps – many with Charles Warren, Iain Ogilvie and myself. After four seasons with routes including the Mittellegigrat on the Eiger, a traverse of Lyskamm, the Hirondelles ridge on the Grandes Jorasses and the Mer de Glace face of the Grépon, he applied for membership of the Alpine Club. His later routes included the Brenva Spur and the Sentinelle Rouge on Mont Blanc, the Frontier Ridge on Mont Maudit, the Nollen on the Mönch, the Triftjigrat on the Breithorn and a traverse of the Meije. He also climbed in the Canadian Rockies and trekked in the Himalaya.

His friends Charles and Iain encouraged him to apply for membership of the Scottish Mountaineering Club. He was told by the Secretary that it was important to enjoy 'gadding about in the hills' – a phrase that described Oliver's approach so very well. He wandered the Scottish hills and took an active role in the club. His enthusiasm for the SMC's Easter meets culminated in his taking on the role of Honorary Meets Secretary. The meets had declined in popularity but Oliver's first meet, in 1996 at Tomdoun Hotel, was a huge success with wonderful weather, ice on the loch and the largest turnout for several years.

Oliver took great trouble choosing which areas to visit and his anticipation and enthusiasm were infectious. For days he would quietly pore over maps and guidebooks, looking up references in his climbing library before telephoning with a firm but thoughtful suggestion. On one occasion he spent hours with his friend Ivan Waller planning his 'Ultimate Challenge' route across Scotland. His friends often said, when he was planning these trips, that you could see his 'tail wagging'. Oliver had many varied interests and an enquiring mind. When travelling, a plan would emerge: go and look at a grand house, visit an art gallery, call on an interesting friend. Even rainy days could be an adventure.

After working for a timber importer in Finland, Newcastle and Liverpool, Oliver moved to Lancaster to work for Courtaulds before settling in Kendal where he owned and managed Titus Wilson, publisher and printers. The Company merged with Dixon Printing and Oliver concentrated on encouraging local authors and the production of antiquarian book catalogues – a job he loved. He had a natural charm and gained the trust and respect of his colleagues and cients, many of whom became friends. He frequently searched through second-hand bookshops and on one occasion found the original CIC hut book on a Kendal bookshelf, which he bought and returned to the club when invited to represent the AC at the SMC's annual dinner. His interest in collecting antiquarian books, particularly early mountaineering association editions, led in his later years to the production of many beautiful book catalogues for international antiquarian booksellers.

We rarely talked during our climbs. Joined by a single rope and purpose, only sharing tea on the Brenva face of Mont Blanc, or a sip from a flask halfway up a Scottish ice climb, or drinking from a crystal-clear stream in the Pyrenees; we chose to be silent and soak up the atmosphere. Oliver didn't talk openly about his climbing plans; he preferred to keep his options open. He only once let a thought slip – the Matterhorn. In the hut after good climbing days he would talk of other routes and mountains and he frequently commented that he didn't want to climb the ordinary route on the Matterhorn, jostling with the crowd. So an ascent had to be by a good route, in good style.

The Zmutt ridge was in poor condition so we walked to Cervinia from Zermatt. Next day we climbed to the Carrel hut on the Italian ridge. Out well before first light the next morning, we set off up the ridge with its fixed ropes and rope ladder; the sun rose as we climbed. We had the ridge to ourselves and were alone on the summit. It was Oliver's 60th birthday. We descended the Hörnli ridge, mostly on the East face avoiding the crowds as they ascended, reaching the hut seven hours later. Tired but elated, Oliver's first thought was to phone his wife, Viv and the children: Lucy, Clare, Sarah and Harry. He was extremely proud of his children and grandchildren.

After he and his wife moved to Suffolk in 1998, he returned to his golf and took up a new interest – silver making. Oliver, who had a classical education and maintained that he wasn't good with his hands, created many lovely gifts for his family. He was quietly proud of his new-found talent. He frequently returned to Kendal for business and pleasure and would delight in walking along the High Street greeting old friends and colleagues on the way.

Oliver took an interest in the Club's paintings and more particularly in its book collection; he was a member of the Library Committee. His own collection of mountaineering books, which was auctioned shortly after his death, comprised 180 lots and was described as 'A Fine Collection', collected over thirty years, including Sir Charles Fellows' own copy of his book *A narrative of an ascent to the summit of Mont Blanc*, a unique copy, arguably the most desirable work on Alpine mountaineering to be offered for sale in recent years.

It is hard to imagine that less than a year before he died from cancer, Oliver walked over 100 miles in the Pyrenees, in both snow and sun. But we will all remember the vibrant, enthusiastic man who shared his wide interests with so many friends. He was always great company, especially on the hills.

Dick Allen

Jean François Saltet 1920-2003

Jan Saltet was born in Kediri, Java, the former Dutch East Indies. His father was a civil engineer, active in the fields of road construction and irrigation. After the death of his father in 1933 his mother returned to the Netherlands with her children. Jan went to school in The Hague and studied medicine at the universities of Leiden and Amsterdam. He was a general practitioner for about ten years, after which he specialized in pathology. Until his retirement he was a pathologist for the hospitals of the city of Gouda. Jan was married to Sjoek van Hees; they had four children.

As a boy Jan made several ascents of volcanoes on Java with his father. In

1937 he visited France with schoolfriends to watch the Tour de France. He felt attracted, however, by the nearby Alps and left the humdrum cycling circus for the Haute Savoie. Except for an interruption during the war and subsequent military service in the Dutch East Indies, his climbing career spanned a period of almost 45 years. He carried out numerous guideless climbs in the French and Swiss Alps. Later he was introduced to the Himalaya and visited Nepal several times: 'Indonesia and Switzerland all in one,' I remember him saying.

He was a member of the committee of the KNAV (Royal Dutch Alpine Club) from 1955 to 1958; editor of 'De Berggids', the journal of the KNAV, from 1953 to 1971; editor of a book published in 1977 on the occasion of the 75th anniversary of the KNAV, and author of a great number of articles about his climbs. Jan was very much at the centre of the Club's activities. He became an honorary member of the KNAV in 1971. He was elected a member of the Alpine Club in 1974.

In 1970 on his return from Nepal, where he led a Dutch expedition to the Himal Chuli area, he described his experiences in a booklet that starts with the following paragraph:

'Air, earth, water and silence still surround man here in all simplicity. To be free from any mechanical device, the absence of any sound of an engine, the absolute dependence on one's own muscular strength and the feeling of being one with the earth: I remember it all with gratitude. To have been part here of the almost untouched life on earth created the incentive to write this book.'

Nepal, the Himalaya, this was where Jan found what he was looking for in life. Perhaps a search for what lies between the stars and the earth? In front of his tent in the dark of a Himalayan night he wrote: '*Om mani padme hum*. When the jewel is in the lotus, the world is perfect and man looks beyond death. I realise the fascination of this prayer at this moment between the Primus stove and the moon.' In search of, perhaps, the world behind the curtains of time? One night he strolled along the Angkhu Khola: 'That night, stumbling in the dark on the path that leads from the camp to the river, I see a light flickering on the steep rocks above. Arriving at the bridge I see a man running to and fro in the water carrying a torch, in his hand a spear, around his middle a rope to which a jar is attached. Within fifteen minutes he has caught eight fish. Lascaux seems to have come to life; I am looking behind the curtains of time.'

Jan has now disappeared behind the curtains of time. In 1994 he sent me a postcard from Les Haudères showing the West Face of the Aiguille de la Tsa, a climb we did together back in 1957. The postcard carried one sentence: 'Finalement ils ne me restent que les images, mais quel souvenir.'

Robbert Leopold

Peter Lloyd CBE 1907-2003

Peter Lloyd, who was born on 26 June 1907 and died on 11 April 2003 aged 95, was the last surviving team member of the pre-war British expeditions to Mount Everest.

Lloyd's climbing apprenticeship began in the Lake District in the 1920s with Gino Watkins, Jack Longland, the brothers H G and L R Wager, Charles Warren, Tony Dummett and others. He was educated at Gresham's School, Holt, and Trinity College, Cambridge, where he read Chemistry and was elected President of the Cambridge University Mountaineering Club 1928-9.

He first went climbing in the Alps in 1926 at the age of 19 when, with Douglas Busk, they engaged a rather autocratic guide, Heinrich Burgener, as described in Busk's book *Delectable Mountains*. Although they did not have much say in the matter, it was a privileged beginning. They climbed the Wetterhorn, Mittelhorn, Mönch, Fletschhorn, Lagginhorn and Nadelhorn. Peter never climbed with a guide again!

His application for membership of the Alpine Club was proposed by Arthur G Whitting, seconded by Jack Longland and supported by Frank Smythe and Peter Bicknell. It listed his climbs over seven years, 1926-32. After 1926, these were all guideless and mostly of a high technical standard for those days, eg in 1928 in the Mont Blanc area: Dent du Requin, Dent du Géant, Le Moine, Les Droites, Le Grépon, and in 1931 in the Swiss Valais: Rothorn, Dent Blanche, Matterhorn (Zmuttgrat), Weisshorn, Obergabelhorn, Wellenkuppe and the Täschhorn-Dom traverse. His principal companions were H G Wager, Charles Warren, G W Harris, C G Smith and G A Dummett. With this alpine record, it is not surprising that he earned a place, together with Tilman, Graham Brown and Noel Odell, on the British-American expedition to Nanda Devi, 25,645ft, which they successfully climbed at the first attempt. Odell and Tilman were the summitters. Lloyd carried a load to the highest bivouac at 23,500ft, proving himself, in Tilman's words, 'capable of dealing with difficult rock at that height'. This was a magnificent team effort. Indeed, until the French ascent of the first 8000m peak, Annapurna, in 1950, it was the highest mountain climbed.

Two years later, in 1938, Lloyd again accompanied Tilman, this time to Everest. After the earlier heavyweight expeditions, this was a great opportunity for Tilman to apply his principles of comparative simplicity. 'Anything beyond what is needed for efficiency and safety is worse than useless.' The expedition cost £2,300. He chose a compact, well-balanced climbing party of seven: Shipton 30, Smythe 37, Odell 47, Warren 32, Lloyd 30, Oliver 32, and himself 40 years old. But despite a high level of fitness, they were foiled by the weather. The upper slabs were covered in huge deposits of powder snow, into which they sank up to their hips, and they were in obvious danger of being swept off the rocks by a snow avalanche. Shipton and Smythe made one attempt and Tilman and Lloyd another, but both attempts petered out at around 27,500ft. However, for the first time, useful comparative trials of open and closed circuit oxygen equipment were made under realistic high-altitude conditions, which very much favoured the former.

On the expedition's return home, the question of oxygen was debated with some heat at the Royal Geographical Society. Despite the fact that his expedition had tested oxygen with some care, Tilman believed that mountaineering was analogous to sailing, and that any attempt on Everest should be made only with man's natural resources. But after Tilman and Lloyd had voiced their lack of enthusiasm, Lloyd rose to declare: 'I have a lot of sympathy with the sentimental objection to its use, and would rather see the mountain climbed without it than with; but, on the other hand, I would rather see the mountain climbed with it than not at all.'

The Second World War intervened, but in 1949 the door to Nepal at last began to open, and permission was secured for the first-ever exploratory climbing party, provided that they also undertook some serious scientific work. Tilman, who had hitherto refused to mingle art with science, swallowed his scruples. A botanist, O Polunin, and a geologist, J S Scott, agreed to accompany Tilman and Lloyd. Tenzing Norgay combined the roles of sirdar and cook. They chose the less well mapped area of the Langtang Himal, close to the Tibetan border across which lay the high peak of Gosainthan, now known as Shishapangma, at 8046m or 26,397ft, the last of the fourteen 8000m peaks to be climbed, in 1964. Lloyd carried out photo-theodolite surveys and they got within 12 miles of it, the closest any climbers had yet been to the mountain. They also climbed Paldor, 19,451ft, which is now one of the popular trekking peaks. They were in the mountains from June to August, so views were restricted by the monsoon weather and, as Tilman wrote, 'Climbing took second place. Neither of us was ready for serious work.'

Although, with advancing age, the ability to tackle challenging climbs diminished, the love of mountains remained strong and there was an opportunity to put something back into the sport. Peter Lloyd seized this to the full. In the preparations before the successful ascent of Everest in 1953, Lloyd was put in charge of the oxygen equipment, assisted by Tom Bourdillon and Alf Bridge. From his experience in 1938, Lloyd distrusted the closed circuit design with its inherent complexity and claustrophobic effect in use. Even though Bourdillon was working on an improved closed-circuit design for 1953, Lloyd felt the right tactic was to concentrate on improving the storage efficiency of a well engineered open-circuit system (ie increasing the ratio of oxygen weight to total weight). In the event, twelve open and eight closed sets were taken for active use on the mountain and other open sets for training, sleeping and spares. Recalling his own sleepless nights at high altitude, it was Lloyd's idea to use oxygen at a low rate as an aid to sleeping. Hillary and Tenzing used the open circuit on their successful summit bid and later on Hunt wrote of the oxygen: 'Only this, in my opinion, was vital to success. But for oxygen, we should certainly not have got to the top.' Over the years, Lloyd's conclusions have proved correct. It was not until 1978 that the first ascents without supplementary oxygen were made by Messner and Habeler. Today, when oxygen is used at all on the highest peaks, it is always with open-circuit equipment, and Russian-built cylinders or ones using composite materials (pressured to 300 bar!) with the highest weight ratio of oxygen are the most popular.

In the Alpine Club, Lloyd was elected Vice-President 1961-62 and President 1977-79, coinciding with the 25th Anniversary celebrations of the first ascent of Everest. It was decided to mark the occasion by raising additional funds for the Mount Everest Foundation. A number of lectures were organised; a reception at the Mansion House, an exhibition at the Science museum and another at the Club entitled 'Man and Mount Everest'. These events raised some £100,000 making a net addition to the Foundation's funds of £89,000 which doubled its existing capital assets. Peter was himself chairman of the Foundation 1982-84 during which he initiated publication of a 1:3,000,000 map and gazetteer of *The Mountains of Central Asia*.

One of the achievements during his term as Alpine Club President which gave him most satisfaction was the resolution of a dispute over Mountain Training which had become acrimonious, with two training boards claiming to do the same job and a threat of legal proceedings between them. Lloyd set up a Tribunal, chaired by Emlyn Jones, the president elect, to investigate and make proposals for a settlement which fortunately was accepted by both parties. He also highlighted the major problem of the Club's leasehold premises in South Audley Street, which led to the move in September 1991 to 55 Charlotte Road, the Club's first freehold property in its 134-year history.

So far I have concentrated on Peter's contribution to mountaineering, but he had an equally distinguished professional career. He worked for the Gas Light and Coke Company in London from 1930 until 1941 on the industrial design of furnaces. Frustrated at being in a reserved occupation when war began in 1939, he got himself posted to the Royal Aircraft Establishment branch at Exeter, where he worked on defences against low-flying aircraft. In 1941 he joined a group working on gas turbine engines under Hayne Constant, developing the new method of propulsion. In 1942 this was merged with Frank Whittle's group, which had been pioneering the pure jet form of propulsion.

The rest of his professional career was devoted to advancing the technology and applications of the gas turbine. Initially a research scientist, he was rapidly promoted to Head of the Combustion Department, by now at the National Gas Turbine Establishment at Pyestock. He was appointed CBE in 1957. In 1961 he moved to London as Director General of Engine Research and Development in the headquarters of the Ministry of Aviation, responsible for administering the Government's extensive involvement in the aero engine industry until 1969. He was particularly proud of two achievements. One was the Spey engine used widely in military and civil aircraft and the progenitor of the successful Tay engine. The other was the

Harrier vertical take-off fighter powered by the remarkable Pegasus engine, a key ingredient of success in the Falklands war. (A Pegasus mascot adorned the bonnet of his car in Toowoomba, Queensland, where he settled in retirement.)

From 1969 to 1972 he was head of the British Defence Research and Supply Staff in Canberra, responsible for guiding the work of British Government officials engaged in cooperative defence projects with Australia and for the sale of British defence equipment. After retiring, he returned to England and became a director of Booth International Holdings, involved in the purchase of hides and skins, until 1979.

Michael Neale, one of Lloyd's professional engineering colleagues, recalled that even though Peter had outlived virtually all his contemporaries, he is well remembered and his legacy to the aeronautical business lives on. 'He could appear austere and somewhat remote. He had the knack of asking the question that went right to the heart of an argument, and not infrequently demolished it. This, combined with a penetrating gaze from beneath formidable eyebrows, could unnerve his juniors particularly if they were seeking to present a less than watertight technical report. To those who knew him well, though, he was kindness personified, ever extending a helping hand to those following in his wake.'

When I moved with my family to Hartley Wintney in 1978 quite close to Peter and his second wife Joyce at Farnham, we came to know and value them as friends and genial hosts. When they decided to move permanently to Australia we had great pleasure in arranging a farewell lunch party for them at our home to which we invited his many Alpine Club friends. I cherish the group photograph which I took at the time and he greatly appreciated the copy I sent him; he assured me it would find a place on his desk. He was a most considerate, warm, generous and gentlemanly person.

In Toowoomba he remained an enthusiastic motorist. When he decided it was time to trade in his old car, the salesman was astonished to find himself delivering a brand new large Volvo to a man aged 92!

George Band

Michael Ward writes:

I would like to add a brief appreciation of Peter Lloyd's contribution to the development of the scientific expertise that resulted in the first ascent of Everest.

In all the accounts before the 1938 expedition there had been no unequivocal nor objective evidence that supplementary oxygen improved performance at great altitude. However, in 1938 Peter Lloyd's ascent to great altitude, using supplementary oxygen and climbing with Bill Tilman who did not use it, showed clearly that his own performance, despite the weight of the set, was better than Tilman's and that he was less fatigued. Although, at the time, he was not fully aware of the significance of this comparison, Peter left an account of the expedition's findings which were noted by Griffith Pugh and myself in 1951 while we were researching the Everest problem at the Medical Research Council. Largely as a result of this data, it was decided on Cho Oyu in 1952 to try a higher flow rate (4 litres rather than 2 litres per minute) than that used previously, and subsequently this higher rate became the norm. It gave sufficient boost to turn 'sick men climbing in a dream' into confident mountaineers capable of climbing through bad weather and overcoming all obstacles.

In 1938 Peter also noted that the amount of urine passed at altitude was minimal and very concentrated, the result of dehydration caused by fluid loss from the lungs due to excessive panting. This was another important observation picked up by the MRC in 1951. Subsequently, on Cho Oyu, it was shown that exhaustion and rapid deterioration at high altitude were preventable by drinking enough fluid during the climb.

The benefits to be gained by the use of oxygen while asleep had been demonstrated by George Finch in 1922, when its use at night at over 25,000ft prevented hypothermia and deterioration. In 1953 it was used again for this purpose by the assault and support parties from as low as 21,000ft and contributed greatly to the relatively good condition of all who went up to the South Col and beyond. This was one of the ideas that Peter supported when he was made oxygen controller in 1952, following Pugh's report to the MRC on the various problems of cold and high-altitude to be expected on Everest.

Peter Lloyd's scientific approach to all these problems not only helped climbers on the first ascent of Everest but also contributed greatly to the improved performance and condition of all subsequent mountaineers at extreme altitude.

Book Reviews

COMPILED BY GEOFFREY TEMPLEMAN

'My Life'
Anderl Heckmair.
Foreword by Reinhold Messner. Translated by Tim Carruthers
The Mountaineers Books / Bâton Wicks,
pp272, with numerous b/w illustrations, £17.99

This is the autobiography of one of the most outstanding figures in the history of alpinism, and certainly one of its greatest survivors. A major part of this story, namely the first ascent of the Eigerwand, has been told before, several times in fact. For instance, as a fifteen year old I spent hours translating a French edition of Heckmair's, *Les trois dernier problemes des Alpes,* and his memoirs, *My life as a Mountaineer,* were first published in English in 1975 by Gollancz, translated by Geoffrey Sutton. However, this present edition has many new photographs, some minor additional material and a fresh translation.

Heckmair's father was killed in the First World War, and he and his older brother Hans were educated at the Munich Orphanage. Like his father before him, he became a gardener and even attended horticultural college, but the climbing bug bit deep after he was introduced to the sport by his brother and this has dominated his long life ever since.

The 1920s and the early 30s were years of poverty and mass unemployment in Germany, creating a breeding-ground for social and political unrest. Managing to get by from taking odd jobs, and with a little help from his brother, Heckmair and many of his contemporaries took to the hills, echoing the situation at that time of some of the working-class climbers in Britain. But what hills the Munich climbers were able to have to go at: the Wetterstein, the Kaisergebirge and the Karwendel! A telling passage in 'My Life' relates how Heckmair, as a youngster, climbed the Laliderer Wand in the Karwendel. He was equipped on that occasion with a description from no less a climber than Welzenbach and had as his rope-mate Gramminger, who was to become one of the most respected figures in the history of mountain rescue. It is a feature of Heckmair's story that many of his friends from the early days subsequently became famous in the annals of mountaineering history, for instance Hans Ertl, Hias Rebitsch, Rudi Peters; and in the main they helped each other out, sharing what little they had in the way of food and equipment.

Heckmair took up skiing, but he quickly learned the hard way from fractured limbs that ski jumping and racing were not for him, and thereafter it was long tours in the mountains at which he excelled. He and his companions travelled everywhere by bicycle and it was by this means that he first visited the Dolomites, went to Switzerland for ski touring and later to the Western Alps. They must have been super-fit and hard as nails physically. In 1931 Heckmair was attempting with his partner Gustl Kroner to make the first climb of the then unclimbed North Face of the Grandes Jorasses, but after several failed attempts the weather was so bad they pedalled off to find some sunshine, rest and relaxation in the south of France. They rode all the way to Marseilles and back, and on their return they made the first ascent of the North Face Direct of the Charmoz. Afterwards, on returning to their major objective the Jorasses, they found the dead bodies of two of their friends, Brehm and Rittler, at the base of the wall. But nothing seems to have put Heckmair off, despite personal suffering, injury and the death of so many of his acquaintances in the mountains.

Many other adventures followed: by cycle and public transport to the Atlas mountains in Morocco and further hard climbs in the Eastern Alps. But then Heckmair, who up until then had lived as a mountain vagabond, took the exams and qualified as a mountain guide. As he observes in his book, 'A man has to live somehow'. And this is how he came to meet the actress and film director, Leni Riefenstahl who, in 1937, engaged him as her guide for a visit to the Brenta Dolomites. After a rather harrowing climb on the Guglia, followed by a forced bivouac, she took him back with her to Nuremburg for a Nazi party rally. Heckmair met Hitler and spent two hours with him on a balcony, saluting as a torchlight procession passed beneath them.

It was the Eiger North Face, however, that obsessed him, and despite its terrible reputation, with many high-profile media fatalities, he was determined to climb it and trained assiduously, some days running as far as 50 kilometres. He spent six weeks beneath the face in 1937 waiting for the right conditions, and returned in 1938 with Wiggerl Vorg who, the previous year, had climbed high on the face with Hias Rebitsch.

The story of Heckmair's successful climb is the meat of this book – perhaps the most discussed event in the history of modern alpinism. The coincidence of his meeting on the face with the Austrians, Kaspareck and Harrer, the incredible performance by Heckmair in finding a route, and leading the rope of four successfully to the summit in the teeth of a storm and the resulting horrific conditions, is surely one of the most outstanding feats in the history of our sport. Despite having read of these achievements many times previously, I found this account as absorbing as ever.

Unfortunately, once the climb was successfully accomplished, politics intervened, and coming after the forced annexation of Austria by the Nazis, this was obviously a public relations coup for that party's officials. Two Germans and two Austrians joining together to climb the most challenging mountain face in the Alps was too good to be true. And soon they were being presented to Hitler, rewarded with a cruise to Scandinavia and other blandishments. Argument has raged ever since as to what was the real depth of political involvement of the climbers. Despite subsequently playing down this aspect or ignoring it altogether, as in Heinrich Harrer's famous book *The White Spider*, the facts that are now known are that the Austrians were Nazi party members, and in Harrer's case he was a member of an elite SS group. This is a worrying testament to a racist element appearing in Austrian mountaineering in that era.

Heckmair and Vorg were employed at the time of the climb as instructors in the Sonthofen Ordensburg, a key Nazi/sporting political training organisation, and they may or may not have been forced to be party members. They did receive some support in the way of equipment provision from that organisation, and this was one of the keys to their success, namely the fact that they were equipped with the very best gear then available, including the new revolutionary twelve point crampons. Nonetheless, after the outbreak of war, both Vorg and Heckmair were sent as ordinary soldiers to the Russian front, where Vorg was killed on the first day of the campaign. This for me supports Heckmair's claim of being totally disinterested in politics, for, if he had been, he could surely have used his connections to avoid this fate. It was a climbing friend who rescued him, for Rudi Peters, the successful pioneer of the North Face of the Grandes Jorasses, was in charge of the army mountain training school at Fulpmes. Six months after first being approached, he managed to get Heckmair transferred to that institution where he spent the rest of the war as an instructor.

After the war Heckmair continued climbing without any let up. Another great climb was an ascent of the Walker Spur on the Grandes Jorasses in 1951, with Hermann Kollensperger, carried through in atrocious conditions of storm and blizzard. During the bivouacs Heckmair contrived to keep out the cold by sipping from a large bottle of brandy, but Kollensperger being a teetotaller refused. Heckmair attributes the fact that he did not get frostbite to this intake of alcohol, whilst his partner suffered second and third degree burns and only narrowly avoided amputations. Many years after this event I met Kollensperger in Munich, heard from him about this great adventure and we ended the evening much the worse for liquor. I think the experience on the Jorasses with Heckmair had convinced him of the latter's point of view, namely, that a drop of the hard stuff can be quite good for you!

The rest of the book deals with the author's expeditions to Rakaposhi (a great disappointment due to his contracting pneumonia), the Ruwenzori, and the Americas, North and South, with continued ascents in his home mountains, and with his work as a guide and instructor. For many years he was Chairman of the German Guide Federation, and was very supportive of the British Guides when they applied for International recognition. He survived a terrible accident in the summer of 1956 on the Matterhorn when, with Gramminger and two other German climbers, he took part in a rescue and was pulled off the mountain when one of the team he was with fell off, resulting in Heckmair fracturing his back, neck, ribs and pelvis. He was in hospital for months, but by that Christmas he was back skiing and climbing. Of such stuff are the legends made, and Heckmair will remain one as long as people are attracted to climbing, and as long as the leitmotif of our sport is the seeking out of adventure, enterprise, comradeship and having fun. And this comes through to me from this inspirational book – its author has enjoyed a hell of a lot of the latter.

Dennis Gray

Tenzing: Hero of Everest
Ed Douglas.
National Geographic, 2003, pp299, £18.99

Ed Douglas begins his biography at the moment Tenzing Norgay and Ed Hillary step on to the summit of Everest. Hillary's photograph of Tenzing brandishing his ice axe became an icon of the 20th century, representing a triumph of human endeavour, made all the more potent by its provenance in the post-war era, when Britain was still coming to terms with the aftermath of conflict while also emerging from austerity into a new expansionist age.

Yet this multi-layered symbol has much that is curious about it. Tenzing's face is masked by his oxygen equipment, so that he comes across as an anonymous, almost sinister being, devoid of all personality. Douglas's achievement is to have written a book which brings Tenzing alive, rendering him as a complex, ambitious character, wrestling with contradictions he could never resolve. Douglas has not done so in the customary modern manner which is to debunk the subject, magnifying faults and flaws. This is a balanced, insightful book, thoroughly researched, skilfully crafted and enticingly written, luring you on with its detail and empathy.

The summit of Everest is an apt starting point in several ways, as Douglas contends that it was the watershed of Tenzing's life. In Douglas's narrative, everything for Tenzing led up to the moment when his life's ambition was realised. Tenzing was rapturously applauded by the crowds which lined the route back to Kathmandu, lionised by the Nepalese and Indian press, feted by politicians. But whereas Hillary adjusted to the demands of celebrity, and found new altruistic purposes in life, Tenzing never did, and died a sad, lonely man.

Some of the book's key revelations concern Tenzing's origins. Douglas has pinned down the identity of his birthplace, which proves not to be Thame in the Khumbu region of Nepal – as both John Hunt and Ed Hillary believed – but the village of Tshechu, 30 miles to the east in Tibet. By the standards of the area, Tenzing was born into relative prosperity, for his family were yak-herders. But when Tenzing was in his early teens – the precise date remains unclear – his father's herd was wiped out by disease. It was a disaster for the family, reducing it to penury. Soon afterwards Tenzing trekked across the border to the Khumbu in search of work. He was reduced to carrying salt for a living and also, as an economic refugee, had to contend with prejudice and rejection. His consequent feelings of alienation and exile both fuelled the ambition that took him to the summit of Everest and haunted the rest of his life.

Tenzing was 19 when he moved on to Darjeeling, joining the ranks of Sherpas who queued for work when mountaineering expeditions came in search of pack-carriers and high-altitude porters. It was Shipton – whimsical as ever – who gave Tenzing his break, awarding him one of the last places on the 1933 Everest expedition largely because he was attracted by Tenzing's enchanting smile. Douglas is excellent on the ambience of the city as the westerners arrived and the Sherpas waited anxiously to see who was hired.

It was a lottery in more ways than one: standing in line to be chosen for a dangerous venture that could well cost their lives. At the same time his cameos of legendary figures such as Shipton and Tilman are skilfully drawn.

Through this period we see the Sherpas advancing their skills and economic status while Tenzing himself begins to emerge as a star. During the 1938 Everest attempt he carried a 30lb load to 27,200ft, establishing his credentials both as climber and as a force among the Sherpas. During the war he worked as an RAF orderly, cook and sometimes batman. When peace came, the travellers and adventurers returned, seeking out Tenzing as their aide and guide. In 1947 Tenzing made his first links with the Swiss, being drawn at once to their easy friendliness and informality. He was racking up significant mountain experience too: Annapurna with the French in 1950; the ascent of Bandarpunch that summer in Jack Gibson's party; a catastrophic British attempt on Nanga Parbat that winter when Jim Thornley and Bill Crace died in a storm; an attempt on Nanda Devi with the French in 1951, which also cost two lives.

Then came Everest, first with the Swiss – twice – in 1952, when he and Raymond Lambert got to 28,200ft on the south-east ridge and might well have succeeded, had the Swiss not made a catastrophic choice of oxygen equipment. It is a commonplace now to relate that Tenzing was impressed by the way Lambert and his colleagues viewed the Sherpas as fellow-mountaineers, displaying none of the colonialist baggage of the pre-war British. Douglas also believes that the Swiss brought Tenzing his epiphany, accepting him on his own terms and validating his view of himself as human and mountaineer.

Even so, Douglas tells how Tenzing was still so wary of the British that he had to be cajoled into being sirdar in 1953. He remained vulnerable to slights: it was he – and only he – who protested after the notorious incident when the Sherpas were lodged in the garage of the British embassy. He was almost as dismayed when the British did not ask him to help push the route through the Khumbu Icefall, despite the experience he had acquired with the Swiss.

Tenzing was burning with the righteous feeling that on this, his seventh Everest expedition – four with the British, one with the maverick Earl Denman, two with the Swiss – the summit should be his. He need not have been so anxious: the canny strategist John Hunt had spotted him as a potential summitter, and paired him with the equally ambitious and determined Hillary. (Hillary had wanted to make the attempt with his fellow New Zealander George Lowe, but accepted that on a British expedition two New Zealanders were not going to be allowed the main summit push.) Tenzing still had to wait out the preliminary attempt by Tom Bourdillon and Charles Evans, who turned back at the South Summit because of oxygen problems: Tenzing could not conceal his disappointment when the rumour spread among the watchers that they had actually made the summit.

Douglas presents a balanced account of incidents such as these, among them the Hillary Step incident, when – as Hillary first told it – he virtually hauled Tenzing to the top. Such a claim struck to the core of Tenzing's sensitivities, and Hillary later altered his account. Then came the summit, and the exhilarating moment when Hillary offered Tenzing his hand, only for Tenzing to embrace him in return. Hillary's curious rejection of Tenzing's offer to photograph him on the summit still troubles Douglas, and it can be read as a disturbingly patronising response on Hillary's part. It can also be taken as modesty, with Hillary neglecting to obtain a photograph of himself in his determination to ensure he had a full set of views of and from the summit, and his anxiety to descend in case their oxygen expired.

It was after the summit that much, for Tenzing, fell apart. There was a heavy political and cultural dimension to the ecstatic Nepalese welcome, with the crowds determined to believe that it was he, not Hillary, who had reached the summit first. Tenzing was acutely troubled by the furore, and by the attempt by the Nepalese to claim him as a political trophy. Hunt, Hillary and Tenzing agreed to stonewall the issue by refusing to disclose who had been the first to step on to the summit. It was partly out of sheer impatience that, two years later, Tenzing finally revealed that Hillary had arrived a few steps ahead.

When Tenzing was invited to Britain with the rest of the victorious team he had an overdue decision to make. He was then still effectively stateless, and had to choose which nationality to adopt. With his home in Darjeeling, and wooed by Nehru, he plumped for an Indian passport. His future seemed secured when Nehru found him a post as director of the Himalayan Mountaineering Institute in Darjeeling. But when Nehru died, he lost his job and, worse, found he had no pension.

His consequent bitterness was compounded by the difficulties of his personal life. He married three times and had eight children in all, including an illegitimate daughter. He took his third wife, whom he had made pregnant, while still married to his second, and Douglas judges this episode to be the one time when he behaved with 'real selfishness'. His new wife was determined to lead an independent life, leaving Tenzing prey to almost disabling jealousy. He lost his fitness and indulged in drinking bouts. Old friends, such as Raymond and Annette Lambert, whom he visited in Geneva, were shocked at how disconsolate and depressed he was. He died of a brain haemorrhage in 1986, aged 72.

In Douglas's hands, this makes a powerful and affecting tale. Douglas's reporting skills have given him an eye for telling detail and he has put himself about assiduously, travelling to the key locations and meeting crucial witnesses. He had one major difficulty to overcome, namely the lack of data to represent Tenzing's voice – biographers of Mallory and Irvine have had a far easier ride. An American reviewer claimed that Douglas had added little to the autobiography ghosted by James Ramsay Ullman in 1955 but this is a travesty. Ullman's account was a product of its time and the author's own biases. Douglas has skilfully deconstructed it as well as correcting its errors and filling its lacunae. My own sole caveat is that Douglas sometimes seems to lack confidence in his own narrative, moving out of chronology a little too often, rather than presenting his storyline as one that is fresh and new. Douglas has a superb track record from almost 20 years of writing about climbing. It can be easier to write for specialist readerships but – as this book demonstrates – Douglas has managed to meet the requirements of lay audiences, making his subject-matter readable and accessible while preserving the needs of accuracy and integrity. His book is a tribute to a true hero of the 20th century, flaws and all, while endorsing Douglas's own reputation as researcher and story-teller.

Peter Gillman

Everest. 50 Years on Top of the World
George Band
HarperCollins, pp256, £20

Everest. Summit of Achievement
Stephen Venables
Bloomsbury, pp252, £35

Chris Bonington's Everest
Chris Bonington
Weidenfeld & Nicolson, pp256, £20

To avoid confusion, let us refer to these three books by their principal author rather than their title and the mountain they celebrate. And let us assume that the essential facts of Everest's story – the sequence of expeditions, rebuffs and successes – are well known. What then does that leave to be gleaned from the more than 750 pages of Everest-ania contained in these

50th anniversary offerings? A surprisingly rich amount, is the short answer. The fascination, particularly with the Band and Venables books, lies in the absorbing fine detail (loads, clothing, acclimatisation tests and much more), the colourful portrayals of sahibs and Sherpas, the human stories and stunningly reproduced photographs from the 1920s and '30s.

The photographs alone make the Venables book a worthwhile investment. In an introductory essay, Joanna Wright, curator of photography at the Royal Geographical Society, emphasises that the early images of places like Kampa Dzong and its inhabitants or the Khumbu are not only astonishing in their ability to transport the viewer to another time and place but 'important as historical documents for the Tibetan and Nepali people'. Nuns, monks, porters, village elders and infants all seem to have been obligingly content to pose for Westerners' cameras. Copies of a photograph of the Abbot of Shekar-Chöte, taken by Lt-Col Howard Bury in 1921, became much sought after by Tibetans who regarded the old abbot as a saint. The monastery of Shegar Dzong, a familiar landmark to the early Everesters, makes repeated appearances. Captain John Noel – 'St Noel of the Cameras' as General Bruce called him – was captivated by the place and hand-tinted one of his lantern slides of the monastery's 'dream towers in the air'. Several of Noel's tinted slides are reproduced here for the first time.

But the Venables book is more than pictures. Stephen has bracketed his own consummate telling of the Everest saga with essays by historian John Keay, AJ editor Ed Douglas and, jointly, by Tashi and Judy Tenzing on the Sherpas' story. Summing up the legacy of that first ascent, Tashi and Judy say Tenzing Norgay, by his inspiration, and Hillary, by transforming education in the Khumbu, have given Sherpas a real choice – 'to climb or not to climb'. Career horizons have been opened in medicine, the law and other fields. The book also includes a gentle reminder from Tenzin Gyatso, the 14th Dalai Lama, that Tibetans aspire to conquer the mind rather than summits (Yes, he uses the 'C' word). Turning around George Mallory's enigmatic reason for climbing Everest, the Dalai Lama observes: 'I imagine that for most Tibetans, "Because it's there" was a very good reason for not making the attempt.' Ed Douglas, in a thought-provoking contribution, enlarges on this philosophical East-West divide. Each has its own myths, he contends. Mallory pursued the western myth that reaching the summit is a worthwhile goal expressing a basic human desire to explore, but missed the myth of the people for whom the Everest region is home.

George Band cites a quotation he came across recently in which Mallory, reportedly, told a questioner he wanted to climb Everest: 'For the stone from the top for geologists, the knowledge of the limits of human endurance for the doctors, but above all for the spirit of adventure to keep alive the soul of man.' The third part of this unsourced reply certainly has shades of the summit 'myth' identified by Douglas.

Band's book bears the imprimatur of the Alpine Club, RGS and Mount Everest Federation. All royalties will go to the MEF to support expeditions, thereby making the book a 'good thing' as well as a good read. Told in George's straightforward manner, it really comes alive with the 1953 expedition and his personal involvement. Diary extracts burst with the enthusiasm of a wide-eyed youngster who can scarce believe his luck in being on such an enterprise. An entry on March 28 at Thyangboche jumps from crampon fitting aided by a blacksmith to a blessing at the monastery, discussion on trapping yetis with poisoned chang, packing food, then listening to the Boat Race on the wireless. Cambridge won by 19 lengths, which delighted the young Band who still had to return to the fens for his third university year. When we know the grand narrative, it is in this sort of intimate detail and the affectionate portraits of his companions that the pleasure of the book resides.

Everest changes the lives of all who come in close contact with her. Band brings us up to date with the 'magnificent seven' of the 1953 cast extant, before jogging through later ascents and ruminating on garbage, crowds and last great problems. He is sure that some day, the Russians or similarly gritty mountaineers, will complete the Everest horseshoe – West Ridge, summit, South Col, traverse of Lhotse and descent of the NW ridge of Nuptse.

'Impossible without supplementary oxygen,' says Chris Bonington, turning to the same 'What is left?' question in his own anniversary book. Everest dominated Sir Chris's life for 15 years until, at the age of 50, he reached the top with Arne Naess's SE ridge expedition of 1985. The snag for the middle-aged among us is that, through lectures and the four books from which this latest volume is drawn, we have accompanied Chris on every kicked step of those Everest years. If you are under 25 or were away on Mars during the '70s and '80s, this distilled version is an eminently readable way of catching up on some fine exploratory mountaineering – notably the South West Face. However long-standing fans already familiar with the Bonington canon might put in a plea for his reflections on commercial expeditions, 21st century life in the Khumbu and the enduring magic of Everest to be published in a modestly-priced supplement.

Stephen Goodwin

The Evidence of Things Not Seen. A Mountaineer's Tale
W H Murray
Bâton Wicks, 2002, pp352, £20

Bill Murray died in 1996 and this book, his autobiography, incomplete at the time, has been finished by his wife Anne, herself a poet with a deep love of the wild places of Scotland. Bill's father was killed at Gallipoli in

1915 yet, as he makes clear, neither he nor his sister Margaret felt short-changed by that loss. This was because his mother was so forceful and quick-witted that she was able to out-manœuvre the bureaucrats and give both children a good education – in Bill's case at Glasgow Academy. Their holidays were spent in the wild places of Ireland, the Isle of Arran and Kintyre.

At school, unlike his contemporaries, Bill enjoyed reading and essay writing, but the turning point of his life came when he was nineteen and he discovered and climbed The Cobbler and made a lone traverse of the Cairngorms. Having no particular sense of vocation and little idea of what he wanted to do in life, he started work in a bank, but the driving force in his life lay in his exploration with a small group of friends of innumerable unknown crags hidden in remote Highland glens. Unusually for the period, they climbed not only in good weather but also in the often polar winter conditions that could turn easy routes into formidable undertakings. Unlike in the Lake District and North Wales, very few climbs had been done in the Highlands, and their unknown riches produced many fine new routes. The overall standard of these discoveries was not always as high as their counterparts south of the border, but they had an added zest of their own, being in deserted glens far from roads and frequently overlooking lochs or the sea. In this Highland country Murray found his vocation.

At the outbreak of the Second World War he joined the Highland Light Infantry and was captured during the retreat to El Alamein. He spent the rest of the war in prison camps dotted around Europe. Here he encountered the Gestapo, the really evil men of Nazism, who routinely shot escaped prisoners and returned their ashes 'in a box'. Here, too, he started to write about his Scottish climbing and of his deep mystical feelings for the Highlands. The preservation of this manuscript through the vicissitudes of the war is a saga of countless setbacks and adventures, but it remained intact and eventually became his best-known book and a classic – *Mountaineering in Scotland*.

Leaving the army at the end of the war, Bill was attracted to writing and a contemplative life in a Benedictine monastery, but having fought to defeat one dictator, it seemed folly to deliver his life to another; instead, he bought a cottage on the shores of Loch Goil and began his life of letters. He also started climbing in the Alps and Himalaya, and it was during this period that I knew him best. In his account of an accident in the Dauphiné, he fills in, for the first time, a missing 36 to 48 hours of my life, when John Barford, a leading British mountaineer of the period, was killed by a rockfall that swept us all several hundred feet into a bergschrund. Bill and I extracted ourselves with extreme difficulty, and there is no doubt that he saved my life. After tottering for several hours down to a hut, we arrived at a clinic run by nuns, whose standard of care was awe-inspiringly poor. We had to wait until we returned to the UK for correct wound dressings and skull X-rays. We both had fractures, and I was *hors de combat* for six months.

For a mild man, Bill's comments on this episode are pretty acidic and he is equally forthright about the Alpine Club and the Royal Geographical Society for disregarding the evidence that I had provided in early 1951 of a new route up Everest from Nepal. Despite Bill Tilman's declared opinion that no route existed, we ignored his advice and later that year proved him wrong during the successful 1951 Reconnaissance.

In 1953 Bill explored the Api-Nampa group in north-west Nepal, with John Tyson and Bentley Beetham of the 1922 Everest party. Murray gives a delightful account of their journey in a region untouched by Europeans since the visit of Arnold Heim and August Gansser, two Swiss geologists, some years earlier.

Two of the most entertaining and riveting chapters are on Ben Humble, an idiosyncratic and totally deaf lover of the Highlands and in particular Skye, and a letter to Tom Patey on stack climbing.

Inevitably drawn into the debate on the conflicting priorities of the use of the Highlands, Bill Murray's greatest contribution seems to many to have been his defining of areas of outstanding natural beauty that should remain inviolate. He defined the especial quality of these by going to each in all weathers and camping with his wife. This meant that their mystery and beauty – and midges – could be described in such a way as to appeal to everyone.

The photographs in this book are arranged to tell the story of Bill's life, and of these the one by Ben Humble of the Cioch on Sron na Ciche on Skye is an old friend, one of the best, and I am so happy to see it again.

Bill Murray was a pioneer, and the Highlands and Islands of Scotland were the paradise he was determined to conserve, so that they could refresh the body and spirit of all who visit them. It would have been a sad loss to us all if Bill Murray's autobiography had been allowed to remain unfinished, and it is a credit to all concerned that it has now been completed and published.

Michael Ward

Fatal Mountaineer
Robert Roper
St Martins Press, 2002, ppxiv+306, £18.99

How would you feel, supposing that you could, if your posthumous biographer used this title for the summation of your life, thought and loves? The title *Fatal Mountaineer* suggests that Willi Unsoeld was doomed from the start to kill not only himself, but possibly also others, including his own daughter Nanda Devi Unsoeld, thus evoking Oscar Wilde's famous line, 'each mountaineer kills the thing he loves'. And the reader has not yet opened a page.

Whatever pressure the publishers and their publicity machine might bring to bear, an author chooses the title of the book. He may not choose the dust jacket blurb about Willi Unsoeld's 'casual fearlessness' leading 'the generation of the sixties to test itself in acts of physical daring'. But he is answerable for his title.

Willi Unsoeld became well known following the American ascent in 1963 of Everest's unclimbed West Ridge. In 1976 his daughter died on the mountain after which she was named. Unsoeld, a former Tetons guide, was a charismatic founder lecturer at the innovative Evergreen State University, Washington State, and he died in an avalanche whilst leading an outdoor education student group from Evergreen on Mount Rainier in winter.

This book, which won the Boardman Tasker Award in 2002, seeks to justify its title. Unsoeld was, says Roper, 'that modern rarity, a philosophy professor with a philosophy'. It is to the author's credit that he takes the trouble to go back to the sources of Unsoeld's philosophy, carefully explaining Unsoeld's position in his PhD thesis on the French philosopher of mysticism, Henri Bergson. But the main thrust of the book aims to show that Unsoeld's idealism was 'undone by a series of catastrophes, fateful reversals out of some dark drama. The philosopher confounded by his philosophy: this is not how exemplary lives are supposed to end.' The tone can already be heard to be as flawed as the logic. Who imposes 'modern rarity', 'fateful', 'dark drama' and 'exemplary' here? Who chooses Mark Twain's phrase 'funeral orgies' to characterise a 'bumptious' memorial event on the 'woodsy' Evergreen campus, 'telling heartening tales out of the Willi-Bible'? This tasteless American journalese has stopped some readers at the Introduction, from which all these quotations have been taken. The racy style of high drama is unrelenting, as is the patronising of the book's subject by its author. Comparisons with the writing of W H Murray, also short-listed for the Boardman Tasker Award in 2002, are hard to ignore.

The bulk of the book is taken up with a retelling of the story of the 1976 expedition to Nanda Devi on which it is hard to imagine a more amazing collection of disparate personalities. Together with Willi Unsoeld and Devi Unsoeld were Ad Carter, John Roskelly, Lou Reichardt, Peter Lev, Dr Jim States, Andy Harvard and a second woman, Marty Hoey. Motivations, approaches to climbing, attitudes to mixed-gender expeditions, even the route itself, were all in tension most of the time. The excruciating disputes and tragic outcomes are recounted from everyone's point of view at every stage with a present-tense edge to the intensity of the drama. King Lear, John Muir, Emerson and the CIA all provide cultural contexts for the fatal narrative drive of *Fatal Mountaineer*. But the outcome is a foregone conclusion since Roper has, sadly, set up his 'Old Guide' as a tragic hero, a flawed philosopher, a too-liberal father, a blinded visionary from the start of his 'frank' biography.

Terry Gifford

Everest. A Thousand Years of Exploration
A Record of Mountaineering, Geographical Exploration,
Medical Research and Mapping
Michael P Ward
The Ernest Press, 17 Carleton Drive, Glasgow G46 6AQ, 2003, pp384, £25

This volume is the exception in the inflationary flood of Everest anniversary books repeating the same old stories over and over again. Michael Ward's history begins at AD 800, reviews the early sources and maps and presents Hermann von Schlagintweit's aquarelle of 1855 showing Makalu described as 'Gaurisánkar or Mount Everest'. It needed the surgeon Ward to dissect the many errors and fantasies surrounding the world's highest point and to separate facts from fancy. Pundits – native explorers – and early smart scientists like A M Kellas, who predicted in 1920 that Everest could be climbed without bottled oxygen, play a lively part in this history and particular attention is paid to the early use of oxygen and to the medical peculiarities of pre-war British expeditions.

In 1951 Ward, doing National Service in the Royal Army Medical Corps in London, was instrumental in the crucial exploration of the south side of Everest by discovering unknown photographs and maps in the archives of the Royal Geographical Society. On the basis of these forgotten documents, a possible ascent route from the south could be identified. In the same year, in a laboratory at the Medical Research Council, Ward, together with Griffith Pugh, solved the 'oxygen problem of the last thousand feet', using open circuit sets and determining a flow rate of four litres of oxygen per minute as optimal.

Michael's 'great days' followed during the reconnaissance expedition of 1951, when a spirited group explored the approach to Mount Everest and climbed most of the icefall, thus opening the route to the Western Cwm. They identified many additional goals, including the option to fantasize about the Yeti and give future parties the idea of financing expeditions by pretending to search for the mysterious monster. This all makes absorbing reading and brings to life an adventure time long gone.

Science led to success in 1953 and Michael, also one of the key players of that expedition, gives a vivid and personal description, supplemented by some critical physiological and medical highlights.

Subsequently, the mysteries of Everest have faded away ... Ward gives no body counts or records of the following 50 years but instead provides exact information on the height of Mount Everest, its topography and the problems of ascents without supplementary oxygen.

The authentic appeal of an original source distinguishes this book from the recycled publications. It is a must for those seriously interested in Mount Everest and a demonstration that the meticulous study of history can be fascinating and an inspiration to those who seek adventure in the future.

Oswald Oelz

Tigers of the Snow
Jonathan Neale
Little Brown, 2002, ppxiv+338, £18.99

Touching my Father's Soul
In the Footsteps of Sherpa Tenzing
Jamling Tenzing Norgay with Broughton Coburn
Ebury Press, 2002, ppxviii+318, £7.99

Tenzing and the Sherpas of Everest
Judy and Tashi Tenzing
Robert Hale, 2002, ppxxvi +211, £25.00

Both *Tigers of the Snow* and *Touching my Father's Soul* highlight the qualities and strengths of the Sherpa, but they also deal with a sad and sorry episode in mountaineering history. Most of Jonathan Neale's book concentrates on the attempted ascent of Nanga Parbat by the Germans in 1934. This was the time of the Nazis and the expedition seems to have been very much politically driven. The author has read widely, so there are many notes and references for each chapter and an additional eight pages providing information on sources and bibliography. In the mid-1930s, at the age of fourteen, I remember reading *Nanga Parbat Adventure* by Fritz Bechtold and being impressed by two things – the beauty of the mountain photography (not available for this book) and the incredible toughness and loyalty of the Sherpas who took part.

Tigers of the Snow deals with this aspect of the Sherpas but the western mountaineers come out of the story with little credit. There are many examples but one of the most telling is the occasion when Schneider and Aschenbrenner, after a storm, untie from the rope, put on their skis and glide down the mountain, leaving their three Sherpa companions to fend for themselves in deep snow. There are other instances but, as one would expect, the book is full of the writer's personal preferences and opinions, so that the reader will need to make up his or her own mind on some of the conclusions. An example of this is the author's reliance on the memory of Ang Tsering who, at the age of 94, was asked for information about incidents in 1934. Some readers may feel that sixty years is a very long time ago for anyone to remember details of an expedition with any clarity. Well researched, the book is a good read, full of interesting information and a valuable contribution to mountaineering history. Happily, it does also tell us much about the Sherpas and why they are called 'Tigers of the Snow'.

Touching my Father's Soul by Jamling Tenzing Norgay is a much more spiritual book, revealing the author's thoughts and aspirations as he makes his journey, really a pilgrimage to the summit of Everest.

To avoid disappointment, a father should beware of refusing to condone the hopes and desires of his progeny and probably it is more essential when the father is such an inspirational person as Sherpa Tenzing Norgay. He climbed Everest, he said, so that others of his family wouldn't have to do so. It didn't work. From his earliest years the desire to emulate his father's ascent was constantly in Jamling's mind, and this is the account of how he achieved his ambition.

Throughout the book it is very evident that the author, like all Sherpas, is a devout Buddhist. There is constant recourse to prophecies and divinations and an important blessing by the Dalai Lama prior to the ascent. However, having spent ten years of his life in the USA, he absorbed much of the materialistic thinking of that Western culture. This didn't seem to sit easily with him so that, in following in the footsteps of his father, he rediscovered his faith in Buddhism and the traditions of the Sherpa people.

The ascent took place in 1996 and Jamling describes the part he played as climbing leader of the David Breashears expedition to make the IMEX film 'Everest'. Their presence on the mountain coincided with several other parties attempting the ascent of Everest. These were mainly commercially (not politically) driven but, as with the Germans on Nanga Parbat in 1934, the effects seem to have been much the same. In trying to achieve and succeed, some of them cast sound mountaineering judgement and principles to one side. At least 17 books have been written about the tragedies of 1996, but Jamling's account is especially interesting because it is written by a Sherpa. Like the Sherpas on Nanga Parbat, he takes a poor view of the callous actions of some of the foreign mountaineers.

Following the disasters early in the month, the weather on the mountain improved from 15 May onwards. Fortified by good divinations, Jamling and the Sherpas, plus the IMEX team, head for the summit. It is there, at the top of Everest, that he describes a mystical meeting with his father, Tenzing Norgay, and the fulfilment of his dream of following in his footsteps. There are many colour illustrations, and a final short chapter on how to help the Sherpas and other peoples of the Himalaya.

Tenzing and the Sherpas of Everest is a readable and informative book about the Sherpa people and the Tenzing family in particular. There is interesting information about Sherpa physiology and a chapter dealing with the nomads of SE Tibet. For a variety of reasons, they migrated across the high passes over the Great Himalayan range and settled in Khumbu, and then later in Sola on the south side of Everest. They are now the people called Sherpas. (Shar = east, pa = people: the people from East Tibet.)

Alexander Kellas was the first to recognise the attributes of the Sherpas, who were not mountaineers in the strict sense, but who were tough, loyal and intelligent mountain dwellers. Today, we know that many have become highly skilled, technical and well-motivated mountaineers. They have followed a similar progression to that of the Swiss mountain porters of the early period of alpine exploration who later became professional guides and some of the best mountaineers of the 19th and 20th century. A chapter towards the end of the book tells us of some of the Sherpas who have made numerous ascents of some of the world's highest mountains. Fortunately, too, Judy and Tashi tell us of the instigation of Tiger Medals by the Himalayan Club in the 1930s. These Sherpas were the first 'Tigers of the Snow'. One of them, Ang Tsering, who died at the age of 98 in May 2002, features in this book and in the one written by Jonathan Neale. The part he played in the ill-fated German expedition on Nanga Parbat in 1934 is well covered. The trauma and physical injuries he suffered at that time meant that for twenty years he mainly worked as a cook on expeditions. I have always been pleased that in 1954 we gave his pride and confidence a boost by having him as Sirdar on the Himalayan Yeti Expedition. This was an entirely British venture and not a German/Swiss/British and American expedition, as incorrectly described in the book.

Dawa Tenzing, Ang Tharkey, Pasang Phutar, Ang Nima, Phu Dorje, Anallu, are all written about briefly and will bring back many memories for older mountaineers. There are so many others, such as Mingma Gyalgen, Ang Dawa V, Khansa Sherpa, Gyalgen Mikjen ('Big Eyes'), Ang Temba and Nima Tenzing. The list goes on, all of them tough, cheerful and steadfast companions adhering constantly to their deeply felt religious beliefs.

As you would expect, the bulk of the book is about Tenzing Norgay, from his earliest days to his part in the first ascent of Everest and what happened afterwards. Some of this background is already to be found in Tenzing's own book *Man of Everest* published in 1955, but Tashi is able to reveal much more of interest about the man and his family, so many of whom have made their own ascents to the summit of Everest. Two of them have twice made the ascent, Nawang Gombu in 1963 and 1965 and Tashi Tenzing himself in 1997 and in 2002, shortly after the publication of his book. A thoughtful final chapter considers the future for the Sherpas. Their way of life is rapidly changing and the hope is that future Sherpa generations will possess the power to preserve and protect their homeland and unique culture. One feels that, with the help of Hillary's Himalayan Trust and with wise advice from the older members of the Sherpa community, such as Nawang Gombu, Dorjee Lhatoo, Jamling Tenzing and Tashi Tenzing himself, these wonderful people will achieve just that.

John Jackson

Gabriel Loppé. Peintre, Photographe et Alpiniste
Marie-Noël Borgeaud
Glénat, 2002, pp.136, npq

Several important events in recent years have helped to bring the name of Gabriel Loppé into re-focus after many years of partial neglect.

In 1981 some 150 of his drawings appeared at public auction in Paris, to be followed two years later by another consignment which helped to confirm his skills as a draughtsman and display the breadth of his subject-matter, since views of the Dolomites, Oberland, Venice and the Lac d'Annecy were included, in addition to his more usual scenes of Mont Blanc and the Chamonix valley.

Then, in early 1998, a major mountain painting exhibition, 'Le Sentiment de la Montagne', was held at the Musée de Grenoble, where the French public and critics alike were surprised by the scale and power of Loppé's depiction of high mountain places.

There followed a great tragedy in 1999 when the Musée Alpin in Chamonix caught fire and of the 34 Loppé canvasses held there, six were completely destroyed and ten others very badly damaged, the rest requiring extensive restoration and cleaning.

More recently, in 2002, Marie-Noël Borgeaud completed several years of painstaking research to produce this excellent book celebrating Gabriel Loppé's life and work and providing an accessible review of his contribution to the mountain scene in all its aspects.

Loppé was one of the earliest painter/photographer/alpinists of the continent. In 1846 Sir Alfred Wills introduced Loppé to the Alpine Club where he was soon elected as the first honorary French member of the Club. Leslie Stephen seconded the motion and, together with James Eccles, became friend and climbing partner on many important Alpine first ascents.

Marguerite, Loppé's first wife, died suddenly in 1874 leaving him with three children. Happily, in 1879, Loppé was re-married, to James Eccles' sister Elizabeth (at that period at the forefront of the suffragette movement).

Loppé found enormous favour in London, becoming one of the few French exhibitors at the Royal Academy, in addition to regular shows at the Alpine Club and elsewhere. Early in his career he remained relatively unknown in his native France and only later on, having built a studio in Chamonix (still standing today, somewhat hidden, in the very centre of the town), did he gradually become recognised as the leading *peintre de haute montagne* in addition to founding the Compagnie de Guides de Haute Montagne as a spin-off from his series of Alpine ascents with local guides and Alpine Club members.

Marie-Noël Borgeaud, art historian and *guide conférencière des monuments historiques*, has delved into all corners of Loppé's life and work, visiting family members, tracing drawings and paintings as far away as America, and unearthing photographs and family anecdotes.

Loppé climbed Mont Blanc some forty times, often painting on the summit as though he was perched on a small hill. He even established a little encampment, complete with all his painting gear, on the top of the Montagne de la Côte which became known as 'Le Chateau de Loppé'. Douglas Freshfield recalled an incident when Loppé, having concentrated on his drawing for so long, found his turn-ups frozen to the snow and had to use his ice-axe to free himself. Leslie Stephen joked 'Gabriel Loppé is the Court Painter to His Majesty Mont Blanc.'

In 1873 a strong party containing Stephen, Kennedy, Dévouassoud,

Almer, Loppé et al reached a new col where, to their surprise, they found some twenty swallows huddled together frozen to death in the snow, no doubt caught in a storm during migration. Consequently Col des Hirondelles seemed the appropriate name.

Gabriel Loppé was much appreciated by the Club members and on occasion Freshfield was heard to remark, 'He only needs to push open the door of the AC for an alpine wind to follow him.'

We can all be grateful to Mme Borgeaud for her perseverance and dedication, in addition to her obvious admiration for this warm and distinguished pupil of François Diday and Alexandre Calame, and hope that in due course the publishers will realise that an English edition of his beautifully produced book would meet with an enthusiastic reception on this side of *La Manche*.

Peter Mallalieu

Climbing Free: My Life in the Vertical World
Lynn Hill
HarperCollins, 2002, pp270, £18.99

'What lies behind us and what lies before us are tiny matters compared to what lies within us.'

Ralph Waldo Emerson

This quotation perfectly sums up Lynn Hill's climbing philosophy. In *Climbing Free* she returns repeatedly to the idea that her sport is 'a kind of moving meditation', which allows her to experience a world beyond the constraints of superficial preoccupations.

Through the many challenges in her life – internal and external – her passion for this state of consciousness is what informs both her climbing and her choices. John Long's affectionate and engaging introduction singles out 'Lynnie's courage, lack of guile and tenacity' as the qualities which have supported her achievements.

Her climbing exploits began when she was fourteen, fuelled by a keen gymnastic ability and a position in a large family which made it necessary for her to work things out for herself when all around her were preoccupied with the frantic minutiae of family life. The departure of her father signalled an end to this close web, and her involvement with the climbing fraternity in Joshu Tree provided her with both a substitute network of support and the chance to experience hard leads.

Greg Child is credited with assisting Lynn Hill in writing the book and his narrative style is firmly stamped on the entertaining anecdotes Hill selects about Long, Bachar and the other climbing notables of those early days. Other sections are not as tellingly constructed: on occasion, descriptions of both competition and free climbs are too insistently detailed, giving them an almost mechanistic quality.

Yosemite in the early '80s was the next stage for Hill's talents – this was her education, her career and her obsession. Free climbs and a larger-than-life cast provide a vivid backdrop to exploits on El Cap and Half Dome and Hill's growing realisation that in a male dominated sport she was both protected and patronised. This predictable duality is clearly acknowledged and challenged – not least by her climbing resume – yet this remains a covert narrative thread, as does her part in the public debate on climbing.

Hill is the consummate all-rounder: multi-discipline challenges, international climbing competitions, bouldering and big wall exploits have all been within her compass. She seems to have been less successful in her intimate relationships – a curious dichotomy, since the warmth and openness which repeatedly draw other climbers towards her seems, at her own admission, absent from her closest liaisons. Her reiteration of a psychologist's report on the reasons for the disintegration of her brief marriage to Russ Raffa cites her as 'detached and emotionally controlled' – perfect qualities for the bold climbing at which she excels but undeniably a death knell to intimacy.

Yet this autobiography speaks much of sincere and quiet passion – for climbing partners, travel and the ethics of her sport. Her greatest delight is achieving that state of heightened awareness which results from sustained and determined application to her climbing, helping her to appreciate more fully the beauties of her spectacular surroundings. In short, *Climbing Free* is the story of an addiction which has underpinned a remarkable and diverse climbing life.

Val Randall

Sikkim Himalaya: Travels in the Cloud Kingdom
David Lang
Pomegranate Press, 2003, pp200, £29.95

Anyone with a general interest in the natural history and culture of the Himalaya in general and Sikkim in particular will be fascinated by David Lang's new book. Recalling four separate journeys to Sikkim, visiting valleys that no western botanist had visited for more than 150 years, Lang's book is really a celebration of Sikkim, weaving together its history, geography, its flora and fauna, and offers a detailed introduction to anyone planning an expedition there. Most compelling of all are the sumptuous illustrations, particularly of Himalayan flowers, but also of the birds and creatures of this stunning region. There is a useful introduction to the history and exploration of the region, while the bulk of the text is given over to Lang's own journeys, beginning in 1987. He lifts the lid on the tortuous complexities not just of travel in Sikkim but also of the political controls on botanical expeditions, which seem to exceed even those for climbing peaks. Lang acknowledges the problems and challenges facing those who live in the eastern Himalaya, but there are opportunities too. He recalls how, while trekking in Bhutan in the autumn of 2000, he explained to some local people who had recently gained access to the internet that he lived in Lewes, a small town in Sussex in the South of England. 'Oh my God,' he was told, 'your town is under water!'

Ed Douglas

Poems From The Edge
Dennis Gray
from 16 Royal Park Ave, Leeds, LS6 1EY, £3.00, incl p&p

'Having measured my limits, / I only want to return to my old haunts,' writes Dennis Gray in the final poem of this collection. But it's not so easy for a poet. If you're writing poetry you're always continuing to 'measure your limits' in the form. There can be no easy nostalgia if the slip into the crevasse of twee verse is to be avoided. Dennis crosses some very flimsy snow bridges across those crevasses at times in this collection.

It is, of course, written in plain Yorkshire, which can come close to what passes for prose in the South:

Watching and waiting can be a rewarding part of climbing
When I was fifteen I saw Arthur Dolphin and Peter Greenwood
Make the first ascent of Hell's Groove on Scafell's East Buttress

Perhaps the lack of punctuation makes a difference to the way it works, but certainly this poem, 'Watching', can use a telling almost-simile:

And truly climbing can be a creative activity that crosses boundaries
Of nationality, cultures, or style and in its execution it might fairly
Be compared to a ballet or even one of the great classic symphonies

A poet, especially a climbing poet, has to push the boat out and take risks. Look at the titles below which Dennis Gray uncoils his rope: 'A Hymn to Harnesses', 'Thrutch', 'Sleeping Bags I have Known', 'The Dead Climb With Me', 'Spoorts Climbing' [sic] and, most poignantly, 'Watch The Bloody Rope'. These poems and others have been infiltrating august publications for years with a breath of fresh Yorkshire air in the riskiest of forms with which a climbing writer can frighten an editor: *Rocksport*, the *Climbers' Club Journal*, *Summit Magazine* (USA), *Granta* and even the *Alpine Journal*. Putting poetry where it isn't normally expected to be is a major achievement in the opening up of a traditionally macho culture, such as the old Rock and Ice that Dennis had infiltrated as a youth. This first collection of the verse of Dennis Gray is a chance to recognise that achievement.

At the last Festival of Mountaineering Literature a strange thing happened. Dennis sold out of copies of this book and had to rush home for some more. What was going on? *Poems From The Edge* are just that. This book was suspected of being an edge worth trying for £3.00. Idiosyncratic in their fun and philosophy, Dennis Gray's poems are both history and present. They are 'The Song of an Old Mountaineer', 'The Song of a Climber returning from a Climb'. How much risk do you want for £3.00, (signed if you ask)?

Terry Gifford

Great Himalaya: Tourism and the Dynamics of Change in Nepal
Sanjay K Nepal, Thomas Kohler & B R Banzhaf
The Swiss Foundation for Alpine Research, 2002.

This publication has been prepared in collaboration with the University of Bern, whose Centre for Development & Environment provided scientific support for a five-year Nepal Tourism Project, during which studies were made for five Masters Degrees and one Ph.D. The book is described by Jürg Marmet, President of the Swiss Foundation, as its contribution to the International Year of Mountains 2002. It owes its appearance to financial support from the Foundation itself, the Binding Foundation and three private donors. It is co-authored by Sanjay K Nepal, who chose the subject for his thesis at Bern University; Thomas Kohler, a lecturer at the University; and B R Banzhaf of Saas Fee, who has been involved with trekking and touring in Nepal for several years. During field work in Nepal vital to the authors' research, they collaborated closely with local officials, project directors, conservation workers, field research assistants, village committees, owners of tourist lodges, ordinary villagers, porters, and others in the Khumbu, Annapurna, and Mustang regions. Although the studies were confined largely to areas most deeply affected by tourism, they provide a broad picture of a new order of development which has swept across the country in a relatively short period – causing a doubling of firewood consumption during the tourist season when the population density rises to 34.45 persons per sq.km for the Annapurna area, and 10.80 for Khumbu. Some traditions of the ancient culture of the inhabitants, as well as a large part of their activities, have altered to a degree that would have seemed unbelievable to the limited numbers who were granted permission to enter the country before the gates were thrown wide open to tourists.

A few years after the Chinese entered Tibet in November 1950, an event which threatened to bring to an end the Sherpas' traditional trading activities, and as a direct outcome of Sir Edmund Hillary's pioneering initiatives in the fields of education and health, dramatic changes began to emerge in the lives and livelihood of the essentially religious Sherpa communities settled in Khumbu for five centuries, involving their adaptation from the tranquillity and simplicity of their former existence as agriculturists and traders to a form of urbanisation (Footnote: I quote from the book's text: 'Tourist shops dominate the streets of Namche Bazar.')

A review of this book is no place to attempt to balance the economic and material gains against the social, cultural, and ecological effects resulting from those changes. The latter have given rise to other considerations such as degradation of forests, protection of the environment, and the spread of aspects of Western culture. The map on page 15 of the book indicates the existence of eight National Parks and four Conservation Areas. Logically such demarcated zones should provide adequate opportunities for local employment of trained personnel under competent management, thereby serving the dual purpose of promoting their tourist appeal. The authors quote the World Tourist Organisation's definition of 'sustainable tourism' as a form that improves the quality of life of the host community, maintaining the quality of the environment, and providing a worthwhile experience for the tourist, without which mountain tourism could be a short-term enterprise of boom and bust. Regrettably, at the current stage of development, the authors' research has shown that in popular areas such as Khumbu and Annapurna, tourists greatly outnumber the local populations, resulting in higher prices for basic goods, benefiting external interests at the expense of local communities, and widening the gap between rich and poor.

The book's four sections deal respectively with Nepal's social, economic, and historical background, followed by the complexity of problems facing planners if the future of tourism, which has expanded six-fold in the past two decades, is to be sustained at an economically viable level. Next comes the Impact of Mountain Tourism, containing the main meat of the book, which details the manner in which many communities have adapted their lives, retaining their traditional activities whilst participating in the benefits brought by tourism – a picture that is not always rosy, but one that reveals the initiative and ingenuity of men and women largely unsupported by official incentives or encouragement. Finally, there are suggestions directed at planners and administrators, researchers and scientists, national and international agencies, emphasizing the strengths and weaknesses revealed by studies carried out so far. The development of tourism is an on-going process, which can only thrive and endure if lessons learnt from past endeavours are heeded.

In spite of the gloomy note on which the book ends, as a result of political unrest in the year 2002 which caused a dramatic decline in the number of tourists, this seems to be an appropriate moment at which to set on record, as the authors have done in this well-researched treatise, the overall effects of tourism in a country with scant other resources, and therefore heavily dependent upon its success. To quote a Khumbu lodge-owner, 'There is no problem for the future of tourism. As long as Mount Everest remains in place people will continue to come here.' Yes – but it is important to take stock during the present hiatus and, benefiting from knowledge gained, to ensure that prospects for the long-term future are built on sound foundations.

As one would expect from the Swiss Foundation, the publication is of high quality, lavishly illustrated with colour photographs and maps. Two minor quibbles. The map of Nepal on page 15 refers to the High Himalaya, although the book's title adopts the term Great Himalaya. Nepal Himalaya would be more appropriate for the former, whilst the latter describes the mountain range which stretches from Bhutan in the east to Kashmir in the north-west. The opening of Nepal to mountaineers did not commence when Arnold Heim flew over Dhaulagiri on 18 october 1949 (page 26), but when H W Tilman set out with a small group on foot from Kathmandu on 29 May 1949 on his first pioneering expedition, followed by his second exploratory expedition in 1950, the latter terminating with the first visit by foreigners, including Charles Houston and his father Oscar, through Khumbu to the south side of Everest.

Trevor Braham

Pale di San Martino Ovest
Lucio de Franceschi
Club Alpino Italiano – Touring Club Italiano, 2003, pp504, €36.50

Pale di San Martino Ovest, the latest in the series of CAI-TCI guides to the Dolomites, was the last production from the long-standing General Editor and our late member Gino Buscaini, who died prematurely in September 2002. This is a definitive guide to the climbs above San Martino, bounded by the Val Canali to the south and Passo di Valles in the north. It therefore includes the great peaks of the Cimon della Pala, Pale di San Martino and Sass Maor. For the Cima Canali, Sasso d'Ortiga and the great Monte Agner and San Lucano massifs, with their huge rock walls, you will have to wait for a long-overdue edition of Pale di San Martino Est, which surprisingly has not been re-written since 1935.

The Pale has long been known as an area of big mountains, long approaches and large limestone walls rising above extensively forested valleys. It is also noted for its rock quality, which is generally of a higher standard than most areas in the Dolomites. As in many parts of the region, particularly those requiring some commitment, the number of climbers here has dropped markedly over the last couple of decades. However, there are magnificent classics that are well-worthy of attention, and despite the passage of time, the best of these still lie in the more accessible grades: the *Solleder routes* on Sass Maor and Pale di San Martino; the *Andrich Route* on the Cimon della Pala; the *Spigolo del Velo* on the Cima della Madonna; the *Grand Pilaster* on the Pale di San Martino; the *Castiglioni-Detassis* and *Corradini-Frisch* on the Pala di Refugio; the *Spigolo di Vecchio* on the Campanile Pradidali, and in the north the *Grey Pillar of Monte Mulaz*. All

these are great routes of UIAA grade VI or below. In this pocket-sized soft-
back all climbs and walks have full written descriptions and are illustrated
by detailed colour photo-diagrams. However, with very few topos, this guide
requires a rudimentary knowledge of 'climbing' Italian.

Pale di San Martino Ovest meets the usual high standard of production
we have come to expect from the Italian Alpine Club. Long may it continue
under a new editor.

Lindsay Griffin

Climb. The History of Rock Climbing in Colorado
Jeff Achey, Dudley Chelton & Bob Godfrey
The Mountaineers/Cordée, 2002, pp256, npq

Fifty Favorite Climbs. The Ultimate North American Tick List
Mark Kroese
The Mountaineers/Cordée, 2001, pp224, $32.95

It is 25 years since Godfrey and Chelton wrote and published the first edition
of *Climb*, which became a classic and changed the face of rock climbing in
Colorado. Jeff Achey has now joined Chelton in bringing the story up to
date, with many new photographs, to give the complete picture of climbing
in the State. The Mountaineers have also brought out *Fifty Favorite Climbs*,
a worthy successor to Steck and Roper's *Fifty Classic Climbs*, published in
1979. The difference is that, whilst in the first book the selection was the
authors' own, here each route is chosen by a different climber, virtually
every well-known climber in North America being represented. Each route
has a description/history, photo of the selector and climb, and a diagram
of the route.

Kinder Scout. Portrait of a Mountain
Ed. Roly Smith
Derbyshire County Council, 2002, pp144, £12.99

The Libraries and Heritage Department of Derbyshire County Council,
jointly with the National Trust and the Peak District National Park, has
published this portrait of Kinder Scout. Inspiration for it came from an
exhibition of photographs by Stephen Lewis held in the New Mills Heritage
Centre in 2001. It was decided to bring out the book in memory of Benny
Rothman, who led the 1932 mass trespass on Kinder and died in January
2002. The book covers geology, natural and human history, access, trespass,
recreation and so on, and the photographs are superb; it is designed in
such a way as to make it an exemplary publication of its type.

Cry from the Highest Mountain
Tess Burrows
Travellers Eye, 2002, pp256, £14.99

When you pick up this book, look at the title and the fact that it has a forward by the Dalai Lama, you assume it is yet another book about Everest. However, the cover picture doesn't look much like Everest, and further investigation shows that the 'highest mountain' is, in fact, 'the point furthest from the centre' of the Earth, ie Chimborazo in Ecuador, 6310m.

The book is about the ascent by Tess Burrows and her companions of Chimborazo 'seen through the eyes of the journey of my body and my spirit and the window of my heart.' As an expedition narrative it is quite an ordinary one, but the climb was carried out by a 'Climb for Tibet' team, promoting earth peace in Millennium year, and this explains the involvement of the Dalai Lama. Some of the proceeds of sales of this book will go towards these objectives.

Vittorio Sella. Ascensioni Fotografiche/Aufstieg in Bildern
Città di Bolzano, 2002, npq.

A superbly produced catalogue of the exhibition, held in the Civic Galleries in Bolzano between June and September 2002, of photos taken by Vittorio Sella in the Tyrol in 1887, 1891 and 1893. Many of the photos exhibited are reproduced full-page in the catalogue, together with a detailed historical introduction. A splendid addition to the ever-growing Sella literature.

Hans Conrad Escher von der Linth. 1767-1823
The First Panoramas of the Alps
Drawings, Views, Panoramas and Maps
Ed. René Brandenberger
Linth-Ercher-Foundation, Mollis, 2002, pp452, npq.

The Zurich-born politician and philanthropist Hans Conrad Escher, given the honour 'von der Linth' for his work on the Linth river, spent the years between 1780 and 1822 drawing panoramas of the complete Alpine chain. This massive undertaking remained undiscovered for over a hundred years, having been stored in a cupboard in the Institute of Geology in Zurich until its importance was realised by Gustav Solar and Jost Hösli in 1971.

This magnificent volume catalogues Escher's complete works, with many fold-out plates, numerous panoramas and drawings in colour, and with a CD-rom of additional material by Escher and Solar.

A Nepalese Journey. On Foot Around the Annapurnas
Andrew Stevenson
Constable, 2002, pp192, £19.99

In 1997 Andrew Stevenson's book *Annapurna Circuit* was published and, in a short review in AJ 1998, I praised the book for its excellent travel writing. At the same time, I rather lamented the lack of illustration. This has now been rectified in the present volume, which shows the author to be an excellent photographer. He has made a number of trips to the Annapurna region, and the photographs (and descriptions) cover the treks to Annapurna base camp, the Annapurna Circuit, and the extension from Kagbeni to the far north in Mustang. Taken together, the two books are a superb record of the region and its people.

Alpinistes Britanniques et Austro-Allemands dans les Ecrins. 1850-1914
Michel Mestre & Michel Tailland
Editions du Fournel, 2002, pp98, €28.00

This is a well-illustrated history of early climbing in the Écrins by British and Austro-German climbers, the authors splitting the writing with Tailland covering the British side. There is no translation into either English or German.

Una Cameron. The Scot of Mont Blanc
Cesare Bieller
Musumeci Editori, 2002, pp102, €20.00

Many members will have known the distinctive and talented Una Cameron, and this book celebrates her life at Villa Cameron above La Palud, and the fact that she bequeathed the villa to the Aosta Valley Region. The book is well illustrated and includes a number of her own drawings.

Wild Winds. Adventures in the Highest Andes.
Ed Darack
Alpenbooks, 2001, pp352, $19.99

Ed Darack describes here his ascents of Aconcagua, the highest mountain in the Andes; Sajama, the highest in Bolivia; Ojos del Salado, the highest in Chile; Cerro Pissis, one of 'the least visited peaks in South America'; and Llullaillaco, a lonely volcano, home to the highest archæological site in the world. As a renowned photographer, the author has not been well served by the mass of small, poorly-reproduced photos.

The High Himalaya
Art Wolfe
The Mountaineers/Wildlands Press, 2001, pp160, $44.95

Art Wolfe is a respected photographer of 'nature in the wild', winner of numerous photographic awards and author of more than forty books. In this volume he has turned his attention to the mountains, people and wildlife of the Himalaya, with more than 120 stunning shots. Full photographic information is given for each photo and, by way of text, Peter Potterfield conducts brief 'conversations' with Reinhold Messner, Doug Scott and Ed Viesturs.

An Unsung Hero. Tom Crean – Antarctic Survivor
Michael Smith
Headline, 2002, pp342, £14.99

Tom Crean's name is one of the lesser-known names in Antarctic exploration, and yet he played a major role in three of the four main expeditions of the 'heroic age'. He was one of the last people to see Scott alive, and returned to bury him in the snow months later. He was on the *Endurance* with Shackleton, later sailing with him in the small open boat across the southern Ocean and then crossing South Georgia. There is a Mount Crean in Victoria Land, and a Crean Glacier in South Georgia. This book tells his story.

The Team.
The story of the Cockermouth Mountain Rescue Team   1953-2003
Sheila Richardson
Mill Field Pub. / Cockermount M.R.T., 2002, pp236, £9.50

The Cockermouth Mountain Rescue Team has published this book to celebrate its 50 years' existence. Starting in 1953 as a small team formed from members of the Cockermouth Rucksack Club, it nearly foundered in 1969 when an accident killed the leader and another member, and severely injured five others; but the remainder of the team struggled on and grew into the professional organisation it is today. Publication coincides with the opening of its new headquarters.

Vanoise. Gran Paradiso. Hiking Guide

No 14 in the new guides and maps issued by 'Alps Without Frontiers', a joint venture of the French and Italian Alpine Clubs, who are issuing twenty guides to the Alps. Contained in a plastic wallet, it includes detailed itineraries in English and German, plus a large map at 1:25 000.

Alpine Club Notes

OFFICERS AND COMMITTEE FOR 2003

PRESIDENT	A Blackshaw
VICE PRESIDENTS	D J Lovatt
	D W Walker
HONORARY SECRETARY	R M Scott
HONORARY TREASURER	I Appuhamy
HONORARY LIBRARIAN	D J Lovatt
HONORARY EDITOR	
OF THE ALPINE JOURNAL	E Douglas
HONORARY GUIDEBOOKS	
COMMISSIONING EDITOR	L N Griffin
COMMITTEE ELECTIVE MEMBERS	W J E Norton
	R L Stephens
	R Turnbull
	P Wickens
	D R Buckle
	M D Eldridge
	T A Gronlund
	P Mallalieu
	W G Thurston

OFFICE BEARERS

LIBRARIAN EMERITUS	R Lawford
HONORARY ARCHIVIST	P T Berg
HONORARY KEEPER OF THE CLUB'S PICTURES	P Mallalieu
HONORARY KEEPER OF THE CLUB'S ARTEFACTS	R Lawford
HONORARY KEEPER OF THE CLUB'S MONUMENTS	W A C Newsom
CHAIRMAN OF THE FINANCE COMMITTEE	R F Morgan
CHAIRMAN OF THE HOUSE COMMITTEE	
CHAIRMAN OF THE LIBRARY COUNCIL	G C Band
CHAIRMAN OF THE MEMBERSHIP COMMITTEE	W G Thurston
CHAIRMAN OF THE GUIDEBOOKS EDITORIAL AND	
PRODUCTION BOARD	L N Griffin
GUIDEBOOKS PRODUCTION MANAGER	J N Slee-Smith
ASSISTANT EDITORS OF THE *Alpine Journal*	J L Bermúdez
	G W Templeman
PRODUCTION EDITOR OF THE *Alpine Journal*	Mrs J Merz

GENERAL, INFORMAL, AND CLIMBING MEETINGS 2002

8 January	General Meeting: Elizabeth Hussey, *Arnold Lunn*
22 January	Informal Meeting: Henry Day, *Travels with a Donkey in the Kun Lun*
23 January	Northern Lecture: Pat Littlejohn, *Big Free Walls in Kenya*
1-2 February	Scottish Winter Meet
12 February	General Meeting: John Town & Derek Buckle, *Up the Kongpo without a paddle*
20 February	Northern Lecture: Members' Night, featuring Ed Douglas, Dick Turnbull et al
26 February	Informal Meeting: Adele Pennington, *Bolivian Climbs*
2 March	'Alpine Style' Symposium
12 March	General Meeting: Richard Goedeke, *'Alpine Odyssey'*
13 March	Northern Lecture: Richard Goedeke, *'Alpine Odyssey'*
26 March	Informal Meeting: Colin Knowles, *The Trident of Shiva*
9 April	General Meeting: Discussion led by Ed Douglas, *The Hidden Face of Everest*
13-14 April	North Wales Meet
23 April	Chris Fitzhugh, *Short Neck in the Hindu Kush*
11-12 May	Peak District Meet
14 May	General Meeting: Allen Steck, *Hummingbird Ridge*
11 June	General Meeting: Sarah Chandler, *Going up in the world*
25 June	Informal Meeting: Terry Kenny, *Cascade Ice in the Rockies*
13-20 July	Alpine Meet (with ABMSAC & CC): Vanoise Alps Haut-Maurienne
20-27 July	Alpine Meet (with ABMSAC & CC): Vanoise Alps, Tarentaise

27 July-17 Aug   Summer Meet: Les Choselets, Chamonix
1-13 September   Alpine Meet (with ABMSAC & CC): Tour de Mont Blanc
10 September   General Meeting: André Hedger, *Ethiopia to Antarctica*
9-16 September   AC/CC Cornwall Meet
27-28 September   Lakes Meet: Rawhead, Langdale
18 September   Northern Lecture: Paul Knott, *Aotearoa NZ – Land of the Long
                  Stripey Thermals*
24 September   Informal Meeting: Paul Knott, *Aotearoa NZ – Land of the Long
                  Stripey Thermals*
27-28 September   Lake District Meet
8 October   General Meeting: Tashi Tenzing, *Tenzing and the Sherpas of
                  Everest*
23 October   Northern Lecture: Mick Fowler, *North Face of Siguniang*
26 October   AC/YR Meet: Yorkshire Dales
8 November   Boardman Tasker Award Ceremony
12 November   General Meeting: David Hamilton, Highlights of 2002
13 November   Northern Lecture: Ian Parnell, *SW Face of Denali*
26 November   Informal Meeting: James Harris, *The Antarctic Peninsula*
6 December   Annual General Meeting
8 December   134th Annual Dinner
11 December   Northern Lecture: ACG Meeting

The 134th Annual London Dinner was held on 7 December at The Great
Hall, St Bartholomew's Hospital. The principal guest was Tom Hornbein.

THE ALPINE CLUB LIBRARY
ANNUAL REPORT 2002

Four Council meetings were held in 2002, but much of the effort involved
two separate work groups: one concerning a redefinition of relationships
between the Club and the Library; the other being an assessment of the
space occupied by the two bodies.

At present, the Library has custody of the Club's books and photographs
and, as a registered charity, is responsible for their care and maintenance.
As the Club owns other 'heritage' items, such as its archives, paintings,
memorabilia, and even some monuments, it was considered that the Library
Council might be a more appropriate body to be granted custody of these
items, provided the relative responsibilities of the two bodies was clarified
in a new Custodial Agreement. This was developed in a joint Work Group
under the chairmanship of Patrick Fagan, a Vice-President of the Club,
and submitted to the Club Committee and Library Council for approval at
year's end. This should help to improve communication and understanding
between the two bodies, particularly for the more transient members of the
Club Committee who may initially have little knowledge of the extent of
the Club's possessions.

On the second issue, previous reports have drawn attention to the cramped facilities tolerated by our professional librarian, Margaret Ecclestone, and the very restricted working space for readers. Responding to this plight, a Space Working Group, set up by the Club Committee under the chairmanship of Richard Morgan, decided after careful consultation that the Club could now afford to take back half of the top floor at Charlotte Road when our tenant's lease expired in mid-2002. This extra space allowed the first floor to be re-arranged to give the Librarian marginally more room and to divide the former office into two compartments. There was also some enthusiasm to create a more sociable Members' Room. A number of permutations were discussed and were being planned under the supervision of our member Hunter Johnson who very tragically died in an Alpine climbing accident in summer 2002. This delayed implementation considerably, until our member Neil Lawton kindly volunteered his services to agree fresh plans with the Club Committee. These placed the Members' Room and Committee Room on the top floor with some welcome fresh furniture. The Club office was also renovated, and the inner compartment proposed for use by the Himalayan Index and the photo library. In fact, very little extra space was gained by the library itself. During 2003 we are hoping to make more efficient use of the basement.

Our professional archivist, Susan Scott, ended her two-year, half-time assignment in mid-2002 by managing to complete the computerised cataloguing of the Club's unique holographic archives, using the special ADLIB software which links the library and archive cataloguing systems together. To continue maintaining the archives, our Honorary Archivist, Peter Berg, has recruited another professional archivist, Margaret Pope, to assist him for two days per month.

The photographic collection has benefited from the great enthusiasm and dedication of Sue Lawford, working voluntarily two or more days per week. Some £13,000 worth of equipment has been purchased to permit digital photography and both flatbed and transparency scanning of images to pre-press specifications. This will enable us to respond more efficiently to media enquiries and earn an increasing stream of income. In order to proceed with the equally important work of computerised cataloguing of the more marketable images, we needed more manpower so, as with the archives, we decided to employ professional help. In March 2003 we recruited Helen Long for a two-year, half-time assignment and she has settled in well, so that Sue Lawford can gradually reduce her voluntary commitment for which we have been exceedingly grateful. We had hoped we might receive a substantial grant from the Pilgrim Trust for cataloguing the images. They have responded positively with an offer of £6,000, but this is to be directed to the conservation of the collection to prevent deterioration, so we are arranging for volunteers from NADFAS to help with this work during the second half of 2003.

More funds will be sought from other charitable bodies to add to a welcome £2,500 received from the Stanley Foundation. The Mount Everest Foundation commissioned the Library Chairman to write an official history of Everest, published by HarperCollins, to mark the 50th Anniversary of the first ascent in May 2003. The book included over 300 images, mostly drawn from the RGS and AC collections, and briefly entered the best-seller lists. Numerous other Everest articles and publications were expected to add to the photo-library's income. Later during 2003 we hope to clarify the somewhat uncertain copyright arrangements between the AC and the RGS for Everest images which have been held for many years by the AC.

Our endowment fund continues to be managed with discretion by Flemings, now a subsidiary of J P Morgan. This has suffered from the recent falls in the stock market, but dividend income has held up well around £20,000 which meets a large part of our operating costs. In the absence of sufficient grants, donations and legacies to fund the balance, we are continuing to erode our capital base by some £20,000 annually which is a cause for concern.

We have received a number of very welcome gifts: £1500 from a fund initiated by Nigella Hall and Elisabeth Parry in memory of the late Peter Ledeboer, to be devoted to an appropriate facility in the Library; a £1000 legacy from the estate of the late Oliver Turnbull together with £3,574 from the sale of books given to him by Charles Warren. Jennifer Bourdillon has kindly donated the 1951 and 1953 Everest diaries kept by her late husband Tom Bourdillon, including the manuscript report of his first ascent of the South Summit with Charles Evans on 26 May 1953, written specially for John Hunt. The executors of Charles Warren's estate have donated his Leica camera with which he took the earliest colour photographs of Everest in 1938.

We are very sad to report the death of Oliver Turnbull who had only recently joined the Library Council and was making a valuable contribution. The AC has nominated Chris Fitzhugh to replace him.

After two years serving as Honorary Secretary, Luke Hughes asked to stand down owing to pressure of work and family, although he agreed to remain on the Council. Margaret Clennett agreed to take on the administrative duties of Honorary Secretary, so that the current membership of the Council is as follows: five nominated by the Alpine Club: George Band, Chairman, Jerry Lovatt, Peter Berg, Chris Fitzhugh, Luke Hughes; Michael Westmacott, nominated by the RGS; Richard Coatsworth nominated by the BMC; Margaret Clennett as Honorary Secretary. Bob Lawford has continued to handle sales of surplus books, which has provided very welcome income over the years, but he has more than earned his retirement from this task, and we are looking for a successor. As always, I am grateful to Margaret Ecclestone and to our hard core of regular volunteers, but we can always use more help!

George Band
Chairman, Alpine Club Library Council

HARISH KAPADIA WINS THE PATRON'S MEDAL

For the year 2003, Her Majesty The Queen approved the award of the Patron's Medal of the Royal Geographical Society to Harish Kapadia 'for contributions to geographical discovery and mountaineering in the Himalayas'. The Patron's Medal is one of two Gold Medals awarded by the Royal Geographical Society. It was presented on 2 June 2003 on the exact day of the 50th anniversary of the Coronation of HM The Queen.

The citation by the President, Professor Sir Ron Cooke DSc, was as follows:

Harish Kapadia has made a unique contribution to our knowledge of the Himalaya: as editor of the *Himalayan Journal*, one of the most authoritative and comprehensive records of exploratory activity in the Himalaya, through his numerous guide books and as a leader and organiser of countless expeditions over the years. He has been assistant editor and then editor of the *Himalayan Journal* since 1978 and has consistently improved both its content and its production. His guidebook and works on the Himalaya are erudite and practical, skilfully combining historical, geographical and practical guidance to increase our understanding of the region.

As an expedition leader, he has initiated a series of joint expeditions with climbers from the United Kingdom, France, Japan and the United States to explore and climb throughout the Indian Himalaya. The quality of exploration and the full and detailed reports that he has issued have provided superb background information about these areas.

Furthermore, Harish has been a tireless compaigner for the resolution of the Kashmir conflict through the Siachen Peace Park initiative in the Karakoram region. He is an outstanding modern explorer in the finest traditions of the great Himalayan pioneers.

It is most fitting, that this year, in which we celebrate the 50th Anniversary of the first ascent of Mount Everest, we honour Harish Kapadia.

Harish Kapadia has dedicated the Award to his son Lieut Nawang Kapadia, a Gurkha officer of the 4th battalion of the 3rd Gurkha Rifles of the Indian army, stating, 'He shared my passion for trekking and love of nature, and he gave his life defending the Himalaya.'

Harish is the first Asian and Indian to receive this Award in the past 125 years. The only other Indian and Asian who has received it was Pundit Nain Singh in 1877.

Past winners of the award include Eric Shipton (1938), H W Tilman (1952), Lord John Hunt (1954), Sir Charles Evans (1956), Professor Ardito Desio (1957), Sir Edmund Hillary (1958), Sir Chris Bonington (1974), Michael Ward (1982), Doug Scott (1999) and Reinhold Messner (2001).

BOARDMAN TASKER AT TWENTY

The Boardman Tasker Charitable Trust marked the twentieth year of its Award for Mountain Literature with a celebration of the lives of the two men in whose memory it was established, Peter Boardman and Joe Tasker. At a packed Royal Geographical Society in November 2002, Pete and Joe's former climbing partners recalled their considerable achievements, from Dunagiri and Changabang to Kangchenjunga and Everest North-East Ridge on which they were lost in 1982. Speakers included John Barry, Sir Chris Bonington, Paul Braithwaite, Dr Charles Clarke, Jim Curran, Doug Scott and Martin Wragg, so it was not surprising there was standing room only in the gallery. John Boardman and Paul Tasker also read pieces from their brothers' books and Hilary Rhodes recalled climbing the Carstensz Pyramid with Pete.

Earlier in the same day the 2002 Award winner was announced at a lunchtime reception at the Alpine Club, generously making their premises available to the Trust for the twentieth year. The first overseas chair of the judges, Dr Mikel Vause of Ogden, Utah, noted that there had been twenty-four entries and from a shortlist of seven the winner was Robert Roper's *Fatal Mountaineer* (St Martin's Press, New York), the story of Willi Unsoeld's obsession with Nanda Devi and the climb he would attempt with his daughter of her namesake mountain, a climb that would claim Devi's life at 24,000 feet on its North-West Face. In his summing up Dr Vause said:

We found Mr Roper's book to be a highly original biography. Its structure gives a new shape to the art of mountaineering biographical writing, taking his readers forward and backward through Unsoeld's intellectual and spiritual philosophies by which he governed his life, both in and out of the mountains. By cutting through layer after layer, Roper breaks down many of the deceptions with which mountaineers are forced to live. In examining what was a very complicated expedition, Roper presents an even-handed analysis of the various personalities of its members and the difficulties they all faced. He avoids accusations and judgments. By linking together anger and happiness, humility and bravado, triumph and tragedy, Roper aptly paints a compassionate picture of a very complex situation as a window into the life of Willi Unsoeld, a very complex individual.

The Boardman Tasker Prize is currently worth £2000 and is awarded annually. The charity appoints three independent judges who, for 2003, are David Hopkins, Eric Major and Chris Smith. For further details see www.boardmantasker.com.

Margaret Body, Honorary Secretary

THE KING ALBERT MEMORIAL FOUNDATION

The Foundation, established in Zürich in 1993 by Walter Amstutz, aims to honour individuals or institutions for exceptional and lasting achievements in a very wide range of activities – sporting, scientific, ecological, social and artistic – relating to mountains. Since 1993 the Foundation has presented twenty-one awards to individuals and societies at ceremonies which have been held in Switzerland every two years. Its First Award Ceremony was held in 1994 when Lord Hunt, Bradford Washburn, and (posthumously) Wanda Rutkiewicz were honoured (see *AJ 100*, 348-350, 1995). At the Second Award Ceremony, held in 1996, presentations were made to Charles Houston, Erhard Loretan, Silvia Metzeltin and Pit Schubert (see *AJ 102*, 367-368, 1997). The winners at the Third Award Ceremony, held in 1998, were Professor Augusto Gansser, Elizabeth Hawley, the Belgian society Intersoc, and the documentary series Land Der Berg (see *AJ 104*, 350-351, 1999).

Fourth Award Ceremony

This was held on 23 June 2000 at Muottas Muragl above Pontresina, when five individuals nominated by the trustees were presented with its Gold Medal and Diploma for outstanding photography, defined in various categories relating to mountains and mountain people. Prior to a dinner held on the eve of the award ceremony, invited guests and members of the public were able to view the work of the award winners which was displayed in the halls of the Alpine Museum in Pontresina. The recipients were:

Simon Carter

The colour photography of Simon Carter, born in Canberra and now living in the Blue Mountains west of Sydney, combines the unique landscape of Australia with brilliant images of climbing skills portraying scenes of great visual beauty. His photographs, which have been published in magazines all over the world, incorporate the action, passion, and commitment of climbers on hard rock and his book *Rock Climbing in Australia* vividly illustrates the high technical quality of his work. Carter's photographs have portrayed several internationally-known climbers, including Lynn Hill and Catherine Destivelle. He describes himself as a climber who takes photographs, as well as a photographer who climbs. For the prizegiving in Pontresina Simon Carter was accompanied by Julian Saunders, a leading rock-climber from Blackheath, New South Wales.

Walter Niedermayr
After training in electrical engineering, computer science and technical drawing, Walter Niedermayr took up photography in 1970; he now works as an architectural photographer in Bolzano, where he lives. His series of large-scale black and white photographs of the Dolomites taken in 1992 and entitled *Die Bleichen Berge* (The Pale Mountains) has been exhibited at the Art Museum in Bolzano and in Austria, France and Switzerland; under the same title it has been published as a book. In 1993 he received the European Photography Award. In 1998 he produced a fresh photographic series of urbanised Alpine landscapes *Reservate des Augenblicks* (Momentary Resorts), followed by a book under that title. During the past ten years Niedermayr's work has been exhibited all over Europe as well as in the USA, Canada, and in London in 1997 and 1998. His photographs subtly analyse the physical and emotional aspects of mountains, highlighting the change and damage to the Alpine environment brought about by the spread of mass tourism.

Didier Ruef
After completing a university course in economics at Geneva, where he was born, Didier Ruef undertook a course of study at the International Center of Photography in New York. His photographs, taken during journeys in Europe, North and South America, the Middle East, Africa, India and South-East Asia, in collaboration with *Médecins sans Frontières* and the World Council of Churches, have been widely displayed in magazines across Britain, the USA, and Europe. He has received a number of Awards, including the Italian *Prix Geoffroy* and the Nikon International Prize for black & white photography. His book *Bauern am Berg* (Mountain Peasants) published in 1998 was awarded the *Prix des Pays du Mont Blanc* in Passy (France). Didier Ruef's expressive black and white photography has won special acclaim for its sensitivity and beauty, portraying the arduous routine in the daily lives of mountain farmers, and the fascination of the alpine environment, now under increasing encroachment owing to expanding tourist demands.

Shiro Shirahata
During a lifetime's devotion which began in 1951 when he was eighteen, Shiro Shirahata has gained wide renown for his brilliant portraiture of mountains. In addition to his extensive photographic coverage of the Japanese Alps, he has made 17 photographic journeys, between 1971 and 1989, to the Nepal and Indian Himalaya, the Karakoram, the Afghan Hindu Kush, the Pamir, Peru, South Korea, and three journeys to the European Alps. He has published several photographic volumes including *Nepal Himalaya*, *The Alps* (translated into seven languages), *Beauty of South Korea* (in four volumes), and *My Southern Alps* which was awarded a prize in 1977 by the Japan Photographic Association. A Shiro Shirahata Museum for

Mountain Photography was opened in 1984 in his home province Otsuki, and a prize for mountain photography, in his name, was established in 1989. Shirahata's photography depicts in brilliant colour the magnificence of mountain peaks in a variety of settings.

Jürgen Winkler

After serving as a photographer's apprentice for three years, Jürgen Winkler won his first photographic prize at a contest in Frankfurt at the age of 21. He held his first exhibition in Münich in 1972. An active climbing career, which developed side by side with his photography, included Mont Blanc's Innominata Ridge and the fifth complete traverse of the Peuterey Ridge. In 1970 he was a member of Karl Herrligkofer's expedition to Nanga Parbat, and later joined expeditions to the Himalaya, New Zealand, Africa and the USA. He qualified as a mountain guide in 1973.

In 1970, with Walter Pause, he co-authored a book about extreme climbing, *Im Extremen Fels*. Winkler's first photographic volume *Nepal* appeared in 1976. His next book *Himalaya* received the European Mountain Book Award in 1989. In 1990 he received an award from the DAV (German Alpine Club) for mountain photography, and in 1993 his book *Aus den Bergen* was awarded the *Prix Mondial de l'Image de Montagne*. The high technical quality of Jürgen Winkler's work illustrates the unique power of black and white photography to emphasize the artistic impact of the mountain scene.

Fifth Award Ceremony

This was held on 31 August 2002 at Zernez in the Swiss National Park region when awards were presented by Jürg Marmet, President of the Foundation, to the following:

Professor Dr Bruno Messerli, Swiss geographer, research scientist and lecturer, who has been described as the doyen of mountain academics. His commitment to the protection of the world's mountains led him to play a leading role in establishing the Mountain Chapter of the United Nations' Agenda 21, emphasising the significance of mountains as vital sources of water, energy, recreation and challenge. His fieldwork has taken him to Africa, the Andes, the Mediterranean, Bangladesh and the Himalaya. His much-appreciated book *Mountains of the World: A Global Priority*, written in collaboration with Professor J D Ives, contains guidelines for presentation to the United Nations General Assemby. He is an honorary member of the Swiss Academy of Sciences, a member of the Swiss National Science Foundation, and Chairman of the Board of Trustees of the International Foundation for Science, Stockholm. In 2002 he was awarded the Founder's Medal of the Royal Geographical Society.

Professor John David Ives, who was born in Grimsby England, emigrated to Canada in 1954 and is now a Canadian citizen. As a geographer and lecturer with a deep commitment to protection and preservation of the fragile ecosystems of mountain regions, he was the founder and first editor of the journal *Mountain Research and Development*, which provides essential source information for students, scientists and political leaders. He authored, jointly with Professor Messerli, the book *Mountains of the World: A Global Priority*. He was Director of the McGill Sub-Arctic Research Laboratory at Schefferville Quebec (1957-60), and of the Canadian Federal Geographical Branch (Energy, Mines & Resources) in Ottawa. He was Professor of Mountain Geoecology at the Universities of Colorado (1979-89) and of California (1989-97). He was Chairman, for two eight-year terms between 1972 and 1996, of the International Geographical Union (Mountain Geoecology); and Chairman of UNESCO's International Working Group for study of the impact of human activities on mountain ecosystems. He founded the International Mountain Society in 1980 and was editor-in-chief (1981-2000) of *Mountain Research & Development*.

Hans Weiss, Swiss conservationist, scientist, and lecturer, has made valuable contributions to the preservation of the Alpine environment by arousing public awareness of the value of mountain ecosystems. He has introduced basic training courses in ecological issues at the Swiss Federal Institute of Technology, Zürich. He is the author of two books, *The Peaceful Destruction of Swiss Landscape and Attempts at Reversal* and *Indivisible Landscape: Enhanced Ecological Awareness*, the publication of which has been responsible for the incorporation of new guidelines into existing laws. He has written numerous articles, and has done invaluable work helping to establish a fund for the preservation of cultivated land, without which the Alpine landscape would present a different picture.

Alliance in the Alps is a project founded in 1997 by CIPRA-International Committee for Protection of the Alps in Schaan (Liechtenstein) and AFI-Alpine Research Institute in Garmisch-Partenkirchen, Bavarian Alps. This pioneer project brings together a network of 27 local authorities in France, Germany, Italy, Austria, Slovenia, Liechtenstein, and Switzerland, with the purpose of advancing environmental initiatives by providing a flow of information between the affiliated communities to assist development of agriculture, energy, transport, and responsible promotion of tourism in the mountains. The objectives are pursued by means of cross-border conventions and workshops aimed at establishing closer communication between community networks towards the improvement of social, economic, and ecological standards, whilst emphasizing the need for sound environmental practices.

ECO Himal, a non-government organisation founded in 1991, based in Salzburg Austria, with a regional office in Kathmandu Nepal, promotes and supports, in partnership with local organisations, social, cultural, educational, and ecological development programmes in Nepal and Tibet which are intended to generate income for the population and to bring long-term benefits to their lives.

• Construction of a 600 Kw Hydropower Plant in Thame which is operated by a trained Sherpa team. Since 1999 the Khumbu power plant has been managed by representatives of local communities, who are its major shareholders. Regional development of the Sagarmatha National Park includes promotion of solar energy, village improvement projects, and provision of drinking water and sewage systems for Namche Bazar.

• Integrated rural development project Arun valley (Makalu-Barun National Park) including building of pathways, bridges, drinking water systems, improved agricultural output, fruit plantation, small-scale health services and literacy systems.

• Since 1992 Tibetan primary schools have been built and furnished in neglected rural areas. Each school will be provided with a flock of sheep in order to generate income for the school and provide food for the pupils.

• Thame mountaineering school provides training for trekking and mountaineering guides, as well as for Nepalese Tourism Management personnel.

• Restoration of an historical garden and architectural ensemble *Keshar Mahal* situated in the centre of Kathmandu, assisted by local and international experts.

Contributors

KEN ALDRED is a mechanical engineer, geologist and lecturer who first visited Austria in 1972 where he developed an interest in Alpine flora. Since then he has walked and climbed in the Alps, Norway, Nepal, the Polish Tatras, Swaziland and the Picos de Europa.

ELAINE ASTILL is a recent arts graduate whose dissertation subject was *The Life and Work of Elijah Walton*. Her passion for the mountains is based upon her study of their artistic representation. She also enjoys walking excursions that have included the Tour of Mont Blanc.

GEORGE BAND was the youngest member of the 1953 Everest team. In 1955 he made the first ascent – with Joe Brown – of Kangchenjunga, and subsequently climbed in Peru and the Caucasus. More recently he has climbed in Bhutan in 1991, and currently leads treks for 'Far Frontiers' in Nepal, Sikkim and Central Asia. AC President from 1987 to 1989, he is currently Chairman of the Library Council and, as President of the British Mountaineering Council from 1996 to 1999, was tasked with setting up the National Mountaineering Exhibition, which opened in July 2001.

JOSÉ LUIS BERMÚDEZ is professor in the Department of Philosophy, University of Stirling. He took up climbing too late and has been making up for lost time in the Alps, Caucasus and Himalaya. In July 1997 he climbed Gasherbrum I. Co-author, with Audrey Salkeld, of *On The Edge of Europe: Mountaineering in the Caucusus*.

WALTER BONATTI was born in Bergamo in 1930, becoming a professional guide in 1954. One of the greatest mountaineers in history, his routes in the Mont Blanc Range, particularly on the Dru, the Capucin and the Grand Pilier d'Angle and on the Matterhorn, are obvious classics. He was caught up in the controversy that followed the first ascent of K2 in 1954, and survived a horrific descent from the Central Pillar of Freney. Since the 1960s he has worked with great success as a photo-journalist.

DEREK BUCKLE is a medicinal chemist in the pharmaceutical industry who now works part time as a private consultant. He has climbed in the Alps, the Caucasus, the USA, Canada, Equador, Kenya, Nepal and Greenland.

NICK BULLOCK is 37 and in the last few years has established himself as one of Britain's leading alpinists. A PE instructor for the Prison Service in Leicestershire, he discovered climbing in 1991 on a work-related course at

Plas y Brenin. A first alpine season included ascents of the Croz Spur and a solo of *The Shroud* on the Grandes Jorasses. Other Alpine ascents include *Beyond Good and Evil* on the Pélérins, and new routes on the Grand Pilier d'Angle and the Sans Nom. Most recently he has done a string of new routes in Peru, this year completing the highly adventurous *Fear and Loathing* on Jirishanca.

ED DOUGLAS is a writer whose first book, *Chomolungma Sings the Blues*, won the Special Jury Award at Banff in 1998. Other publications include *Regions of the Heart: The Triumph and Tragedy of Alison Hargreaves*, co-authored with David Rose. His latest book, published in 2003 for National Geographic, is *Tenzing. Hero of Everest*. He has been Honorary Editor of the *Alpine Journal* since 1999 and retires at the end of the current year.

EVELIO ECHEVARRÍA was born in Santiago, Chile, and teaches Hispanic Literature at Colorado State University. He has climbed in North and South America, and has contributed numerous articles to Andean, North American and European journals.

DEREK FORDHAM When not dreaming of the Arctic, Derek practises as an architect and runs an Arctic photographic library. He is secretary of the Arctic Club and has led 21 expeditions to the Canadian Arctic, Greenland and Svalbard to ski, climb or share the life of the Inuit.

JULIAN FREEMAN-ATTWOOD is a forestry manager who lives on the Shropshire/Welsh border. He has climbed in the Himalaya, Africa, the Antarctic and Sub-Antarctic, specialising in unclimbed peaks in little-known areas.

DENNIS GRAY was born in Leeds and started climbing on local gritstone outcrops aged eleven. He has climbed in and travelled to over sixty countries, most recently China, Southern Africa and Hungary. He is a former General Secretary of the BMC and Chairman of Leeds Wall. He is the author of four books about climbing. He recently published a volume of poetry and organised an exhibition of photographs taken from fifty years of travel and mountaineering.

DENIS GREENALD is an educational psychologist and has been climbing since 1948, almost always with Gwen, his wife and equal partner on and off the rope. They have three children. Their best alpine route was an early British ascent of the South Ridge of the Aiguille Noire in 1953, and they were together on the LSE Karakoram Expedition in 1956, making the first attempt on Lukpe Lawo Brakk or Snow Lake Peak.

LINDSAY GRIFFIN is a magazine editor and jouranlist living in North Wales who, despite dwindling ability, still pursues all aspects of cimbing with undiiished enthusiasm. Exploratory visits to the Greater Ranges are his main love, and his last two expeditions have taken him to previously unclimbed mountains in Central Alaska.

LIEUTENANT COLONEL JAMES HARRIS joined the Army in 1981 leading his first team to climb Mt Rainer in 1983. He has climbed extensively in the European Alps, in the US and Canadian Rockies, Norway and South Georgia. He was elected to the Alpine Club in 1991. He continues to serve in the Army and lead expeditions whenever time allows. He lives in Devon with his wife and two children.

TONY HOWARD led the first ascent of Norway's Troll Wall in 1965 and wrote the Romsdal guide. His expeditions include Arctic Norway, Canada, South Georgia and Greenland. He has climbed extensively across North Africa and the Middle East from Morocco to Iran. He 'discovered' and wrote the guide to Wadi Rum.

JOHN JACKSON has climbed and explored in the Alps, Greenland, Africa and the Andes. His experience in the Himalaya dates from 1944 and includes first ascents in Kashmir, Ladakh, Garhwal, Sikkim and Nepal. A reserve member of the 1953 Everest expedition, he was also a member of the British team which made the first ascent of Kangchenjunga in 1955.

HARISH KAPADIA has climbed in the Himalaya since 1960, with ascents up to 6800m. He is Hon Editor of both the *Himalayan Journal* and the *HC Newsletter*. In 1993 he was awarded the IMF's Gold Medal and in 1996 was made an Hon Member of the Alpine Club. He has written several books including *High Himalaya Unknown Valleys*, *Spiti: Adventures in the Trans-Himalaya* and, with Soli Mehta, *Exploring the Hidden Himalaya*. In 2003 he was awarded the Patron's Gold Medal by the Royal Geographical Society.

PAUL KNOTT has recently made several changes of continent and now lectures at the University of Canterbury, New Zealand. He delights in visiting obscure mountain ranges and has climbed in most regions of Russia and Central Asia. After three successful trips he also enjoys the adventure provided by the big snowy peaks of the St Elias range in the Yukon.

PAT LITTLEJOHN began climbing in the Alps in 1968, aged 17, and has since spent virtually every summer there. He qualified as a Mountain Guide in 1983. Partnered by Steve Jones, in the early 1970s he achieved free ascents of the Hemming-Robbins on the Dru , the W Ridge of Salbitschijen, the Fou S Face and many major Dolomite routes. Pat has made over 1000 first ascents worldwide.

JOHANNA MERZ was over 50 when she took up mountaineering. After qualifying for membership of the Alpine Club, she devoted most of her energies to the Alpine Journal, first as Assistant Editor, then as Honorary Editor from 1992 to 1998, and currently as Production Editor.

ADE MILLER currently lives, climbs and sometimes works in Seattle, Washington. He has visited and climbed in numerous mountain ranges but has spent the last few years sampling the delights of climbing in the Pacific Northwest, the Yukon and Alaska.

MARTIN MORAN is a qualified mountain guide whose interests range from mountain running to making new routes on technical peaks in the Garhwal. In 1985 he made the first winter traverse of the Munros and in 1993, with Simon Jenkins, the first continuous traverse of all the 4000m peaks in the Alps. In 2000 he made the first ascent of the W Ridge of Nilkanth (6596m).

ALAN MULLIN is one of Scotland's most exciting – and controversial – mixed climbers, repeating and then adding some of the hardest mixed routes in the world. He made first winter ascents of *The Steeple* on Shelter Stone (IX, 9) and soloed *Rolling Thunder* (VIII, 8) on Lochnagar. His winter ascent of an E4 on Lochnagar gave a route graded X, 11. He has also climbed in the United States and Patagonia, where he made the first free ascent of the *Czech Route* on the West Face of Cerro Torre.

TAMOTSU NAKAMURA was born in Tokyo in 1934 and has been climbing new routes in the greater ranges since his first successes in the Cordillera Blanca of Peru in 1961. He has lived in Pakistan, Mexico, New Zealand and Hong Kong and in the last ten years has made 19 trips to the Hengduan mountains of Yunnan, Sichuan and South-east Tibet. He is currently auditor of the Japanese Alpine Club.

IAN PARNELL worked for the British Mountaineering Council and is now a writer and photographer. An all-round climber, having climbed E6 on sight, Scottish VII and ED2, in 1999 he led an expedition to Kyrgyzstan which established ten new routes. In 2000 he and Jules Cartwright put up a new route on Mount Hunter in Alaska.

ANDREW POLLARD is a paediatrician and research fellow in the Department of Paediatric Infectious Diseases at St Mary's Hospital, London. He began climbing as a medical student and has made first British ascents of Jaonli (6632m) in 1988 and Chamang (7319m) in 1991. He reached 8600m on Everest as the deputy leader of the 1994 British Mount Everest Medical Expedition. He is co-author (with David R Murdoch) of *The High Altitude Medicine Handbook*.

PAUL RAMSDEN is 33 and works, appropriately enough, as a Health and Safety Consultant whose credits include the last James Bond film. He lives in Nottingham with his wife Mary. He has been mountaineering since childhood and climbed the Walker Spur and the Eiger's North Face before his nineteenth birthday. His climbing interests are now a bit more remote. Highlights include new routes on Denali, Foraker and Thunder in Alaska, Jebel Misht in Oman, the first winter ascent of Cerro Poincenot, and the Peuterey Integrale in a long weekend from home.

SIMON RICHARDSON is a petroleum engineer based in Aberdeen. Experience gained climbing in the Alps, Andes, Himalaya and Alaska is put to good use most winter weekends whilst exploring and climbing in the the Scottish Highlands.

GUY ROBERTSON is 32 and lives in Aberdeen where he works for the Scottish Environment Protection Agency. He is a very active climber both in Scotland and in the Alps, where early in his career he climbed the North Face of the Lauterbrunnen Breithorn. He has been on trips to the Middle East and Peru and like many of the current crop of British alpinists puts great emphasis on an ethic of adventure.

ROY RUDDLE leads the Virtual Reality Research Group at the University of Wales, Cardiff. He enjoys climbing on sea-cliffs, gritstone and the big mountains, especially first ascents in Greenland. ACG Hon Secretary from 1989. Assistant Editor 1992-1996.

C A RUSSELL, who formerly worked with a City bank, devotes much of his time to mountaineering and related activities. He has climbed in many regions of the Alps, in the Pyrenees, East Africa, North America and the Himalaya.

BILL RUTHVEN has been Honorary Secretary of the Mount Everest Foundation since 1985. Now confined to a wheelchair, the MEF has provided him with a lap-top computer to ensure that it still gets its 'pound of flesh' from him even during his not infrequent periods in hospital. He is always happy to talk to expeditioners about projects past, present and future.

GEOFFREY TEMPLEMAN, a retired chartered surveyor, has greatly enjoyed being an Assistant Editor of the Alpine Journal for the past thirty years. A love of mountain literature is coupled with excursions into the hills, which are becoming less and less energetic.

JOHN TOWN is Director of Planning at the University of Bradford. He has a preference for little-explored mountain areas and has climbed in the Alps, Caucasus, Eastern Turkey, Siberian and Mongolian Altai, Kamchatka, Yunnan, the Andes, and most recently in the Kongpo region of Tibet.

MICHAEL WARD CBE was a member and Medical Officer of the 1951 and 1953 Everest Expeditions. He is a retired consultant surgeon who has combined exploration in Nepal, Bhutan, Kunlun and Tibet with high-altitude research. Master, Society of Apothecaries of London, 1993-94. He was made an Honorary Member of the Alpine Club in 1972. He was awarded the Founder's Medal of the RGS in 1984. His monograph *Everest. A Thousand Years of Exploration* was published in 2003.

BRADFORD WASHBURN, an Honorary Member of the AC, was born in 1910 and started climbing aged 16, making ascents of the Matterhorn, Mont Blanc and Monte Rosa. Soon afterwards he was elected to the Groupe de Haute Montagne. The publication of his first guidebook, to the White Mountains, helped to establish his reputation as a fine photographer. For 41 years he was the Director of Boston's Museum of Science, and his map-making, notably of the Everest region, has made him internationally famous. He is still at work figuring out the region's plate tectonics.

JOHN B WEST is Professor of Medicine and Physiology at the University of California at San Diego. He was born in Adelaide in 1928 and spent 15 years at the Hammersmith Hospital. He applied to join Edmund Hillary's 'Silver Hut' expedition and despite no climbing experience was accepted. This began his long interest in high-altitude medicine, which has included the 1981 American Medical Research Expedition. He edits *High Altitude Medicine & Biology* and is a former President of the American Physiology Society.

DAVE WILKINSON has been a member of the AC/ACG for over 30 years. During the 1970s and 80s he was very active in the Alps, particularly in winter. More recently he has been involved in first ascents in the greater ranges, especially low-key alpine-style ascents in the Karakoram and Greenland.

DUNCAN WILSON works as a Management Consultant in Paris, where he lives with his French wife, Véronique. He climbs regularly in the Alps, and occasionally in his native British Isles. He has written mountaineering articles for various magazines and journals, mostly based in France.

SHARON WOOD became the first North American woman to climb Everest on 20 May, 1986, via the West Ridge and North Face. Born in Nova Scotia, she started climbing aged 12 and at the age of 20 joined an all-female expedition to Mount Logan. In 1983 she climbed the Cassin Ridge on Denali which pushed her into tackling the Himalayan giants, including Everest and Makalu in 1984. She lives in the Rockies with her two sons.

Index

NOTES FOR CONTRIBUTORS

The *Alpine Journal* records all aspects of mountains and mountaineering, including expeditions, adventure, art, literature, geography, history, geology, medicine, ethics and the mountain environment.

Articles Contributions in English are invited. They should be sent to the Hon Editor, Stephen Goodwin, 1 Ivy Cottages, Edenhall, Penrith, Cumbria CA11 8SN (Steve Goodwin, sg@stephengoodwin.demon.co.uk). Articles should preferably be sent on a disk with accompanying hard copy or as an e-mail attachment (in Word) with hard copy sent separately by post. They will also be accepted as plain typed copy. Their length should not exceed 3000 words without prior approval of the Editor **and may be edited or shortened at his discretion.** It is regretted that the *Alpine Journal* is unable to offer a fee for articles published, but authors receive a complimentary copy of the issue of the *Alpine Journal* in which their article appears.

Articles and book reviews should not have been published in substantially the same form by any other publication.

Maps These should be well researched, accurate, and finished ready for printing. They should show the most important place-names mentioned in the text. It is the authors' responsibility to get their maps redrawn if necessary. This can be arranged through the Production Editor if required.

Photographs Prints (any size) should be numbered (in pencil) on the back and accompanied by captions on a separate sheet (see below). Colour transparencies, in 35m format or larger, should be originals (**not copies**).

Captions Please list these **on a separate sheet** and give title and author of the article to which they refer.

Copyright It is the author's responsibility to obtain copyright clearance for text, photographs and maps, to pay any fees involved and to ensure that acknowledgements are in the form required by the copyright owner.

Summaries A brief summary, helpful to researchers, may be included with 'expedition' articles.

Biographies Authors are asked to provide a short biography, in about 60 words, listing the most noteworthy items in their climbing career and anything else they wish to mention.

Deadline: copy and photographs should reach the Editor by 1 January of the year of publication.